The Letters of Randolph Bourne:

a Comprehensive Edition

The Letters of Randolph Bourne:

a Comprehensive Edition

edited by

Eric J. Sandeen

The Whitston Publishing Company
Troy, New York
1981

to my parents

Acknowledgments

I would like to express my thanks to Prof. Robert F. Sayre of the University of Iowa, whose advice sustained me throughout the process of editing and annotating these letters. His Preface to this collection will give the reader an idea of what an astute and lively resource he was. The contents of this collection are drawn primarily from three University archives, and I am thus indebted to the Curators of Rare Books and Manuscripts at these institutions for making the resources of their holdings available to me. Kenneth A. Lohf at Columbia University gave me access to both the Randolph Bourne Papers and the John Erskine Collection and has answered many tedious questions over the past four years. Neda Westlake, of the Van Pelt Library at the University of Pennsylvania, has given me help and encouragement which exceeds even the excellence of the Carl Zigrosser, Van Wyck Brooks, Waldo Frank, and Theodore Dreiser papers the Pennsylvania archive holds. Donald Gallup at Yale University kindly made the Alyse Gregory and Elizabeth Shepley Sergeant papers available to me. The newly-discovered letter from Bourne to William Wirt was released from the William Wirt Collection at the Lilly Library at Indiana University. I would also like to acknowledge the co-operation of Mrs. Theodore Dreiser, and Mrs. Arthur Macmahon, who released to me the previously unpublished letters from Bourne to her husband; Clara Zigrosser, Rosemary Manning, executrix of the Alyse Gregory estate; Mrs. Van Wyck Brooks; and Mrs. Waldo Frank. Mr. Read Lewis, a remarkable man, took time off from his work to give me his invaluable reminiscences of Bourne, and of New York life in 1913.

I would like to acknowledge gratefully the co-operation of the following publishing houses: The University of Minnesota Press has given me permission to quote material from Sherman Paul, *Randolph Bourne* and from David Noble, *The Paradox of Progressive Thought*. From the Oxford University Press I received permission to use material from Charles Forcey, *The Crossroads of Liberalism*.

Finally, Mrs. John Dos Passos has allowed me to use her husband's description of Bourne, taken from *1919*.

The University of Iowa sustained my research with a fellowship which allowed me the leisure of enjoying these letters while I worked on them. The American Studies Program at the University of Iowa graciously allowed me access to their computer funds so that this volume could be prepared; I appreciate the ATS text editing program even more in retrospect, since all the revisions have had to be made laboriously by hand. Mr. Stephen Goode of the Whitston Publishing Company allowed me time to return from my Fulbright year in Germany and collect my thoughts before tackling the revision of this collection. Finally, my wife Susan helped me with the most tedious details of this volume's preparation—proof-reading and indexing.

Eric J. Sandeen
Idaho State University

Preface

Of all the qualities necessary to a superb letter-writer, Randolph Bourne definitely possessed two of the biggest. He had a great affection for his friends and an uncanny skill for being open and personal. These traits, which are so abundantly illustrated in this collection, are also evident in his essays, and they may be the most important factors in his revived reputation as a cultural critic and social thinker.

In his essay "The Handicapped," published in *The Atlantic Monthly* in September, 1911, when he was twenty-five and just emerging as a writer, though still an undergraduate at Columbia, Bourne wrote of himself that "The doors of the deformed man are always locked, and the key is on the outside. He may have treasures of charm inside, but they will never be revealed unless the person outside cooperates with him in unlocking the door. A friend becomes, to a much greater degree than with the ordinary man, the indispensable means of discovering one's own personality. One only exists, so to speak, with friends." His own deformity was what he called "a crooked back and an unsightly face." He could "move about freely," and had great energy and ambition—indeed, too much of this restlessness, he complained—but being sensitive about his appearance, he felt unfit for the rough worlds of business and the professions. He preferred not having to deal with strangers' "first impressions." He was offended by the way strangers and new acquaintances had of "discounting in advance" what he had to say. Yet this made him all the more appreciative of true friends, who, feeling unthreatened by him and feeling no need to impress him, were less reticent to him than to other people. And Bourne, we can be sure, reciprocated, so that he always felt his friendships were unusually "genuine and sincere," adding that this was particularly true of his friendships with young women. There was no romantic interest to interfere with "a charming companionship."

The pictures in this book present their own evidence of

Bourne's physical deformity. His hunchback was the result of spinal tuberculosis when he was four. His misshapen face and one badly deformed ear were the result of a messy birth, as he called it. The preponderance of letters to young women also demonstrates his spiritual and intellectual intimacy with them, even though this preponderance could result only from his female correspondents' having saved more letters. If so, this in itself would be indicative of the intimacy. But what is more important is that in all these letters Bourne somehow shares both the burden and the pleasure of his youthful insights, his enthusiasms, his disappointments, and his ambition. Whether to young women or young men, he writes as if he expected them usually to be fully sympathetic. With some people he is ironic, with others more direct and straight. Some he expects to share his pacifism, others his socialism, his feminism, or whatever. Different ones engage particular facets of his own diversity. But he seldom really argues or debates. He just describes what he has seen or done or felt and expects to convince. And most remarkable of all, perhaps, he writes this way to an extraordinary number of people. He wasn't just intimate with one or two and newsy and chatty with all the rest. He was intimate and confiding with almost all.

This assumed sympathy and trust in the letters helps us, I think, to recognize it better in his essays. The underlying reason for Bourne's revival in the 1960s, after neglect during the Depression, World War II, and the Cold War era, was not the sudden contemporaneity of his ideas. True, he was against interventionist war and the imperial state ("War is the health of the State"). He saw the contradictions in supposedly liberal universities and raged against the connivance of intellectuals in the policies of a wartime state. Against these he advocated and appealed to the idealism of youth. He was for the cultural self-determination of minorities. He reported on developments in progressive education. On one point after another, he seems almost like the inventor of SDS and the Student Left. And he wrote with much more authority and clarity than was generally found in underground newspapers and campus manifestoes. But the common feature in all these essays is Bourne's openness, his way of being explicitly Out Front, to use an appropriate 1960s idiom. You know his own interests and values. He does not hide behind a pose of objectivity or a jargon of social science. And so, being out front about his own passions, he leads his readers to feel their own. Rather than the relevance of his political and social positions, what is most appealing, ultimately, is the inner urgency with which they are expressed. He arouses us because he makes us see how large national choices really can affect us as single persons.

There is no other American essayist to whom culture and the meaning of culture are more personal words. Thoreau, Whitman, and even Emerson were more isolated, each in his way an independent majority of one who could go on alone. They created their own cultures. And since Bourne's time we have not been so sure what the common intellectual culture in America is. Specialization has brought fragmentation. But Bourne, though he constantly complains in these letters about being unheard and ineffectual, still felt that some vital link connected all good artists and the advocates of all good causes. All modern artists and political progressives were, in a spiritual sense, his friends. He writes as if he were really corresponding with them. Wherever new ideas were exciting and being tried out—Boston, Gary, Indiana, or Madison, Wisconsin—Bourne was there. Culture was friendship.

An obvious value of these letters, therefore, is that they admit us to the even closer world of Bourne's actual friends: the Columbia classmates, the independent young women, the other young writers, artists, and reformers with whom he regularly associated. A complete collection like this gives a unique social and historical picture of what these people did. It shows them going to plays and concerts, spending their summer vacations in the country, looking for jobs and inexpensive apartments in New York, and, like Bourne himself, making all he can of his year's travelling fellowship in Europe. It reveals what they read (or what Bourne read and enthusiastically urged on his friends). And it suggests the hours that they spent listening to Bourne play the piano or sitting in his or a friend's rooms and talking. This, perhaps, is what they really lived for, or what Bourne lived for. As he wrote when bored in Bloomfield, New Jersey, September 1, 1912, "I am unhappy unless I have friends around me, . . . My good times and happiness mean more to me, I think, than they do to some people, . . ." Friends provided the conversation on which he lived. " 'The lack of a conversable person,' " he wrote from Paris on March 18, 1914, quoting Lady Gregory, " 'is the abomination of misery.' " So when he did not have friends around to converse with, he wrote letters. "You see," he wrote to Prudence Winterrowd in March, 1913, "I am going through your letter trying to converse with it just as if I were hearing it in person." The fact that when he wrote this long letter he and Miss Winterrowd had not even met proves how extremely hungry for conversation both of them were. She had grown up in a dull town in the Middle West, as he had in depressing Bloomfield, and their need was desperate. The comic part of the affair was that when they met, she did not fulfill his expectations. Bourne had imagined her to be more interesting than she was!

On the other hand, this pen-pal friendship is yet one more example of the good-natured, possibly naive earnestness of so many of these people. The outstanding difference between Bourne and his friends and the circles of young intellectuals all around the country today may indeed be this greater seriousness and dedication. Bourne and his group did not have movies and television, stereo sets and canned entertainment, so they made their own. They could not experiment as much sexually. They had no drugs and seldom drank excessively. Their evenings of conversation and their long excursions to the country seem to have the earnest purity of Emerson's and Margaret Fuller's Concord, the Transcendentalist Club. In fact, as these letters show, they did have various discussion clubs, and Bourne's group was also involved with magazines, including a new *Dial*.

So one of the other values of this fine collection is that it documents the persistence, at least through Bourne's short but exciting era, of a certain style in the American intellectual tradition. It has been argued—most provocatively by Christopher Lasch in *The New Radicalism in America, 1889-1963: The Intellectual as a Social Type*—that Bourne and the other intellectuals of his time were too preoccupied with their own revolt against middle-class gentility ever to engage in serious political thought and power. They muddled their politics with their bohemianism and made a radical life-style a substitute for radical politics. As a result, they were also pretty well cut off from the rest of Americn society. Revolt really meant more to them than reform. A further effect of this was that they extended their conception of politics into "the most intimate areas of existence." Bourne's definition of politics, a "means to life," was hopelessly and also dangerously broad: hopeless because it wasn't very practical, dangerous because it might someday bring political intervention and retaliation against people's personal behavior. Lasch's chapter on Bourne, "Randolph Bourne and the Experimental Life," aggressively challenges all Bourne's personalism, from its origins to its potential consequences.

Sherman Paul's pamphlet on *Randolph Bourne* (which is also referred to in Eric Sandeen's informative Introduction) makes an almost diametrically opposite case for Bourne's recognition of the limits of politics, as usually perceived, and the necessity of his engagement in the many other fields where he might eventually exert influence. Paul also indicates Bourne's affinity to the older intellectual styles of Emerson, Whitman and Thoreau—especially as restated by William James and John Dewey. To him Bourne is not a curious case of the New Radicalism but a new flower on the old personalist, organic, and pragmatic traditions.

As this Preface shows, I mostly side with Sherman Paul's analysis. Bourne does not seem very bohemian to me, and I like Bourne's recognition of the profound political implications in culture. His self-consciousness and his personal voice seem to me virtues more than defects. Bourne was so strongly present and reflexsive in everything he wrote that he was a great autobiographical writer, even though he never wrote what could be called a formal autobiography. He did not need to. He was also too young. His essays and these letters are all a reader can legitimately ask for. In addition, I am moved, *humbled* by Bourne's courage. There are very few signs in these letters of his succumbing to weaknesses which might have been caused by his physical deformities. The most we learn is that in Europe his stronger travelling companions generally carried his suitcase and that he sometimes sought special help from friends in finding apartments or places to go in the summer. But more muscular complainers than he have done that. And despite his handicaps, he travelled alone a good deal of the time he was in Europe and even eagerly climbed in the Alps. When he defines "my zest for the experimental life—a life lived in conflict with my natural constitutional timidity" (in the letter to Arthur Macmahon of December 23, 1913), I think we should consider that it had this physical basis. He zestfully drove himself not to be timid. He says in his essay on his physical handicap that it filled him "with a profound sympathy for all who are despised and ignored in the world . . . all the horde of the unpresentable and unemployable, the incompetent and the ugly, the queer and crotchety people who make up so large a proportion of human folk." But he spent relatively little such sympathy on himself. Indeed, Sherman Paul attributes Bourne's reprinting of this essay in Bourne's first book to the insistence of Ellery Sedgwick, editor of the *Atlantic.*

Regardless of one's own interpretation of Bourne, however, there can be no doubt that he will continue to be a controversial American writer. The publication of these letters, while answering some questions about him and making his life a little clearer, will also provoke new ones and new research. Little is known, for example, of his childhood; and we would like to know more about the final period of his life when he seems to have had less time for writing letters. But Eric Sandeen has performed an immense service by tracking down so many letters and presenting them in such a well informed, balanced manner. A great letter-writer like Bourne deserved this comprehensive, illustrated edition.

Robert F. Sayre
The University of Iowa

Table of Contents

List Of Figures

Timely Papers:
An Introduction to the Letters of Randolph Bourne

In his brief, thirty-two year life Randolph Bourne wrote many vigorous, well argued essays which redefined the role of youth in twentieth century America. Even as early as 1911, when he was a 27 year old undergraduate at Columbia University, he proclaimed that the rising generation had a vision, a mandate to carry out a reformation of the obsolete traditions of their elders, who were products of the nineteenth century. Early in his career, while still a student at Columbia University, he was known as the voice of youth. He fought for educational reform which would facilitate social action—allying himself with the Progressive school of education, he advocated learning through doing. Most fame has come to Bourne, however, through his principled opposition to the First World War. Using the short-lived magazine, The *Seven Arts*, as a forum, he preached his form of pacifism and anarchism in the face of diminishing popular support for his cause. Even his physical make-up gave evidence of struggle. Bourne was only five feet tall, having contracted a spinal disease at an early age which left him a hunchback. The contrast between his physique and the strength of both his ideas and his prose was unforgettable.

Many commentators have dealt with Bourne's published work, and have therefore been concerned with Bourne's public figure, but, due to the limited amount of biographical and autobiographical material, only a few have concentrated on the courageous and conflict-filled life which Bourne led. As interesting as his published essays remain, questions relating to how he led his life deserve exploration. It is important to know, for example, that while Bourne was formulating his public statements against the war his letters show that he was attempting to avoid coming to grips with the conflict, and was, in fact, going through a period of personal turmoil. It is crucial to realize that, while he advocated the experimental life in his published writings, he found it very difficult to follow his pronouncements, not through disingenuousness, but because of the contrary forces of adventurousness and dependence playing on his mind. His letters reveal that, underlying the forceful prose of Bourne's published work, was a feeling of inarticulateness with which he constantly had to wrestle. The letters, therefore, are important not only as a source of autobiographical statement from a man who did not write a formal autobiography, but also as a complement to his published work. Through an examination of critical appraisals of Bourne's achievements, the circle of friends in which he operated, the function which letters played in his life, and the development of his personality as seen through the letters, we can come to a better understanding of the importance of these documents.

I

> More than any other of our fellows, he pointed the path of fusion which American leadership must take. His political discussions were actually lit by a spiritual human soul, the individual soul, the values of *being*. Through him, men who had lost touch with the spiritual base of life were led in its direction, since his discussions upon actual events, his discussions of the Machine, furnished a channel they could follow.
>
> —Waldo Frank on Bourne[1]

The stature which Randolph Bourne has attained as a commentator on American society largely reflects the judgment of his distinguished friends—Van Wyck Brooks, Paul Rosenfeld, and Waldo Frank—who were themselves cultural critics. The music critic Paul Rosenfeld voiced an opinion shared by most of Bourne's contemporaries that Bourne was "a dialectical machine."[2] By the power of his personality Bourne held together his many interests. With his masterful intellect "he made himself a wedge of crimson into the dun, the timorousness, the cheap self-satisfaction of his community."[3] In Rosenfeld's view, Bourne's power to organize the contrary forces of his times, to categorize influences, to act as the cutting edge in the search for truth, surmounted the disorienting chaos of the cultural material with which he was working. For Rosenfeld, Bourne represented the ideal of the socially responsible intellectual—one who is able to exert influence on social conditions through the forceful application of the power of his mind.

Van Wyck Brooks also described Bourne in terms of a cultural dialectic, but for Brooks this polarity was present explicitly within Bourne's thought, rather than implicitly in the tensions of Bourne's position. Brooks admired Bourne's ability to draw together the sociological and the artistic perspectives of society into one all-encompassing, comprehensive vision. "No other of our younger critics," he said, "had cast so wide a net."[4] Brooks, too, lauded Bourne's social responsibility; in fact, Bourne was the leader of what Brooks called the young intelligentsia. For Brooks, the dialectic in which Bourne was engaged lay within and was function of the ability of the intellectual to internalize the complexities of society.[5] Sooner or later, Brooks conjectured, Bourne would have had to choose either the life of the political activist, or the role of the artist. Brooks considered Bourne's opposition to the First World War as a necessary interlude in Bourne's career as an artist; Bourne's task in the twenties, according to Brooks, would have been to develop a great American literary tradition linked to a specifically American way of life.[6] Even though Brooks may have impressed Bourne into the service of the intellectual mission he favored, it is true that Bourne would have found it difficult to maintain the equilibrium of his central position in the cultural battle, between, as Waldo Frank puts it, the political rebel and the artist.

Bourne was a leader for these men, because he showed them the power of the intellect, made doubly impressive by the fact that this brilliant mind was trapped in a misshapen body. More than that, Bourne demonstrated to them that a way could be found through the contrary forces of society, that "a path of fusion" could be made, which the intellectual alone could construct. Bourne alone could choose the middle path between what Frank calls the Machine and the Recluse. Like the political activist, Bourne could be concerned with the world, which is the Machine, but, like the artist, he could withdraw from the world in order to find that Life on which the artist feeds. Frank concluded that this dialectic between the artistic and the sociological is unique to the United States; in Europe these are united into the integer of culture. Alone among Americans, Bourne was able to embrace the two and was, thus, in the best position to synthesize our intellectual life into the unit "culture."[7] "He was a humanist," Rosenfeld lamented, "and the men left us are sociologists, political thinkers, professors, and critics."[8]

Because of both descriptions of his appearance and his effectiveness as a cultural critic, Bourne became a mythical figure to critics who were acquainted with him only intellectually. The keynote in the creation of the myth of Randolph Bourne was delivered by Lewis Mumford in 1930. In Mumford's view, "Randolph Bourne was precious to us because of what he was, rather than because of what he had actually written."[9] Mumford, who did not know Bourne personally, was less interested in the creative tension within Bourne than he was in the effect which Bourne had on an audience of intellectuals. In Mumford's view, there was little doubt that Bourne died with his potential as a cultural critic unfulfilled; he classfies most of what Bourne had produced as "journalism," rather than enduring analysis.[10] Far more important to Mumford was Bourne's function in the awakening of a generation to its role in American culture, "that mingling of passionate resolve and critical inquiry which was the very spirit of America in 1914."[11] Mumford lamented that the vitality of Bourne's image decreased as the audience became more removed from this spirit. To reacquaint an audience with Bourne in a vital way would be to retrieve that receding spirit. Mumford's account is sympathetic and laudatory, but it does not do the greatest service to an understanding of the man whose memory he wishes to preserve.

Mumford's reaction to Bourne is based on the effect on the reader rather than on the thoughts of the author. For him Bourne is the spirit of the "Aufklärung of 1910"[12] whose works should be preserved as historical documents which would inspire more than they could instruct. To relegate Bourne to obscurity would be to deny a range of possibilities in American life; even though Bourne did not have the chance to write the works which either existed as germs within his published essays or were discovered as posthumous fragments, Americans need the vista which Bourne's work painted of American society:

His view of life was maturing, deepening, not yet ready for rounded expression, it was still a promise; a cool luminous dawn was spreading
across the skies, but the landscape was still in silhouette, and one could
only guess what shapes, what vistas, what living creatures it might show
and what inviting roads might lead away through it.[13]

In the view of the myth-makers, represented by Mumford, Bourne
appears as a mysterious figure, a representative of his times, yet
killed by them, a harbinger of the decade which could have followed,
but didn't; Bourne becomes a caricature, a sketch frequently made
lovingly, but an incomplete figure nonetheless. Dos Passos' poem in
1919 presents the most extreme portrayal of that outline:

If any man has a ghost
Bourne has a ghost
A tiny twisted unscared ghost in a black cloak
hopping along the grimy old brick and brownstone
streets still left in downtown New York,
crying out in a shrill soundless giggle:
war is the health of the state.[14]

Recent critics have both returned to and amplified the view of
Bourne's contemporaries. For these men—Christopher Lasch, Sherman Paul and Henry F. May—Bourne is a representative thinker of
his times, but he has been stripped of his mythical qualities. No longer does Bourne stand for a decade of cultural conflict, but he is one
perhaps prime example of the toll which society took from the cultural critic of the period. Lasch, and other critics, have succeeded in
re-humanizing Bourne, in creating what Lillian Schlissel calls a
usuable Bourne, distinct from the Bourne myth which had developed, and have used Bourne's letters as an element of this humaniza-
tion. These critics, too, realize that Bourne is the prototypical intellectual of the period, one for whom, as Christopher Lasch puts it,
"thinking fulfills the function of work and play."[15] Bourne believed
in Progressive education, that learning existed as a continuum from
the earliest years through higher education and that at every stage of
development contact with the society beyond the classroom led to
valuable experiences which would not only shape the student but
which would, eventually, lead to the reformation of society through
the collective vision of the students. The developing intellectual,
therefore, was placed in an organic, functional relationship with a

society in which there was a clear relationship between thought and action. The problem for Bourne, as Lasch sees it, was how to take the spirit of youth with him into middle age, how to maintain the stance of the reformer, separated from the social structure by both age and perspective, while at the same time assuming social responsibility.[16] Bourne represents the problematics of a radicalism propounding a generational critique of society. For Lasch the dialectic was between the urge of the intellectual to participate in the workings of society and the necessity for critical distance:

> Because his vocation is to be a critic of society, in the most general sense, and because the value of his criticism is presumed to rest on a measure of detachment from the current scene, the intellectual's relation to the rest of society is never entirely comfortable.[17]

His essays on youth made Bourne a representative of his generation. In Henry F. May's analysis, Bourne belonged both to the Liberation, which employed European ideas as a fulcrum to displace the American genteel tradition, and to the Innocent Rebellion, which stressed generational revolution. Bourne helped to popularize such thinkers as Henri Bergson, Friedrich Nietzsche, H. G. Wells, G. B. Shaw, and, to a lesser extent, Freud, and thus aided the attack of European thought upon American genteel culture.[18] He believed in the function of spiritual and artistic liberation, which would be achieved primarily through the upheaval of generational change, and was thus a member of the Innocent Rebellion.[19] May's list of thinkers who were important to the Liberation and the Innocent Rebellion reads like a compilation of Bourne's most respected authors— Shaw, Ibsen, Dostoievsky, Nietzsche, James, Dewey, Bergson, and Freud.[20]

If thought was work and play for Bourne, it was also a responsibility; if this position as the representative of youth gave Bourne a specific voice, it also presented him with the onus of speaking for his generation. As Sherman Paul summarizes, "What is impressive in Bourne's career, finally, is the attempt to master disillusionment and despair by recovering the very history of his generation, by learning the lessons it had to teach and plotting the course it might take."[21] Bourne's position, therefore, necessitated a continual confrontation with the different alternatives of social development. While he was able to state his views on political, cultural, and literary matters articulately in his published work, he found the exploration of the tensions within himself tumultuous and unsettling; paradoxically, his central position could also lead to inarticulateness.

As Paul and Lasch point out, this exertion resulted in a great reliance upon his friends,[22] who had been considered less important when Bourne was depicted as the embodiment of the Spirit of 1910. These confidants served specific, recuperative functions: to one he confided his political views, to another his artistic values, and to a third he complained of his inarticulateness. Indeed, it is his ability to act as the cutting edge while experiencing the stress of his position that is so impressive. It is through Bourne's letters that the effort which the life of the socially responsible intellectual exacted can be seen. These letters counterbalance the forceful, persuasive essays which Bourne published. Together, the published work and the letters present the reader with a more complete portrait of a complex, impressive, and human thinker.

II

Very little is known about Bourne's early years. Even the extensive research of John Moreau, who wrote a critical biography of Bourne in the early '60's, has produced little information. There is scanty record of Bourne's father, Charles, who had left the family before Bourne reached his teens. From an early age, therefore, Randolph was in the company of women: his mother and grandmother, and his two sisters. The one male authority figure, his maternal uncle Halsey Bennett, was a wealthy Newark lawyer who supported the family. For him Bourne did not have kind feelings. Randolph was not a protected child. Moreau notes evidence which indicates that from the time he contracted his handicap until his graduation from high school, Randolph insisted on participating in all activities and overlooked his physical disabilities.

After his graduation from high school the situation changed, however. Randolph did not go off to college directly, but endeavored to earn money to support himself and his family. It is unclear exactly how many jobs he held, but he did work in a Morristown office for a period, and then obtained work in a piano roll cutting shop, about which he was later to write. Indeed, this experience, along with his perception of the town of Bloomfield, helped drive him to college. Bloomfield was transforming itself from an independent town, with a full range of social positions, to a commuter suburb dependent on New York. While it had contained factories controlled by families which were held in high esteem within the community, it was becoming increasingly middle class—homogeneous and dominated by New York businesses. Bourne had nothing but scorn for these businesses—his father may have left the family because of business failures—and regarded living in Bloomfield as stultifying. The piano roll job sealed his distaste for the life of the manual laborer. Bourne felt exploited here, because he and his co-worker were paid increasingly smaller amounts for their piece-work by their employer, who spent his time amusing himself on the piano. In 1909, Bourne succeeded in getting a scholarship to Columbia and entered the freshman class, six years older than his classmates.

At Columbia Bourne took both social science and literature courses, but quickly became disenchanted with the literature department, which was oriented toward the classics. Little he found in his literature courses pertained to contemporary life. The last straw came, he relates in "The History of a Literary Radical," when his class undertook an intensive study of Tennyson while he was discovering "the poignant torture" of Tolstoi.[23] After that he found it impossible to associate with the formal study of literature, and instead turned to the social sciences, where James Harvey Robinson, Charles Beard, Franklin Giddings, Franz Boaz, and James T. Shotwell offered him courses more related to contemporary society. Bourne retained his interest in literature; however, he demanded writing which was anchored in a realistic approach to social problems. Realists, naturalists, European writers on social problems, political essayists, and anarchists—none of whose books were discussed in literature courses—therefore became his fare.

He did not abandon his concern for literature; only his taste changed. He did not jettison literature for sociology, but attempted to find sociological literature, writing which responded to the social setting in which it was composed. Thus, while he classified himself as a literary radical, he could not endure radical works which were not good literature. He looked for "the vigor of literary form, the value of sincerity and freshness of style" in the works he read. His mission in life, and the function that literature played in its fulfillment, had been transformed. Literature was now a tool in his search for cultural understanding: "He was to put literature into its proper place, making all 'culture' serve its apprenticeship for him as interpretation of things larger than itself, of the course of individual lives and the great tides of society."[24]

During this time his career as an essayist began. Bourne had always eagerly sought the opportunity to voice his ideas; he had belonged to several discussion groups and had edited the Columbia literary magazine, the *Monthly*, during 1911. In that year, however, a professor, Frederick Woodbridge, suggested that he submit articles to *The Atlantic*, which Bourne did. By the time of his graduation from Columbia in 1912 Bourne was considered one of the leading spokesmen for the younger generation. During the 1912-1913 academic year Bourne worked on a Masters degree, for which he wrote a paper about Bloomfield, later published as "The Social Order in an American Town." More important for his development, however, he succeeded in getting a Gilder Fellowship, which provided him with the funds for a year's travel in Europe.

Also during his college years he met three friends, and made one additional acquaintance, who were to exert a strong influence on his life. Carl Zigrosser was an artist and fellow Columbia man. His later career culminated in the Curatorship of the Philadelphia Museum of Fine Art. During this time, however, Zigrosser worked at Keppel's, a print gallery run by the brother of one of Bourne's college deans. Arthur Macmahon, the second friend, was a classmate of Bourne's. He began teaching at Columbia in the Political Science Department in 1913. He eventually became the President of the American Political Science Association. Both men were roommates of Bourne, Macmahon during the 1912-1913 school year, and Zigrosser during 1915.

Alyse Gregory, Bourne's closest female confidant, first contacted Bourne as a result of his essay, "The Excitement of Friendship." Miss Gregory had nothing to do with the Columbia-Barnard circle, but introduced Bourne to a variety of people and activities in the area of Greenwich Village in which she lived. At the time she was engaged in suffragette activities. She became the managing editor of *The Dial* in the 1920's and then moved to England. Also because of "The Excitement of Friendship" Bourne exchanged letters with Prudence Winterrowd during 1913 and 1914. He tried to persuade the Indiana girl to come to Columbia, which she did, but only after Bourne had left for Europe. The correspondence diminishes after her abortive attempt to enter his milieu—she stayed at Columbia only a week and returned to Indiana, where she eventually became an employee of the state government.

Bourne left for the Continent in July 1913, hoping that a secure environment would greet his return—a stable circle of friends and stimulating employment—but determined to grasp this opportunity to lead the experimental life. During the year Bourne traveled throughout the Continent and spent three-month stints in both London and Paris. He attended many women's suffrage meetings, met with socialists and anarchists, and sampled the culture of the avant garde. He also received an initiation into the coming war; he was in Germany just before the war broke out and arrived in Berlin as war was declared. He escaped to Denmark before the initial chaos of war closed the borders temporarily and arrived back in the United States in August.

The *New Republic* served as a home for Bourne for the next two years. For it he wrote several of his educational articles—he traveled to Gary in 1915 and wrote *The Gary Schools* under the magazine's auspices—and contributed many book reviews. Nevertheless, Bourne felt frustrated on the staff of the magazine. He was not given freedom to speak to political issues, but was designated as the expert on educational matters. Therefore, during late 1916 Bourne began to focus more of his attention on *The Dial*, a magazine which had recently moved its editorial office to New York and which promised him more freedom. Once again, Bourne contributed mostly reviews, but the books he considered were drawn from a broader range of subjects. He also received the opportunity to write articles on more overtly political subjects. Most notable were his attack on

John Dewey's capitulation to the war logic, "Conscience and Intelligence in War," and his defense of Theodore Dreiser, "The Art of Theodore Dreiser." Still, his relationship with the magazine was not altogether harmonious, particularly as American involvement in the War grew. His attention therefore turned to a new and short-lived journal, the *Seven Arts*, for which he wrote the most famous of his anti-war articles. During 1917 he contributed such attacks as "The Puritan's Will to Power," "War and the Intellectuals," and "Twilight of the Idols," but, many conjectured, contributed to the demise of the magazine as well. For the rest of his life he continued to write for *The Dial* and was starting an autobiographical novel at the time of his death in the influenza epidemic of 1918, on December 22nd.

III

> Each man must have his "I"; it is more
> necessary than bread.
> —from Bourne's journal

In the 1930's Lewis Mumford tried unsuccessfully to interest a publisher in the letters of Randolph Bourne; "it appeared," he lamented, "that they were too meager in content to give any sufficient clue to his mind."[25] Since then, a substantial collection of Bourne's letters has been donated to the Columbia University library, disproving Mumford's opinion. The reassessment of Bourne which has taken place in the last fifteen years also demonstrates the value of Bourne's letters as a reflection of his personality. In fact, they emerge as documents of equal importance to the published work. Through the letters we see Bourne as he builds up the rhetorical position which he articulates so well in his tightly argued essays. In the letters we ascertain the strain of his position as the vacillations of his ego. The letters are important for the themes they elicit. For example, many letters which remain from Bourne's year in Europe present a perceptive picture of European civilization just before the outbreak of war. Most of all, though, the letters are engrossing. They are written in a self-analytical, yet precise style which continues to hold the attention of the reader.

These are consistently youthful letters, full of exuberance, searching, and turmoil. In his college letters, which most closely reflect the confidence of his essays, Bourne demonstrates his intellectual sophistication. Letters to Carl Zigrosser, and, especially, to Prudence Winterrowd reflected the eagerness with which Bourne sought and assimilated knowledge. In Europe he proved that he was both an enthusiastic and perceptive observer. He received a vision of the degree of commitment which true radicalism entailed during this year, in which he witnessed suffragette rallies, the emergence of the English Labor Party, and the anti-militarism demonstrations in France. His position on the *New Republic*, however, offered him only frustration; what he had thought to be a platform for his plans for social action devolved into a routine job of reviewing books as his views became increasingly unpopular in the climate of mounting war sentiment. Until his association with the *Seven Arts* began in 1917, Bourne felt increasingly restless and ineffective. Only during 1917 and 1918, in the *Seven Arts* and *The Dial*, did Bourne finally have the opportunity to express his principles. As his commitment to essays which reflected his maturing principles increased, the importance of his letters declined. Early in his career he had used letters to try out new ideas on friends and to record the development of his sensibilities. Especially during the European year his letters attained the stature of essays. By the time the war approached, however, Bourne had matured. He was able to stabilize himself and to respond to the attack upon his principles which the war represented. Throughout most of his career, Bourne had weighed his degree of commitment to causes—and, conversely, his sense of his own hypocrisy—in his letters. With the advent of the war these functions were surrendered to his essays.

Two forces are remarkable in Bourne's public life: the power of his vision in sorting through the forces he saw operating in society, and the strength of intellect directing that vision. Yet, in his correspondence Bourne vacillates in a way seldom seen in his essays. His letters reveal a struggling, dialectical mind which managed to unify itself into a forceful model of wholeness when it faced the world publicly. It is in the letters that we best see Bourne's mind in opposition to itself, searching for a consistent set of values, plagued by feelings of inarticulateness. These enormous tensions critics have sensed in Bourne's published work; but it is through the resource of his remarkable letters that these stresses can best be illuminated.

Bourne's obvious physical handicap, his philosopher's sense of the importance of ideas, and his Progressive belief in the obligation of intellectuals to social action form the major tensions in his life. Bourne was justly proud of the way in which he had overcome severe physical deformities. On the other hand, Bourne felt the distance in which this deformity often resulted. While the writings of William James and Henri Bergson excited Bourne, who thrived on philosophical discussions at Columbia, theoretical discussions encouraged in him a feeling of being socially handicapped. His friends—Alyse Gregory, who delivered feminist lectures, for example—could balance strictly intellectual concerns with strenous social action; he could not. In his most forceful prose, this sense of handicap transcends personal references as Bourne condemns a society which, despite its apparent devotion to principle and to the rule of the expert, handicapped all intellectuals.

Bourne searches for a consistent public identity in his letters. He both issues a call for action and realizes that he must be a spectator. Before the war he questions his allegiance to some of the values of American culture—family mores, religious beliefs, standards of criticism. From these letters a consistent "I" does not emerge; rather, the reader views Bourne as he constantly reworks his position. Bourne identifies with both the social worker, who must show how a personal moral conviction takes shape as a social attitude and in social action, and the poet, who constantly struggles to engage his vision in society.[26] With the search for a profession, sociological and aesthetic interpretations of his moral convictions battle for supremacy within Bourne. Along with defining his role in society, he must identify himself intellectually without mirroring the limitations of his physical existence:

I wish I was artist enough to use my experience without tangling myself up too much again in my imagination. The reformer got such a terrific start in my youth over the artist that I'm afraid the latter is handicapped for life. The reformer with an amour-propre is a temperament pretty quenching for any upflow of art in one, isn't it? (12/6/16)

Bourne's tendency to analyze himself was not only caused by his reliance on his own philosophy, but also by his vision of the unique place of the intellectual of his generation in society. Taking a mediating position between society and the dispassionate observer, the intellectual was subject to suasion by both the sociological and the aesthetic points of view. The year which Bourne spent in Europe proved to be the turning point in this regard; his Wanderjahr offered him the opportunity to refine his conception of profession against European models and to test the resolve of his conviction in an unfamiliar environment.

At the beginning of this year he expresses many of the same sentiments he had voiced at Columbia. He associates the qualities of understanding and feeling with action, while his own imagining, tied as it is to observation, breeds only inaction and—implicitly— uselessness. While Bourne does not use these terms in any rigorous way, it is clear that his sense of action is still bound to the life of the social worker, to the person whose social activism is immediately demonstrable. In a short time, however, he is able to reconstruct his conception of action, to refocus the target of his reforming spirit. In order to have an effect on the world, one must be able to base "intellectual and emotional expression" upon a specific personality "with something to say and something to do." (11/3/13) The initial focus of activity must be the self; articulation must be based on the action of self-knowledge. Bourne has now found a new metaphor for the public self. No longer is he the soul of youth, gestating in the college environment, promising the reformation of the world; he is now the embattled self, drawing power from his ability to assimilate different experiences into his personality, and, with the strength of that personality, to confront ideas which must be reformed. The self has been activated. No longer is there a sense of ironic detachment from the world; rather, the self searches for a general context, a role, a specific function through which it can express itself. This resolve underlies his comments to Van Wyck Brooks written four years later:

> There is a certain superb arrogance in your implication that it is we and
> our friends who are to be the masters. Your coming book [*Letters and
> Leadership*] is a pretty comprehensive demolition of the claims of any
> type or class of American, past or present, to hold this membership for

us. You leave nobody, so that by mere process of elimination, it must be we fearless ones—and self-conscious ones—who are to hold it. (3/27/18)

Bourne has a mature, reflective vision of American intellectual life, and presented these conclusions as results of his own experience. What is more impressive is his ability to make general statements of the responsibilities of the intellectual in modern society which spring from his own development as one of the "self-conscious ones."

Bourne's letters reflect his ability to learn from experiences. During his year abroad, specific incidents, such as his experience with Stanley M. Bligh, helped Bourne to mature both his vision of the world and his definition of himself. Bourne was invited to Wales to spend a fortnight at the country estate of Bligh, a psychologist with whom he had corresponded, to talk about social psychology. Bourne looked forward to participating in the salon which such a rich, intelligent man would inevitably attract. His expectations were not fulfilled, however. Bligh turned out to be a militarist and a laissez-faire capitalist who lived on inherited wealth and had little sympathy for the poor. Immediately the two clashed, much to the embarrassment of all the guests and Mrs. Bligh, who turned Bourne out after a visit of only four days.

Initally, Bourne was shocked at this rebuff, but his letters show how he was able to justify both his and Bligh's actions, and how he was able to learn from the experience. His mood progresses from a feeling of triumph because he had not compromised any of his principles, through a period of resentment at Bligh's lack of courtesy, to an admission that "I had a hell of a time emotionally, though a wonderful time educationally." (9/13/13) This insight into the life of an English country gentleman convinced him of the decadence of English civilization, a feeling he was predisposed to hold, and revealed to him the workings of the English mind, which was able to segregate intellectual beliefs from political and cultural attitudes in a way which Bourne found unnatural. Chiefly because of the Bligh episode Bourne understood that England did not offer him the model of the intellectual for which he was searching; he turned, instead, to France. Through this episode, we also view the deep hurt that Bourne could feel at a personal affront, but the resiliency of his character, which could draw valuable experience out of even this situation.

It was in France that Bourne found the model for intellectual involvement in society. The intellectual was so respected in that country that the author was relieved of the basic concern over the existence of an audience for his thoughts, and was able to concentrate on the way in which these thoughts were to be presented. In the United States, Bourne had lamented over the fact that his ability to see all sides of an argument hindered his ability to express himself. During his experience in France he found that he could be more concerned with the style in which he expressed himself: "I am always conscious of the different ways in which the idea could be expressed or embodied, and, worse, what this or that type of person will think of it." (3/13/14) There are perils in writing—the creative process can never be effortless—but at least the position of the self is now clearly defined.

Bourne admired French civilization. An opera, he observed, was cheaper for the common man to attend than a motion picture, and, indeed, one saw many working class people at cultural events. With such an educated populace, the intellectual could have influence. Unlike the English, the French did not shrink from an argument and they were not inhibited by the Puritan sensibility which so permeated English civilization. (1/19/14) In France there was the sense of a national culture, in which everyone participated. As the capstone of this stood the national university, one of the institutions Bourne most admired. This represented to him the good aspects of French culture—the free access of the people of the country to the cultural institutions.

Although Bourne succeeds in finding a model for the interaction between a national culture and its intellectuals he is still occasionally trapped within the old dialectic of action and inaction, between the activist social philosophy and the ironic critique. Even after he has seen the admirable French example of intellectual participation in society he is able to say that when he comes into contact with "real people" he is struck with "the impossible philosophicalness of my ideas and the really dreadful seriousness of my attitudes." (2/16/14) He fears that he may accept himself as he is, "instead of building careers, and of feeling that I ought to make prodigious efforts to be somewhere else and be something else." He should have written more during this year in Europe, but, he apologizes for himself, it is hard to conceive of the audience for which he is writing, and also, it is difficult to compose essays when so much time is spent adapting to the foreign environment. Bourne still longs for a satisfying routine, a shelter from the self-pity into which he occasionally falls.

Often, though, Bourne feels a great sense of potential, a potential which is being increased each day as experience is stored, and which will inevitably be expressed. For the present, he explains to Carl Zigrosser, "we all are Hamlets," but soon "our will will begin to operate freely and creatively. Our task," he concludes, "is now bent to getting that poise and understanding [of] the chaotic world about us." (11/16/13) He now has a feeling of consistent activity— he is struggling against decadence, he explains. The intellectual has become the rejuvenator of culture.

In Europe Bourne turned from the basic problems of self-definition to the more external questions of audience and social climate. Without an audience for which to write, he realizes, "Writing . . . must lack real vitality as I feel all mine does." (1/5/14) He feels that in order to write he must find an audience and know it more clearly than before; this conception relies heavily on his definition of friendship. The problem then becomes to be able to identify with a socially significant group which is intellectually stimulating. (1/19/14) The status of the intellectual in America, then, becomes more of an issue. Bourne laments the American inarticulateness. (3/23/14) He accuses American universities of not training a class of intellectuals who will attain a position of leadership in society:

> Our Universities still tend to produce as professors the hard-working patient mediocre scholar, or the clear-sighted skeptical critic, rather than the intellectual leader. Our intellectuals will have to sharpen up their knowledge, and stiffen their fibre a good deal, it seems to me, before they can take the commanding place of leadership which they fill in France. (3/11/14)

If only he had been educated in such a society as France where intellectuals were trained to expect leadership roles he would not be plagued by the feeling that he will be coming home "a supercillious intellectual snob." (4/6/14)

In Bourne's letters we see his effort to control his present, and to transform his conception of the past into useful experience, as the dialectic between drift and mastery, a metaphor which, for Bourne, resonated with the terms of the Walter Lippmann analysis by that name. He struggled, once again, with the tensions he set up in his early essay, "The Experimental Life": how to order the course of a life which was inherently beyond the control of the individual. Europe confirmed to Bourne that the role of the intellectual in society could be active. He developed both his sociological sense and his aesthetic appreciation during this year and was now ready to assume the position of cultural critic. The question was whether he could master the specific circumstances which would allow him to attain this position, or whether he would drift from one position to another in search of a profession.

And, in fact, a position on the staff of the *New Republic* awaited his return. His doubts about his ability to produce, and, more deeply, to control the flow of his own life, continued to concern him, however, throughout his tenure on the *New Republic*, *the Dial*, and the *Seven Arts*. His concerns about his position dominate the letters; seldom do the letters mention progressive education, which was Bourne's major interest in his published work. Rather, he attempts to live out the implications of his philosophy.

Bourne found that the establishment of a routine did not assure mastery. More important than a secure profession was his ability to justify his role as a productive intellectual. With the feeling of territory came the assurance of boundaries, limits which could threaten creativity. "Must one look forward," he asks, "to a gradually shrinking horizon of stimulating pretenses, a gradual drying up of this 'outside' which has seemed so wonderful and glowing to me?" (12/1/14) Many of the constrictions of the scope of his creativity stemmed from the *New Republic*; articles he wrote for them were pure drudgery, he explains, and, besides, few of them saw the light of day. The danger is, he fears, that he will "drift off into peevishness" if this adversary relationship continues. (12/1/14) Occasionally he feels persecuted by the magazine and does lapse into the peevishness he wishes to avoid. He complains of starvation wages, although evidently the magazine paid him adequately. (8/24/16) By the middle of 1915, by his own assessment, he had published over 31,000 words in the *New Republic*, but this creditable production did not satisfy him because he did not feel in control. "I drift so horribly pulling myself up with a start, only to slip the oar again somehow. Place would help, but it would have to be people too and then some smashing victory, which just to think of would give me a feeling of power." (6/25/15) It is this feeling of powerlessness which prevents him from satisfying himself with his writing.

Yet, characteristically, in the next letter he writes that he is working well. (7/24/15) Bourne realizes, in moments of penetration, that his friction with the world represents a constant and fathomless resource of creativity, if only he can learn to tap it. (11/15/14) After all, he decides in the summer of 1915, there must be some centrifugal force which prohibits him from being at the center of any organization. As his European experience fades, he realizes that the best procedure for him would be to recognize that the locus of his self lies in the poet and not in the social worker—outside the boundaries of social action in the realm of ideas. He is born to be a commentator, not a participant. The problems of place and audience remain. How is he to find a location from which to write which will not exhaust him just from the tension between his position and society? Further, how is he to assure that society will want the writings of one who defines himself as an observer? (9/20/16)

Nevertheless, there is new realization that this position he has selected is an active one; all of the turbulence of his early years has led him to precisely the sort of delicate position which he would not consciously have chosen. This sense of destiny, which originates in Bourne's concern for youth, permeates these letters. As he explains to his niece, Dorothy Teall, "let butterfly self grow up in chrysalis family and burst with the emancipating years." (8/19/15) There is a sense of inevitability in this development which is linked to little conscious effort on the part of the self. The major task for the self becomes, in fact, to recognize the tendencies of this development, to master the attributes which destiny develops. In one letter, which demonstrates his ability to analyze himself, Bourne explains his present position:

> I wore myself thin against an immovable wall, got into habits of despair
> and futility that are riveting me still, and all to no purpose. Nothing that
> I planned and made for did I get, but gradually my own seemed to find
> me. My labor to settle myself in the world was really worse than wasted.
> If I had merely sat down calmly and read and written and thought as best
> I could, and made the most of what was lying around me, I would be
> infinitely better off now in the work that finally found me. In spite of all
> my desperate efforts to renounce college, to be content with my poverty,
> to get a good routine position, to work hard and support myself and help
> my family, to give up all thought of writing or ambition, I now find my-
> self exactly where a few years ago I should have considered it Quixotic
> even to pose as an ideal. (7/9/15)

The solution, he realizes, both for the problems he experiences at
the *New Republic* and for the uncertainties he feels is self-confidence
and pride: "the only solution is to get so somehow proud of myself
that I cannot bear to have the world deprived of what I could tell
them." (8/17/15)

Bourne's estrangement from Carl Zigrosser was the sort of
dislocating event which threatened his faith in his ability to master
his destiny. The argument, which centered on the character of Florence King and an accusation of a broken confidence, was very complicated. As with most disputes among friends, it is very hard to
assess the truth and distribute the blame; in any case, the dynamics
of the argument are not as significant as the effect these events had
on Bourne. Again Bourne becomes the searcher—"O, for that calm
stability of comfort, place and mood, which I keep looking forward
to, where I can work and really live!" (1/3/16) Most often, Bourne
mourns the loss of his friend through the labyrinth of this complex
argument, but he can also assert that "I am the victim, lonely and
scorned" (1/4/16) His inclination, he realizes, is toward melodrama,
to "flit around from one [friend] to another, a homeless, helpless
waif, eternally passing out into the cold from their warm and confident firesides." (1/21/16) He knows that he must write, and yet
he cannot rid himself of these domestic complications which induce
self-indulgence and which distract him from larger, cultural questions: "24 hours a day and the strength of ten wouldn't achieve the
work I want to do. And I spend my time drinking tea, talking about

my woes, of psychologizing privately about my domestic complications." The incident, he laments, has so consumed him that his life has developed into the meticulous, self-analytical intricacies of a Henry James novel. Here Bourne wars with his own tendencies to "psychologize," to look into himself and to be concerned with his own sensitivity.

Bourne also resists the opposite strain of active participation in the political world. A conflict was inevitable, however, when Bourne, a pacifist, was confronted with the government's participation in World War I. Bourne continually voices his restiveness at the role which he is forced to play: "I seem to disagree on the war with every rational and benevolent person I meet. I crave some pagan monastery, some 'great, good place' where I can go and stay till the war is over." (9/17) While the war does give Bourne a specific voice, it increases his self-consciousness. However, this time, Bourne's awareness of the singularness of his position is accurate, not distorted:

> I feel very much secluded from the world, very much out of touch with my times, except perhaps with the Bolsheviki. The magazines I write for die violent deaths, and all my thoughts seem unprintable. If I start to write on public matters I discover that my ideas are seditious, and if I start to write a novel I discover that my outlook is immoral if not obscene. (11/26/17)

The reward for this separation from society is, however, that while the rest of the country is enslaved to a war-mentality, he is free. This reward is far from pleasant—"It is not fun being a free man in a slave world" (5/31/18)—but it does afford Bourne a strong, consistent, moral voice with which to speak.

Bourne's letters lay the foundation for his public writing, both in their content and in the self-conscious use of the genre of letter writing. Bourne allows his letters to ramble as freely as ordinary dialogue in an attempt to follow more closely the workings of his mind. While some of the letters are developed logically, other range

through many subjects. "Now I had no idea when I started this
letter that I should come out where I am," he comments (6/30/13);
he realizes that this haphazard development is what he must expect
when he is "going through [a] letter trying to converse with it just
as if I were hearing it in person." (3/2/13) Bourne also uses letters
as a theraputic monologue—an analysis which a friend is privileged to
overhear. After meeting Alyse Gregory, for example, Bourne explains
that he has painted an artificially black picture of himself for her. He
does this so that "as soon as I begin to describe it, the whole thing
incurably lightens." (6/14/13) He realizes that any form of expression is subject to the egotism of the author and therefore must be
taken as a version of the truth which is sometimes clouded over with
obfuscations, or, more likely, is distorted by self-advertisement:
"One has only to take pen in hand, and every word instinctively becomes a flatterer of one's egotism, the sentences conspire to make
the writer better, braver, nobler than he ever was or hopes to be, and,
not only that, but fixes that noble character in black and white."
(4/10/13)

Bourne was aware of both the benefits and the drawbacks of
self-reflective letters. Though his ability to bare himself before his
correspondents does not falter, his faith in his ability to portray
accurately the condition of his ego wavers. A Tantalus theme runs
through his life. He feels that there is a disparity between the ideals
he has set for himself and his achievements. While he can be proud
of himself occasionally, more often he is disappointed that he constantly judges his accomplishments "by unobtainable standards"
which deny him the "solid satisfaction of achievement" and cause
his horizons to recede as fast as he progresses toward them.
(6/30/13)

More than external or formal concerns dominate these letters.
We see Bourne concerned with himself. While he does deal with
social problems, current events, and the position of what he considered to be a class of intellectuals in American society, he is primarily
concerned with his ability to grow, to continue to learn, and to
express himself. While he was unable to resolve his relationship with
society to his satisfaction, he was able to articulate through his letters his varying moods and lasting feelings.

To Alyse Gregory he admits his envy of her commitment to the cause of women's rights. He sees that this must produce a sense of stability, a feeling of identification, which he feels he lacks. For him "everything beckons, the air seems filled with winged spirits of opportunity, yet until one is seized and flung into something, one never can get oneself quite committed." While Bourne's ironic critique relies on a separate perspective on society, he finds himself unable to achieve those habits of persistent work which he longs for without this feeling of participation. The threat here is more than uncertainty; his ability to follow the life of writing is called into question. These tensions are evident from the beginning of his career. He acknowledges that *the Atlantic* has encouraged him, even suggested articles for him to write, but he recognizes that he must be able to assume his profession without their "coddling." Both personal achievement and social responsibility demand that he do this— "There is so much to be done, so much to be said, while I don't seem quite able to make the connections, close the switch that will set the current flowing." (6/1/13)

For this fulfillment, Bourne concludes at the end of his senior year, college did not prepare him. The voice he assumed through his published work, the voice of youth, proclaimed that the new generation would undo the onerous traditions of the old. But, while this gave him a consistent voice during his twenties, the passage of time did not promise him a vocation in life based on this generational stance. The tension between his philosophy and his search for a profession was thus set up: "My success in life depends so largely upon my growing up that I don't like to think that I am still impressing people as an infant prodigy." (5/18/13)

On the one hand he strives for a routine which will assure production, while on the other he seeks to surpass the limitations of his own perspective, to live by the mandate in "Youth" that life not be ruled by the conventional: "Perhaps there is some spirit that makes every person with the gift of articulation say more than he is, speak clearly and authoritatively what he but dimly strives to reach, describe the heights seen by him in moments of penetration, though from far down the mountain side." (6/14/13)

During most of his career, therefore, Bourne's letters reflect

a constant struggle. He redefines the role of the intellectual in society and his particular role within this group. From his position as
an observer he battles with feelings of inarticulateness, the development of his identity, and his assessment of his own egotism. His
reactions to his own essays reflect the uncertainties of this struggle.
He sometimes feels the exhilaration of the mountain top, but then,
when he sees his ideas in print, he can "stumble and roll the full
length of the mountain-side." (4/19/13) On the other hand, essays
could offer reassurance. "The Life of Irony" was agony for him to
write, but once he saw it in print he was charmed by it. There is
more than the insecurity of the novice at work in these vacillations;
he could see his writing as a clear call for action or as the articulation
of a rigid—and therefore handicapped—philosophical position.
Opposition to the war gave Bourne such a strong, visceral sense of
commitment to a moral cause—a commitment he most effectively
expressed in essays rather than in letters—that the number of surviving letters declines sharply after September 1917. Few of the
remaining letters refer to the war issue; during this time Bourne was
much more preoccupied with his love for Esther Cornell. Throughout
his life Bourne had used his letters as vehicles for working out the
ambiguities of his own existence, the seeming contradictions between
his confident published work and his private insecurities. With the
advent of the war, however, all his attention turned toward opposition to intervention and his need for letter writing as a means of
maintaining his intellectual equilibrium declined.

IV

Any marked personal deficiency sufficiently noticeable to interrupt easy
and familiar intercourse with others, & make people talk *about* or *to* a
person rather than *with* him causes isolation & makes him feel chilled,
fearful & suspicious.

—from Bourne's journal

The problem of Bourne's handicap must be recognized but should not be overemphasized. While Bourne does not mention his disabilities frequently—he does occasionally refer to his "uninspiring self"—the influence of his handicap surfaces as an element of tone in the letters, as what he calls many times his tendency toward "peevishness." This self-indulgence and severe introspection are related to his disabilities. Many commentators have followed the portrayal of Bourne constructed by Dos Passos and have depicted Bourne as a courageous, but doomed, misshapen youth chastising America. Nevertheless, these handicaps did have a profound effect on Bourne's life, as can be seen in the tensions which exist in the letters. These tensions influence both the dynamics of Bourne's friendships and the tone of his letters, which varies from the celebratory to the self-pitying. There is a tension in these letters between the feeling of friendship for his correspondents—his ability to talk with them—and the uncertainty he felt about his relationships with them—his premonition that he was being talked about or talked to.

This thread of self-pity and self-consciousness running through his letters transcends the introspection one expects to see in the writings of an intellectual. He describes himself to Alyse Gregory as "a man cruelly blasted by the powers that brought him into the world," one for whom the "comradeship of men and women" is impossible, though he is "doubly endowed with desire." In this letter Bourne throws himself at the feet of Gregory and begs for emotional nurture; he proceeds to a lyrically self-conscious passage which is painful in its self-deprecation:

> Encase that soul, which is myself, in Puritan morality, and you produce a refined species of spiritual torture, which is relieved only by the demands and appeals, fortunately strong, of philosophy and music, and heaven-sent irony which softens and heals the wounds. But, to complete the job, make him poor and deny him the thorough satisfaction of the higher appeals, deny him steady work and thus make easy the sway of desire, and you force all his self-impelled action, all his thinking and constructive work to be done in hampering struggle with the unrealized desire, which yet—another irony—colors all his appreciations, motivates his love of personality, and fills his life with a sort of smouldering beauty. (1/19/14)

After returning from Europe the problems Bourne experienced

with friendship became more acute. While in Europe he had anticipated that his friends would remain a stable group which would
support him upon his return. In fact, the situation was much alter-
ed. When he resettled in New York, he moved to the lower East
Side, far from Columbia University, and was no longer directly connected with the academic community he had found so invigorating.
Alyse Gregory, Elizabeth Shepley Sergeant, and other career persons,
became his confidants. The dislocation which he felt affected him
deeply. "It is bad enough to be lonely away from your friends, but
what are you to do when you find yourself lonely in the midst of
them?" Bourne queries in November 1914. He feels like a mis-
anthrope, wonders if he is forcing himself on his unwilling acquaintances, and almost decides to assume a passive role and wait for them
to seek him out. He also assumes the role of the noble—and abused—
quester seeking out true companions: "Chase the fine, the true,
expressive people," he advises, "and let the rest slide to perdition.
Chase them indefatigably and find yourself in them. . . . They will
never completely satisfy, but perhaps you won't satisfy them."
(2/21/15) Bourne applies this metaphor of the quest through many
of his letters regarding friendship. After all, he admits, he doesn't
know himself very well; why should his relationships with his friends
be any more stable. On the other hand, he feels it dangerous to his
stability to be buffetted from one circle of friendship to another, to
suffer through alternating feelings of camaraderie and alienation.

Most often, though, his friends sustain Bourne, and he, in
turn, inspired them. Beulah Amidon, a close friend of Bourne's after
his return from Europe, voices sentiments which are common to
many reminiscences of Bourne written by his friends:

> It is as a conversationalist, I suppose, that I most often think of him, and
> I have heard many other friends say the same. There was no redeeming
> feature in his appearance—even his eyes had no magnetism, and his hands
> were clumsy and undistinguished. And yet when he talked one forgot the
> misshapen body, the scarred head and face, the awkward gestures. So
> many topics kindled him—not only the few things in which he passion-
> ately believed (pacifism, education, individual integrity) but the books
> he read, the people he met, the things the literary critics did and didn't
> say, flags on Fifth Avenue, a ferry boat trip across the harbor, Greenwich
> Village history, the Greek dramatists—there is no end to the list. He

talked with a slow, relentless flow of words, with pauses made necessary
by his difficult breathing. And he listened, too. What he said was sometimes acid, often brilliant, almost always provocative. Also, he seemed
able to draw out of his listeners more than they knew, and to endow
them with an unaccustomed gift of speech. Then his response lifted the
talk to a new level.[27]

Indeed, Bourne's friends have been revitalized through these letters,
even as they preserved these documents for posterity through their
care and respect. Although Bourne corresponded with many famous
individuals, the most perceptive of the letters which survive were
written to confidants who are less familiar to present day readers.
Bourne confided most in Alyse Gregory, whom he met through her
comments on his article, "The Excitement of Friendship." They
met briefly in June 1913 and Bourne sent her some of his most
sensitive, perceptive, and self-analytical letters during his European
year. Gregory was active as a feminist lecturer and as a journalist.
For Bourne she possessed the qualities of empathy and emotion he
associated with women and also represented the active, productive
radical, who, unlike himself, was constantly involved in the political
activities of society. Bourne's concept of the perfect comrade was
female, and Gregory most closely approximated this ideal. Bourne
believed that through women the self could be liberated from the
restraints which male sexuality imposed on it; the feminine sensibility could free men from the "Crudities of this hard, hierarchical,
over-organized, anarchic . . . civilization" through "the more personal, social, emotional attitude toward things." (1/19/14)

Second among his closest friends was Carl Zigrosser, whom
Bourne met while attending Columbia. During his college years,
Bourne felt close to Zigrosser, who, like him, was older and more
mature than Bourne's classmates, and wrote him very confidential,
sometimes anecdotal letters. Later, during his European year, he
began to concentrate on artistic and architectural subjects, with
which he knew Zigrosser would be most familiar. Gradually the two
became less familiar until the final argument at the end of 1915 over
Zigrosser's fiancée dealt a blow from which the friendship never
recovered.

Another college companion who received several good letters,

particularly from Europe, was Arthur Macmahon, who had roomed
with Bourne in 1911. Because of Macmahon's professional interest
in political science, it is to him that Bourne directed his political
analyses. Primarily, though, Bourne relied on Macmahon to keep him
in touch with the Columbia scene, so his letters to Macmahon ring
with the overtones of college camaraderie.

Many letters remain from an undoubtedly lengthy correspondence which Bourne had with his mother, Sarah Bourne. These letters
are mostly informational; during his year in Europe, for example,
Bourne informed his mother of where he had been—drawing extensively from a notebook he kept during that year—but reserved more
personal embellishments for other correspondents.

To other recipients Bourne parcelled out his personality more
specifically. His letters to a close friend of the family, Dorothy Teall,
were avuncular. He gave her advice from Europe on how to lead her
life at Barnard College, at which she enrolled in 1913, and, later, he
tried to secure her a job as a secretary to a psychiatrist friend, Dr.
Beatrice Hinkle. In the letters to Prudence Winterrowd Bourne
plays the teacher, guiding her to Columbia and drawing her further
into radical thought. Remarkable letters survive from 1913 in which
Bourne lays out for her his beliefs in both the instrumentalism of
the American pragmatists and the Bergsonian mysticism he found so
attractive. It is also interesting to see how Bourne, who did not
meet Winterrowd until 1915, quickly warmed to the task of explaining his positions, and, indeed, of analyzing himself for his admirer.
Finally, during 1916 Bourne fell in love with Esther Cornell, an
actress, and a few warm, self-conscious letters survive from the two
years of their friendship.

Little of Bourne's professional correspondence remains. The
most significant contribution are several letters written to Van Wyck
Brooks, who was both a friend and a fellow critic. In these letters
Bourne discusses his intellectual beliefs, outlines his own work, and
gives Brooks valuable advice. The magnificent letter of March 27,
1918 remains one of Bourne's best. Beyond that, little remains of
what was undoubtedly a significant body of letters. A short note
written to Theodore Dreiser survives, congratulating him on the
publication of *A Hoosier Holiday*. Only one note to Waldo Frank

remains as evidence of a friendship which was—for Bourne's legacy, regretfully—carried out over the telephone and in person. There is evidence that Bourne corresponded with Henri Bergson, John Burroughs, the English psychologist Stanley Bligh, and the American ethnologist Elsie Clews Parsons, but no letters have been found.

The letters which survive complete the image of Bourne; they round out his personality. Here we see Bourne revealing to his friends aspects of himself which are not dealt with in the published work. Through these documents we see Bourne as he experiments with the life of the college intellectual, the editor, the European adventurer, the radical, the writer, the musician, and the misunderstood soul.

V

Bourne died at such an early age that few autobiographical fragments remain. Therefore, authors have relied on the letters for their biographical information. Prior to 1955, any information gleaned from letters must have come either from the private collections held by individual correspondents of Bourne, or from those letters published in *Twice-a-Year* in the late 1930's and early 1940's. Among the approximately thirty letters published at that time were excerpts from letters which were lost before 1955. The only other pre-1955 anthology generally available in which Bourne's letters appeared is Philip Rahv's book, *The Discovery of Europe.*[28] Rahv's selections, which were drawn exclusively from the *Twice-a-Year*[29] compilation, helped establish Bourne as a perceptive commentator on European life. In 1965 Lillian Schlissel edited *The World of Randolph Bourne,*[30] which included long excerpts from over twenty letters drawn from the Columbia Collection. Unfortunately, this book is presently out of print. Thus, while the letters have been rediscovered by scholars as a valuable element of Bourne's intellectual output, no more than fifty letters have been made available and no edition of letters is currently in print.

The major resource for Bourne's letters is the Columbia

Collection, which contains a set of transcriptions donated by Agnes de Lima in 1955. While Miss de Lima did scholars a great service by collecting versions of letters from some of Bourne's correspondents, the collection has some significant drawbacks. Of the entire collection of over 200 letters, less than a dozen exist in manuscript form; all of the other letters are transcriptions. When the collection was being compiled, many of the correspondents were asked to submit copies of the letters they held. Thus, not only are the letters transcriptions, but they are copies transcribed by several hands; Bourne's occasionally difficult handwriting has been subjected to several different interpretations. In the case of three correspondents' transcriptions—Teall, Macmahon, Gregory—ellipses appeared in the typescript. In the case of Gregory's letters, however, it has been possible to consult the original letters, available at the Yale Library, in order to restore these omissions.

The Carl Zigrosser papers at the University of Pennsylvania contain all of the letters which Mr. Zigrosser transcribed for Columbia. Also at the Van Pelt Library are the nine letters which Bourne wrote to Van Wyck Brooks, only two of which were copied for the Columbia collection, one note written to Waldo Frank, and a letter to Theodore Dreiser, neither of which is represented in the transcriptions. Separate from the Bourne collections at Columbia are three letters written to the Columbia Professor of English, John Erskine. The Yale University Beinecke Library contains the important collection of the letters written to Alyse Gregory, and many letters addressed to Elizabeth Shepley Sergeant. Three newly discovered letters are included in this edition: two letters addressed to Arthur Macmahon were brought to my attention by Mrs. Macmahon, and one note to William Wirt, the educational reformer, was discovered among the Wirt papers at the Lilly Library of Indiana University.

The letters written to Alyse Gregory, Carl Zigrosser, Van Wyck Brooks, Waldo Frank, Theodore Dreiser, Karl D. Robinson, Joseph C. Green, Edward Murray, John Erskine, Elizabeth Shepley Sergeant, and William Wirt have been checked for accuracy against the manuscript letters. In the case of all other letters, with the exception of the two Arthur Macmahon letters noted above, the present text has been checked against the transcripts in the Columbia Collection. I have followed the transcriptions of the various correspondents exactly with only two exceptions. I have taken the liberty of correcting obvious typographical errors on the part of transcribers. Also, in the case of the letters written to Prudence Winterrowd I have broken the text of the letters into more coherent paragraphs. Throughout his letters, and especially in the European letters, when space was dear, Bourne used a six or eight character space to designate a paragraph break. Miss Winterrowd was an especially diligent transcriber who duplicated these long spaces. Where the sense of the letter corroborated Bourne's stylistic habits, I have interpreted these breaks as indications for the beginnings of new paragraphs.

The present edition presents for the first time all the presently known surviving letters of Randolph Bourne, many of which have been checked for textual accuracy, and the majority of which are appearing in print for the first time. I can only echo the wish of Lewis Mumford: "It was the good furtune of American society to produce this man. We must not toss that luck away."[31]

Notes

[1]Waldo Frank, *The New America*, (London, 1921), p. 218.

[2]Paul Rosenfeld, "Randolph Bourne," in *Port of New York*, (New York, 1924), p. 212.

[3]*Ibid.*, p. 217.

[4]Van Wyck Brooks, "Introduction," *History of a Literary Radical*, (New York, 1956), p. 2.

[5]*Ibid.*, pp. 16-17.

[6]*Ibid.*, p. 18.

[7]Frank, p. 217.

8Rosenfeld, p. 235.

9Louis Mumford, "The Image of Randolph Bourne," *New Republic* LXIV (September 24, 1930), p. 152. I am excluding from this category the many eulogies Bourne received, because this form encourages lionizing the subject and is therefore directed toward the formation of a myth more by convention than by the choice of the author.

10*Ibid.*, p. 152.

11*Ibid.*, p. 151.

12*Ibid.*, p. 151.

13*Ibid.*, p. 152.

14John Dos Passos, *1919*, (New York, 1932), pp. 105-6.

15Christopher Lasch, *The New Radicalism in America*, (New York, 1965), p. ix.

16*Ibid.*, p. 85.

17*Ibid.*, p. ix.

18Henry F. May, *The End of American Innocence*, (New York, 1959), p. 248.

19*Ibid.*, p. 326.

20*Ibid.*, pp. 303, 304.

21Sherman Paul, *Randolph Bourne*, (Minneapolis, 1966), p. 43.

22*Ibid.*, p. 16, Lasch, pp. 99-100.

23Randolph Bourne, "History of a Literary Radical," in Van Wyck Brooks, *op. cit.*, pp. 29-30.

24*Ibid.*, p. 34.

25Mumford, p. 152.

26Roy Pascal, *Design and Truth in Autobiography*, (Cambridge, Mass., 1960), pp. 126, 135. Pascal explores the possibilities within these classifications in detail.

27Beulah Amidon to Alyse Gregory, October 4, 1948, Bourne Collection, Columbia University.

28Philip Rahv, *The Discovery of Europe*, (Cambridge, Mass., 1947).

29"Randolph Bourne: Some Pre-War Letters (1912-1914)," *Twice-a-Year* II (Spring-Summer 1939), 79-102. "Randolph Bourne: Letters (1913-14)," *Twice-a-Year* V-VI (Fall-Winter 1940, Spring-Summer 1941), 79-88. "Randolph Bourne: Letters (1913-1916)," *Twice-a Year* VII (Fall-Winter 1941), 76-90.

30Lillian Schlissel, *The World of Randolph Bourne*, (New York, 1965).

31Mumford, p. 152.

The College Years (1911-1913):
The Young Intellectual

When Bourne entered Columbia University at the age of 23, he was eager to make the most of these years. He had a traditional impression of the function of a college education; college represented access to a higher level of knowledge. These years also brought about a different focus for this loftier vision, however; "it has all quite revolutionized my life," (1/16/13) Bourne realized near the end of his career. From this higher vantage point, the difference between principle and practice became more obvious and less tolerable. While Columbia preached social ethics in the classroom, for example, the administration still exploited the labor force at the University. Bourne felt restless in such an institution. At the end of his last semester at Columbia, facing the prospect of entering the world outside the University, Bourne wrote that Columbia had not trained him to apply his knowledge to any specific vocation. He did not feel prepared for "literary labor and [felt] untrained for sociological research." (6/16/13) At the end of a career which had been, on the whole, very rewarding, Bourne felt suspended between appreciation for the intellectual advantages gained during his college years, and dissatisfaction because this four year investment had not brought him useful knowledge with which he could act in the world.

The atmosphere at Columbia University during this time justified Bourne's perceptions. There can be no doubt that the Columbia University which Bourne attended between 1909 and 1913 offered a rich environment full of intellectual activity. The University had expanded dramatically since its move to Morningside Heights in the 1890's and, with over 6,000 students, was the largest university in the United States. Columbia and Johns Hopkins were the only universities in the country in which the graduate school was larger than the undergraduate college. Clearly, one of the great advantages for an ambitious student was the proximity of a graduate college in which intellectuals were being trained. Edwin Slosson, popularizer of reform movements in American higher education, asserted that Columbia was potentially the greatest institution of higher learning in the country.[1] The two reasons given by Slosson for the ascendency are indicative of the way in which Columbia was perceived. Since the University was large, eccentricity and unorthodoxy could be tolerated.[2] Also, since Columbia was situated in the country's largest city, a symbiotic relationship could be established whereby the University could help the city initiate programs, as the University of Wisconsin did for that state, and the metropolis would furnish the diverse cultural opportunities which would assure a lively atmosphere on campus.[3]

Indeed, there was ample reason for Columbia to take pride in its position in American higher education, and in American intellectual life in general. Illustrious faculty members filled virtually every department, especially the social sciences, in which Bourne was most interested: Franz Boaz, James Harvey Robinson, Charles Beard, John Dewey, and James T. Shotwell were among those to whom Bourne was attracted. Popular administrators, such as Frederick Keppel, Dean of the Undergraduate College and patron of many student gatherings, and Frederick J. Woodbridge, Professor and Dean of the Faculty of Philosophy, offered encouragement to students; it was Woodbridge, in fact, who first suggested that Bourne write the letter to *The Atlantic* which started Bourne's career as an essayist. Student discussion groups, such as the Boar's Head, the Philolexian Society, and the Academy, in all of which Bourne participated, allowed students to sound out new ideas and to create a feeling of scholarly conviviality on campus. Bourne thought that it was among his fellow students that the most profitable moments were spent.

Yet, the fact of Columbia's size, and the personality of its President, Nicholas Murray Butler, caused many problems, most of which Bourne recognized. The philosophy expressed by the admininstration through Butler emphasized the function of the University in increasing the sphere of knowledge. The 19th century college, Butler said, educated young men to become gentlemen, while the 20th century University served a different purpose:

> Its chief function is the conservation, the advancement, and the dissemination of knowledge, the pushing out of that border-line between the

known and the unknown which constitutes the human horizon.[4]

Advanced research with the emphasis on the theoretical bases of social action, and not on that activity itself, was the hallmark of the University. Therefore, while the University prided itself on the intimate connection between Columbia and the city of New York, the linkage was cultural and intellectual, and was not based upon the social action—legislative agendas and extension courses, for example —which emanated from other progressive Universities, such as the University of Wisconsin. Columbia was a private University, and, through its independent means of support, was able to dictate the terms of interchange between the University and the city in a way in which the majority of State-owned, Progressive universities could not. As Lawrence Veysey summarizes, there was, in fact, a barrier separating the University from the city.[5]

Because the rapid expansion of the University demanded full-time attention, Butler assumed the role for which he was, in fact, most suited—that of academic administrator.[6] The President played a conservative function; he protected the smooth operation of the institution, and adopted the principles of corporate management.[7] Conflicts with dissident or non-bureaucratically attuned faculty members preceded the famous Charles Beard resignation during the World War I period. At least three professors, including Bourne's favorite American composer, Edward Macdowell, were removed from their positions because they proved difficult to handle.[8] Butler would allow for intellectual eccentricity, but he would not tolerate impediments to the efficient operation of the institution. Bourne would later describe these inconsistencies in his article, "One of Our Conquerors." According to one historian, Butler exhibited "an inconsistency between expressed ideals and autocratic administrative function, which was visible in his failure to tolerate human dissent and imperfectibility."[9] The radical discussions in which Bourne and his Academy friends engaged—the social force of Religion, the effect of the Protestant ethic—could be tolerated, but agitation for more pay for University employees could not. It is little wonder, then, that Bourne felt privileged to attend a University where ideas could be discussed so freely, but that he sensed the oppression of this institution.

I

Bourne held an advantage not enjoyed by other Columbia undergraduates—his voice was heard outside the University. During this period he succeeded in placing several articles in The *Atlantic Monthly*, a journal of high reputation which had, until the turn of the century, remained conservative in its editorial standards.[10] In 1908, however, Ellery Sedgwick took control of the magazine and articles began to show more concern for contemporary issues.[11] Meanwhile, literary subjects continued to be dealt with. For example, in the volume containing Bourne's most famous essay of the period, "Youth," articles by H. G. Wells, Hugo Münsterberg, and Havelock Ellis appeared. Mary Antin's autobiography was serialized through the volume, which also contained fiction by Edith Wharton and John Galsworthy. Sedgwick and Woodbridge suggested topics for Bourne's essays, thus assuring his productivity by their willingness to consider him as the representative of the younger generation.

Bourne thought of his articles as autobiographical. Indeed, the string of essays, which were collected in 1913 as *Youth and Life*,[12] corroborates and extends the self-confidence in his philosophy which Bourne expressed in his letters. The self-doubts which appear in some of his letters are only implied in this published work. Both the essays and the letters give the impression of being preached rather than merely delivered. The Bourne who speaks through *The Atlantic* to the growing readership of that magazine was strong, celebratory of youth, and contemptuous of intellectual weakness. The letters, while not inconsistent, show periods of self-doubt.

Three essays which demonstrate the scope of Bourne's argument, outline the form of his philosophy, and reveal inconsistencies in his pronouncements are "Youth," "The Experimental Life," and "The Life of Irony." In "Youth" Bourne entered into the dialogue over a generational critique of society. In his celebration of the "self-expression" of youth (3)[13] Bourne set up a tension between creative self-consciousness and tradition which remained unrelieved in his written work. The creative life of the individual parallels organic development through youth, (7) a stage of life in which self-consciousness develops. It is during this period that struggle develops between the ideals of the youth and the traditions of society. As the individual ages, however, it is necessary to retain this self-consciousness or else the struggle has been lost; the individual must free himself from the traditional influence of time. The inclination to plan a life, to limit experimentation, to react stereotypically must be resisted. (12) For Bourne, experience was no virtue; the cardinal virtue was to confront the tradition-bound world with the strength of youthful ideas.

The keys to a youthful life lay in the willingness to experiment and in the use of the ironic critique which stipulated that life is inherently irrational. (227)[14] The greatest fallacy is that any reward is proportional to the amount of effort exerted. Bourne believed in a naturalistic universe, one in which large forces beyond human comprehension were at work. At best, individuals could guide their lives in the directions which apparently corresponded to their aptitudes; under no circumstances should they believe that they were able to direct their lives. (231) Bourne reacted to this universe not with resignation, but with the spirit of adventure experienced by the scientist. "Life is not a campaign of battle, but a laboratory. (233-4) An optimistic outlook is essential, for failure must be met with indifference. (238-9) But in this essay Bourne did not address the problem of the individual faced with the imperative to maintain this optimistic self-consciousness in such an environment.

In "Youth" Bourne delivered his world view. "The Experimental Life" presented his battle plan, while "The Life of Irony" supplied him with an intellectual critique. Irony enabled Bourne to test experience—to point out inconsistencies, to set up juxtapositions. (102)[15] For him irony is, in short, "the science of comparative experience." (105) Irony should not be confused with cynicism, because this technique enables the critic to see the strengths of any argument and to be able to synthesize established beliefs with another point of view. (107) The ironist is an impartial judge. Through this technique real events can be compared to ideal situations, so the ironist can project a social vision. (111) Irony helps preserve self-consciousness, for the ironist is able to view himself as dispassionately as he does other people. (125) An audience is guaranteed to such a person, because he can democratically appeal to everyone's way of thinking.

Despite Bourne's proclamation of the ironic technique, more tensions appeared than those set up in the juxtapositions upon which the method relies. Bourne believed in the social function of the ironic critique, yet irony is predicated on the separation of the writer from society. Similarly, Bourne advocated irony as a method of creating sympathy with friends, yet the technique relies on the ability of the writer to play off the thoughts of others, to show weaknesses along with strengths. To say that ideas fall of their own accord may be intellectually satisfying, but this critique seldom creates good will in the interchange of friendly discourse. Bourne's concern for the effect of the ironic critique upon his friendships is initially voiced in the earliest surviving letter and continues throughout his correspondence. Finally, there is a parasitic aspect of this philosophy, of which Bourne spoke most clearly in his letters. The ironist does not create experience, he feeds on it. Were the source of experience, which lies outside of himself, to dry up (130) the ironist would be lost. This technique forced him to remain a spectator, he explained to Alyse Gregory, but he could not help longing for a sense of participation. In his essays Bourne stated that the ironist "is conscious only of the shifting light and play of life; his world is dynamic, energetic, changing." (130-1) The letters point out that this dynamism and participation could be based on observation and not action.

Bourne's letters of this period most closely parallel his published work in both tone and content. Both Prudence Winterrowd and Carl Zigrosser received letters which had more of the characteristics of essays; for Prudence Bourne outlined extensive readings in the philosophy of William James and corrected what he thought were her spurious conclusions. Carl Zigrosser received a treatise on Bergsonian intuition and science. Bourne also recounted for Zigrosser many of the intellectual conversations he had had, both within the Academy discussion group, and with individuals, such as Roderick Seidenberg. So long as Bourne's profession remained that of a college intellectual his letters reflect confidence. As he approached graduation, and the inevitable dislocation from this college identity, doubts began to surface in his letters. He expressed the normal anxiety of a graduate seeking a job—"I have no idea where I shall be next year" (2/5/13)— but he also faced the more basic problem of defining his function as an intellectual in terms of participation in a cause. "I would give almost anything for that feeling of *participation* in something that you must wonderfully have," he exclaimed to Alyse Gregory in June 1913. "I haven't the will or the power to force myself into it, and must drift somehow along the line of least resistance." Bourne then voices a theme which was to become more prominent in subsequent years: "That is why I feel my book [*Youth and Life*] is so hypocritical; it purports to represent me, when it only represents my ideals." Thus from an initial position of intellectual security Bourne moved by the end of his last college year to the realization that he was abandoning the shelter of youthful potential and was going to have to live out his ideas.

Notes

[1] Edwin Slosson, *Great American Universities*, (New York City, 1910), p. 446.

[2] *Ibid.*, p. 445.

[3] *Ibid.*, p. 446. Bourne also shared this view; see 3/2/13, for example.

[4] Nicholas Murray Butler, *Scholarship and Service*, (New York City, 1921), p. 62.

[5] Lawrence Veysey, *The Emergence of the American University*, (Chicago, 1965), p. 333.

[6] *Ibid.*, p. 365.

[7] *Ibid.*, p. 366. See also the contemporary analysis, "The Higher Learning in America," in *Theory of the Leisure Class* by Thorstein Veblen.

[8]*Ibid.*,pp. 426-27.

[9]William Summerscales, *Affirmation and Dissent: Columbia's Response to the Crisis of the First World War*, (New York City, 1970), p. 35.

[10]Frank Luther Mott, *A History of American Magazines*, II, (Cambridge, Mass., 1938), p. 511.

[11]*Ibid.*, p. 513.

[12]*Youth and Life*, (Boston, 1913).

[13]All page numbers given in parentheses in this paragraph refer to the essay "Youth."

[14]All page numbers given in parentheses in this paragraph refer to the essay "The Experimental Life."

[15]All page numbers given in parentheses in this paragraph refer to the essay "The Life of Irony."

1

to Carl Zigrosser
(Ms Pennsylvania)

Dear Carl,

Thank you very much indeed for your kind and really beautiful letter. None of my friends, and certainly none of my Columbia friends, have the slightest cause to fear that they have ever hurt me. They have all been so good to me that I bless my good fortune for having found them, and hope that I shall not lose them. The danger, I fear, is very much the other way. It is *I* who say cutting, sarcastic things and wound them, most of the time quite out of inadvertence, and through a diabolical weakness of trying to be clever. I had a reputation for a sharp tongue long before I had a reputation for anything else, and I am terribly afraid it flashes out on friend and foe alike. That is what gives me a guilty conscience to be praised for what I write, for I can write things that, while I believe I am sincere in saying them, are mighty hard to live up to sometimes in concrete cases. I guess we all, however, preach a nobler philosophy than we ever practice. I can truthfully say that what I put into that article[1] is the way things look to me a considerable part of the time, and they are at all times my ideals, or some of them, even if I often and flagrantly and disappointingly fail to live up to them. You are certainly curious to complain of your fortunate life. It has seemed to me quite ideal, uncheckered enough to stimulate your growth, and not too rosy or pampered to make you lazy. Mediocrity! Bosh! I have the greatest confidence in your success. I only wish mine was as sure and definite as yours is.

I have been half-laid-up with a horrid cold, and gave myself a little recreation to-day by going to Greenwood Lake, most conventionally, of course, by rail & steamer. Took my lunch and ate it on the parapet of the Chapel Island, and walked over to the village later. The air was lovely, the clouds and water delicious, and the whole day the fairest picture, I think, in my whole summer. I used to bore myself horribly when travelling alone, but am getting more interesting, or is it Hazlitt? whose Table-Talk I took along and read by the very edge of the water. When would I find you at home if I came down, or don't you want to come up youself? My piano has been tuned, and I am trying to convince myself that it is improved.

As ever,

R. S. B.

[1]Probably "The Two Generations," *The Atlantic* (May 1911), CVII, 590-98, in which Bourne outlines the virtues of youth, later expanded in his influential essay, "Youth."

2

to Karl Robinson[1]
(Ms Columbia)

Dec. 23, 1911

My dear K. D. R.

After long cogitation by the assembled board, your Arnold Bennett went into the drawer; and for the following reasons: —

1. Although it was beautifully written, the subject had lost the charm of novelty. The Old Wives' Tale is rather an old tale to be treated in that particular way, that is, with fulness of plot and elaborate quotation. It would be an admirable way, if the book was new, and were to be brought to the reader's attention.

2. I think we would have taken it, if you had assumed a knowledge of the book on the part of the reader, and had contributed a new and original point of view.

3. Deducting quotations, and what Mr. Howells said, left about 2½ pages of K. D. R. out of 11. We can stand a lot less literary modesty, you know; even 99% pure, at times. We dote on fresh, untrammelled, original reaction to things. Now, I would very much like to see a serious, strong, long essay on some coming man of letters of to-day, somebody who is little known and yet out to be known better. Do you know John Masefield? His name one sees often, but he hasn't penetrated over here yet. Or Leonard Merrick? Or a very original American writer, John Jay Chapman, essayist? I should dote on an essay on any of these, but very particularly Masefield. A[lfred] A. K[nopf][2] will lend you some of his works. Barr[3] has his plays. Work it up for the February number, and gain

the eternal gratitude of

R. S. Bourne
Editor-in-chief
of that organ of
light and learning,
the Columbia
Monthly

[1]Karl Robinson was an Associate Editor of *Monthly*, the Columbia student literary magazine, in 1913. After graduation he joined the staff of *Harper's Weekly*.

[2]Alfred A. Knopf was then Circulation Manager of *Monthly*. Later he founded the Knopf publishing house. Knopf and Bourne were never close friends.

[3]Simon Pelham Barr succeeded Bourne as Editor of *Monthly*. During the 1909-10 school year he and Bourne were roommates. Barr's literary efforts, mostly poetry, appeared only in *Monthly*.

3

to Carl Zigrosser
(Ms Pennsylvania)

Hartley [Hall]
Feb. 7, 1912

Dear Carl,

You would not recognize our poor little denuded apartment now that the rugs and pictures have departed with their proud owner. We did not know how attached we were to that rug, and when we came back and found our furniture all cowering and shivering in the midst of the bleak vastness, we felt positively homesick, or as if a great joy had passed out of our lives. Mac[mahon] dreamed he was in a prison—all that night. We are gradually becoming acclimated again, however, and with the delectable vision of a big yellow rug from home, we are brightening again.

College began again to-day to my great relief—I have been loafing and need something steady to do again. I think I got these uninitiative habits by being a factory hand for so long, and doing nothing except what I was told to do. My debauch this last week included standing up to hear Tetrazzini in "Lucia," and an unexpected visit to "Sumurun." We went down to stand at

"Rigoletto"—Tet. and Caruso and Renaud—and found a howling mob being turned away by a squad of policemen.[1] We stood on the other side of the street for a while watching the line go in one door and out the other, and then consoled ourselves at the Casino. But I enjoyed it hugely, the barbaric colors, and the fair forms and the music which makes it a "singless opera" rather than a "wordless play."

The Academy had a brilliant meeting at Elsasser's[2] Saturday. Springer was the event of the evening with a paper on Scholasticism. The idea was to give Springer, who talks a good deal, a chance to show what he had. As a showdown, he was a failure. We rendered him positively humble before the evening was over. Murray brought his violin and we played Beethoven sonatas together. Beer and lemonade furnished a fitting climax. Seidenberg failed to appear—"was afraid he would not be welcome at E's." Really he is a little difficult, sometimes.

This is just a little gossip dashed off. You must write me a literary letter, and I will try to reply in kind. The John Burroughs episode[3] turned out to be a semi-almost. Perhaps in the Spring. When you go over to see him, just remind him of me, will you? And write me just what you are doing, that is, the petty details, if they are petty, but the details anyway? You know mine, so I will only hit the high places. But a Monthly editor, an art connoisseur, etc. on a farm in February I should really like to watch. And many of us envy you.

[signature omitted]

[1]The concert was one of the social events of the season. See the account in the *New York Times* for February 7, 1912, page 11, column 3.

[2]Henry W. Elsasser, a brilliant friend of Bourne's, who committed suicide in 1921. Although the two talked about every subject, Elsasser was especially valuable to Bourne for his knowledge of science and mathematics.

[3]John Burroughs, a critic, poet, and naturalist. The specific episode to which Bourne alludes is unclear.

4

to Carl Zigrosser
(Ms Pennsylvania)

Feb. 23, 1912

Dear Carl,

A mighty issue has been decided this day—I have carried out my threat and resigned as High Mogul of Col. Monthly. The political pot has been buzzing this last week as a result. My ticket was Andy, with Gove H[ambidge] as Secretary and heir apparent.[1] Henle,[2] I found, had abandoned Barr and had flown to Elsasser. Barr also was making mysterious references to Lyman Abbott Elsasser and T. R. Bourne.[3] Anything to prevent a Philo man from getting in. It looked like a deadlock, 3-3, with both sides writing up to you and waiting with bated breath while you cast the deciding vote. A little private conversation with H. Wolfgang Elsasser however elicited the fact that while he would like the nomination he was ready to make the great refusal. I didn't attempt to persuade him from such abnegation, and suggested my ticket. He disapproved strongly of Andy's light-and-airy propensities, wanted no Pan-like editorials, and was most generally unpropitious. He announced that he would vote for Hambidge, however, and as it was easy to swing Hambidge and Andy the same way, I transposed my ticket, and prepared to control the convention. Barr and Henle seemed about to perform the "Die Hard" act, and were filled with a despairing rage at the treachery of their ally. They were going to vote for Elsasser in spite of everything. But the meeting occurred. The threatened split failed to materialize. Hambidge was absent, and as the vote went around, every one meekly answered, Yes, for Hambidge. I am glad to be out. I have some hard courses this term, want to write some essays, and am getting just the least bit tired of the crowd. I feel sometimes as if I was growing up faster than they were. Now with a headquarters in Hartley, I am not so dependent on Monthly office, and leave with real admiration for my good sense in not working a good thing to death, and having a very pleasant experience turn to ashes on one's hands.

I don't know just how much Columbia news you hear, or what New York papers. You certainly won't get the above inner history in them. Perhaps you read of my election to ΦΒΚ along with five others of whom J. P. Wilson was the first and I last.

The Times the other Sunday had a very complimentary review of Joyce Kilmer's verse, styling him "A New Davidson."[4] I should like to get his book and review it with Wupperman's[5] for Monthly. Seidenberg's didn't really make good. He brought it around when almost completed, and asked for an honest editorial opinion of it. Not realizing that he did not mean what he said, I let him know that it seemed to me lacking in coherence, and too majestic in style for so humble a book. He went up in the air so high that I have not seen him since—

and Monthly loses a much-heralded article. It really wouldn't have done, however, you know.

We heard the Chopin concerto the other night played by Adriano Ariani. I wonder what you think of it. Not a dissonance in the whole thing. Like sugar and honey mixed. Too much for me. Also, a posthumous symphony of Dvořák which I thought very fine, but the paper said was amateurish.[5]

You in your rural leisure can write me a better letter than this. I can only jot down gossip. I am in a rush.

As ever,

Randolph

[1]Probably Henry H. Anderson, who was then Secretary of *Monthly*, and who became Editor-in-Chief in 1912. Hambidge did, in fact, succeed Anderson in 1913.

[2]James Henle, later head of the Vanguard Press.

[3]Bourne is alluding to the political situation within the Republican Party which culminated in the split between Taft and Roosevelt at the August 1912 convention. The Die Hards stayed with Taft, even though they felt he would be defeated by Wilson in the general election. Roosevelt formed the Progressive (Bull Moose) Party and ran in the November election on a third party ticket. Roosevelt received the support of Lyman Abbott, liberal Congregational minister and Editor of *The Outlook*, even though he risked losing subscribers.

[4]The review appeared in the New York *Times* on February 11, 1912, page 70, column 2. Kilmer's only book of poetry at that time was *Summer of Love* (1911).

[5]Probably Carlos Wupperman's 1912 volume of poetry, *Quiet Places*. Wupperman had appeared before the Philolexian Society.

[6]A review appeared in the New York *Times* on February 16, 1912, page 9, column 3. The program included Dvořák's Symphony in E flat and Chopin's Concerto #2 in F major. This review did not call this Dvořák amateurish, but immature.

5

to Carl Zigrosser
(Ms Pennsylvania)

Hartley
March 16, 1912

Dear Carl,

If you found the February no. so uninspiring, you will not even read the March. Although it isn't so bad. The new administration falls to with vigor, and the flow of manuscripts begins again, as I knew it would. Wait till you see the April no. just gone to press. Thanks for your review. It goes in for March; they have delayed us horribly at Princeton. Your guess at "Old Chilton" was a critical lapse; it was our old friend Simon[1],—a page out of his English boyhood, he says. Our dinner was a fair success,—Joyce Kilmer, sort of a frost, but R[ockwell] Kent and Prof. Baldwin[2] hit it up splendidly; talked Art, while we listened spellbound. Kent quite mystical, and very fervent; Baldwin cool, and excessively ethical; Elsasser was delighted because Kent seemed to attain a reductio ad absurdum of theories of Art. It was after all, Kent said, and aesthetic feeling that was hard to define in concrete terms. Elsasser agreed and I told him he was a mystic! Bergson throws some light, I think, on the subject by his idea of "intuition," which is nothing mystical, but simply our ability to perceive the qualities as well as the quantities of things. We can see color intellectually as ether vibrations, or intuitively as color; art as an arrangement of lines, or sounds, or words, or as beauty and individuality. Both kinds of knowledge are valuable, but a sharp distinction should always be kept between them. Of course in Art the qualitative side is infinitely more important than the quantitative, just as for our daily life color is more important as color than as ether vibrations. But art may always be analyzed to see how it is done, just as color may always be analyzed into vibrations. On the other hand, color is not the sum of the vibrations, but a quite incommensurable, unique experience; so a work of art is not the sum of its parts, or its technical materials and processes, but an incommensurable, and unique appeal. Although it is incommunicable, just as the idea of color is incommunicable, yet the distinctions of color are communicable, and distinctions of art are communicable. Thus a person cannot make a blind person understand what he means when he says, "I see 'color' "; but he *can* make a normal person understand when he says, "I see red here, and blue there." Now artistic genres are just this distinction between different colors, and, although criticism cannot communicate the quality of an art-work itself, yet it can helpfully, though roughly, make the distinction of shades or aspects of the same quality. Thus, if I say, In this artwork, I find unity of idea, harmony of form, proportion of tone, charm of appeal, etc., I am doing the same as if I described to a friend the colors of a landscape. I can make rather minute distinctions of shading, and get an approximate, but only approximate, impression of my vision, on my friend's mind. The exact shadings, the exact quality will of course always elude my expression; at my best, my approximation will be a very imperfect one. But that is not to say that it is not necessary and significant. Criticism has a very subordinate place to creation. What Spingarn[3] meant by Criticism was simply aesthetic appreciation, which of course eludes communication. Criticism is the attempt to express that appreciation, constantly conscious, however, of its limitations, and indeed its impossibilities. It is struggling heroically and resolutely up a path to a goal that it knows it will never achieve. And yet somehow that march, predestined as it is to failure, aids countless wayfarers, whose eyes would be otherwise fixed stonily on the ground, to see the vision at the goal and be glad.

I don't know whether I am clear at all; it is a rather impromptu analogy. Some day, perhaps I will develop it.

What are you reading nowadays? Or writing? My essay on "Youth," if I understood the Editor right, heads the April "Atlantic." He seems to like it;— Barr not very much.— (He read it in manuscript, and thought it feeble.) I, on the contrary, thought it rather overdone, flamboyant.

As Ever,

R. S. B.

[1]"Old Chilton" was an essay by Barr. The Princeton University Press bought a three-quarter page advertisement in the March number of *Monthly*. Perhaps Bourne is alluding to this advertisement in reference to the delay at Princeton.

[2]Rockwell Kent, American painter and author of adventure novels. Charles Sears Baldwin, English Professor at Columbia who was noted for his teaching ability, his concern for composition and rhetoric, and his love for medieval literature.

[3]Joel Spingarn, Comparative Literature Professor at Columbia until 1911, when he was dismissed after a disagreement over the status of the Comparative Literature Department. Spingarn's conception of criticism, which emphasized attention to the text of a literary work, Bourne considered incomplete because of its lack of concern for the social context of literature.

6

to Carl Zigrosser
(Ms Pennsylvania)

Hartley Hall
Apr. 2, 1912

Dear Carl,

Your manuscripts have been duly read, and I am flattered with my new role of literary censor; it is soothing after the harsh criticisms I received at Monthly to know that somebody believes in my critical faculty, such as it is. I like the essay better than the story; it is a very charming and original idea, and well worked out. The only question would be whether it did not assume too much knowledge of the songs to make it intelligible to the general reader. The Board, most of whom are quite unmusical, will be able to settle that. Personally, I enjoyed it very much. The story, I cannot say seemed to throw very much new light on an old "triangle." It's a pretty common dramatic motive, and has to reveal some unexpected aspect of life, some rather subtle point of psychology, to get an effect of freshness and vitality. The woman's deed does not seem to be motivated quite intensely enough; you want some hint of passion and rage and remorse to make it plausible, or rather convincing. She is just a little too matter-of-fact about it all. She tells all the details and the facts, but few of the little suggestive things that would show the enormous emotional disturbance that such a deed must inevitably involve. In her attempt to explain and justify, she is too rational, too lucid and too candid. You would not get that in real life; her story would be shot through with sudden little irrelevant [sic] outbursts that would reveal the slumbering volcano in her heart. She would be either triumphant or remorseful, or both, and you have made her neither. That would be my criticism, and you must remember that I have never set eyes on Seidenberg again, so that I am paying you a big compliment in knowing that you will not be as foolish as he was.

About Murray, you were perfectly right. I told him that you would answer him frankly, and that it would have to be a cold business proposition. I did not know enough about farm labor to be able to tell whether you would find him useful or not, so I said, It won't do any harm to find out; nothing is at stake in the matter at all. It was a good deal of a spasm with him, I guess. He is the most unworldly person I ever met, and has musical ambitions which are crushed by the routine of drudgery. It won't hurt him to wait a while, I guess. Other people do.

Have you seen my essay on Youth in the April Atlantic? I am curious to know what people think of it. I'm afraid it's rather exaggerated and few youths will find it strike a responsive chord in their breasts. It seems really more typical of the feminines I have known than the youths. It might apply to Barr, certainly not to Elsasser. People find it hard to reconcile with my prosaic and unyouthful self.

As ever,

Randolph

7

to Carl Zigrosser
(Ms Pennsylvania)

Hartley Hall
Apr. 19, 1912

Dear Carl,

The Dean[1] tells me you are going to be in New York soon again. This is great news, and we must have a Monthly dinner or at least an Academy in your honor. The last Academy was very select. At Murray's house, on "Religion"; Swain, Elsasser, Seidenberg & myself only—Seidenberg appeared in fine form, and you would never have been able to discover that there had been the faintest ripple in our relations. I read a few thoughts on Religion, with most of which he agreed; neither he nor Elsasser would approve my rather disparaging attitude towards Science as needing to be checked in its tyrannous career, and relegated strictly to its practical sphere.

Your own assaults on the inner citadel of S's unsophistication I heard a little about from Murray, to whom he had confided his disappointment in your ability to appreciate childhood. If we did not know S., we might wonder at his anxiety to keep himself unsophisticated, and his frantic attempts to remain childlike; do they not seem at times rather sophisticated themselves?

[Frank] Essig's misfortune seems to be one of those incomprehensible tragedies that are inseparably bound up with the machinery of institutional red-tape. Perhaps, however, it will do him good to get some regular work to do, and get into some touch with the real world.

Don't fail to let me know when you are coming. Mac has gone to Ithaca to compete for the State Intercollegiate Oratorical Peace Prize; is, at this moment, I trust, winning it. He beat out a field of ten down here, & has a great speech.

As ever,

R. S. Bourne

[1]Probably Frederick Keppel, Dean of the Undergraduate College.

8

to Carl Zigrosser
(Ms Pennsylvania)

290 Belleville Ave.
Bloomfield, N. J.
[June ?] 1912

Dear Carl,
Your account of the trip was most entertaining and romantic; most of the points were corroborated by Seidenberg,[1] with a few details added, which you were either too modest to mention or forgot about,—for instance, the new form of vice which you chose to indulge in on this outing. When Seidenberg began to hint darkly at the new species of dissipation, I immediately jumped to the conclusion that you had been learning three-card monte and had turned the tables by fleecing some poor unsophisticated city boys or college men by the roadside. But he assured me you were incapable of such malice, and that all the vice consisted in was a propensity to cheer the inner man on Arctic days the frigidity of which he still shudders to think of. The picture of S[eidenberg] gallantly kissing the flower flung to him by the fair delighted me beyond measure. Why did you nip such a promising romance so cruelly in the bud?
By the way, he and Murray[2] intend to return to the scene of the exploits, and are about to start for East Windham for two weeks. I am just on the point of making up my mind to start next Thursday, spend a week with them, then drop down to friends in Milton for the boat-races, and come to your place on Tuesday, July 2, or thereabouts, if convenient to you. I appreciate very much your taking me, and hope you will find no occasion to regret your kindness. All the terms are just what I should want, and you must also reserve the privilege to send me home whenever you want "without giving reasons." You certainly show an extraordinary insight into my character when you mention the "people and girls" that I will be deprived of. It is perfectly true that I may have become so

city-debauched that the quiet of the country life will pall upon me. But that is one of the things I want to find out; and another is whether I have any more ideas in me to turn into some essays, and whether the "monotony and solitude" which Arnold Bennett says are so necessary for writing will really inspire me, or merely stupify me. You have your piano, haven't you? and you won't be working so hard that there won't be time for an occasional tune. And a more than occasional walk. I don't believe I will be very stupified with them.

I just left Macmahon[3] struggling with his furniture, and trying to clear out our rooms. He worked so hard packing up my things that he had no time for his own. Very discouraging work, and all the more disheartening because he thinks his family will take an apartment in the city, and I will lose him for a room-mate,—a very serious loss to me.

Write to me at the proper time how to come, etc. If you address me here, they will forward the letter.

Randolph

[1]Roderick Seidenberg, a college friend of both Bourne's and Zigrosser's. Seidenberg became an architect and remained a close friend of Zigrosser's until Seidenberg's death in 1973. Their tradition of hiking together continued for many years.

[2]Edward Murray was an accomplished musician and composer. He later played violin in the Philadelphia Symphony Orchestra. With Murray Bourne played many duets.

[3]Macmahon was a close friend of both Bourne's and Zigrosser's. After graduation Macmahon became a member of the faculty of the Political Science Department at Columbia.

9

to Carl Zigrosser
(Ms Pennsylvania)

Bloomfield
June 5, 1912

Dear Carl,

Come up Friday night and we will play five-hundred. Come to dinner too, any time after 4 P. M., when I expect to arrive from New York; we will have time for a little music. This is the way to get to my house: get off the Bloomfield car at Bloomfield *Centre*: then walk north along the single track trolley-line to (Broad St.) to Belleville Ave.; turn to the right and we are 290, first house before the railroad. Do I insult you by my explicitness?

Hastily,

R. S. B.

10

to Carl Zigrosser
(Ms Pennsylvania)

Bloomfield, N. J.
Sept. 1, 1912

Dear Carl:—
I certainly hope you haven't had the weather on your trip that we have had here yesterday and to-day,—rain and cold and mist. I am practicing on my new typewriter, and have just finished a long anti-Wilson letter to the Editor of the Bloomfield "Citizen", jumping in with both feet into a discussion which has been raging all summer, although it is only fair to say that the discussion has been practically a monologue, conducted by a fervid Princetonian Wilsonite. There is also a rather warm argument running epistolarily with reference to the recent abolition of hell, but I think I will keep out of that.
I enclose a realistic picture clipped from Collier's[1] which Mrs. Smith, who originally jeered at my going to the country and quite terrified me with her description of the lowering darkness and quiet, has given me. That I am not the person sitting on the bed is evident from the hour at which I was wont to arise in the morning, as your mother will testify. Nor do I wish to insult any members of the family by insinuating that I see any resemblance to them in the picture. Only the ducks; I must say they come right home to the bone, as John Masefield would say. The cow is of course a wicked caricature on beautiful Reedy, but the pigs are even more Butlerish than your present representative. And there were no milk cans. Otherwise the picture goes far to corroborate my impressions that there was nothing dull or monotonous about country life.
The sail was delightful, except that the light was so intense that I arrived in New York with a fine head ache. One of the first persons I met was Barr, who was engaged in reading Frank Weltenkampf's "How To Appreciate Prints"; by the way, the frontispiece of that book is Whistler's "Etcher", that I brought you. Barr, too, is evidently conquering the fields of appreciation and knowledge, one

by one. He had most to say of the return of A[fred] A. K[nopf] from Europe, with dazzling accounts of visits to Galsworthy in Devonshire, and lunch and theatre with Granville Barker, Ollivant,[2] etc. Also many pictures of the great, taken by himself.

Next I ran into Kovar, and surprised him very much by telling him that he had been at Washingtonville, and that Babbitt[3] had visited him there. He is evidently Weaver's most intimate friend, spoke of Weaver's asking his advice and taking it, and of the good it would do him to soak himself in the aesthetic atmosphere of old Japan. All the same, I continue to remain profoundly unimpressed by Mr. Kovar. Sachs, after that little séance we had with him at Murray's in May, asked Murray in his honest, philosophical way,—"Murray, why did you want me to meet Mr. Kovar?" Of course Murray was shocked and hurt, but it was just the question I should myself have liked to ask. It seems he tried for a Ph.D. at Columbia and failed. Of course that in itself is no discredit, but that he should be always talking about it, or that it should always be popping up like a family scandal, gives me a very uncomfortable impression of him. Then he sings, in a warm, caressing tenor voice, and talks about that a good deal; he even attempted to sing that night without music and without accompaniment, with painful results, which, however, did not check his perseverence and ardor. But enough of him, until you meet him. He gets on my nerves a little, because I feel that he is appreciable, and that I am missing something choice in the way of personality.

The next adventure was with Erskine.[4] He stole coyly up behind me as I was working in the Library, and greeted me from the rear with such effusiveness of demeanor that I jumped up to embrace Elsasser or at least Hambidge. I was unable, when I saw who it was, to check my headlong torrent of enthusiasm, so we both fairly oozed affection and interest. He had been back for some time, and I asked whether life at Sparta, N. J. was not too Spartan and rigorous for him, and had not driven him back to old Athens. He said I could put it that way if I liked, and did not smile. I learned afterwards from K[arl] D. R[obinson] that he (Erskine) had actually not had enough to eat, boarding with an aged couple whose larders were not suited to those who had been reared on the fleshpots of Egypt. So it was a peculiarly unfortunate witticism for me to make, implying that I already knew of his early retreat from the land of famine, and had perhaps talked it all over in the ribald halls of Monthly. He expressed sorrow at the seeming termination of your academic career, but I did not discuss you loosely and freely. He has moved to 115th St., and I had all sorts of cordial invitations to come and see him.

I have been able so far to drown my homesickness in two days of work, but I know the time will come when there will be real pangs. I can never thank all of you enough for your kindness in making such a pleasant vacation possible to me. It really meant more to me both in body and mind than you imagine. I am unhappy unless I have friends around me, and Bloomfield depresses me. Between these two contingencies I don't know what I would have done, if I had not been able to come to your place. Whatever else happened I should certainly have passed otherwise a most miserable summer. As it was, it was one of the most delightful I ever had. My good times and happinesses mean more to me, I think, than they do to some people, and this summer will give material to brood over and scenes and faces and little things to bring back to mind that will last me through a whole winter.

Please give my regards to everybody, and tell your mother particarly [sic] how grateful I am for her good care of me.

As ever,

Randolph

[1]Bourne treats as caricatures the animals in a barnyard scene presented in *Collier's* XLIX (August 31, 1912), p. 13. His identification of Nicholas Murray Butler with a fat, heavy-jowled pig demonstrates his disdain for Columbia's President.

[2]Harley Granville-Barker, an English dramatist and drama critic. He managed the Court Theatre, which produced plays by Shaw and Ibsen. Alfred Ollivant, an English novelist. His most famous work, *Bob, Son of Battle* (1898), was a best-seller in the United States.

[3]Irving Babbitt, noted literary critic and college professor. He was the recognized leader of the literary custodians of the Genteel Tradition. His theory of literature, which eschewed social themes and literary realism, was abhorrent to Bourne.

[4]John Erskine was a popular English Professor at Columbia, who encouraged student discussion groups such as The Academy. He wrote verse, novels, and devised the Great Books program for Columbia. He and Bourne became estranged and later clashed over educational theory.

11

to Carl Zigrosser
(Ms Pennsylvania)

Bloomfield
Sept 10, 1912

Dear Carl,

This is to let you know that the valise arrived safely; many thanks to you and the others who took trouble for me. The typewriter I suppose I will find in

N. Y. when I go to pay an installment on my new machine. I should have apologized for typewriting my letter; but I was a child with a new toy and had to address the envelope too, you see. I could also write much more than by hand.

Many things have happened since I came down. Friday I went to New York primarily to fix up my courses with Prof. Woodbridge.[1] I called on Elsasser, paid my doctor's bill, and then prepared for the grand climax with Seidenberg. He was out, so I left a note, telling him to find me in the Library. Which he did, and we hurried to his room, and after we had removed our coats and made ourselves comfortable, there poured forth the wonderful Arabian Nights tale of your adventures. I was delighted to find you had visited Mr. Burroughs, (I thought I saw it in your eye before you left), and that you had spent a night there and heard about Whitman, etc. Who was the lady that was there? Seidenberg could remember no names, and his description did not quite fit Dr. Barrus.[2]

S's account became so interesting that when I left, I pleaded with him to come out to Blfd. Sunday and finish it. He came, (it was a glorious day) and we spent no less than five hours walking. He read one of my essays, but I could not quite bring myself to let him take the whole batch in to New York to read. While out walking, we had an adventure at the Glen Ridge Country Club. He became very thirsty, and snooping around a little to find some water, we stumbled upon a charming little keller and asked the waiter if we could get something to drink, or rather he asked. The waiter was most obsequious. Seidenberg waved away a mere glass of sarsaparilla and demanded a bottle apiece. They were all poured out in the tall glasses, with the ice clinking deliciously, before us, when R. S. said, "How much?" The waiter murmured something about being members —and signing a check. Well, no, we weren't exactly members, but we knew it would be all right. I had a cousin, anyway, who was a member. The waiter looked at the glasses, and then he looked at us; we must have looked thristy, so he said, "I'll call the manager." So there we sat like two naughty schoolboys caught in the act, with the stolen fruit before us, while this very dapper young man in a Tuxedo cross-examined us. Even if we had a cousin-member, had he "extended to us the privileges of the club?" We blushed and stammered, mentioned our mere innocent desire to quench our thirst. Suddenly he turned and in the most imperial manner, said in a loud voice to the waiter, "Make out a cash check!" Then he left us without a word, and strode over to another table where two young bloods were sipping various colors, and conversed ostentatiously with them, while we furtively and guiltily sipped our drink. The waiter looked as if he thought he ought to apologize to somebody for serving it. We paid our check, and slunk out, with a propitiating glance in the direction of the manager. R. S. stammered some words of thanks as we passed him, but he did not deign to look around. After we got out we congratulated each other that we did not move smoothly in the atmosphere of flunkeyism.

I saw Keppel to-day and he mentioned you. David,[3] he said, is engaged to be married, and is not responsible. Nothing can be done with him until he gets married, which will be about Dec. 1st. He seemed to think you made a good impression, and did not doubt he, Dr. K., would want you eventually. F. P. certainly didn't get the idea from his brother that the jig was up. His manner gave indication of that. I don't believe he need be discounted so very much.

I'm sorry to hear Mr. Evans is not well; this good weather ought to bring him around again. It was good of you to write even as much. The account of the roast brought every golden moment vividly back to me again. That page is worthy of a special shrine in your note-book. I look forward to your account of the latest journey over Slide to see Burroughs and to Roxbury.

My regards to your good family. With Allen and Elmer gone, the place must seem very strange.

As ever,

Randolph

[1]Woodbridge was Professor of Philosophy and Dean of the Faculty of Philosophy, one of the three faculties of the University.

[2]Dr. Clara Barrus was Burroughs' literary secretary and was his biographer. Zigrosser visited Burroughs several times in Roxbury.

[3]Dean Frederick Keppel's younger brother who helped manage the family's art gallery. Zigrosser worked at the gallery from 1912 to 1918.

12

to Carl Zigrosser
(Ms Pennsylvania)

Hartley [Hall]
Oct 3, 1912

Dear Carl,

Whether it was the effects of the birthday party, or a reaction from Vedder's[1] suffering, R[oderick] S[eidenberg] and I came back to my room Sunday night and talked one of the most brilliant talks that we ever had. It was really quite wonderful and impressed me so much that I started to make an article out of it, with what success remains still to be seen.[2] It started off with Catholicism, of course, and ran gently into Protestantism, discussing the two ideals, the two conceptions of a church, the appeal of the two bodies to young men, ending up with an extraordinarily acute psychological analysis of Mr. Babbitt as the typical non-Catholic and Vedder as the typical Catholic. Never was religion treated so sympathetically by Jew and Infidel before, never was such comprehension of ideals and motives and purposes exhibited by outsiders, and, best of all, never did R. S. and R. S. B. react to each other so harmoniously, so stimulatingly, so lucidly. Altogether a high and elevating experience. If you don't believe me, ask him. I hope he was similarly impressed.

Previous to this, we had made the trip uneventfully; Vedder slept and dozed fortunately, and I read Figgis.[3] We got him safely lodged in St. Luke's, after all the fearful red tape that had to be gone through, and his biography and genealogical tree all safely inscribed on the records. Not till then was he permitted to rest from his sufferings. While we were waiting, in walked my old landlady of 124th St. Her little boy, my musical star, had appendicitis, and had to be operated on immediately. They sent the ambulance for him, and in the excitement, as perhaps V. wrote you, they got the two cases all mixed up, so that when he went in to have his ear examined, he had to fight desperately to prevent them from removing his appendix, and I suppose the little boy, Georgie, was given the impression at first, when he arrived, that his appendix was in his ear. However, it seems to have been straightened out all right, and both patients well taken care of. Vedder escaped Wed. morning and I saw him in the afternoon in Shotwell's[4] class. He did not seem so much the worse for wear either, but how very unfortunate of him to have his old ear coincide with your birthday party. We could have had such a good time Sunday afternoon. As it is, we have the rare birthday evening to look back on, and all its delights. I hardly dare think of those little cakes, they fill me with such desire.

Monday night Read Lewis[5] and I saw "Fanny's First Play." Of course, it is the richest humor, with much sound ironic philosophy. The contrast between 18th, 19th & 20th cent. ideals is beautifully brought out. Shaw seems to say, "I am showing you the 20th cent. You may not like it, but I can't help that; I'm not responsible for it; I didn't create it. I don't like it any better than you do, not much better than I like the 19th cent. in fact. But what are you going to do about it? I am simply showing you, showing you up, in fact. But don't blame me for it." The religious lady is really very convincing, although the ribald audience howled whenever any one mentioned the word; "religion." The acting is very fine, and the scene with the critics, of course inimitable.

We are to have a new literary authority in the Times Book Review. A[fred] A. K[nopf] "is doing Galsworthy's Inn of Tranquility for them." The talk of the great pagan battle rages with undiminished vigor. Joyce is a little hero in the Monthly office, in spite of his religious conversion.[6] I dropped in to-day, for the first time in a week.

We are looking forward to your return. Please think a great deal before you decide to take a room downtown, as you so very ominously threaten to do. You do not intend to throw us all over when you come. And also those Philharmonics—If you change your mind, do please let me know, so I can get seats. If you are going to court my Lady Poverty, do it in some other way than with timbrel and harp—

My regards to all your people.

As ever,

R. S. B.

[1]Vedder Van Dyke was a college friend of Bourne's. Van Dyke came to Columbia to study politics, but left after three years to enter the General Theological Seminary. He was ordained an Episcopalian minister and eventually became the Bishop of Vermont. According to Zigrosser, Van Dyke spoke of the unification of the Roman Catholic and the Anglican church. Zigrosser called him the most religious person he knew during that period.

[2]Possibly "Socialism and the Catholic Ideal," which appeared in the November 1912 *Monthly.*

[3]Probably Darrel Figgis, Irish nationalist and poet. His *A Vision of Life* was published in 1909. Less likely is John Figgis, a Catholic theologian who was influenced by Bergson. He had lectured at Harvard in 1911 and had achieved some popularity.

[4]James T. Shotwell, Professor of History and one of Bourne's favorite teachers.

[5]Then a graduate student, Read Lewis received a law degree in 1914. He later headed the American Council for Nationalities Service, which sought to ease the transition of immigrants into American society.

[6]Bourne is probably referring to Joyce Kilmer, although Kilmer did not officially convert to Catholicism until 1913.

13

to Prudence Winterrowd
(Transcript Columbia)

Hartley [Hall]
Columbia Univ.
New York City
Dec. 18, 1912

My Dear Miss Winterrowd,

I am filled with remorse that my charge of grapeshot fired at random should have hit the kind of woman who didn't love to talk about funerals and sorrow, and that I should have pilloried the whole sex for the guilt of a few. The fact that you appreciated "Youth" makes you immortally young. I apologize to you as the representative of young women, for it was really only about the old, the old in spirit, as well as years that I was thinking when I wrote that unlucky paragraph. Other letters have shown me how wrong I was, and I think I shall have to expatiate my guilt by writing a whole essay about women. If I had not touched the subject in my essay of "The Handicapped", I should have said something more about what my friendships with women have meant to me. Some girls have a magic charm not only of transfiguring you to yourself, and you love them for what they make you. This is one side of what women are constantly accusing men of doing, that is, just using her graciousness and intuition to minister to their own self-esteem, only liking a woman as long as she acts as a sympathetic reflection of his glow. But with the best friendships both the glow and reflection are mutual. You take as much delight in reflecting her glow as she does in yours. You glory in her personality and individuality as much as in your own. The ministrations are mutual.

I cannot tell you how proud your letter made me. I wish I could learn more of how life looks to a girl of 25.

Sincerely yours,

Randolph Bourne

14
to Alyse Gregory
(Ms Yale)

Hartley Hall
Columbia University
16 January 1913

My dear Miss Gregory,

I meant to answer before this your most interesting letter and my tardiness does not mean that I was not very much pleased and flattered to hear from you. I am afraid that my paper was read very much more carefully than it deserved, for it was in reality rather irresponsibly written, my only care being to skirt the triteness of the subject.[1] I am willing to stand by all I say of the golden glow of friendship, even if I have to admit that my notions of women's friendship were based largely on certain remembered dinner tables of feminine relatives whose conversation turned and lingered, it seemed to me, lovingly, on the sufferings of dying neighbors. There is a more serious indictment to be brought against me, I find. Many people, women particularly, are much more controlled by inner moods in their intercourse with people. With me, for instance, the presence of a friend is sufficient to dispel automatically my mood and put me into the ordinary tone of feeling which seems to be ours, that "pre-established harmony" I speak of. Or the presence of a person I am intuitively out of sympathy with is sufficient to dispel my buoyant self-assertion, and put me into the painful, tongue-tied condition I speak of. But many people, I find, are not like that; their mood is not automatically dispelled, but continues to control the situation. Though they may love and be thoroughly interested in the friend there will be many moments when they will be unable to establish that *rapport* which seems so inevitable for me. This is a side of things that I had not considered, and has explained to me many of my dislikes of really interesting people. When I met them, perhaps, they were not in the mood of my dominant interests; yet later, we might, under different conditions, have established the most perfect understandings. I have been too inclined to dismiss them impatiently. Although often I do feel an attraction, largely physical, which in spite of their seemingly forbidding spiritual demeanor, makes me curious to pursue them and stimulate that sympathy which may be there. People with that inner command of moods do not need friends so keenly as I do; they are more self-sufficing. What would seem to me "a prison with a life of penal solitude" is to them simply the four walls of their own home, where they dwell among their interesting moods and ideas. I lack this and I generalized far too sweepingly on my own poverty of inner resources.

What you say about men disburdening themselves of their disappointments and suffering with women not having this same advantage with men, is profoundly true. Men are habitual exploiters of the sympathy of women, and use them constantly to salve their wounded self-pride and justify their incapacities. They suspect of course that many girls rather enjoy this role of spiritual nurse, but this does not excuse their brutal and insatiable demands. Much of the "charm" which youth finds in girls is simply this power of flattery and justification. Of course, if there is to be this, it ought to be mutual. It is ruinous to the girl's personality to play this role without return. The charm must be mutual, and the comfort and stimulus reciprocal.

I should like to hear more about your ideas on people. I am interested in nothing else, and all my studies are valueless except as they throw light on people's souls and personalities. I want to know more about these moods, about people's attractions for each other, about a hundred things that come up in friendship, and arouse curiosity. You, I feel, could tell me much if you would. I wish that you might.

Thank you again for writing me,

Sincerely yours,

Randolph Bourne

[1]Probably "The Excitement of Friendship" which was published in *the Atlantic* in December 1912.

15

to Prudence Winterrowd
(Transcript Columbia)

Hartley Hall
Columbia University
Jan. 16, 1913

My Dear Miss Winterrowd,

It was very pleasant to hear from you again, and it was still pleasanter to have you tell me so much of your experience. It sounded almost like a page out of my own life, even to the pipe organ, for I nearly got a position as organist, and only gave up all idea of it when I decided it was a little too much of a physical strain. Your town, I imagine, is very much like mine, although we were near New York, and so had some stimulation from a freer atmosphere. But how well I know that silent "sect-pressure", ceaselessly trying to mould you to their ways of thinking and acting! A church, to those who have individuality and in- dependence, is one of the most subtle tyrannies there is, because all its codes and manners are invested, in the minds of the directing spirits, with a peculiarly im- pressive, divine sanction. If you question the minister's beliefs or prejudices, you seem to be questioning God himself, or at least your master, Jesus Christ. Of course the process is much less conscious than this, but there is this vague feeling. The minister himself finds it hard to distinguish between your loyalty to his particular church organization and your loyalty to religion and God. In- stead of talking with you and endeavoring to reconcile your doubts with perhaps a broader synthesis, he will only pray for you or with you, when it is the very efficacy of prayer which you are questioning. I am convinced, however, that most of the people in the churches, who are not there for soical and worldly reasons, get a peculiar comfort out of this group spirit. Instead of being a *pres- sure, as it is to you and me*, it is *a support and a shelter*. They have a vague feel- ing of safety, in the evangelical denominations, and much more powerfully in the Catholic church. Many women, I think, like that sense of merging their individuality in a larger group! The church is a symbol of that measureless sea of divinity in which their ideal is to lose themselves. This may sound rather poetical to you, and of course the whole feeling is not nearly so clear and de- fined as I make it here. I am simply trying to explain to myself the satisfactions that people do get out of church. It does not in any way solve your difficulties, or the difficulties of people like you, who think for themselves and resist the submerging stream of group opinion. Where the church is the core and social centre of the community, one's position is very hard. One has no opportunity to work free of the pressure, and must remain in a permanently rebellious and unsettled frame of mind. Unless—you can rise to a higher level, get at the es- sential things in religion and church life, be constructive instead of destructive, and exercise a real influence in radiating broader views, and in making religious life more human, more vivid and more vital. I used to feel the same way about hurting people's feelings, and alienating good and friendly, if narrow and unen- lightened, neighbors. Has it ever occurred to you, however, that it is always the radical, the questioner, who seems to have this sensitiveness about other people's feelings? The bigot, and the narrow conservative never have the slightest com- punction about the feelings of the sincere seeker after truth. He preaches at him as a traitor and a renegade, pursues the "sinner" quite regardless of the latter's discomfort. Don't you suppose your feelings are as cruelly lacerated by having to listen to a three week's revival, as those of any pious elder would be by any- thing you might say against his creed? Of course I don't mean that you have carte blanche to ridicule and denounce his beliefs. But if you have something really vitalizing and liberalizing to offer, you should feel perfectly free to offer it for what it is worth. His feelings will not be hurt any more than it is good for them to be hurt, and you may open his eyes and enlarge his ideals. I will tell you how it worked out with me. I went to the Unitarian church in a neighboring town for a while, although still a member of the Presbyterian church in my town. I must confess I felt very guilty and uncomfortable, but I struggled manfully in C[hristian] E[ndeavor][1] meetings to liberalize the subjects that were discussed, and so justify my divided allegiance. Then I became interested in socialism, saw the inspiring union that was possible; how socialism was really applied Christianity, in all the best sense of the letter. Now I had a constructive programme and when a Young Men's Bible Class was organized in our Church, I persuaded them to adopt "Studies in Social Christianity" and proceeded to preach social service as hard as I could. I found I was listened to with interest if not agreement, and although the class aroused opposition and finally died through the loss of the leader and my personal inability to keep it going, I am convinced that considerable good was done by our agitation. Social service at least became a live issue, and a beginning has been made in a Boy Scout movement, etc. to make the church a socialized force in the community. If you are to spend your life in the community, I should think you would try to become some such socializing, liberalizing force in the church, and whatever other organizations there are. To be effective, you must of course be absolutely convinced of something positive; you must have some sort of vision, and be known as preaching some definite gospel. Society (?) is contagious, and you will be listened to with respect if you are felt to be thoroughly sure of your message and sincere. So I should say to give up Tom Paine and Buckle[2] and all the other eighteenth century sceptics and nineteenth century flounderers, and read the living men of today. You probably know Wm. James' books, but read them again with a passionate interest, as the most inspiring modern outlook on life and reality. *"The Varieties of Religious Experience"* will explain religion to you as vital *human experience;* *"The Will to Believe"* will clear up some foolish dilemmas; *"Talks to Teachers"* will show you the possibilities of human nature; *"Memories and Studies"* has some priceless things; *"Pragmatism"* gives you the philosophic basis for a dynamic, creative attitude towards life. I should like to know your reaction to James; he has settled so many of my own worries that I preach him as a prophet. Then there is H. G. Wells; his *"First and Last Things"* is an "apotheosical" book. (I love that word: you have done a great deed in coining it.) His *"New Worlds for Old"* is a good exposition of Socialism, and his recent fiction has much in it that is suggestive of the modern viewpoint. G. Lowes Dickinson[3] I like very much, although he is less positive and rather too calm and Platonic. But his *"Letters from a Chinese Official"* impressed me tremendously when I read it in 1906, I think, and his *"Modern Symposium"* and *"Justice and Liberty"* are noble and beautiful books. Chesterton's[4] *"Heretics,"* while paradoxical and often irritating, gives one a surer sense of the power of vital conviction. Dewey and Frifts (?) Tufts (?) *"Ethics"*[5] is a noble book. Much of Maeterlinck is stimulating, although he may strike you as too mystical. If you like Philosophy, Bergson's *"Creative Evolution"* is very inspiring. I am just mentioning, you see, books that have immensely impressed me, although they do not converge along any particular lines. I must differ with you; agnosticism *is* or *ought* to be dead. We may not know much, and can never know the most, but at least have the positive material of our human experience to interpret. That at least is assured to us, and it is only when we try to interpret the world in terms of pure cognition, pure thought, that we get into trouble. But our feelings and appreciations and values are what really count. Your Religion of Humanity I would transfigure into a Religion of Socialism, moving towards an ever more perfect socialized human life on earth. Science is purely instrumental, giving us the tools with which to control our environment; it is in no sense valid as an interpretation of life and life's meanings. Its description of the world is a description simply of the machinery, the behavior of that world, not of its palpitating life. This we know only by feeling it and living it. Religion and art have simply been human attempts to catch and fix and make intelligible that life. Like all institutions, the church has become stereotyped and artificial, has killed the spirit with the letter. The churches to-day, most of them, represent about the same quality of religion that a picture-postal does of art. But we know that art is not dead, and we should not be willing to believe that religion is dead. All theological controversies are futile, because they do not teach the living reality. Modern philosophy and psychology give us the materials for a broader, more hopeful, truly spiritual Weltanschauung than the crude agnosticism of Spencer and the early evolutionists.

You see when I get a text I preach a regular sermon. I doubt, after all I have said, that I have made myself clear. One has to live through various attitudes, I suppose, and cannot jump all at once. But I think the process may be hastened. Your letter made a great impression on me, because it so closely touched my own experience. I know the bewildering, cramping effect of not having anyone to talk to or understand. I don't know really what I should have done if I had not come to college. Socialism was almost as tabooed a subject as liberal religion in the town where I lived. At college I met for the first time, not only one person but many who thought as I did, and formed an interesting social group [The Academy], in which the members constantly stimulated each other. Most of my education has come thus from talk and argument here, with brilliant, interested young people. Not only that, but the greatest comfort of all comes from finding most of the professors more or less in sympathy with you so that you found yourself no longer an alien, but one in thought with the people who are doing the thinking of the world. It has all quite revolutionized my life, and I cannot imagine myself back now in the little complacent society where I was brought up, although I think I could, if needs were, go back with a certain prestige and certainly comprehension, and live quite actively (?) in the community. I do not know, of course, your finances and opportunities, but I should think a year, or even half-a-year at a University, where you could get in touch with interesting people who have a zest in things intellectual would prove the greatest experience you could have. The lectures would be stimulating and the life would in general give you a poise and familiarity in this world of ideas and broader interests in which you have already begun to live. There is no society quite like a big University for this. It goes without saying of course that I should be only too happy to make you acquainted at Columbia. Here one can take courses as a non-matriculated student; the term begins Feb. 5. All this seems, on the whole, a highly impertinent suggestion; but I am going to let it stand, knowing you will forgive me if I have erred.

Anyway I hope I may hear from you again. There are many things you can tell me; and I want a chance to write a better and more coherent sermon.

Faithfully yours,

Randolph S. Bourne

[1]Christian Endeavor was a Presbyterian young adult's study group which also engaged in social functions.

[2]Henry Buckle, amateur British historian and rationalist.

[3]G. Lowes Dickinson, an English essayist, and an enthusiastic pacifist.

[4]Gilbert K. Chesterton, essayist and social critic. He was especially critical of corruption in government during this stage of his career. Bourne was apparently less interested in Chesterton's literary criticism.

[5]Winterrowd apparently mistranscribed the author of this work. James Hayden Tufts co-authored *Ethics* (1909) with John Dewey.

16

to Prudence Winterrowd
(Transcript Columbia)

Hartley Hall
Columbia Univ.
Feb. 5, 1913

Dear Miss Winterrowd,

I opened your letter with considerable trepidation, because I did not know what mischief I might have done. "There"! I said, "I may have implanted in her mind a desire which it is impossible for her to gratify, and will proceed to devour her alive." So I was much relieved to find that your situation was no worse than it is. I understand just how you feel about it all, and admire your large and healthy point of view. Although I myself have never felt these controlling influences of old people in the family, I do think that the unconsciously selfish tyranny of the old over the young and their unconscious dependence upon them, is in many cases a real tragedy. Some of my friends, eager, talented, and restless, are uncomplainingly chafing their lives away because they will not renounce the obligations of support and constant ministration that the old people have imposed on them. They are in a fearful dilemma; they cannot manfully and justly throw on their resources people of failing strength who have ministered so kindly to them in their childhood. Yet the confining life and wearing devotion and responsibility suck their young life-blood out, and they are released only when their youth and freshness of interest has forever vanished. Your case is different and more fortunate; because your people have resources, and yet they probably count your presence as worth more than all their resources. Still it does not seem to me that they will be defrauded by a year of your absence at college of as much value as you yourself will be the gainer. (Excuse this horrible bungling sentence.) From what you say, if you were to be married and go away, they would feel few pangs, but would consider that you had fulfilled your proper destiny. They might even feel a slight pride in such an eminently suitable consummation of your career. Why should they object if you should go away to "prepare for life", not forever but for only a short year. I had an intuition that my suggestion would fall in line with your own vague intentions, and was delighted to find I was right. No one ever felt the need of being "boosted up the tree of knowledge" more than I, and college, I feel, has settled so many things for me that I want to spread the good word.

About Columbia—unless you have a college training or equivalent, you could not enter the graduate school *as a matriculated student*. But "students of mature age who give evidence of earnest purpose and special fitness may register, with permission of the Dean, for any of the courses without matriculating as candidates for a degree."[1] That is, you could *take the courses* just as the others, but you would not be labelled A.M. or Ph.D. at the completion of them. The only other alternative is to enter Barnard College, but then you would have to pass entrance exams and be thrown only with girls of 16-20. The graduate work would be the thing for you, and there is no doubt of your being able to convince Dean of "your purpose and fitness." The tuition is 150.00 for the year, room 3-4, and board 5-6. There is nothing particularly cheap about it and if it were not for the fact that I have been supported by scholarships and have obtained work in the city from time to time, I would never be here at all. I will send you bulletins of the Philosophy and Political Science Dept. in which I presume you would be most interested.

If you are going to come next year, I only wish I knew that I was going to be here. That conversation is no more desired by you than by myself. You write so awfully well, that if a letter is "a miserable travesty on a personal conversation", as a certain obscure essay writer recently said, the idea of that personal conversation quite thrills me with anticipation. This college year is the jumping-off place for me. I have no idea where I shall be next year. It will be difficult for me to obtain a teaching position and the literary jobs seem thoroughly occupied. The "Atlantic" is a dubious support and life on the whole presents almost the same forbidding front that it did when I broke the ranks and came to college. To be sure, I have now more philosophy and a tenuous literary reputation, which my college superiors amuse me very much by cudgeling their brains in an effort to capitalize for our mutual profit. They are very slow, however, about offering me any job here, and prefer to speak optimistically of a "far-off divine event." If worst comes to worst perhaps they will give me a scholarship again. But I am becoming a bit restless after four years of leisurely study, and would like to do something direct and useful in the world, occupy some steady position where I could get back some habits of persistent work. Academic study is a little too much of an invitation to dawdle, and every now and then it strikes me as an effective waste of time in a world where there are as many things to be done and done at once. And never was there a less qualified person to do them! If I only had some confidence in my ability to persuade by writing, but I lack that; after I have written a thing, suddenly all the other points of view come trooping before me and jeer at my puny, exaggerated one sided ideas until I turn almost sick within me. So that some of my theories which sound so bold are really written with the most shame-faced timorousness, and sent off to the editor with a forced and desperate bravado. Now this is no attitude for a would-be man-of-letters, a would-be man with a message, who wants to be a preacher, and even a prophet. But how is one going to change it? I feel particularly badly because I have just finished the first draft of an article on which I have been thinking for some time; I was quite pleased with it as long as I kept in my room, but when I stepped out on the street, the rushing life there made all ideas turn suddenly hollow and stale, and I shudder now to think of typing it and sending it away to a scornful editor.[2] Can you give me any advice as to how to cure this inhibitory disease which is now the chiefest of my troubles?

I wonder is Shelbyville anything like Bloomfield? If you see the Atlantic for this month, you will find a very bumptious analysis of the town where I was born and "raised", calculated to rouse the ire of any stolid notable, I think, who reads it.[3] I owe most of my political, social, and psychological education to that town. The only things I find to write about in essays are sort of generalized autobiographical data of my youthful life there. Its church, its social classes, prejudices, conservatism, moral codes, personalities—all furnish the background against which I throw all my experience, and in terms of which I find I still see life and suppose always shall. If you want to do something of permanent value, you will sit down one day and write up the kind of world that you were brought up to believe in, the moral and social codes, and in general, the social philosophy your circle and family believed in. A girl feels these things more, or has in general, more conventions imposed upon her, and I want very much to know in detail what those conventions are. Which reminds you (?), that if that January zero weather froze your desire for writing, it was about the most unfortunate weather Shelbyville has had. You really should write, if it's only a copious diary, because you seem to see so many things in life that other people don't, and, most important of all, they seem to be just the things in which I am interested.

But this letter was to be a discussion of the pamphlet you sent me about James. You will have to read James' books yourself and then see whether you consider this to be a fair exposition and criticism. Since the whole point of the pragmatic philosophy is "just what do we mean by truth," this writer, Mr. Mangasarian,[4] seems to me to dodge the whole question by assuming as he does, an external, absolute Truth, "from everlasting to everlasting." This seems to me simply substituting Reason and Truth for God; the process is just as theological a one as that of the religious person who thinks of a changeless, external God. What is this capitalized Truth which we must seek, love and live? James attempts to bring truth down to earth and make it something we can understand. Truth to him is thoroughly comprehended *experience*; it is created as we go along, it is what proves its verity by being verified. We thus speak of *more truth* or *less truth*, not of Truth and Error. Relativity is thoroughly scientific; it is the absolutest way of thinking that is theological, and my quarrel with the rationalist is that, in spite of his lip-service to science, he is fundamentally unscientific. James' attitude towards the supernatural is subtly caricatured in the pamphlet. He does not use his "Will to Believe" to "prop up the belief in immortality", but he examines the evidence impartially;—there are certain amazing phenomena, religious experiences, psychic experiences, occurring all through the ages; how are we to explain them? To dismiss them as pure illusion is not to ennoble human life but to cheapen and degrade it. We must somehow comprehend a world where both the cold, mechanical facts of the physical plane exist and the warm emotional and conscious life of desires and ideals and hopes. They are just as real as the other, more real for our human purposes. Now this means that the rigid distinction between the Super-natural and natural breaks down, and becomes of less importance. Human experience is now what we have to study, and out of that we have to form our values and ideals. The very essence of James' doctrine is to destroy other-worldliness, while the Rationalist seems to me to be really keeping the idea of the other world alive, by constantly attempting to disprove it. The point is not Is there another world? but What are we to think of a world where amazing regenerations of the vital and spiritual forces of man take place, and which, in spite of all analysis remains so incorrigibly alive and so incorrigibly mystical? I don't believe I make myself clear at all. You will have to read James himself and get his point-of-view which is so different from the rationalistic that they can hardly argue on the same ground, for their ideas are of fixed, solid mutually exclusive things,—Truth and Error (simply a furbishing up of God and the Devil), Mind and Matter, Soul and Body, this world and the other, etc., while his ideas are of fluid, interpenetrating, creative things, of a dynamic world flowing and creative like Time and Life themselves.

It is such a pleasure to write to you that I run on forever. I hope you will pay me in the same coin.

Sincerely,

Randolph Bourne

P. S. I send you some pamphlets you may be interested in.

P. P. S. James never implied that life without immortality was not worth living; he was too good a psychologist for that. All he said was that the balance of probabilities judged by human experience was in favor of it. He would indorse the views of Kropotkin,[5] I think.

---

[1]This policy appears to have been initiated by Woodbridge; in effect it divided graduate students into a group which only sought extra course work and those who were actually pursuing degrees.

[2]Probably "The Life of Irony" published in the March 1913 number of *The Atlantic*.

[3]"The Social Order in an American Town."

[4]Mangasar Mugurditch Mangasarian, tract writer and free thinker. Winterrowd was probably familiar with his pamphlets because she was an agnostic and lived near Chicago, where Mangasarian published his pamphlets.

[5]Peter Kropotkin, Russian mystic and anarchist, who believed in the fundamental good will of human nature. He opposed the Darwinistic conception of a universe of struggle.

17

to Prudence Winterrowd
(Transcript Columbia)

Hartley [Hall]
March 2, 1913

Dear Miss Winterrowd,

I meant you to keep the pamphlets, but if you have really "pored" over them, you must have them graven on your mind by this time. Now I am sending a clipping, which just hits you off beautifully, it sounds almost as if it had been written for your special benefit. It is by a pupil of James, a very brilliant young Socialist, whom I have been conspiring to get acquainted with, but have not yet succeeded. Pore over this and then read "The Will to Believe."

I am glad and yet a little alarmed to see the University virus working so violently, afraid, you see, that your life will be shrouded with gloom if you do not succeed in coming, and, more seriously, that you will be disappointed when you do come, from having idealized the experience so highly. But then I can't tell; only experiment will show. I am a little vexed with Columbia just now, so am not a good judge of what she means to others. I feel myself growing a little stale here, and am in trouble over some impassioned letters I wrote to the college daily protesting against the poor treatment of the scrub women, and the low wages of the children employed around the campus. With all its "sweetness and light", Columbia, like other Universities too, I suppose, does not hesitate to teach Social Ethics in the class-room and exploit its labor force on the side. Any one who points out the inconsistency is denounced as a sentimental idealist and a crank. I feel pretty certain that I have destroyed my chances for preferment here, and will have to go out and earn an honest living at the end of this college year. This worries me a good deal too, because I do not forget my ineffectual struggles to get a place in the world before I came to college. And if I alienate all my powerful friends by being a radical and a crank, there is nothing for me, I'm afraid, but the "bread-line".

Two of your suggested courses I like, but Dewey's Psychological Ethics I doubt if you would get much out of, and Socialist Economy is one of those courses given by a man with a big name who has no conception of teaching, and just talks to fill up time; it would be a waste of time. I would suggest History 121-2, which is considered *the* great course (you will like the anti-Religious bias of Robinson's interpretation of history); and Giddings' Sociology 257-8, a good survey by a very able lecturer; and possibly Shotwell's History 156. You could easily take 4 courses each term and do as much reading as you cared to. I wish I knew I was going to be here next year, because your coming would then be one of the big events to look forward to. It would be great fun to be the one to lead you to the Promised Land, and give you a boost up the Tree of Knowledge. I can see that you have a sort of reverential respect for this place and the people, which is not borne out by the facts. The students here are the greatest medley you ever saw. Few of them are the intellectual giants which your fancy, I imagine, paints them. Most of the professional students are quite hopeless; and those who are studying the "humanities" are most of them from little colleges from the South and West, and have about as many modern ideas and as broad an outlook on life as a child of two. Why, just your rationalism and your philosophical way of thinking will put you at once among the intellectual elite. Robinson (if I may speak so undignifiedly about a distinguished professor) will fall on your neck in delight at the appearance of a "free-thinker" among the swarm of theologies and Southern Baptists that clutter up his courses. (Why, I didn't realize that I could speak with such malicious animus about my fellow-students.) Some of them are really unbelievable, however, and many pass entirely through the course without acquiring a single new idea, or having their intellectual stolidity shaken up for a moment. They are impervious, watertight, immune; some good preacher has seen to that before they started. But, you will say, where are those beings of fire and intelligence that I dangled before your dazzled eyes at first. Well, they are here too, but not many of them; you see here I am assuming that all my friends are highly endowed, interesting, and charming and that outside my circle, such creatures don't exist. You will forgive my delusion that my dozen or more intimate friends are the cream of the students here, and that the rest fall without the pale of interest. But it is these that I should want you to meet, and I think you would find that I had not exaggerated their charm. One difficulty is, we are all of one sex. The girls here give point to the charge that intelligence and beauty are rarely found together. The majority are women who have taught, I presume, for ten or fifteen years, and earned enough to enable them to study for a higher degree. And avid they are for knowledge, and so hopelessly uncritical! I myself am a fearful critic, staying my hand at no man, and taking the greatest delight in hurling the mighty from their seats. But all the women students I have seen drink in every word and never compare, or feel the slightest inadequacy with anything. I simply scandalize them with my free-handed way of discussing all things sacred and profane, and do not get on far with friendships. And I am so keen on girls' friendships. A charming girl, if by any miracle she does have a mind of the same texture as yours, is simply a heaven-sent companion, and the blessedest gift of the gods. One I knew went home to Montana last year, and left me lamenting. Although my eyes have searched the campus ever since, not one face have I seen that even looked as if there was a mind of light behind it. They all look preoccupied and bowed down with the weight of learning which they have not been able to assimilate with their lives and which merely oppresses them, and exhausts them and does not vivify and enkindle, as ideas should. I love people of quick, roving intelligence, who carry their learning lightly, and use it as weapons to fight with, as handles to grasp new ideas and situations with, and as fuel to warm them into a sympathy with all sorts and conditions of men. The reason I can carry my own so lightly is because I have so little, but I don't object to people having little as long as it is all being put to use; and in our campus walks and talks and over our dinner-tables, we put a lot of it to use. Columbia too overflows so easily into the city, and it is easy to meet interesting, unacademic people who make up for the heavy-laden people here.

I was immensely taken with your harrowing experience on the music-stool. You shouldn't reproach yourself with "spineless behavior" that was simply automatic, instinctive, impossible-to-be-avoided "stage-fright." Do you know I never suffered this way? I never played the piano well enough to be shown off publicly, but I spoke many pieces in school, and have made speeches since with hardly a tremor or even a look at the audience. And in writing, I am much more courageous if I think I *am* going to have a public. I have never, until last week, shown anything I have written to a friend, and I used to hate to have my professor read my English themes. I cannot bear to think of the individual personal disapproval, while on the other hand I rather thrive with public abuse. This may come from having anticipated in a long debate on Socialism conducted in the columns of the "Bloomfield Citizen" several years ago, in which my radical views got soundly trounced by my fellow-citizens' sturdy pens. Private praise I always deeply suspect as insincere but the public comment makes me very elated. Newspaper praise of an article *sets me up*. On the other hand, I cannot talk to more than two or three in conversations, and I never could bring myself to speak in class-rooms. So you see I am quite inconsistently developed. I fear my own self-criticism most of all. My own contempt for the work which I feel unable or too lazy to improve, is the bitterest pill I have to swallow in writing. I don't know quite what to call it, except my over-critical sense, my "perfectionist" standpoint, turned inwards upon myself. Because really when I read my work over again much later it seems quite different and I rub my eyes. This last essay, "The Life of Irony", I hurried off to the publisher without reading over and slunk around for a day or two, feeling what a fool and incapable I was, and sure that it would be summarily rejected, and with such scorn that I should never get even another hearing. And now as I read it over it quite charms me; I wonder how I could ever have expressed so completely the apotheosis of a whole side of me which makes my talk and comment on friends and events and books, with my friends, such a sparkling joy to me. The fact is, each of my essays has expressed an aspect of me, horribly idealized I must admit, and the new essays in "Youth and Life" will express some more. But altogether, I really can't see that they express any kind of a unity; they sound like many different personalities, or like many insincere aspects of one personality. I would have great difficulty in convincing anybody that they were all thoroughly and almost uncannily autobiographical. You don't know how much it means to me to think

that you will read them, I hope you will—and understand them. For I do watch
the appearance of the book with a good deal of foreboding. I don't mind abuse,
but I don't want to be laughed at, and some of the naive confessions of my
heart, I am afraid, will sound awfully silly to the academic people up here. I am
afraid both of that, and that some of it sounds like the preaching of a prig. I am
so glad that you want to be a "prophetess" because I want to be a prophet, if
only a minor one. I can almost see now that my path in life will be on the outside of things, poking holes in the holy, criticizing the established, satirizing the
self-respecting and contented. Never being competent to direct and manage any
of the affairs of the world myself, I will be forced to sit off by myself in the
wilderness, howling like a coyote that everything is being run wrong. I think I
have a real genius for making trouble, for getting under people's skin; I have
proved it in my various assaults on things up here. Between an Ezekiel and an
Ishmael, it is a little hard to draw the line; I mean, one can start out to be the
first, and end only by becoming the latter.

Really you tease me by misrepresenting James; he was very far from
being a defender of existing conditions; indeed he wrote one of the most effective and practicable Utopias that has been suggested—"The Moral Equivalent
for War", which I will try to get and send you. He never wrote directly on Ethics, and mentions socialism rarely, although with approval; but all his work is
infused with the ideal of free individuality, developed through a spontaneous
social life, which is the ideal of Socialist and Anarchists alike. You *are* "in bad";
and even the claims of the giddiest Shelbyville social season must not prevent
you from reading at least some of the shorter papers. A book recently reprinted
by Henry Holt & Co. of N. Y. called "on Some of Life's Ideals" is of his best,
and "Memories and Studies" contains some very beautiful papers. By the way,
can't you introduce James to your literary clubs as pre-eminently the best
American writer since Emerson. There is chance for missionary work. If it is not
indecently curious I should really like to know what subjects they do discuss.
(This is my sociological aspect appearing.) If you've read John Muir's[1] articles
in the "Atlantic" recently, you know what he did—I got up at 1 A.M., so as to
have five long hours for reading and inventing. I humbly recommend this method to you as means of meeting both your social and intellectual responsibilities;
or, if you prefer, you can wait till you come to Columbia, and then sit up all
night studying, like my old room-mate used to do. Then you'll have the drop on
old John Muir by two or three hours.

You see I am going through your letter trying to converse with it just as
if I were hearing it in person. And now I come to that awful remark of your
"enfant terrible" friend—"The less one knows the happier is one." Only a person
of uncanny insight or exquisite naiéveté could have said that. As I said the other
day, "A *little* knowledge may be a dangerous thing, but *more* is quite fatal."
You do get an ungodly number of new doubts and problems that you would
never have thought of without, but then you get that sense of widening your

universe, of exploring dangerous and uncharted seas, of living in a world of real peril, where not only you do not know the answer, but nobody does. This is borne in upon you as you ascend the ladder of any one branch of knowledge. It is the beginners, the elementary instructors who are certain and dogmatic; the further you go, the more shaky the authorities become, until you find it is those who know the most who have the least certitude. But by being a philosopher, you can be contented with tentative certainties, with intuitions, and by a judicious mixture of reason and faith based on what seems the balance of probabilities and on the effective workableness of your principles,—you can extract a surprising amount of satisfaction out of the boundless puzzling world; you can live it and feel it with imaginative sympathy, and thus "understand" it, even if you feel you don't really "*know*" it.

The answer to your fears of verbosity is this portentiously long letter. Both our educations will be neglected if we take such an enormous epistolary interest in each other. But please continue to neglect yours!

I think you probably endow your people with more disapproval of the project than they really feel. I used to have much the same consciousness of my relatives' abiding disapproval, much of which I found later was a mere chimera of mine. They may be a little ironical about the "uninteresting family", and are just amusing themselves quietly. I would take the risk anyway and act as if such were the case.

I haven't the fortune of knowing Mr. C. but will try to meet him.

Ever sincerely yours,

Randolph S. Bourne

[1]John Muir was a famous naturalist and writer. He was a proponent of the National Park system. The article to which Bourne is referring is probably "Lessons of the Wilderness," in the January 1913 issue of *the Atlantic*.

18

to Prudence Winterrowd
(Transcript Columbia)

Hartley Hall
April 10, 1913

Dear Miss Prudence,

All you need is a little more of James and you'll be a full-fledged religico-philosophico-sociological pragmatist, knowing the value of all things, and willing to look on dusty Positivism as a step to a more breezy and inspiring height. For the Positivist has everything except the verve, the color, the music of life, and anybody with any artistic sense feels that a philosophy of life must have a great deal of these things. I thought I made a very shrewd hit—although you quietly ignored it—when I said that the Rationalist simply substituted for the theological God and the Devil, a Theological Truth and Error of his own. The modern philosophy is all dynamic, vital; thinks of everything in terms of change and purpose and will and instinct, that is vital processes rather than physical changes.

You know I have no acquaintance who is so thoroughly Jamesian in style as yourself, with so much zest and sweep of life, and to think that you should be nourished on Tom Paine and the dry, keen, clear but not very warming philosophy of the Positivists. Well, it's almost a miracle, and I hesitate to think what you'll be when the virus of the Bergson-James-Schiller-instrumental-pragmatism has really got into your blood. You are so susceptible, I can see, to it, that you are probably now, as I write, already down with the disease. Of course I began in the same way as you, although I did have the mild and healing salve of Unitarianism to aid me in my work of reconstruction. My enthusiasm for James is really comparatively recent, for two years ago when I was studying a philosophy course with a wonderful teacher [Woodbridge], the best we have here, who, by the way, suggested several of the titles of my essays, I was a rank materialist and took great delight in lacerating a rather tender and green young man whose delight was in Emerson and Plato, whom I despised. But my readings of James and Bergson since then and my studies in primitive psychology have led me to give the feelings and aesthetic perceptions a much higher place in the world than I had, with a corresponding reduction of the intellect and reason. This sounds, I know, like an awful backsliding, and to those who believe that Bergson is the last of a school, rather than the first, any such giving of any claim at all to anything outside of the intellect and reason must look like sheer reaction. It would be great fun to give you a detailed history of my philosophy, in person I mean; although I realize that I am a very bad practitiser [sic] of it. I am rather dull, and cannot talk very much; my fate seems to lie in poking holes in what other people are saying. They flow on in steady stream, and I stand aside and jab a sentence in now and then which I mean to dislocate them, and which often does. I don't think anybody ever listened to me say more than two consecutive sentences. When the situation demands or permits my talking I find myself insensibly drifting into a cross-examination of the other person; they begin to squirm perhaps or look uneasy and then I suddenly realize that I have not been converting but cajoling and browbeating a witness. I can never manufacture talk; if the other person won't fence with me, or occupy the witness stand, or flatter me, I am simply helpless. And this reminds me that your flattery of "The Life of Irony" was so electric and vivid that it gave me a genuine thrill, of a sort that I didn't know I could get. Have I spoiled the charm by telling you? Your style quite annihilates distance and I have so vivid a sense of your personality that I pointed out to my room-mate the other day as we were waling (?) a girl we met on the street, and said with the most assured conviction, "That girl looks very much like my friend in Shelbyville!" He was astounded, "Why, how do you know? I thought you said you had never seen her!" But she looked as if she could talk atwest (?), and I knew that I should like to interpolate ironical jabs in her discourse. If you really "sputter", and could thus provide all the body of discourse, while I danced around your mind, how famously we should get on! You might make me somewhat paternal and professional, I fear, since you imply that I lack these mental inhibitions and conflicting tendencies to action, and am a sort of integrated person of poise of mind and clarity and sanity of purpose. But this is simply another instance of that unconscious hypocrisy with which writing endows a person. One has only to take pen in hand, and every word instinctively becomes a flatterer of one's egotism, the sentences conspire to make the writer better, braver, nobler than he ever was or hopes to be, and, not only that, but fixes that noble character in black and white, like a heroically idealized pen and ink sketch. I look sometimes at my book and think —"What a divine caricature you are of the personality of R. S. B.? Who would recognize in you there the puny, timid, lazy, hypochondriacal wretch who really wrote those words of courage and idealism"? And then, instead of straining heroically to reach those lofty levels, I go out and do some foolish thing or waste a day or put off my work, or have a day-dream or mope about how my friends are getting ahead of me, and I'll never be able to learn regular habits of work, or accomplish anything worth while. I have been unhappy for so many hours of my life over my weakness of will, and inhibitions, and melancholy even over my melancholy itself, that sometimes the privilege of chanting a lay of the ideal and pretending that it is you, seems a just revenge for all the low-lying days. Sometimes I think I'll just break up housekeeping and leave these mouldy valleys and go up on the mountains of my book-world and camp there for awhile, perhaps always? There must be a path there, indeed I have climbed it occasionally and know the way. After I had written "The Handicapped", a girl friend wrote me the most ecstatic letter saying I had been living on the mountains. I was stunned and humiliated. What an awful lie, I thought! As I saw the valleys where I had dwelt and the silly avoidable misery I had suffered owing to my little faith and I could not reply to her without shame. Well, I say I will go camp on the mountains and I start. And then someone neglects me, or I have a pain or I hear a dull lecture, or I don't see any of my friends for a whole afternoon and I stumble and roll the full length of the mountain side. That is "Youth and Life" from one who was never young, and has only partly lived. Why does a severe attempt at honesty like this always end in pessimism? But I'll play Ulysses to you if you'll play the person—I forget who it was—who got Christian out of the Slough of Despond.

The description of the literary activity in your town was highly entertaining. I can see now why Indiana is called the literary centre of America. Why, my poor town, which I imagine, is larger than Shelbyville, only has one woman's club and that isn't very big. I think our town must have been fearfully unstimulating, though where I achieved an interest in books and ideas I can't imagine. I certainly didn't read much when I was young, and I had absolutely no intellectual conversation around me. I often wonder myself about my going to college; I can't settle whether the gnawings of ineffectiveness would have forced me to try to write, or whether I would have just sunk down into a stagnation of despair. But you are right, I had to. Although it was rather hard work to decide, I felt like a criminal because it meant my withdrawing from the possibility of earning money for my family. They didn't particularly approve, but it turned out all right, and when I found out how easy it was, I wondered why I hadn't done it before, with a lot of other bold things that timidity and that awful glowering family eye of rich guarding relatives inhibited me from doing.

And now to top off with the "white lies". Rather than tell them I often keep still, and then of course get a reputation for rudeness. When I am home and a bustling neighbor gets into the room before I can escape, I am supposed to tell her how delighted I am to see her and warm into a genial glow. Whereas I am unable to do anything of the kind; she interfered with my playing the piano in the parlor and I am generally cross with her. But then when I merely say "How do" in a sepulchral voice and pass on, the whole family descends at supper table in an avalanche on my head, and I am made to realize that my manners are outré and my whole social bearing quite eccentric and bizarre. There I should say I am moved and will try to do better in the future; but I am not moved at all, so I don't say anything, and get into an awful scrape again for my callousness. This has convinced me that white lies are an invention of the Devil, or rather of womankind in order to feed their own egotism on every occasion, and to keep up an elaborate network of social relations which has lost all sense of values and spontaneity. It must be horrible to have to tell people you don't like how pleased you are to see them and ask about their health which is evidently good or they wouldn't be there. I shall try to escape ever being caught in such a system. This may sound fearfully undemocratic but it is not really so, for the white lie is a way of concealing all true equality by mixing people artificially and preventing their personalities from really touching.

Your friend,

Randolph S. Bourne

19

to Karl D. Robinson
(Ms Columbia)

Hartley [Hall]
April 16, 1913

Dear Karl,

I shall be glad to come. Your other letter I have meant to answer, but its flattery quite overcame me, and I did not know just how to react. How did you know so cunningly the way to my self-esteem? You put your fingers on so many qualities that I wanted to believe were there, and indeed warmed the cockles of my heart.

As ever,

R. S. Bourne

20

to Prudence Winterrowd
(Transcript Columbia)

Hartley Hall
April 28, 1913

Dear Miss Prudence,

Here is a picture of the preacher if you will accept it. The photographer chose the pose, I didn't, but I fell for it when I saw the proof in spite of the jeers of my friends, who do not appreciate my dignity always in just the way they should.[1]

I have been mixed in my mind lately concerning my future, and have been coquetting with a Fellowship which has been tentatively awarded me. It would give me enough to study abroad upon, and thus I could realize one of my earliest ambitions. On the other hand I have been living here in such a kindly sheltering circle of friends that it chills me, especially in the night-time, to think of exposing myself to a foreign world, and putting my friendship-forming capacities to so cruel and new a test. The experimental life calls, it is true, especially when the sun is bright and warm, and I comfort myself with the feeling that my friends will be here when I come back, and they cannot change very much in a year. If you are to come here next winter, though, it discourages me to think that I would not be here to aid your assimilation, and immerse myself in that flood of good talk which I know we are saving up for each other. You would doubtless soon discover for yourself circles and poeple quite as stimulating as any I could point out, and so it will be wholly my loss if I go away. I have a curious feeling, in fact, when I think of Europe, of being *coerced* into doing the thing that my heart is set upon.

Speaking of circles, there is the most delightful group of young women here who constitute a real "salon".[2] Three or four of them live together in an old house down in the Greenwich section, while the rest have rooms in the neighborhood and come to the house for meals. They are all social workers, or magazine writers in a small way. They are decidedly emancipated and advanced, and so thoroughly healthy and zestful, or at least so it seems to my unsophisticated masculine sense. They shock you constantly, or would if you didn't, as I am afraid I do, judge things and people by other standards than their predictability and good form. They have an amazing combination of wisdom and youthfulness, of humor and ability, and innocence and self-reliance, which absolutely belies everything you will read in the story-books or any other description of womankind. They are of course all self-supporting and independent; and they enjoy the adventure of life; the full, reliant, audacious way in which they go about makes you wonder if the new woman isn't to be a very splendid sort of person, and whether much of this talk about the hard road which the woman finds in the world, the dangers and difficulties and constraints, are really in the nature of things, and not the reflections of her own timidities and constraints and conventions. They talk much about the "Human Sex", which they claim to have invented, and which is simply a generic name for those whose masculine brutalities and egotisms and feminine pettinesses and stupidities have been purged away so that there is left stuff for a genuine comradeship and healthy frank regard and understanding. This is, of course, the great ideal, but to most people such talk, I find, seems the merest humbug, and you might think so yourself until you sense the reality of these delightful people, and are converted. Such a circle you would of course have to know, and I should love to see how you took to it or didn't. Because nobody is perfect and it may be I like them because I put so high a value on irony and such a low one on conventionality. It is true that you shall not look for romantic passions in my salon, but I really believe that much of what we call romantic passion simply doesn't exist outside of the story book world; and this story book world is the worst sort of training for people growing-up. We translate all our experiences into those terms, and get such a thoroughly distorted view of sex-relationships that it takes up years to straighten out. Not in the terms of romance and passion which poets have sung in, and novelists have agonized and rhapsodized in for so long that we are incurably sick with it all, should these things be seen, but in terms of equality and camaraderie and frank hearty delight in personality and all the charm, physiological and spiritual, that goes with it. My salon says that their object is to restore "charm" to life, and that is one of the greatest revolutions that could be accomplished. I was brought up in a society where everybody seemed to think it a duty to fall in love with each other and then either desperately conceal it, or express it in a peculiarly hypocritical and insincere way. The whole thing instead of being based on a whole-hearted camaraderie and interest and attraction for each other's personality, which would grow and expand with friendship, was simply the working of a crude instinct plus a lot of conventions as to how it was "proper" to behave, and what people would think of you.

Well, I don't know how I could go off on this very important subject. It quite works me up to talk on it. I shall look forward to your letter. Do you not owe me two or its equivalent?

Sincerely,

Randolph S. Bourne

[1]See the frontispiece to this volume.

[2]Probably the salon at Patchin Place, an eating club formed by Elizabeth Westwood and other feminists. Among the women who frequented the club were Frances Lundquist, Louise Deming, and, perhaps, Alyse Gregory. Carl Zigrosser was also a frequent guest.

21

to Prudence Winterrowd
(Transcript Columbia)

Hartley Hall
May 18, 1913

My Dear Miss Prudence,

Your second letter was most welcome, cancelling as it did all the remorse and guilt into which your very disturbing news had plunged me. I began to feel like those terrible persons in Ibsen who go about breaking up happy families with the "claims of the ideal." It makes one suspect ones ideals when they create so much misunderstanding and do so much damage. Fortunately the damage is not so much as it threatened to be, but I feel as if I had had a narrow escape. If my book is to go like an agitator, stirring up the perfectly contented and happy and changing all their outlook into a fancied glare of oppression, I shall have to think long and reasonably before setting down my thoughts on paper, and if I did that many of them wouldn't get written. But you see I suspect that you were very fertile soil for agitation; you must have believed these things, or some of them, all the time, or you wouldn't have written me, wouldn't have reacted. As for the older generation, they do demand and deserve a great deal of devotion and the flattery of agreement in ideals and beliefs, in return for the sacrifice and tenderness they have lavished on us. But it is just that fanatical propensity to sacrifice with its ensuing overwhelming claims of obligation and support in this after life when, having lived for their children, their children will now live for them—it is just this (as I expounded to a young Southerner last night, who thought I was very wicked), that I hope is a waning ideal. I want to see independent, self-reliant progressive generations, not eating each others' hearts out, but complementing each other and assuming a spiritual division of labor; I want the father and mother besides raising the children to lead independent lives of their own, (this "I have nothing to live for but my children" that one hears so much is most demoralizing, I think), to add their own life-works of art to the great picture gallery of personality of the past. Much of the modern restiveness of youth is a desire to get away from the enervating spiritual coddling and demands for an exaggerated affection which parents of the old school think is respectively the proper attitude for parents and children. This restiveness seems of course like the basest of ingratitudes, but it is really the healthy insurgency of a new morality which will call people to a new robust sense of family relations in the world. It is the working-out of it, however, that causes so much pain and despair. You see much of it among the immigrant families whose sons and daughters go to Columbia or City College and become innoculated with new ideas that produce a constant guerilla warfare with the irreconcilable traditions of the parents. I think your little flurry probably cleared the air. Have they read the book itself?

Though "Prudence may be a hateful thing in youth", youth is certainly a most delightful thing in Prudence. You see in the matter of name I have the advantage of you, for I can drift almost insensibly into "Miss Prudence" while "Mr. B." is quite bungling and crude. But Mr. B. is horrible; I have never gotten over the humiliation of being called "Mr. Bourne" in High School. I could always seem to detect a sardonic lurk in the eye of the teacher when she applied that ponderous epithet to my fragile, and shrinking self, and I can hardly hear myself called it now without wincing. So there is nothing left, I guess, but a plain acceptance of the least offensive epithet of my Norman cognomen. If we could only use of German phrases, "Hochgechiter" [sic], or whatever they use, and automatically approach the nickname as our acquaintance got better and better—although I am perfectly sure that you are one of those guaranteed-always-existing, sprung-full-blown-friends that I wrote about. I cannot imagine knowing you any better than I did on your first letter, I hope that through the pulpit atmosphere there appears occasionally a little of my real self. You certainly seem to know the preacher. I appreciate your remarks on the babes and sucklings, although I can't say I was much flattered. My success in life depends so largely upon my growing up that I don't like to think I am still impressing people as an infant prodigy. When I look at my last years roommate *four* years younger than myself, and my most admired and, I think, admiring friend, I feel how the slipping years have passed me. He is to teach politics at Columbia, next year, while I am still wandering around trying to get scraps of knowledge, and pin myself down to one activity at which I can grow and develop. "Youth" may have been preposterous as a picture of youth, but it was a very accurate revelation of my own chaotic inwards, which—and this is the menacing thing—seem to remain almost as chaotic. My kind University is giving me every opportunity to succeed and show what I have in me, but sometimes I despair of there ever coming out anything solid, profitable, worthy, reliable.

I certainly appreciate your experience with Easton. It is all much more difficult for a girl. But these things must wait for talk.

I am so glad you like Burroughs.[1] I had the great pleasure of spending a few days with him last summer up at his old birthplace in Roxbury, and also took him to some of the Bergson lectures[2] here in February, with a never to be forgotten little supper with him and two of my enthusiastic friends at the "Copper Kettle". He was so delighted with Bergson and it was great to see them together at the University tea to which I smuggled him and got him introduced to the great philosopher. He is a noble old man, very simple and modest, likes simple, childish people best. I am sorry he is not a better letter-writer, dislikes it, in fact, so that you get rather cursory little notes for your long letters. He looks at the world with the eye of the artist, and uses his science to illumine his artistic insight, which I believe is the eternally right way and attitude of the intellectual life.

I have not read Pratt's book, but will look it up. I am probably so hypnotized by James that I do not see the point of these bright objections that his colleagues bring against him. You will find usually, I think, that they are not merely the objections of common sense, but have some philosophical presuppositions at the basis of them. It seems to me that James does anything but accept the old religious beliefs, except as they seem to express and interpret some age-long and eternal experience of the race. Belief for him is not a cold intellectual acquiescence but a motive for action, a basis for behavior, a program, rather than a creed. Chesterton's attitude is somewhat similar, though I agree with you that his backhanded somersaults into Christianity are exasperating. He does so much good, though, in loosening up the vicious logicalism of thought that I can forgive him. We are all instrumentalists here at Columbia. Thought is a practical organ of adaptation to environment; knowledge is a tool to encompass this adaptation, rather than a picture of reality. Bergson carries this a step further and says we can only know that reality through the feelings, through appreciation, through observing the world rather as a work of art than a scientific, logical schema. My little metaphor at the end of "Religion" is not so meaningless. The religious person (?) an extreme and basks eternally in the art-atmosphere. But life is primarily action, and he thus misses the deepest meaning.

It is great news that you will be in New York. My going depends entirely on my getting a companion to travel a little with me, which doesn't look probable now. I had thought of sailing about the middle of July and spending a few weeks at the French University. My correspondent, Mr. Bligh,[3] invites me to Wales for September and then classes begin at London in October. I wish you might be here for a week early in July, when the Summer Session was open and you could see Columbia in action. You must plan to stay longer than a "day or so". You could get very nice lodgings like the Summer Session people have— teachers, you know, from all over the country—and you could get a little epitome of our Bohemian life for a wk. for the price of two days in a hotel. It would certainly be unwise to come to Columbia for a year without financial sufficiency and go without the things that New York offers in the way of opera, etc. I feel rather remorseful for unsettling your mind; the Columbia scheme was thrown off in one of my audacious moments, the motive being largely the thought of having so delightful a friend here. But if you could come and look the ground over, I should then lose my responsibility and feel acquitted of complicity in the matter. You will notice how my enthusiasm for your being here next winter wanes in the light of my European trip, which takes me to other parts. But all that can be better talked about. Please do let me know your plans because I would postpone my departure quite delightedly if you were to take in New York for a week surely. And we sometimes have the most charming weather in July, and a wonderful park overlooking the noble Hudson and the lordly Palisades, and a beautiful little campus. The prospect makes me enthusiastic. Do let it materialize.

Sincerely yours,

Randolph S. Bourne

[1]See note to the letter of February 5, 1912.

[2]These lectures given by the famous French mystical philosopher were the intellectual event of the year.

[3]For a summary of this visit, see the general introduction.

22

to Alyse Gregory
(Ms Yale)

Hartley [Hall]
1 June 1913

Dear Miss Gregory,

    I want to tell you in turn what a great treat it was to meet you, all the more so for its entire unexpectedness. I had, as I told you, puzzled over you a good deal, and it was so delightful to meet you as you are, and not as you had colored yourself in the somewhat grey tones that belied you, or some of you. For I went home with the elated feeling that I had found a new friend, and one with so much achievement and personality. Indeed, I can't quite understand these "questionings" and inhibitions of yours. You don't know how I envy you your activity and the chance to reach people with a vital message and in such a direct way. I seem to be merely mooning along the wayside of life, helpless and unachieving, while you are on the battle-line expressing yourself, expressing your convictions and ideals in the most effective, and—I should think—soul-satisfying way. What is cold writing in comparison with direct campaigning? I would give almost anything for that feeling of *participation*, something that you must wonderfully have. But I haven't the will or the power to force myself into it, and must drift somehow along the line of least resistance. That is why I feel my book [*Youth and Life*] is so hypocritical; it purports to represent me, when it only represents my ideals. Without *participation*, one's mind is kept constantly

unsettled; everything beckons, the air seems filled with winged spirits of opportunity, yet until one is seized and flung into something, one never can get oneself quite committed. I almost dread another year of assaults on my initiative,
which is too disintigrative and perplexed to concentrate on anything. You may
not believe it, but just at this time I am quite at a loss as to what I shall write
or could write next. I cannot give myself whole-heartedly to the scholarly labor
that would win academic preferment, for I get restless over details and indignant
with academic attitudes and ideals. On the other hand, I haven't the insistent
creative imagination to enable me to picture vividly and concretely the life that
I see and feel. And there I am, nicely deadlocked, passively and rather miserably
waiting for some one to force upon me a regular routine of definite writing. The
"Atlantic" has been my good angel, poking topics at me which I bit with the
eagerness of a fish, and coddling me along until now it feels, I think, that I
ought to stand on my own feet. And there is so much to be done, so much to be
said, while I don't seem quite able to make the connections, close the switch
that will set the current flowing.

But now it is I who am boring. I hope I may see you at least once before
I go. Are you ever in New York, and free—for a walk? You know, I never made
my speech at all; everybody seemed so happy talking that it seemed a pity to
disturb them. I hope Miss Rodman[1] was not offended at the readiness with
which I accepted the suggestion not to give it. It was a poor speech, and marked
me as an academic.

Sincerely,

Randolph S. Bourne

[1]Henrietta Rodman, a prominent feminist and inhabitant of Greenwich Village.
Bourne could be referring to a meeting held during the week of June 2-9, a period designated by suffrage organizations as a time for demonstrations.

23

to Alyse Gregory
(Ms Yale)

290 Belleville Ave.
Bloomfield, N. J.
June 14, 1913

Dear Miss Gregory,

I was sorry to grovel so hopelessly on such a bright and brilliant morning, when there was really no occasion at all for recounting one's failings and per-plexities. I don't know whether you will forgive me, but perhaps you will when you know that your stern contempt cheered me up wonderfully. Starting in with a firm determination to conceal nothing from you, to throw myself from the pedestal with as reckless an abandon as possible, I soon found it was quite delicious to paint the picture as black as possible in order to get your sniffs of scorn. You must have seen all this, so that is why I tell you about it. In my lone moments the picture is pretty black, but as soon as I begin to describe it, the whole thing incurable lightens. Friends are dreadful for pessimism; mine simply will not endure in their company. But as yet I have found no substitute for them, and an hour's loneliness is enough to start a host of spectres of ambitions, and regrets, and genuine weaknesses that keep one busy fighting for the rest of the day.

I have been reading Whitman the last few days. If one could keep per-manently that wonderful mood of serene democratic wisdom, that integration and understanding, I think everything one did would be beautiful and right. But it is this wanting to do beyond one's power to do or opportunity to do, or courage to try to do, that makes all the trouble. Perhaps he didn't attain his poise till after struggle. He didn't write till he was 33, did he? and perhaps he longed to write and couldn't until he had worked out his life and gotten a firm footing. Traubel[1] says he was never sure of himself, that is of the permanency of his message, and that is very encouraging. Perhaps there is some spirit that makes every person with the gift of articulation say more than he is, speak clearly and authoritatively what he but dimly strives to reach, describe the heights seen by him in moments of penetration, though from a point far down the mountain side.

A friend has offered us a cottage near Redding, and I shall probably come up the latter part of this week. Will you be in that part of Connecticut at all now? I should like to see you again if you are. I really enjoyed that walk more than I can say.

Sincerely yours,

Randolph Bourne

[1]Horace Traubel, friend, publicizer, and critic of Walt Whitman.

24

to Simon Pelham Barr
(Transcript Columbia)

Bloomfield, N. J.
June 16, 1913

Dear Barr:
    I did not realize you would be sending stuff so soon, and really have
nothing ready. I never felt so uninspired as I do now. My graduate work has just
about ruined me, I guess, unfitted me for literary labor and not trained me for
scientific sociology. Still I will try to have something this week; if Darrow cuts
up there ought to be considerable time, and anyway Summer School doesn't
close till middle of August. Have you any hustling business manager to sell
copies? You ought to dispose of 300 or more on the Campus, if you get out an
artistic product. Ask H[enry] W. E[lsasser] if he hasn't changed his mind about
going to Europe. The enclosed "poem" is for your private perusal only. You will
see the influence of Barr and Giovannitti; of course you saw The Cage in the June
Atlantic. Didn't you think it magnificent; or is your blasé mood, induced by the
pageant,[1] still strong upon you? Please return this with comments.

R. S. Bourne

[1]Bourne is probably referring to the pageant staged to dramatize the plight of the
Paterson, New Jersey strikers. See also note 4, letter 42. Arturo Giovannitti was an Italian
born syndicalist. He was imprisoned during the Paterson strike and wrote "The Cage," a
poem commenting on the oppression of contemporary society, while incarcerated.

25

to Carl Zigrosser
(Ms Pennsylvania)

Bloomfield
June 28, [1913]

Dear Carl,

I should have answered your kind invitation before this, but I was waiting to see when we would go to Europe, and how I could work this invitation in with another. However, they both fall through, I am sorry to say, because we (that is Ward Swain,[1] whom I have raked up as a companion) have been constrained to sail next Saturday, July 5, on the "Rochambeau." It seemed an excellent chance to go on this very fine ship, with far better accomodations than we would get for two weeks or more. It gets on one's nerves to wait around for such an event as embarking for Europe, so we jumped at the good opportunity. I am sorry enough to miss a week with you at Ulster Park, and hope that I shall have another invitation in 1914 or 1915. We are to take a rapid survey of Belgium, Holland, Germany and Switzerland, perhaps landing up in Grenoble, France, and studying some French. Ward is planning to attend the Sorbonne, and will need the French before beginning in November. I go to Wales for September, and then to London. Three months will be all I can stand of their infernal weather, when I will go to Paris for a few months probably. And if we have any money we will travel some more in the Spring.

I ran across R[oderick] S[eidenberg] in the Columbia Library the other evening. He discoursed with great subtlety on the militants in England. Spoke also of a walking trip with you over the Fourth.

Write me a steamer letter if you have time to tear yourself from your bucolic occupations. I suppose you are haying already and enjoying to the full the pleasures of the country and farming life which a knowledge that you can get away from them is sure to give you. I wish I was going to Europe with half your artistic knowledge and appreciation. When I think how much I shall miss, it quite staggers me.

I wish it was you that were going with me. We should enjoy it in quite a different sense from what I will with Ward, who is an amusing kid, but not exactly inspirational. However, "es hat nicht sollen sein." My best regards to your family, and hoping to hear often from you.

Adieu!

Randolph

[1]Joseph Ward Swain was a graduate student in history at Columbia. Swain later became a professor of history at the University of Illinois.

26

to Prudence Winterrowd
(Transcript Columbia)

Bloomfield, N. J.
Monday, June 30, [1913]

Dear Miss Prudence,

It just occurs to me that, as I am sailing Saturday, and I want to hear from you before I go—and I do—that I had better not leave you to think I am completely lost, but write at once. I was rather disgusted, to tell the truth, to find you would not be in New York in July, for I had counted so much on seeing you before I went and having at least one of those long talks which have been reverberating through our correspondence. But like so many good things, it was not so to be, and now I am off across the water, with a callous indifference to impending situations which I know in a few weeks will cause me all sorts of trepidations. Fortunately I have a companion who will travel with me this summer and then settle at the Sorbonne for the winter to study history. While not the most stimulating friend I could choose, he seemed to be the only one of my, as I thought, numerous and feasible acquaintance, who had either the inclination or the opportunity to go. He is a Columbia graduate in my class, A. M. Harvard this year,—one of those mixtures of shyness and childishness and old thoughts and precociousness that I know so well and always have a soft spot in my heart for, although the world seems to consider them genuine pariahs. I feel myself so wise and fatherly by his side, having in a way passed beyond that stage, that perhaps he will be a much more valuable companion than a person of real personality who would depress me by his greatness. I don't think I ever asked you whether you had ever been abroad. When I survey the wilderness of things that are to be seen and known about, I feel mad at myself for not spending these few months industriously studying up history and politics and social conditions instead of going off half-cocked like this. Of course, I know what I expect to see in a vague sort of way, but when I imagine describing to anyone the government or legislation or history or social organization of any of the countries, I realize how large and misty are the outlines of the structure I have carried away from college. The terms of my Fellowship are delightfully free and easy—indeed the whole attitude towards me is quite amazing, one would think I were receiving a pension instead of a commission of useful intellectual labor—and so this gives me a soft spot to land on if I get so immersed in the whirl of impressions or so daunted by the foreign atmosphere that I fritter away my time and accomplish nothing, as I have done this year at Columbia. It has taken me two months to recover from the bad attack of remorsefulness at my unprofitable year, and have driven my friends, who were sympathetic enough to listen to me, almost crazy with my vivid delineations of my helplessness and hopelessness. Why cannot one take oneself as one is, instead of trying forever to judge ones accomplishments by unattainable standards, so that as one advances one never has the solid satisfaction of achievement but must see the horizon recede as fast as one travels towards it? And what is worse, there seem to gravitate towards me friends of exactly the same temperament so that we are like a group of hypochondriacs, perpetually recounting to one another their symptoms. This sounds very dreary, doesn't it? and the only ray of light on the situation is that, although my condition is probably chronic, there are so many things to talk about and think about than one's own greatness or lack of it, that I am only unhappy part of the time. I shall miss dreadfully my piano, which I thump and pound until my dejection passes and the blood flows again and my spirits are righted. I have just been playing the third act of "Meistersinger" almost entirely through and the divine music warms me like wine. There is no music so beautiful on earth and I never get tired of its delight. Do you know it? It's strange that, although you told me you played, that we have never touched upon music. Somehow I was never able to write about music, never able to mix it up with words; it seems so entirely apart from the world of ordinary speech and action, an essentially untranslatable language, which ordinarily words quite ludicrously fail even so much as to describe. Music is a real inner sanctuary to which one retires alone, I think; certainly I have never felt that it was very communicable, perhaps because I have been always with unmusical people, or people that I knew were not getting it in the way I was. This winter I have had however a most appreciative friend to whom I often played on the grand piano in the dormitories. He is the first and only person with whom I have felt absolute musical sympathy, that is, felt that we were hearing the same thing and that he was appreciating in just the key and to just the quality that I was.[1] I had only a limited repertoire of my music over there—Sinding Album, which we grew to love; some Schumann, and some delicious pieces of Schult, which some people must think sentimental, but which are so richly harmonized and slip so charmingly off the fingers that I have gotten into a fond and foolish ecstatic state about them. The Sindings are so robust and splendid intellectual, yet without austerity or coldness. We liked him much better than Grieg, could play him every night in fact. Then we had the Brahms Rhapsodies, which are just a little beyond my technique, but which were always demanded, and my ever-beloved Macdowell, one of my first musical loves, and one who never palls. These we would play over and over till we knew them by heart, and although I don't think "the happy hearty healthy college boy" who frequented the lobby always liked the deluge of "classical" music which I poured out, my friend and I and such others who strolled in with us had evenings which I shall find it hard to forget. There was a sort of rapture about being thoroughly musically understood and it would give me at times a feeling that the material keys had dissolved away and one was evoking pure spirit without effort and simply by the movement of one's appreciating will. Only at times, however, and alas! Only when the piece was in my powers and the touch was light; there were times when the muddy carnality of the keys and the hammers and the pedal all asserted itself, and one was met with resistance and baffled. But for the golden moments! they were worth waiting for and cherishing.

Now I had no idea when I started this letter that I should come out where I am, and I may have many more important things that I wanted to tell you. But I shall close here, with the wish that my going to Europe will not injure our correspondence, which I have enjoyed and quite eagerly awaited—that is, of course, your letters. I am going to give you my addresses, letters written before Aug. 5, can go to American Express Co., Geneva; Aug. 5- Sept. 20, c/o S. M. Bligh, Builth Wells, Wales; after Oct. 1, American Express Co., London.

Faithfully yours,

Randolph S. Bourne

[1]Bourne is probably referring to Edward Murray.

27

to Simon Pelham Barr
(Transcript Columbia)

Bloomfield, N. J.
July 4, 1913

I am a scoundrel and a traitor, but really this fearful excitement of getting away has unhinged my mind. I expect to write on the steamer but that will be too late, I suppose. Come down and see us off, Pier 57, N. R. 15th St., Sat. 5th, 3 P.M. Str. "Rochambeau," or else write me a steamer letter; address till Sept. 1, American Express Co., 6 Haymarket, W. C. London.

R. S. B.

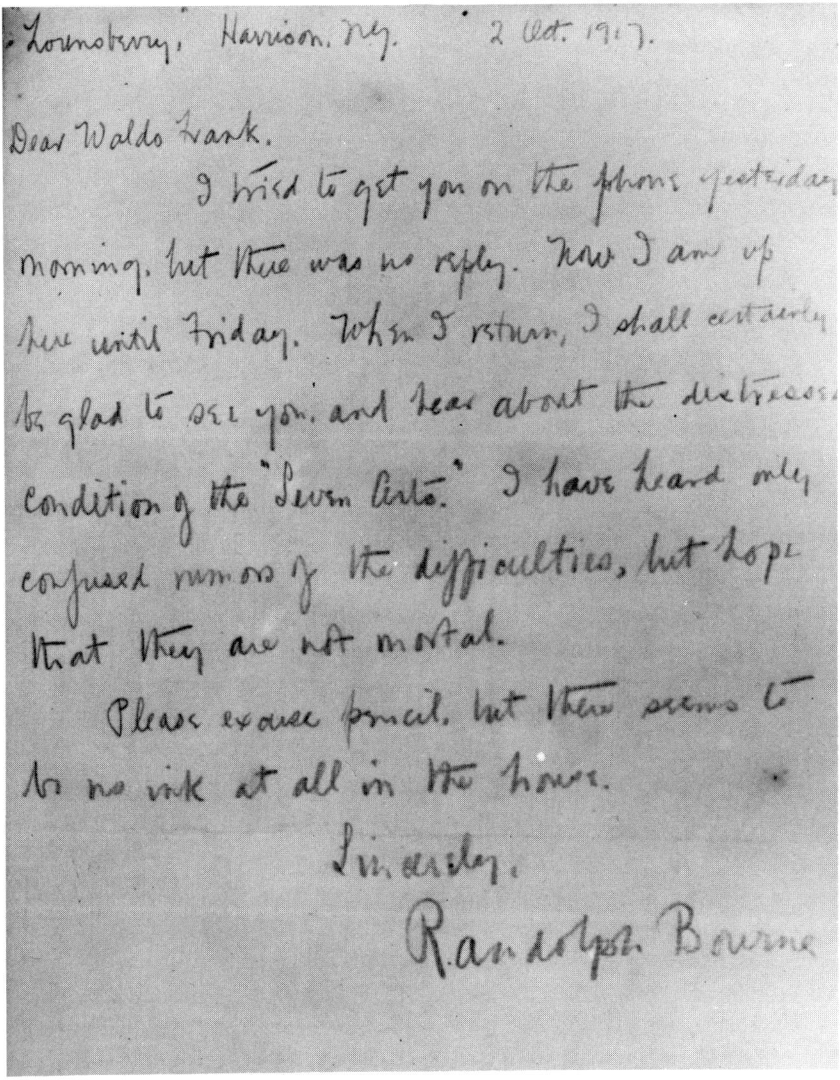

Lounsbury, Harrison. N.Y.   2 Oct. 1917.

Dear Waldo Frank.

I tried to get you on the phone yesterday morning, but there was no reply. Now I am up here until Friday. When I return, I shall certainly be glad to see you, and hear about the distressed condition of the "Seven Arts." I have heard only confused rumors of the difficulties, but hope that they are not mortal.

Please excuse pencil, but there seems to be no ink at all in the house.

Sincerely,

Randolph Bourne

Figure 2. The only surviving letter to Waldo Frank. Courtesy of the Waldo Frank Collection, University of Pennsylvania Library.

Figure 3. Bourne and some of his college friends, (1911). Upper row, from left to right: unidentified, Henry Elsasser, partly obscured by Bourne, Arthur Macmahon, Henry Anderson. Lower row: Carl Zigrosser, Roderick Seidenberg, Nelson Van Horn. Photograph courtesy of the Carl Zigrosser Collection, University of Pennsylvania Library.

Figure 4. Carl Zigrosser (c. 1914), a close friend. Photograph courtesy of the Carl Zigrosser Collection, University of Pennsylvania Library.

Figure 5. Bourne and Joseph C. Green at Carl Zigrosser's farm (c. 1914). Photograph courtesy of the Carl Zigrosser Collection, University of Pennsylvania.

Figure 6. Bourne and Louisa James near Mont Blanc. Photograph courtesy of the Randolph Bourne Collection, Columbia University Library.

Europe (1913-1914):

The Radical Vision

Bourne's reflections on his European year are contained in the many letters he wrote, and in the report which his Fellowship required him to submit to the Columbia trustees.[1] While he wrote few articles while on the Continent, the intellectual material garnered there nourished many of his subsequent essays. Europe had a profound effect on Bourne, an influence which operated on three levels. First, he familiarized himself with the European physical and cultural landscape. He sought out parts of each country which were not inundated with tourists in an effort to discover the authentic way of life of the country's inhabitants. He also tried to sample the intellectual climate of each country. Particularly in England and France he was interested in social psychology, the attitudes of the people, and the class structure of each society. Finally, he was struck with the presence of a national mind which permeated each of the countries he visited. This insight into the unique contributions which each of these cultures could make underlay such essays as "Trans-National America" which he wrote after his return.

From his earliest European letters, it is evident that Bourne was greatly concerned with the European land itself. Like most American writers of European travel accounts, he compared what he saw to familiar American scenes; the Rhine, he reported, was more impressive than the Hudson, despite what some of his friends had told him to expect. The letters present more than this superficial vision, however. Bourne contrasted his impressions with those of his travelling companion, Ward Swain, who was inclined to regard the Alps as just like Montana, or to refer to the Danube as just another river. Bourne's description of Belgium soon after his arrival was representative of the discerning nature of his eye; not only did he show an artist's attention to detail, he also populated his picture with the inhabitants going about their daily business:

> We walked for two miles or more along the most charming brick road
> imaginable, thronged with bicyclists and children with white wooden
> shoes, and lined with old farmhouses hidden in a little wood, with little
> canals stretching away through the green meadows, and a windmill and
> a sail on the horizon. . . . All the old world life, the trolley conductors,
> the shops and streets and vistas, the village roofs and churches and gar-
> dens,—this is what interests me, and what, I am sure, the person who
> whisks from one grand hotel to another must miss. (7/22/13)

Both a reading of the letters, and an examination of the note-
book which he kept during this year abroad leave one with an
appreciation of the vigorous way in which Bourne sought out what
he called "the attitudes, social and political, of various classes, the
social psychology of the different peoples." (77) Both England and
France offered him rich territory for his investigations. The English
political situation, centering on the development of the Labor Party,
was one focus of his attention. Bourne's three-month stay in England
corresponded to a particularly tumultuous period of English political history. Therefore, his comment to the Columbia trustees that
"politically, London was dead that autumn" (84) did not adequately
reflect the depth of his experiences.

Due to his political leanings, Bourne was most concerned with
the many liberal and radical movements which had not yet found
their way into the power structure of the major parties. Bourne
sought out Graham Wallas, George Bernard Shaw, Beatrice and Sidney Webb, and H. G. Wells, all of whom were leaders of the Fabian
Socialists, a movement which had gained much prominence in Britain
more because of the stature of these intellectuals than for the coherence of its plan for social action.

Bourne witnessed some of the rallies of the suffragettes, who,
under the leadership of the Pankhursts, Emmeline and her daughters
Christabel and Sylvia, were condoning acts of civil disobedience in an
effort to force the Liberal Party, which at that time was the ruling
majority under the leadership of Lord Asquith, to give women the
vote. He saw women who had engaged in hunger strikes in prison and
who had been force-fed by their jailers. He empathized with the
women's outrage over the bogus Cat-and-Mouse Act, which released
ill hunger-strikers from prison long enough for them to regain their

health, only to rearrest them to serve out the remainders of their terms. He also endorsed the heroism of such men as George Lansbury, who stood by the women. This experience—more, certainly, than his acquaintance with the Fabians, who were, for the most part, of the genteel class—showed him the price of radicalism.

While he was in England he also heard of the great Dublin dock strike, led by Jim Larkin, a union organizer who had learned the tactic of the general strike from the I. W. W. in the United States. Even though the strike eventually failed, the stir it created in the Liberal government, which was saddled with growing commitments to both Home Rule for Ireland and to organized labor, provided him with an insight into the complexities of English politics. Bourne had witnessed this sort of syndicalist-inspired strike in Paterson, New Jersey; these two experiences gave him an ambivalent opinion of the efficacy of the general strike.

Bourne was thus interested in groups which were just finding political consciousness. On a strictly party level, he was correct in his assessment that not much was happening in the autumn of 1913. There had been a Liberal government since 1906, and its tenure was not in immediate jeopardy. The emergence of the Labor Party, which was tied to all of the labor unrest and women's rights agitation, was in the process of changing the party structure in Britain, however. The Labor Party had evolved from the Trade Union movement, from the Fabian Socialists, and from the radical wing of the Liberal Party. It was separated from the majority chiefly in its clear rejection of laissez faire and in its attention to the needs of the laboring classes. While its power base was still coalescing, Bourne could see the indecision which this new party was creating in the Liberals, whose essential question had become how they were to distinguish themselves from both the Conservatives and the Laborites. In fact, at this time the Liberal Party was finding that, increasingly, it had little to say which was not contained in the platforms of the other two parties. Bourne was witnessing the dissolution of a political party and the invigorating emergence of a new parliamentary force.

In France, Bourne did not find the same sense of unrest. Here too he sought out socialists, labor leaders, and feminists, but he found that they fit more amicably into the French political system. There were crises here, too, however. The Saverne affair, which symbolized both the dominance of Germany over French territory and the oppression by the military of civilian populations, was a major event during that time. Also, Bourne witnessed the vigorous protests over the Three Years Law, which extended the military obligation of Frenchmen from two to three years. Bourne empathized with Socialist leaders such as Juares and the more radical Guesde in their campaign against the increase in militarism in France. Here Bourne's political interest was divided between Socialistic programs and the opposition to the ineluctable remilitarization of Europe prior to World War I.

In France more than in England Bourne was interested in cultural affairs. In England he had visited Oxford, but found it inferior to American universities. His experience at the Sorbonne, which he saw as full of new ideas and eager students, made English education seem all the more archaic and aristocratic. He attended the lectures of both Mauss and Durkheim and was thus introduced to the most stimulating of the French sociologists. The many famous galleries of Paris were available for his perusal. His notebooks indicate that he sought out both the famous pieces of art and the most avant garde. He also lauded the accessibility of cultural events to each member of society and he endorsed government subsidy of the cultural life of the nation. More than in England, Bourne abandoned his role as the sociological observer and immersed himself in the national culture.

Indeed, it is his realization of the existence of national cultures in Europe which is most striking in his observations. Bourne corroborated this in his assessment of his European year: "My most striking impression was the extraordinary toughness and homogeneity of the cultural fabric in the different countries." (79) For him England was dominated by a "fatuous cheerfulness." (82) He was struck by the "permanent derangement of intellect from emotion" (83) which he saw in English intellectuals. It was distressing to him that the intellectual life of the country was being directed by people for whom the life of the mind was an avocation. This created both social irresponsibility and, finally, insensitivity in that society; one symptom of this, he remarked, was the violence of the suffrage movement: "Suffragettism is what you get when you turn your whole national psychic energy into divorcing emotion from expression and from intellect." (85) In England he saw the necessary resource which committed intellectuals could furnish to such an impoverished society—only the intellectual could fuse the emotion with the intellect and reforge a socially responsible society.

"In England, unless you were a 'social reformer,' you did not know anything about anybody but your own class," Bourne remarked, while "in France, there seemed to be scarcely any social reformers, but everybody assumed an intelligent interest in everything." (86) Indeed, France presented him with the model of a society in which the intellectual played a recognized role. "The distinction between the 'intellectual' and the non-intellectual seems to have quite broken down." (87) France was a more open society. While in England dissenting ideas could not be aired except in the context of violent civil disobedience, in France all opinions were allowed their time at the rostrum. This created a more unstructured society, one in which specific reform movements were not needed, and a society which was willing to change some ideas and stand behind others with all the strength of the emotions, a degree of commitment which Englishmen could never muster.

Bourne gave little attention to Germany, either in the letters or in the report which he produced. No doubt this is due in part to the fact that he considered the discussion of his experiences in a country which was then at war with the favored Allies to be too sensitive to bother broaching with the Columbia trustees. Also, his travel in Germany had been quite limited, so his impressions were not as well formed there as elsewhere. What impressions he had of Germany were more tightly organized around one concept—that this country represented the most advanced point of modern social planning. In his report he stated that his experience in Germany was almost entirely sociological. (97) He saw the evidences of town planning which had drawn him to Germany originally, and his notebook indicates that he talked to many local officials about urban growth. He also commented on the modern style in civic architecture, which he appreciated. (97) Germany presented him with a country in which there was "a government between whom and the people there seemed to exist some profound and subtle sympathy, a harmony of

spirit and ends." (99) His analysis of this harmonious society, however, was ruined by the irrationality of war. The greatest disappointment for Bourne was the surrendering to irrationality of the German
nation. This attribute Bourne did not limit to Germany alone; his
experience in Berlin on July 31st, however, gave him the clearest
indication of the irrational capabilities of a crowd, a sociological
maxim he had learned in his college classes.

Thus, Bourne's experience in Europe was to serve as the
groundwork for many of his subsequent essays. Throughout this
year, he lamented his inability to produce essays, but, truly, his
priorities were correctly centered on the experience of a year's
travel. The letters absorb some of the intellectual heft of essays and
present the reader with an impressive account of Bourne's most
active year.

Notes

[1]"Impressions of Europe: 1913-1914," in *The History of a Literary
Radical*, Van Wyck Brooks, ed.., (New York, 1956), pp. 75-101. All references
to this essay will be given in parentheses in the text.

28

to Sarah Bourne[1]
(Transcript Columbia)

[S. S.] Rochambeau
Sunday Night
July 13 [1913]

There was much jollity. Half of the 450 cabin passengers are French and Italian, so the foreign atmosphere is very prevalent. Then there are two Cook's parties, with old ladies who look very uncomfortable and out of place, and a sprinkling of free lances like ourselves. There are several priests and mass is celebrated at 6 every morning in the salon. This morning I attended and played the piano for a girl to sing two sacred songs as interludes. The scene was most picturesque with the improvised altar on the table and the rich robed priest and the kneeling people. It was the same room which the night before had resounded to the music of the dance, following a song recital at which I accompanied, and which the elite all attended in their finest gowns, as they did the night before at a benefit concert for the benefit of the shipwrecked sailors. I played two pieces at this, and have been giving a little impromptu concert every day after luncheon, which seemed to be greatly appreciated by the audience, and indeed which served as a general introduction to the entire ship. Indeed too much so, for many old ladies would beseige me to play pieces I never heard of, and I was rounded up by a Cook party to accompany one of their number who was inspired to sing, and I got roped into all these concerts.

But the friends I met! Saturday, we felt rather low-spirited, not especially blue, or scared; the getting off struck me as rather insipid with the silly people waving their handkerchiefs. I was glad to have some to see us on the boat, however, and think it was really charming of Mrs. Macmahon to come down. It was awfully hot all that evening and night. Next morning, however, was cooler, and I soon struck up an acquaintance with a young Universalist minister named Skinner, from Lowell, with a pleasant wife. He is interested in Sociology and is going over practically the same ground we planned, so I hope to see them again. Ward and I played cards with them, and we have found them most delightful. They introduced me to four girls who live in a settlement in Brooklyn. One of them is delightfully Irish, literary, (went to Barnard), and knows a good many of my friends in New York. I have seen a good deal of them and we may go to Rouen with them. Then I came across Professor Mead[2] of Wesleyan, who I remembered having given courses at Summer Session at Columbia in 1911. He remembered me as having asked him for some stories for the "Monthly" and his wife had heard of my writing. (The Skinners also had read my articles.) Mrs. Mead is very pleasant and gave me a lot of good advice and information. Then I met, through her adorable children, a charming Catholic young woman from St. Louis. Ward and I are both enamored and hope to see her again in Switzerland. She and he have talked theology by the hour, and she has been very lovely to me. There is also aboard a remarkable woman doctor from New York, a Hungarian Jewess of great personality; wears her grey hair short like a man, and has a wonderful stride and verve about her; very cosmopolitan and has the most decided opinions on everything. She immediately took the greatest motherly and sisterly interest in me, and we have been neat chums. The best thing about most of these interesting people is that they will be in New York when I return! I shall not let them forget me. Ward I have hardly seen except at meals; he has pursued a victorious career of feminine conquest, and has met most of the "jeunes filles" on the ship. The Skinners, who have been over before on the Anchor Line say that the whole crowd is unusually pleasant and congenial.

[no signature]

1The letters to Mrs. Bourne must have been excerpted in the process of furnishing a transcription to Agnes de Lima.

2William Mead specialized in English Medieval and 17th century literature.

29

to Arthur Macmahon
(Transcript Columbia)

Grande Hotel
de la Providence
Brussels
16 July 1913

Dear Arthur,

We are stuck at present (10:30 A.M.) in a pouring rain in a most unappealing quarter of the station region of Brussels. It is perhaps a mistake to arrive in a strange town at 10:30 P.M. and snap the first hotel you see. We had such a nice little one at Paris, or "snapped" one too, but it was most satisfactory. We were in Paris just long enough to feel how delightfully you can live there on a pittance. Breakfast for 6 cents (chocolate and any no. of rolls) taken with the other Parisians standing up at the marvellous [sic] little café bars or out on the sidewalk at a table, a luncheon or dinner of soup, meat and vegetables and dessert for 20 cts., at any number of good little restaurants, and then all sorts of patisseries where you can get cakes and things. Excuse my dwelling on the culinary aspects, but after years of Commons and Coopers and Vics.[1] it does appeal to me. To start more nearly at the beginning, our ocean trip was delightful. The boat was all it was said to be, and acquaintances increased in a geometrical ratio. A lovely grand piano in the salon at which I puttered for a while the first day out served as an introduction to the entire ship. They got up a little concert and I had to play at that and for various singing people on board, and in a short time had met a dozen interesting people and any number of others. A party of four girls from a settlement in Brooklyn proved especially interesting. I hope to keep up the acquaintance when I get back. A young Universalist minister and his wife from Lowell played shuffleboard and 500 with us, although--- [Swain] got quite indignant with her because she teased him about the "Jeunes filles" which he pursued with an amazing and indefatigable ardor. Indeed I saw little of him, for we had our own private friends and spent most of the time with them. The crowd was most Cosmopolitan, French and Italian predominating and we worked off some of our French on whom we could. We did not get any real practice, however. All the predictions of mal de mer were falsified; I did not see a single sick person, although many old ladies were said to be remaining in their cabins through deadly fear during the whole voyage. The weather was showery much of the time, though there were some wonderful afternoons of sparkling blue water with whitecaps and a glorious surge to the boat which made a promenade exciting sport. In fact, I hardly had a dull moment on board, and would have been glad to have the voyage twice as long. There was such a charming atmosphere of congeniality and kindness, and everything was so comfortable, and we had no responsibility except going to meals when the bell rang. The whole trip grows even more idyllic as we get into these bad hotels and have to think about time tables and bags and cars.---[Swain] gets fearfully excited while I am taking the opportunity to take many lessons in imperterbability. For two greenhorns without Baedekers we have done well. I think our French has gotten us around, although we only understand about 1/3 of what they say to us. I was very proud of buying a pocket book ("Une pochette de porc") in Paris for 29 cts. which I was pricing for a dollar or more in New York the day before I sailed. And I asked in several stores for it too, before a girl directed me to the "Galeries Lafayette". And a neck tie for 13 cts. which my family might not consider most stylish but which pleases me.

  For a stay of 28 hours in Paris, 9 of which were spent in bed, we saw a good deal. With a bus and tram map as my only guide, I went poking about the

Opera and Place Vendome, Garden of the Tuilleries, the Louvre, Palais Royal, Notre Dame, etc while yesterday [. . .] we took a bus to Montmartre with the most wonderful view of all Paris. At a tiny shop I bought several socialist papers, and thought it would be interesting to sit in the great church of the Sacred Heart up on the hill and read Jaures' "L'Humanité".[2] But—[Swain] was so devout that I refrained. Then we went over the river to the Sorbonne and College de France and then back for the train here. Just a skim of the externals, but a good way of getting things placed for our return. Paris was of course quite different from what I expected, more ancient looking and picturesque, with curious narrow and very prim streets, reminding me much of Quebec which I had not connected with Paris before. The most obvious thing is the homogeneous height of the buildings, never more than five or six stories, no "office buildings" at all, everywhere apartments and stores beneath. Then there is much color; kiosks with advertisements, many of them artistic posters; many little squares with fountains, trees along the boulevards; and everywhere the cafés with little tables and chairs and people eating their dinners or drinking their coffee and wine on the narrowest sidewalks. Little boys, even up to 13 or 14 with bare legs and socks, many men in high hats, clerks in the department stores in Prince Alberts, otherwise a perfectly American looking crowd, and everywhere such clean streets and houses. The policemen look like soldiers, and the station guards too. The buses are very rapid and cheap (2 cts. for a whole route) and the trams with seats on top too go lumbering along, but make excellent time. In fact everything seems to move much faster here than in New York, in spite of the proverbial hustle. No policeman to stop traffic, but taxis and buses shooting around corners and somehow missing you, though you don't see why. We had a wild ride to Brussels flying through the night at 60 miles an hour, with the car lurching and jumping like mad. I like the compartments, though the cars are too silly to look at. In the corridor cars you can move about and standing at the window in the corridor get the most superb view of the country. The trip from Havre to Paris was entrancing, through Normandy villages, too good to be true, every house with a personality of its own, and walled gardens, and thatched barns and red poppies everywhere in the fields and the placid Seine, and Cathedral towers, and red roofs, and patchwork checkerboard fields, and haymowing and the little stations, the yard planted with rows of trimmed catalpas, and the white hard roads, etc.

I shall never stop.---[Swain] says it has stopped raining, so will have to go. We go to Bruges to-morrow.

Regards to all. I can't say how we appreciated your mother's kindness in coming down to the steamer. Thank her again for us.

Randolph

¹Commons was a student eating place on campus noted for its inexpensive fare. Presumably, Coopers and Vics were also eating places of the same variety.

²*L'Humanité,* a newspaper which preached democratic Socialism, was founded by the French Socialist Jaures.

30

to Sarah Bourne
(Transcript Columbia)

Bruges
Friday
July 18, 1913

If you will excuse this paper, I will write you a letter while I am waiting for the rain to stop, a little pastime that we have indulged in every day this week. It is what they are used to in these low countries, I suppose, and the old houses and streets really look more picturesque than in the bright sunlight. Monday night in Paris we got caught in a heavy shower and crept home damp and dejected to bed. We had a very comfortable room, however, with hot and cold water for 3 fr. apiece, and the next day was clear. After getting some money at the American Express Co., I distinguished myself by getting a pigskin purse, la pochette de porc, for 1 fr. 45 c., or $.29, of a kind that I was pricing for $1 and up, the day before we sailed, in New York. Breakfast, I forgot to mention, we took at one of the cafés, standing up with the other Parisians a-round the bar; we had chocolat and several delicious sweet rools for $.06. Lunch we had about 11:30 at a very nice restaurant, soup, meat and vegetables and a kind of waffle cake called a "gaufrette", all for about $.21. Then we took a bus ride to Montmartre, climbed the hill on which stands the new church of the Sa-cred Heart, with a wonderful view over the entire city. Then a bus across the riv-er to look at the University, and back to the station where we left for Brussels at four o'clock. Paris we felt quite familiar with, although we had been there only a day; but we saw the principal centres, the Opera, Madeleine, Garden of the Tuil-leries, Louvre, Place Vendome, Palais-Royal, Notre Dame, St. Germaine-des-Pres. We did not have the time to go through the Louvre and Notre Dame, leaving that for our return. Paris, of course, is quite different from anything I have seen, the great contrast with New York being the crooked streets and countless little squares, and the uniform height of the buildings, none of them more than 5 or 6 stories. There seem to be no office buildings in our sense of the word, offices being scattered all over the apartment houses. Then the architecture is rather uniform, straight up from the sidewalk, rather ornate, and usually a light gray or cream color. The oldest buildings are a remarkable dark gary, ranging from a deep black to a white so that the palaces have a startling streaked appearance sometimes, like a minstrel's face that the black has washed off in places. These things are obliterated in the picture postals, so that the effect of a building you have foreseen to be magnificent is at times rather disappointing. The churches are very magnificent; nothing to compare with them in New York, and the boulevards are planted with trees, and adorned with bright advertising kiosks all of which give much more of an effect of vivid color and life than we find in New York. The taxis go shooting around making a fearful racket with the horns, and the buses go very fast,—no holding up by policemen. That is the advantage of having so many little streets running at every angle; you can get around almost anywhere, instead of being forced to take the long rectangular blocks as in New York. The trolleys and buses are the things your wealthy friends never tell you about, for they are used, I suppose, to riding in cabs or taking a carriage about to see the sights. Certainly I had no idea there was any such complete system of fast trolleys that we found in Paris and Brussels where you can travel all around the city for 2*d* and there is a line in every direction.

Brussels I enjoyed very much. We reached there about 10:30 p.m. Tuesday after a rainy and very wild ride in the preposterous French cars which are hardly bigger than a stage coach, and yet which are carried bouncing and rolling along at 60 miles an hour, until you hang on for dear life and think every moment will be your last. The ride was pleasant, however, for the compartment was not full, and I could move around and stand at the window and see the country. In our compartment were two Dartmouth fellows, one from Newark, making a flying trip. We compared notes, and had quite a chat. We took the first hotel we saw, and got a rather uncomfortable room, where we were stuck until 11 a.m. by a pouring rain. It stopped then, and we took a remarkable horse car, which ran not on tracks, and resembled a big circus van, up to the North Station. Near here we took another room, which was quite palatial, and persuaded the landlady to take our laundry and do it for us, so that we could get it when we pass thro [sic] Brussels to-morrow on our way to Antwerp. She was very nice about it; indeed everybody had been unusually kind and genial, quite different from the grasping extortion which we were taught to expect by our traveling friends at home. Whether they are touched by our youth and innocence, I don't know, or whether they want a tip; but I think I can distinguish a natural politeness, which is rather wanting in America. It is hard to understand why the railway cars and trolleys are not more crowded, and there is not more pushing and jolting and confusion, but everything moves with utmost ease. You can imagine what the subway would be like if the fare was 2 cents. (You know what it is now.) Here you step on a delightful little low open car, with plenty of room, and go flying around the city. The absence of heavy traffic is a perpetual mystery; they must do all their carting early in the morning or late at night. Both in

Paris and Brussels there was not congestion at all that I could see. We did a good deal of walking in Brussels, perhaps 8 or 10 miles, but I was not tired because we were constantly seeing something interesting or picturesque. It is a comfortable and marvelously prosperous-looking city with many old houses and beautiful gardens and parks. We went through the Art Gallery and saw many beautiful Rubens, and saw the great church of St. Gudule, which we entered while a most impressive funeral mass was in progress, almost appaling [sic] in its solemnity, with the chanting priests and unearthly bell. At the Park in front of the King's Palace, before which were pacing very splendid gendarmes, we heard a fine band concert in the afternoon. We spent some time in the great square of the Hotel de Ville, a very rich Gothic building with a great tower, surrounded by elaborately decorated and gilded old houses. The square is used as a great flower market and was a mass of bloom. We could have had a dozen red roses for 20 cents, but alas! we had no one to give them to. We have no Baedeker for Belgium and Holland and are depending on the little maps which I pick up. Ward makes a fearful fuss because I walk along the street with an opened map, but I am quite without shame. I intend to acquire a geographical and aesthetic sense of each place we visit, even if I haven't the historical learning or the guide book information about each building that we see. It is much easier to acquire that after you have seen the place than before, I think.

Bruges we reached yesterday afternoon about 5 after a delightful ride through garden country that looks just like the pictures of the old Flemish painters,—canals lined with tall trees, little farmhouses, many carts, wagons drawn by dogs, little boys with wooden shoes. Even in Brussels we saw many carts with a dog harnessed underneath and helping the man pull the cart. Bruges is of course very quaint, with many Dutch-gabled houses and grim lofty churches, and old canals. We have a room over a little Patissene [sic] right on the great square facing the great Belfry tower and hall built in 1619. The chimes, however, ring every fifteen minutes all night long, and ring for about two minutes each time, so we had very little sleep. The place is shockingly tourist-ridden, every other person carrying a Baedeker, and there are many stores, obviously catering to the American trade. It is also priest-ridden; many of the nuns and monks who were driven from France have settled here, and the streets are full of priests with their remarkable low-crowned, broad-brimmed hats and enormous flowing black gowns. We came up in the train with one from Brussels, a haughty fellow. I don't like them, but Ward is quite enamoured of the Church, and makes his humble devotions in every cathedral we enter. He is a very curious companion, and so moody and monstrously non-congenial that he is just a little better than no companion at all. I find myself almost ignoring him at times, and he doesn't seem to mind. He loses his head at exciting crises, while I am taking lessons in imperterbability. I can not figure out what a truly congenial friend would mean to me on a trip like this, but since it was impossible, I am fortunate in at least having someone, for the mere fact of there being that someone has relieved my mind from all worry and timorousness.

[no signature]

31

to Prudence Winterrowd
(Transcript Columbia)

Amsterdam
July 22, 1913

My dear Miss Prudence,

If you will forgive this note paper, I will write you a little letter while I have a moment in this very remarkable little old Hotel Prins Hendrik overlooking the canals and brightly lighted quays of Amsterdam. We are still green enough travellers to jump at the first hotel we see near the station, particularly when the price is 70 cents for room and breakfast. We have had the most surprising ups and downs of fortune in one first week of it, and will eventually learn, I hope, to "size up" the place at first sight and not go through the drudgery of walking about, looking for a place to lay our head. My friend, who is very young, both in age and manners, is good about carrying my bag but I feel that he thinks there are limits to all good things. We had such a frightful experience in Ghent where we were attacked upon leaving the station by a red-coated hotel agent, who implored us in the most tearful voice to come with him. I had visions of a big hotel, and besides the price was too high. So we said no and started off, with him at our heels, beseeching and imploring. My friend, tall, lanky, lugubrious and red-haired, lost his head and started off at a breakneck pace through the town. Every time we stopped for breath, the fellow was upon us, and as we raced we could see him over our shoulder, lurking behind us, ready to pounce, whenever he saw us stop to look at a map or directory. My friend's terror of him was awfully funny. We actually drew the wretch over half a mile into the town, before we could summon the proper authority in our voices to bid him begone forever. When he left us, we sank exhausted into the first place we could see.

But this may not seem so funny to you. As for the trip, it is all that I looked forward to and more. Every moment is interesting, and there is just enough of the familiar and the anticipated, and the unexpected and disturbing to make the experience very piquant. Your pre–formed picture of Europe you find was very spotted. Now all the gaps are filled in indiscriminately. What you want to see, and what you don't, for of course there are plenty of ugly things in

Europe, though you only imagine the beauties before you go. All the people I know who have been have given thoroughly hodge-podge accounts of their trip, partly because they have been conducted, only hitting the "points of interest", and letting the in-between go. Then they scorn trolley-cars and third-class cars, both of which are the picked ways of seeing the country. I am enjoying the travelling very much; the trolleys are delightful, and the railroad cars built so you obtain the finest view, as fine as you would almost from an observation-car. I always did adore going and seeing new sights; just the physical sensation of riding in a railway-car is as keenly delightful as it was when I was ever so little. And to start off for a stroll around a strange city simply dilates my heart. To-night, we took a chance trolley, which dropped us at the extreme edge of the city, whence we walked for two miles or more along the most charming brick road imaginable, thronged with bicyclists and children with white wooden shoes, and lined with old farmhouses hidden in a little wood, with little canals stretching away through the green meadows, and a windmill and a sail on the horizon. In Bruges I poked about in the rain through the old streets of one storey cottages, where women were sitting at the doorways making lace in the most primitive fashion, with dozens of little spindles which they worked with lightening speed. All the old world life, the milk-carts in the morning, the postman, the policeman, the trolley conductors, the shops and streets and vistas, the village roofs and churches and gardens,—this is what interests me, and what, I am sure, the person who whisks from one grand hotel to another must miss. And then I have a deep sociological interest, even though an amateur one; I am constantly trying to gauge the prosperity, the living conditions, get some feeling for the classes and social divisions, and the daily common life of them all, and I am constantly trying to compare and contrast what I see with what I know of at home. So far I cannot get over the incredibly bright, animated, brilliant appearance of the cities we have seen, to which there is nothing comparable in New York. The modern houses and store buildings (everything is low; no "office buildings") in Belgium and France are very distinctive and bright in architecture; much color, and most of it light. In Holland, it is all a peculiarly atrocious brick, so that the Dutch cities, except for the old quarters, are as hideous as anything I hope to look upon. But Antwerp and Brussels with their streets of creamy-colored stately houses and their miles of small shining shops, (shops such as would only be seen on Fifth Avenue in New York), most brilliantly illuminated at night, made a great impression on me. Such troops of people, such absence of heavy traffic, such speed and ease of their trolley cars, such politeness—everything one thinks of as "Charm", (to which I find myself peculiarly responsive), is here. The country-side is, however, most primitive; a Flemish landscape is a copy of Hobbema or Ruiyjsdael [Ruisdael],[1] and I fear that the low pitched thatched roofs hide much privation and disease. My impression of Europe will be worth more when I have been longer than a week here. Let me here thank you for the letter and the pictures; they are a rather tantalizing suggestion, the difficulty being that they look like two different people. About Mr. C., I found *him* difficult, because I was trying to pump him about *you*, without making the fact too obvious. He said that you were attractive, and played the piano, and had accompanied him to his violin. *Finis.* He was very pleasant, but I did not feel a rush of welcome towards him, and his most remarkable room-mate distracted my attention. Mr. C. was interesting to me just because you *had* mentioned him, but he seemed to lack the intuition to make that interest the central feature of our conversation. He didn't feel the possibilities of making an artistic thing of the whole affair, and so I had to let him go by default. I, of course, gave him a most colorless impression of myself, and so this negative, so to speak, in which we were to see each other, quite failed to develop on either side.

I wish it was Paris you were coming to instead of Columbia. That would be a real experience, and much more justifiable in the eyes of the world, would it not? And then I should not have another of those appalling reasons, which have so inhibited me, for wanting to be in New York next winter. Europe would be a fine "cataclysm" to "impend", wouldn't it? But if you do go to Columbia, my friends there will make you acquainted, I know. In fact Mr. C's successor in the Politics Dept. is my room-mate of 1912, one of the greatest men in the world, both brilliant and thoughtful and eternally fine and good. And coming over on the steamer I met some delightful girls from Brooklyn, just my sort, know about my friends, etc. And I shall not be there. A woe! Europe will have to do much for me to compensate all these losses.

I am afraid I gave you some wrong addresses: better write, if you will, always to American Express Co., 11 Rue Scribe, Paris; they, I am told, will forward, though I am skeptical till I see it done. I have counted up an incredible number of things I was told before starting that have proven absolutely false.

Sincerely yours,

Randolph Bourne

[1]Both were famous 17th century painters of rural scenes. Meindert Hobbema was the pupil of Jacob van Ruisdael. Often they painted the same scenes.

32

to Sarah Bourne
(Transcript Columbia)

Cöln [Cologne]
July 23, 1913

We reached here about **8**:30 after a very strenuous day, but I am not too tired to write a letter to you and must use my stamp before I get into a country where it is no good. This is our fourth country in nine days, and my only consolation for the excessive speed is that I hope to take it all again extensively. Swain, I find, is not really interested in traveling at all; his one thought is to get to Grenoble and study French, so we may part in a week or two. We have been getting along very well, however, inspite of the fact that we approach things in such a different way; often we each go our own road, and then meet at a stated hour. The weather has been awful; several showers every day, and a couple of days of steady downpour in Brussels and Bruges. And cold! I would give anything for a thick pair of flannels (the overcoat is a poor substitute), but hesitate to buy them for fear it will get warm again. We had some laundry done at Brussels and then returned there to get it on Saturday after our trip to Bruges and Ghent. The porteress of the hotel took charge of it, and we had a great laugh as she made out the list and tried to translate our respective garments into French. Swain's B.V.D.'s gave her a lot of trouble. They were evidently a quite unrecognized garment. We thought her price marvelously cheap, and discovered after we got in the train for Antwerp, that some one had neglected to add in 2 fr. 50 c., so we made 50 cents in that unavoidable manner.

From Bruges, we went to Ghent, and had a thrilling experience with a hotel agent, who pursued us half a mile into town imploring us in the most tearful way to go with him. Swain went tearing along with the two bags, and every time we would look back, the fellow would be lurking in our rear, ready to pounce upon us. Our lack of a destination was so apparent that he thought he would eventually get us, but we beat him and put up over a little café most uncomfortably, delighted at having beaten him, and yet vaguely conscious that it would have been better for us to have taken his terms. Ghent I wish we had given more time to, for it has the canals of Holland, the stately streets of Belgium, and in addition, three of the most magnificent Gothic towers we have seen. Then there is a fine old grim mediaeval castle rising out of the water, many of the halls and towers perfectly preserved. We went through it for ten cents, and were rewarded at the top with a beautiful view of the city. In the great cathedral, we saw a family of Flemish peasants, father and mother, son and two daughters, in the picturesque costumes that you have probably seen in books, flowing white caps on the women, with great brass plates and beads on the fore-head, flowing skirt and tight bodice. They were so striking that it seemed as if they could scarcely be real. The streets of Ghent in the morning are alive with milk-carts drawn by dogs harnessed underneath, with the milk in half a dozen of the most beautifully polished brass jugs. In Holland they are larger and shaped like a great vase, and they draw the milk from a spigot. It is fine rich milk, and I had a delicious lunch at the Hague for 15 cents of a cup of Dutch chocolate, two "broodjes" or large rolls, a glass of milk and two boiled eggs.

Antwerp we found very gay, with a big parade, and great Belgian flags of red, yellow and black, floating everywhere. The twilights here are wonderful, still a light in the western sky at 10 o'clock, and that Saturday night with the great tower of the cathedral seen in the setting sun from the river, with the flags flying and the bands playing and the brilliant streets thronged with people, was one of the great moments of my trip. Sunday morning we went to Mass and saw the great Rubens pictures, "The Descent from the Cross," and the "Erection of the Cross," vast and glowing canvasses that are unveiled on Sunday mornings. That afternoon we went to Holland; it was clear, and the green meadows simply sprinkled with black and white cattle and horses, with the canals and villages seen at a distance, looked very lovely. The Dutch towns, however, are hideous (except in certain of the older quarters), long streets of straight brick houses, without any character or charm. The people too are so ugly, and the language such a caricature of English, that we longed for the charm of Belgium, and the smart little houses of the suburbs of Antwerp and Brussels. We did Rotterdam, however, rather thoroughly, took a car out of the city limits, and walked along the Aude Dijk, a road, bordered on both sides by canals, over which hung little drawbridges leading to the houses that line the streams. In to one of these canals sailed my gray hat, and I had given it up for lost, when a doughty passer-by ran for a rake, and to the encouragement of a crowd of little Dutch boys, fished it out for me. It dried coming home in the trolley, and is as good as it ever was, which, in spite of Ruth's[1] admiration, is not very much. In this ugliest of towns we had the most charming hotel, with a big room opening on a park, and the most comfortable beds I had felt for weeks. Everything exceptionally clean and neat, and for it we paid, with a fine Dutch breakfast of chocolate, and zuieback, and bread, and butter, and jam, and cheese, and two kinds of cold meat, all thrown in,—80 cents a piece. Curious that at the Hague, we found identical furniture and almost identical breakfast. Here, however, there was but one bed, and we paid 90 cents. The Hague was of course charming with its old courts and guilt [sic] lakes and prim walks and beautiful parks and woods. But even here the outskirts were ugly. It was the only Dutch town we saw that was really clean, and we saw Amsterdam, Leiden, and Delft, (the latter in hurried tours enroute). The canals have a great deal of unnecessary and vile-looking scum, and the Dutchmen don't care particularly what they throw into them. They are thronged with boats poled along by boys, or pulled by men, harnessed as we would a mule. The old boaters are very picturesque, and a boat piled with round yellow cheeses, or simply covered with pots of geraniums, is not a sight we would see along the Morris Canal. The picturesque villages you read about, I'm afraid are not the rule, however, in Holland, and you see much that is very unpicturesque. We walked out in the country from Amsterdam last evening about two miles or more along a typical brickpaved country road, lined with trees, with little canals stretching away through the meadows, and dark farmhouses, bowered in trees, all along the road. But except for the enormous white wooden shoes of the children and the windmills, there was little of the charm and color that I had always thought of as typically Dutch. It is a low-toned, drab country and it has a great monotony and general pervasiveness which makes three days enough to spend on your first tour.

And now we are in Germany, having come from Amsterdam this afternoon to Düsseldorf, walked around there for an hour or two and then came to Cologne, where we saw the great Cathedral (one of the things I used to think I wanted most to see in Europe) before it was dark. It is very fine, but somehow lacks the grim majesty of those churches of Bruges and Ghent. The city seems much quieter, too, than the brilliant streets of Belgium; and in Holland too the narrow streets, with the shops all lighted with a skill and brightness that seems superior to American ways, were crowded all the evening like Nassau St. in New York is in the day time. But Germany seems more dignified and quiet. These big towns that we have seen, have really been very exciting, and I think we shall have to try to seek some smaller places and get a rest. We have been taking hotels we saw near the station, and have been inclined to take the first we came across. Only twice, however, have they been really poor, and we had the consolation that it was for only one night anyway. And the good ones we have found have been so good as to make up for it.

The trip is costing me about what I expected. I spent about $20 the first week and about $9 for my three days in Holland, and this includes everything, R. R. fare, hotel and meals. We have had plenty to eat, and some very fine meals. We sometimes have to roam a good deal to find a cheap restaurant, but we usually find it.

[no signature]

[1]Ruth Bourne Branstater, his sister.

33

to Carl Zigrosser
(Ms Pennsylvania)

Mainz
July 25 [1913]

Dear Carl,

We have been on such a rush since we landed ten days ago that I have hardly had time to write a letter. We have seen Paris, Brussels, Bruges, Ghent, Antwerp, Rotterdam, The Hague, Delft, Leyden, Amsterdam, Düsseldorf, Cologne, Bonn, Coblenz and have just finished an enchanting boat trip on the Rhine. I had heard that the Rhine was disappointing to those who had seen the Hudson, but the characters are so different that it is unprofitable to compare them. Certainly the lovely rocky vineyard terraces, and little valleys, and old ruins, and incredible mediaeval villages and stately towns, all seen under the most brilliant summer sun with fleecy clouds all over the sky,—this is a Rhein which I had hardly dreamed of, and which is far more picturesque than any scene of the Hudson. For I am very partial to architecture, and feel a landscape incomplete without a cluster of houses. And all this country is so gloriously peopled! Villages and towns flung in the greatest profusion, each with its personality and individuality, indeed, almost every house with its own. And great stately vistas that I delight in, and cultivated land, and a dignity and style! These things our American scene lacks, and it is what I came to Europe to see. In truth, a great many surprises have been mine. I was not prepared for the strange black and white smeared effect of the old Gothic buildings in France and Belgium; (surely the picture postcard is one of the most ingenious of liars); nor for the hideousness of the Dutch towns, (I'm glad I did not land in Rotterdam, for the first impression would have almost blasted my trip). Instead, my first sight of Europe was the white roads, and walled gardens, and thatched farmhouses and peaceful Seine valley and square towers of Normandy, a land of such picturesque beauty that it seemed almost like a dream, and a land of such seeming prosperity, which became a perfect riot of smart steep little colored houses perched dizzily on hillsides, as the train swept past their garden walls with the fruit-trees trained along them and all glowing in the sun. Northern France was grayer and sadder with big factory towns, and into Belgium we were plunged in the "World of Work"; forests of the tallest chimneys and glowing furnaces, as our tiny French train went jumping and bumping at sixty miles an hour towards Brussels. (And there I saw, by the way, the great bas-reliefs of Meunier, and some smaller bronze statues of workers, very fine.) And in the same museum are the great Rubens, and the other Dutch & Flemish masters; in Amsterdam were the great Rembrandts and some Vermeers, but I could not appreciate the oceans of other Dutchmen they had. To tell the truth, I admired the beautiful halls of the Museum more than I did the pictures. But Brussels was a joy. You see my interest so far has been aesthetic more than sociological. But I have had time to be impressed with the general air of prosperity one finds in the cities. We have covered all kinds of districts and have found nothing at all comparable with the outward squalor of sections of Newark or Jersey City, for instance. They may exist, but I have looked for them hard. And then life seems to move with more ease over here, the machinery is better oiled, so to speak. The absence of heavy traffic in the streets, (much of it done in little carts, drawn by dogs in Belgium & Holland); the magnificent systems of speedy trolley-cars, (of course, they do not carry so many people, and only stop at certain points on the line, but they are very comfortable and the fare is from 2-3 cents), and even a small city like The Hague will have its ten or more lines reaching all parts of the city and suburbs. So with a map, and a little guide of the city, and ten cents in small change, we can get a remarkable acquaintance with a city in a day. We usually reach a place about supper time, go to a small hotel near the station, then stroll around town looking for a supper, after which we walk in the lovely long twilight; next day we sightsee, together or separately, and go on in the afternoon to our next place. We shall take it much more leisurely after we get to Munich and down into Switzerland. I expect to go to Wales about Sept. 7, and Swain wants to go to Grenoble to study French about the middle of August. Between those times I will stay in Switzerland or join some friends who are coming over.

The trip over on the "Rochambeau" was quite idyllic. People were very congenial and pleasant, and I made more friends than I ever imagined I would, and had not a dull moment all the time. There was a fine piano in the salon, at which I played, and we had a concert, and I accompanied for a very charming French girl who sang two anthems at Mass (most picturesque, by the way, with the improvised altar & candles, and robed priest, and people kneeling in the salon). I was quite sad when it was all over, and we were thrown again on our own resources. I can hardly realize that I am away for so long; I will repent in time, I suppose. Just now I am enjoying hugely the travel and the seeing of the things that I have wanted so long to see. Write to me care of the American Express Co., 11 Rue Scribe, Paris.

As ever,

Randolph

34

to Sarah Bourne
(Transcript Columbia)

Munich
July 29, 1913

I haven't seen an American newspaper since I left home, and know not a word of what has been happening. It is a new experience to be cut off like this from all my world, but I have been so busy seeing things that I have not had time to think about missing it all. To-day we accidentally spent the whole day more or less, coming about 90 miles from Ulm; we got a slow train by mistake, which stopped for many minutes at every station, unloading pigs in bags and milk cans and vegetables, and dowdy peasants, and children. It was a lovely summer day, however, and it was like spending a day in the country, for I stood on the platform as we went jogging along through the hay fields, with the peasants, men and women at work, and the countryside just dotted with villages, each with its clustered white houses with red or brown roofs and tall white cylindrical church steeple. The people all live in villages, there are no isolated farmhouses at all, so the landscape is very picturesque with four or five villages in view at a time, separated by great yellow and green fields, or woods of slim fir trees. In Munich we had quite a time looking for a pension. One, very delightful, was full, another, even more charming, would only give pension and Swain insists he wants to meet some friends and take some of his meals with them. So we are content with a second-best at 2 marks apiece for a big room, but on the 5th floor. He will leave me here, and go straight to France. I will stay here for several days and then go to Switzerland.

The morning after I wrote you from Cologne we visited the great cathedral, and found its interior quite indescribably impressive. The most wonderful lofty reaches and forests of pillars and arches, all blending in such harmony and sublimity! It was quite the most beautiful church we had seen. I find the picture post-card a most ingenious liar, and some of my most piquant moments are when we see the long-familiar building or square, (long-familiar through a post-card) as it is, and note how much more homely or gross or colored or splendid it is than I had conceived it. Next day we went to Coblenz, stopping off at Bonn, an old university-town, with comfortable streets and beautiful lawns, and the great low rambling University building, with students walking about with canes, and rows of bulletin boards which we read with much interest, comparing them with Columbia ways and manners. Going to Coblenz after supper, we jumped on a train moving from the station, and were followed by a very much excited guard. I thought we had gotten on a Schnellzieg [Schnellzug] (which is a train where you have a special ticket) and that we would be taken off at the next station and put in a military prison. But we finally understood him to say that this was a very slow train, and the next one would bring us to Coblenz much earlier. So we got off at Godesberg and had a delightful twilight view of the "Siebengebirge"[1] and the Rhine, and reached Coblenz in time to take a trolley ride over the river to the great fortress Ehrenbreitstein. The next day we spent on the Rhine boat. The weather was perfect, and I can't see how the river with its steep terraced vineyards and old mediaeval villages and ruined castles (just what you expect, but all so fresh and lovely and clear) could ever have looked more lovely. There was nothing to mar the perfection of the picture, and those Americans who are disappointed in the Rhine must be insensible to enchantment. The night we spent in Mainz and went the next day to Heidelberg (Saturday). This we found so attractive, lying in the Neckar valley with mountains on each side, that we stayed till Monday morning. We went, of course, to the Castle, but oh such crowds! Half of Germany's peasantry must have been there, awe-struck and gaping. The Germans seem to be the greatest travelers afloat; Americans are not in it at all. Every other person you meet in Germany is a German with a Baedeker seeing his own country. And most of them are walking with knapsack on back, green hat with feather in it, bicycle stockings and bare knees, and staff in hand. All ages, men and women; to-day we saw a dozen girls of 15 or 16 trudging through the street with knapsacks and staffs. The woods and gardens about Heidelberg were very lovely, although the castle is rather flaringly modern looking. There are lovely views over the town and up the valley. But the students are the most picturesque feature of the place. Dressed in blue coats or Prince Alberts, with the most outlandish caps of all colors on their heads, (representing their clubs, I suppose) and their faces all smeared with salve pastes. They salute each other on the streets or take off their hats with a very low flourish, and are sufficiently theatrical and picturesque to satisfy the most romantic. We saw one of their "Kammers" Sunday morning on the terrace of the castle, where they entertained their lady friends with beer and song. The girls with their mothers or chaperones came in and were introduced with funny little bows and duckings of the head. Then they all sat down at long tables, and were served with foaming flagons of beer, everybody. Then there were speeches, and songs and much drinking in Honor of Old Heidelberg. The rabble outside, of which we were two, watched the proceedings with much interest. In the evening I went to the open-air concert of the city orchestra, held in a beautiful garden, with fountains and lights, (admission 12 cents including a seat). The music was very fine, and the scene was most brilliant, with people promenading ceaselessly about, and the bright blue coats of the army officers and cadets giving color to the scene. Monday we had an early morning ride to Stuttgart, where we spent several hours, finding it an unexpectedly delightful, characteristically German city, with great palaces and gardens, and a fine old market-place and castle, with a beautiful court yard and old, old houses, each story overlapping the one below it, as you see in pictures, and crowds of soldiers, often marching with bands playing, and streets of the striking new German architecture, built in large masses and fine strong lines,—in fact, all these things that we have found characteristic of German cities, we found in Stuttgart. Ulm where we stopped over night, is very old, with narrow streets and overlapping houses, and a beautiful Gothic church, with the tallest spire in the world. Nuremberg was out of our way, and I think we found in Stuttgart and Ulm, most of the things we would have found there. At Ulm we saw the Danube, very green and rushing along at a great pace, but otherwise "just like any other river," as Swain's favorite comment would be.

[no signature]

---

¹The Seven Mountains, seven peaks near Bonn which are interesting geologically and which form the Western terminus of the scenic Westerwald region.

35

to Sarah Bourne
(Transcript Columbia)

Bellagio
Aug. 5, 1913

In Munich we stayed at the Pension Feldhutter, a pretty good place for 50¢ apiece (for room) per day; our meals we got in restaurants. We took in one of the great beer-gardens, with a concert of fine music by a large military band, and perhaps a thousand people sitting about in the garden and terraces and halls drinking beer and eating supper. I saw the picture-gallery, toured the city, and made several excursions round about. The weather was perfect, as delightful as I have ever seen it, but the city I did not like as much as I expected. Beer and art everywhere, but dingy streets and funny dowdy palaces. The city represents the ideals of a Germany of the last century architecturally and has a colorless look, which is neither the picturesqueness of the old German style, nor the strikingness of the new. And the country around is very tame, a great flat plain, from which you are supposed to see the Alps, but we never saw them. Ninety miles south, however, on the way to Innsbruck, you enter the most gorgeous broad valley of the River Inn, with great mountains sloping down to it, and broad low Swiss-looking farm houses. Innsbruck I enjoyed very much. The mountains tower above it very high, and are very rocky, with patches of snow. The houses are more Italian in character, pink and yellow stucco, some of them, built over the side walks, with Arcades of shops underneath. In the afternoon, I took a mountain trolley line up the Stubai valley, winding up 1500 feet, crossing great gorges, and skirting forest hillsides, until it finally brought you to a little Tyrolean village with a wonder view of mountains and a great white glacier in the distance. The next day I went down to Bogen [Bozen] through wonderful mountain scenery; the railroad climbs up over the high Brenner pass, where you suddenly lose the river you have been following, and soon come upon a new river, the Adige, flowing the other way to the Mediterranean, while the Inn goes to the Danube. From there down to Bogen is a series of the most luxuriant valleys I ever say, hillsides simply covered with vines, trained on trellises so that they grow horizontal, and form what looks like a green undulating carpet. And vistas of snow mountains and ruined castles, and villages perched high on the side of the hills. And the river flowing through the midst in a turbulent plunge of white rapids. Bogen [Bozen] is in one of the loveliest parts, with great green mountains all around, and to the east, a great wall of rocky peaks, white and shining—the Dolomites—and turning pink and then gray as the sun went down. The sun was very hot, and after being stuck with a dinner, I found a funicular railroad which promised a view, and spent the afternoon on the heights among the vineyards, coming down after sunset, when I had supper at the most adorable Pension,—I should like to stay there a month, and wish now I had stayed a few days. My impression is that that region is infinitely more beautiful than the Italian Lakes. I came up here from Como this afternoon, but it was hazy and there was no color in the picture. August is not the time to visit Italy, and I am trying to get out of it as fast as I can. I had meant to stay at Verona overnight, but having to leave Bozen at 6:09 A.M., I stopped at Verona for a few hours and then went on to Milan. The view from the train of the city was very striking with the towers and the villas [sic], but its interior is quite dilapidatedly Italian. And it was fearfully hot. I poked about (with my umbrella over my head) as much as I dared in the hot sun, and saw the market place and some old churches and the crowded streets and the dark little shops and tall houses. To Milan then, by a very fast train through very beautiful Italian country. Milan I was much delighted with. I found a very good hotel near the station and then took a trolley up to the town, saw the wonderful cathedral, quite the loveliest building I have seen in Europe, and then had spaghetti and veal and fruit at the famous Biffi's in the Arcade, and listened to the orchestra. When I left about 10:15, I looked around for a trolley, but none to be had or seen. I tried to ask a policeman in Italian when it would come, and he said what I understood as "ne piu", "no more". So I had to take a cab home, but it only cost me a lire (twenty cents), and gave me a most enjoyable ride. The cabs are delightful in the European cities; they are open carriages like a victoria with one seat; you roll along luxuriously in the open, quite differently from the stupid, shut up cabs of New York. And they are far cheaper. This morning I visited the interior of the castle and climbed the tower; then walked around the city until it got too hot, and came on to Como and here. The Germans with their knickerbockers, Norfolk suits, green felt hats with feathers, knapsack and stick, have all vanished, and their places are filled by conducted American tourists, being brought up through Italy. Two parties in Milan Cathedral, and the boat today on Lake Como almost filled with them. They are funny, make the most inane remarks, look over their picture postals, and have the general look of a herd that feels all right as long as it is together, but would be wholly lost if separated. How much more fun to plunge ahead alone, reading your own time tables and streetsigns and asking for your rooms, and ordering your dinner. At first I felt a little timid about starting alone through Austria and Italy, especially when I didn't know Italian and didn't have a passport. But I have had no difficulty, except sometimes in finding cheap restaurants. I am on my way now to Lausanne where I expect to stay about three weeks and study French.

[no signature]

36

to Arthur Macmahon
(Transcript Columbia)

Lugano
6 August 1913

Dear Arthur,

Since writing you from Brussels, we have seen very many things, but had few adventures, the only one being the horrible affair with the hotel agent at Ghent which --- [Swain] probably wrote you about. To have seen the latter racing through the town with the two valises, the agent, who had nabbed us at the station, lurking darkly in our rear, tearfully imploring us to come with him and taunting us with the taunt that we could do no better, would have made you chortle. --- [Swain] would stop and order him begone, while I would furtively glance at my book of hotels to see if I couldn't find one to which we might act as if we were going. Finally after half a mile or so, we lost him, and finally put up at a miserable café in a most uncomfortable bed, and a damp cold night.

Having begun with this tale, I must now relate that I am travelling alone, --- [Swain] having left me at Munich with the intention of going straight to Grenoble to study French. Travelling bored him quite unutterably; the novelties, which were all my quest, were quite lost on him, and his favorite remarks were, "Just like any other river." "It looks like Montana.", etc. He spurned guidebooks and maps and indignantly refused to accompany me around in an attempt to get a speaking acquaintance with a city. I don't know anyone whom I have repeatedly outraged as I have that poor lad in the two weeks we were together, with my innocent expressions of appreciation of people and houses and landscapes and pictures; with my mild attempts to be comfortable in trains (avoiding Rauchers and Fumeurs [smoking compartments]) and restaurants and hotels; with my personal idiocyncrasies such as using an umbrella as a walking stick, promenading on public streets with a map in my hand, and such like. He betrayed a passionate abhorrence of many things, which abhorrence interested me mildly and furnished the text for some small disquisitions on Stoicism vs. Epicureanism. He was the perfect stoic, answering all rhetorical questions, of which I perhaps am too fond, with a curt, "I haven't the slightest idea" and boasting that he didn't care a "razzle-dazzle what happened". He did prove to be conversational on all subjects connected with a girl Nora, who furnished the leit-motif for the tour, and then basely neglected to appear in Munich. We were lured from place to place by postals and then the great denouement, for she was to be in Munich the time we were, absolutely failed to take place. Her history and that of her family in all its branches and aspects furnished food for --- [Swain]'s most genial hours and long and harmonious monologues. Since she was a Catholic, she always led somehow into a theological discussion in which I was the stern rationalist and --- [Swain] the apologist. This theology was also inclined to make him sullen, so we would have to get back to the sunny uplands of Nora and all her works. On all subjects of my own I disappointed him greatly; he had pictured me as an "intellectual", whereas all he got was "mush". I had never realized I was such a thorough-going epicure, until I went with --- [Swain]. I only live to enjoy life, to have feelings and express them to infuriated rational ears. --- [Swain] was certainly a funny experience; to come together at night after a day of separate rambling, without having the slightest interest expressed in one's goings-about, and to have an attempt at dramatic recital cut short with the most unmistakable indication that it was devoid of interest—this was an odd novelty in companionship. I thought—Oh, how I thought of you or Harry Chase[1]! But his impossibilities I soon learned quite to ignore and I believe my own imperterbability and private enjoyment of everything I saw was positively heightened by the contrast with his queer crossness. Anyway I got nicely broken in for travel alone, and have found the past week most enjoyable. I came down through the Tyrol stopping at Innsbruck and Bozen in the loveliest of vine-covered valleys with towering mountains and vistas of snow peaks and the great shiny rocky Dolomites, and villages perched on the hills. The weather was gorgeous too. In Verona I saw a typical Italian town, very imposing from afar, but monstrously huddled and faded when you thread its narrow streets. Then too Milan, where it was very hot, but where I stayed long enough to see the incredibly beautiful cathedral with its myriad of little Gothic spires and richly decorated tower, and noble interior. The whole church is so beautiful as positively to overcome you. Mass was being said in the morning with organ and male choir, very sumptuous, and the same evening I was in a little old stone church at Bellagio, dimly lighted at the side by an electric arc light. The walls were very bare and dingy but the altar very rich and golden with many candles; the kneeling priest was saying mass in a loud nasal voice, with the congregation making the responses, until all of a sudden they burst into a wonderful strident chant which rose and fell and wandered, with just the men's voices and then the women's voices prominent, a sound unlike anything I ever heard before. The village people kept coming and going, the girls all with black kerchiefs in their heads, the children making their funny little duckings before the altar, and being soundly cuffed if they did not dip their hand in the holy water and make the sign of the cross properly. Bellagio, very famous for some unknowable reason as the garden spot of the Italian lakes,[2] is built in tiers up from the lake, with streets which are simply broad flights of cobbled steps climbing under arches and between garden walls to the market place. An hour after I went to bed, these streets became foaming cascades from a terrific thunderstorm which was still going at five in the morning. The roar of the water past my window which looked out on one of them was quite appalling. And to-day, in which I came on here, and had my view of Como and Lake Lugano quite ruined, has been one of the wettest days I ever saw, with a series of thunderstorms that chased each other around the sky. Weather that would disgrace Scotland, and on the lakes of sunny Italy in August, seems positively malevolent, and designed to cure me of my thirst for beautiful scenery. These lakes too are just saturated with American tourist parties, whose inane remarks, inappropriate dress, and hazy knowledge of where they are or just where they are going gives me a kind of sick feeling. "There but by the grace of God"—I had seen few Americans, except for isolated individuals, until we got to Munich, where parties were being hustled through the Pinakothek. You can tell them anywhere. I was sitting on a bench in a Platz in Munich when along came the happiest heartiest chubby college freshman, and lo! his watchfob displayed a large enamelled Star-Spangled Banner. We helped a minister buy some cherries at a station in Germany, and added confusion to the situation of a minister in Cologne who had left his shirt behind and was trying to get it forwarded to him, and we lunched in Mainz with a man from Massachusetts and an old minister from Pittsburg who was wondering whether it would hurt his morals to try one glass of German beer before he left the country. — [Swain] and I had to take in a beer-garden in Munich and heard a very fine band concert. But the beer becomes positively oppressive, it is so ubiquitous and they slop it around so, it is a sight that you want to see but once, the great Hofbrauhaus at noon with its thousands (literally) of guzzlers and the reeking old stone floors. And a nation that will serve up "Ochsenfleisch" as a course in a fine table d'hote dinner with a pork chop following, and a heavy soup preceding, and a salad and a currant pie at the end and a liter of beer all the time absolutely surpasses my comprehension. Yet twice I paid 2.50 m. for such a dinner in Heidelberg and Stuttgart. But the people look very fine, so many fine clear headed women of forty to fifty and clean, charming children, and striking modern architecture and cheap railway fares. But I must stop. Regards to all.

Randolph

[1]Chase came from Colorado and had seen bitter labor disputes in the mines there. He joined the I. W. W. and remained a Socialist the rest of his life.

[2]Bellagio is located at the tip of a point which divides Lake Como into two very narrow branches.

37

to Alyse Gregory
(Ms Yale)

Lausanne
Aug. 10, 1913

Dear Miss Gregory,
    In the hurry and excitement of leaving I think I must have written some sort of reply to your letter, which I carried with me as a sort of steamer letter and have before me now. And yet remorse and doubt smite me; that day of leaving is all very dim, and I could not swear that I have not given you cause to think me the very worst correspondent in the world. But I have thought of you very often, and intended to write when I should have acquired some vista to look back upon, and rested somewhere in this mad rush of travelling. Now I am at Lausanne, expecting to begin tomorrow a three-weeks vacation course in French here at the University; I don't know how much I shall learn, for my faltering accents are scarcely enough now to procure me a bed, a meal, and a railroad ticket, and I lose my head entirely when a fluent stream is poured out at me by a voluble native. O, why did I not learn all these languages at home before I came! There was a great general strike of some sort just beginning at Milan when I was there last week, and I could not even read the newspapers or ask any one about it. The French and German I can read, but' my wits desert me when I think of framing talk myself. And your railroad companions are so voluble and bright and dramatic too. I feel very humble, and can appreciate the humility of

the "ignorant foreigner" in our country.

My lot has so far been purely that of the sight-seer, and a very superficial one at that. We reached Paris (Havre) on the 14th of July and since then
have raced through Brussels, Bruges, Ghent, Antwerp, Rotterdam, Hague, Amsterdam, Düsseldorf, Cologne, Bonn, Coblenz, the Rhine trip, Mainz, Heidelberg, Stuttgart, Ulm, Munich. Here [at Munich] my companion left me, and I
went down to Italy, stopping at Innsbruck, Bozen, Verona, Milan, Bellagio,
Lugano, and Domodossola, coming here yesterday. It has all been very wonderful to one who has imagined it for so many years, it seems, and looked forward
to seeing it. And the most piquant surprises, of course, were in store; the picture
post card is a most ingenious liar. It takes no account of weather, for instance,—
and we have had our share of mist and showers,—and it does not give the setting
and the coloring and the streakings and the funny shabbiness that so many of
these long-awaited buildings show. And our weather has at times behaved most
malevolently. A sickly mist hung over Como when I passed through it—on the
same boat with an enormous and inane Cook's party—and the most fearful all-
night thunderstorm broke on Bellagio that night, so that the quaint steep streets
became foaming cascades that roared past my window like a waterfall. And the
Borromean Isles in a drab sunset looked hopelessly prosaic, so much so that I
lingered not at all at Baveno, but took the first train for Domodossola, in a vain
attempt—misguided as it turned out—to catch the morning diligence over the
Simplon.

My companion soon sized me up as a hopeless epicure, whose one object in life was to enjoy himself; so perhaps all this was a reminder that I should
give up idle, voluptuous sight-seeing, and settle down for some real work. One of
the delights of travelling is that you forget yourself so completely. It all seems so
completely its own excuse for being, and to me it never leaves a taste of futility behind, like some other pleasures, although I realize there is nothing remaining but memories and pictures—nothing tangible has been created. I can go for
hours and hours without fatigue. Of course, one reason for its pleasantness is
that is all so easy, that is, provided you are of my sex and travel with little baggage, and surprisingly cheap. I have really fared better since I have been alone,
I think, because my companion, who had a heavy suit-case, would insist upon
diving into the first hotel he saw near the station, and it would not always be
the cheapest or the best. He prided himself, anyway, upon his Stoicism, was
enthusiastic about nothing, followed me grudgingly about, and was unhappy
unless he was talking about religion or a girl he expected to meet in Munich. He
is the last person I would have chosen for a companion for my first trip to
Europe, and I wish his queer crossness did not quite so obtrusively permeate my
memory of the trip. He is a Columbia man, very young and bashful and lugubrious, and our combination was a purely fortuitous one, due on my part to a
timidity about starting on a long trip alone, and thinking too that intimately
he would show unsuspected depths of personality. But I disappointed him; he

expected "intellectuality," he said, and he got nothing but "mush." My feminine appreciations were too much for him; I took the tour as the thing, instead of as a necessary evil, preparatory to his settling in Paris for the winter to study history. Our parting was therefore mutually happy, and I have been most contented since I have been alone. Of course, rocks loom up ahead; I have sort of stumped myself to write some essays while I am here, and I know I shall be very rusty and ragged. My mind has been a perfect blank since I left home; if that's what you call getting back one's serenity. I met some very delightful people on the boat, who cheered me a great deal and banished many of the black clouds of foreboding that hung over Europe. If I am homesick now, it is for the "Rochambeau," I am afraid, and that idyllic time that was past so soon.

My European impressions will, I fear, bear no fruit further than a series of letters for the "Bloomfield Citizen." I feel far too green to endeavor to instruct any other public, and I think I should be more appreciated there, and that it might work towards expiating the unfilial sin I committed against the town.

I shall have to do a great deal of reading this year abroad, and make up for my social hours at Columbia. I began well with James' "The American," on the steamer,—recommendation, was it not?—and was absolutely charmed by the smooth and golden art of the thing. I started a couple of novels by Gissing[1] and Masefield after this, and gave up the flabby things in sheer revulsion. These great men are dangerous, for they spoil you for the little fellows, who may have something to say. Now I have been reading some of Andrejew's [Andreyev's] [2] and Gorky's[3] stories in a German translation; they are powerful and haunting, and have a tang of real life that we Americans are afraid of.

And now back to your letter. Your voice is such a friendly one that I wish I could expect to hear from you somewhat regularly often. You must know that I admire your work and the sacrifice it is for you more than I can say. It is the sort of thing that I admire so much that I can hardly imagine the power and joy it would be giving me to have had circumstances come so, or to have been able to make circumstances come so as to do some such pioneering propaganda work myself, instead of always preparing and fumbling. And I am dreadfully curious to know of the course by which you came into it. I have been babbling all my story to everybody, but you have been very silent, and it is only by these dark hints of miasmas that I get suggestions of struggle and bewilderment. What put you going? I am sure enough that you are working out triumphantly the "processes" you are in, but I would like so much to know about them.

Through September I shall be at Mr. S. M. Bligh's Cilmery, Builth Wells, Breconshire. I should love to meet your friend,[4] but wonder if I shall get to Scotland.

Yours most sincerely,

Randolph S. Bourne

P.S. After Oct. 1, c/o American Express Co., London.

[1]Geroge Gissing, author and friend of Masefield and Wells. Gissing was brilliant but was unable to discipline his life. He wrote many novels, some of them pot-boilers, which depicted his hate for the rich. He was mistakenly considered a champion of the poor, whereas he was merely expressing his disillusionment with life.

[2]Leonid Andreyev, novelist, essayist, and short story writer, was discovered by Gorky. He was attacked by more conventional writers because he wrote about the "filth" of common life. He was anti-social, rather than radical. He was categorized as an apostle of gloom and was likened to Poe.

[3]Maxim Gorky, novelist, playwright, and short story writer. He came from a lower class background and became popular at the turn of the century because of his portrayal of common life. He became a revolutionary figure. In 1905 he came to the United States, but was considered too radical to be received popularly.

[4]Bourne may be referring to Elizabeth Westwood, whom he met in Rickmansworth after his stay with Bligh. See my note to letter # 41.

38

to Sarah Bourne
(Transcript Columbia)

Lausanne
Aug. 19, 1913

I moved into a pension in a delightful quarter of the town which I had not seen before. I have a little view of the lake from my window, and only a few doors away is a park with benches and a truly glorious veiw of the whole northern end of the lake. It is tantalizing, however, for the mountains are veiled in mist most of the time, and the climate is not at all generally what Switzerland should be,—for it is cloudy most of the time, and even when the sun shines, the mountains are very coy. So I am afraid I shall have to depend on my remembrances of the gorgeous weather and clear towering mountains of the Tyrol, where alas! I spent only two days—for my impressions of the mountain scenery of Switzerland. I had thought of going to England by way of Interlaken and Lucerne, but it would be quite hopeless with weather like this. One day, a week ago, was clear, and I was clever enough to take the boat up to the end of the lake and see the Castle of Chillon, with the wonderful views that you have from that part of the lake of snow mountains and bare jagged rocky peaks.

The apartment houses are large and square (this one is rather old fashioned and dingy), four or five stories, with a spiral staircase in the center of the house and an apartment on each side. Mme. Chollet, a most attractive pleasant woman, lives on the first floor right; my room is on the third floor, very plain indeed, but comfortable, and the cooking is most excellent and bountiful, and there is a piano; so that I am well content, particularly as I am only paying $.90 a day.

[no signature]

39

to Alyse Gregory
(Ms Yale)

Cilmery
Builth Wells
REO
8 Sept. 1913

Dear Miss Gregory,
I should surely be up in Connecticut if I were home, to see your "Players." What administrative genius you must have to run an affair like this? You will surely have proved your right to be a radical; for the world demands first this business genius and refuses to take one seriously without it. I am visiting a country gentleman who has been listening all the morning with stupified incredulity to my preachments of Socialism, and then gave me an exposition of the most delightful creed of business success to which I ever listened. Laissez-faire, individualism, the absolute justice and perfection of the present industrial system (for the reason that the country needs men who can make money and therefore it is right that the shrewdest should be the most heavily rewarded,) came with exquisite humor from a man who had inherited a large estate, and never worked in his life. The stupid and the "rotters" have to work for their

living; the shrewd man can "make" money, as he does by buying and selling Canadian real estate. I became almost converted to this glorious gospel of success, which sweeps away at a glance all the miasmas of concern for evil social conditions, for unjust exploitation of ignorant and untrained masses, for the spiritual chaos of a class-civilization pretending to be democratic,—for is not everybody rewarded exactly in proportion to their deserts [sic]? I thought of my impossible essays in the light of this that all the world was believing and practicing, and wondered what perverse fate had imposed on me a philosophy so cross-grained, so desperately unpractical as mine of scorn for institutions, combined with a belief in their reform,—of scorn of exploitation combined with a need of the wherewithal to live,—of a fanatical belief in mass-movements and mass-ideals, combined with a sensitiveness to unique and distinctive personality. But I was delighted to find that my real faith didn't waver an instant before the deluge; it only served to bring out more clearly,—indeed more than ever before,— the contrast between my Socialism and the old ideals, and make me want to crush the latter all the more completely.

My friend, however, is a very delightful and keen-sighted psychologist of personality, of great intellectual vigor, and I am having a royal time of talk with him. I think I will recommend to you his books, "The Direction of Desire," "The Desire for Qualities," "The Ability to Converse," by S. M. Bligh, which to me are both quaint and illuminating analyses of human nature, unlike anything I have seen. I became acquainted with him through a review of the second book which I wrote for the Journal of Philosophy,[1] and took advantage of my coming to England to accept an invitation to visit him. If you don't like that (or those) read Allen Upward's "The New Word," a divine book of human philosophizing.[2] I wonder if you wouldn't be interested too in Prof. Ross's books on "Social Psychology" and "Social Control," brilliantly written, and to me as interesting as any books in the world.[3] But perhaps you have read them. In turn, you must tell me what to read of novels and plays, for having sampled your judgment, I come back for more. I want to do so much this winter, I know I am preparing a great disappointment for myself, as I always do—by undertaking far too much, and letting the various interests choke each other to death. My summer has been so perfect a holiday that I'm afraid my taste for serious work is destroyed, though I find myself here in England with a curious audacity, having little of that fear of making a fool of myself which keeps me low before my countrymen. Does one always talk to foreigners as to a rather dull child, whom one does not expect to appreciate one's own irony and subtleties, but whom one is enormously interested in educating? This English brusqueness is very encouraging, for one is thereby relieved from taking thought about one's own manners, and the extreme volubility and self-interest of my friend prevents the necessity of my making any impression myself. He has too those bright, half-satirical, interested eyes, which always stimulate me to heroic efforts at explaining myself, and doing it at considerable length and with accuracy. So I am now in a great bold mood, and only hope it will not slump when I get to London.

My friend calls himself a consulting psychologist, and has a long list of questions which he uses about your personality, ambitions, interests, habits, complexes, and so gives you a psychological diagnosis. I am being done now, with great enjoyment to myself, and much interesting comment and advice from him. He goes after people's spiritual insides in a much more scientific manner than I do, and has the most amazing knowledge of the constitution and fabric of the average human soul that I have ever seen. The diagram of my personality, when finished, will be a most interesting document,—to me, at any rate, and just the little way we have gone has thrown a flood of light on the contrast between the fabric of his ideas and mine. The effect of economic security on personality has come out repeatedly in the strongest way. I feel that I can size him up and put him into my philosophy much better than he can me, and so am confirmed in my Socialism, which is practically that of Kropotkin. Tell me you have not read him and I will send you his wonderful pamphlets from London.

Many thanks for the card, which I shall avail myself of if I possibly get to Scotland.

Sincerely your friend,

Randolph S. Bourne

[1]*Journal of Philosophy, Psychology and Scientific Methods* IX (Sept 1912), 530-31.

[2]This book, published in 1908, was an idealist's attack on the exactness of scientific knowledge.

[3]E. A. Ross was a pioneering social theorist and social reformer. *Social Control* was considered a definitive work on social constraints and *Social Psychology* was one of the first American explorations of the field.

40

to Prudence Winterrowd
(Transcript Columbia)

Almery [Cilmery]
Builth Wells
Wales
8 Sept. 1913

My Dear Miss Prudence,
Are you really going to New York? And do you absolve me from all
responsibilities for luring your intellectual life away from home; for I honestly
meant myself to be there when you should come, and do not want to think of
the maledictions you may be inclined to heap upon my head when you have
really arrived. Do not take the entrance to the Graduate School too seriously;
the Dean [Woodbridge] is one of the greatest and kindest of men, and will
treat you humanly and interestedly—that is, if you see him at all. You had better
write in advance, telling exactly your preparation and the courses you want to
take and have it all settled before you go. If he gives a graduate course in the
history of philosophy, by all means take it, for he is my great hero-teacher there
at Columbia, whose course I still think of as a great event in my life, and who
has helped and encouraged me literarily in as many ways. It gives me considerable disquiet to think you are really coming and I shall not be there to mix you
in to the life that I know, but perhaps by this time has all but forgotten me; I
can recommend you to some of my trusty friends, and I know you will have the
greatest sort of a time anyway in New York. It is myself I am selfishly thinking
of.
I am still on the verge of my winter, anticipating it partly with dread,
partly with excited wonder whether anything will happen of definite significance, or suggest what I am to do on my return. My summer has been so delightful that I am a little afraid of my disinclination to settle down to work and
study. And there is so much to be done and seen and read that I am bound
to have a constant sense of failure to grasp the whole of my opportunity. My
experience at Lausanne in trying to learn French was most humiliating, for in
my three weeks I made no discoverable progress, and was forced to the conclusion that I must take a much longer time and begin much further back. This
may mean that if the weather is at all suitable I may want to stay in London all
winter, for I shall find the books there I want, and talkable people, without
whom I starve. I saw London at 7 a.m. of a cold drizzly morning, on my way up
here, and was unexpectedly pleased with the broad dignity of the Westminster
region and the pleasant working people and suburbanites who soon come
hurrying out from Charing Cross Station. The weather cleared and I had a

charming journey all across England—and England all of fields and small trees and canals and funny red-brick houses and not at all the England of thatched cottages and hedgerows and forests that I had expected. This rolling country with broad fields and hills dotted with cattle and horses and sheep is much more attractive than the England that I saw, and the country-house life with visitors and much riding and fishing and banter and the informal daring English manners, and help-yourself breakfasts and lunches, and dogs, and people who are like you, but just aren't is very interesting. My host is a country gentleman with a great taste for making money in land, and a most marvellous [sic] psychological interest and talent. I got acquainted with him by reviewing one of his books for the Journal of Philosophy and we had a voluminous correspondence all winter, and this chance for a visit. We disagree absolutely on Socialism and all related subjects, but agree very much in our observations about people and our interest in personalities. He does the most extraordinary things in analysis, and is full of quaint and illuminatory insight into motives and interests. Just now he is conducting a psychological investigation and diagnosis of my personality in about 250 questions, most of which suggest interesting points for discussion. We shall have a document interesting to us, indeed, but whether it will represent anything more than my idea of myself remains to be seen. When you get to Columbia you might look up his book, S. M. Bligh,—"Desire for Qualities", or "The Direction of Desire", and see the unusual and stimulating stuff he writes. I meant to do a lot of reading here, but these discussions are so fascinating that I am afraid they will fill my time. I feel, though, that I am learning much about the English mind.

I think I wrote you from Lausanne, at the end of my travels, and have done little since then, except come on here by an almost continuous trip of 30 hours, which, strangely enough, fatigued me scarcely at all. I stopped at Berne, surely one of the most charming towns in Europe, with the brightest houses all built over arcades, with rows of flowers in the windows, and many mediaeval fountains and green river in which the bridges and clouds make purple shadows, and a view of the snowy Alps of the Uberland.

Write me much about Columbia. I am very interested and anxious—and quite wistful.

Sincerely your friend,

Randolph S. Bourne

41

to Sarah Bourne
(Transcript Columbia)

Rickmansworth, England
Friday, Sept. 12, 1913

I reached Cilmery about 5, having been going about 32 hours. Mr. Bligh met me in a funny old trap, drawn by two horses. He had with him a Welsh girl of the neighborhood, very charming, with a mass of red hair, and a manner so much like Grace Wade,[1]—and her friend, a Russian girl from St. Petersburg. He himself is large, with a brown beard and funny little spectacles; he wears atrociously shabby clothes, and talks all the time. He reminded me of a combination of Uncle Halsey and Prof. Erskine at Columbia (whom I cordially dislike), with a dash of Cousin John Canfield, Hoschke, Powers, and all the dominating people who have put it over me in the past.[2] In other words, instead of the shy, sympathetic student, that I had pictured him from his letters and books, the congenial and understanding soul whose interests and ideals matched mine, I found a masterful English country gentleman, tremendously interested in making money, despising anybody who couldn't make money, and surrounded by a circle of very successful and sophisticated people, as unlike anybody I know, or can handle as anything in the world. Well, you can imagine the result. I put myself in wrong from the start. The funny thing was they didn't abash me at all. I talked at them all with rather more fluency and lucidity than usual. The first night after dinner we got on peace and war; I went after militarism, hardly realizing that Mrs. B. was the daughter of a general and all the guests were believers in England's military and naval power to the last degree. We had a great argument; they didn't get mad, English people never get ruffled in the slightest way, but I was exposed to their minds as some sort of foreign lunatic whom it was hardly profitable to bother with. Later, Mr. Bligh went over with me a list of headings for a new book he was writing, and we had a very interesting time. But my whole Socialist viewpoint kept coming out, and I found myself explaining myself with great care and accuracy. Now he considers the least taint of a Socialistic idea as a symptom not only of a disordered but a feeble intellect, so it was quite evident that we were not to get on. After Sunday morning, he completely lost interest in me, and a great art-critic from London arriving, whom he was very fond of and thought one of the best talkers in London, but who seemed to me an insufferable snob and filled with the most amazing platitudes; I was left to read or write or walk. The other people were civil, but made no attempt to get me in. I didn't mind particularly, for when I did get a hearing, for some reason, I talked, as it seemed to me, rather well. But it was all a different language; they couldn't or wouldn't understand. I had two very delightful walks with the red-haired girl, Hilda, whom Mr. B. claims to have educated, but who sees through him and all the prejudices of his class quite beautifully. I got all sorts of sympathy from her and understanding, so that I did not feel lonely. The climax came Tuesday when Mrs. B. said she hoped I would not think her inhospitable, but her parents were coming down suddenly and would my visit terminate Thursday? Mind you I had been invited by them for "at least a fortnight". I told him later that I was sorry that I had to leave so soon, and all he said was that his wife had just told him. I can't make out whether they did need the room, and the barbarian, who had no claims and no rights and feelings, was the one to be thrown over board, or whether I was such a case that I had to be packed off as soon as possible. Anyway it was all most amazing. I felt horribly chilled and chagrinned at first, but I could not see how I had not behaved with dignity and all the good manners I possess, and so I soon recovered, after a talk with Hilda who apologized for the English nation, and gave me a beautiful psychological sketch of her own class—the country gentleman. The whole experience was most educational; the talk around the table was brilliant, and I got an insight into the English mind that was quite unsurpassed. Mr. B. gave me a lot of good advice about becoming strong and decided and definite and rich like him, and my general childishness did show up in striking contrast to him. He made it quite plain that I could expect nothing from his London set, (and they must be monstrously successful and clever, and, as it seems to me, quite futile), and told me all about London society and his whole life, revealing a wholly new world to me. Withal it was a great experience. I returned to London yesterday, a little bruised, and hungry for some friend to tell it all to. I knew that my friend Elizabeth Westwood[3] was to be at this country inn in September, and thought it was worth the risk to run up to see. I found her here recovering from an appendicitis complaint; we were mutually delighted, and I decided to stay a week. She has all sorts of valuable points to give me about the people in London, radicals and students, that I will find congenial, and which I would not know how to find; she knows some of them and will give me cards; so this looks like a nice piece of fortune to counterbalance the Bligh tragedy.

[no signature]

[1]Grace Wade was a close childhood friend.

[2]Bourne did not like Erskine, as some of his earlier letters suggest. Bourne felt special anitpathy toward Frederick Hoschke, his employer at a piano roll factory at which he had worked before entering Columbia, because he felt that Hoschke had exploited his talents. Uncle Halsey Bennett was the dominant male figure in Bourne's family; he dis-

approved of Bourne's entrance into college.

³Elizabeth Westwood was one of the women who frequented the Patchin Place salon Alyse Gregory took Bourne to in 1913.

42

to Simon Pelham Barr
(Transcript Columbia)

Rickmansworth
Herts. [Hertfordshire]
Saturday
13 September 1913

Dear Simon

Your letter saved my spiritual life, and was therefore the most grateful of all I had had from home. It reached me while I was visiting an English country gentleman whom I had been cultivating under the delusion that he was a sympathetic amateur psychologist. He does write books filled with acute observation on personality, etc. but he is mostly a very definite, ruthless man of affairs, and I certainly had a hell of a time emotionally, though a wonderful time educationally, in my five days at his country house. Before me paraded in the best, near-brilliant talk I have ever heard, the smart, artistic, sophisticated world of London, shot through with all the most disgusting militaristic, capitalistic, English, and psychological prejudices and illusions of the age. I talked myself, and soon got shown up as a young prophet of perfectly impossible and impractical ideals and a possessor of a hazy, muddled mind. I don't know yet just how I shall literize this experience; it is too good to be lost, but presents so many possible aspects that I hardly know how to take hold of it.

I was delighted to hear of your success. Of course it is a little hard to imagine your intensely personal style adapted to the needs of a municipal journal. You must be even a greater genius than I took you for. Do send me some of your professional writings, and also that review in the Survey which of course I am crazy to see.¹ Also anything else you see or hear about me. The "Monthly" hasn't come but will, I suppose. You don't mention finances so I presume it was a great success, and everything from last year came out all right. I cannot quite reconcile myself to P[reston] W. S[losson]² on the editorial board! Should like to see H[enry] W. E[lsasser] to cuss a little duet with him about it. P. W. S. with J[ohn] E[rskine] were my pet prejudices at college, and one hates to give up old friends that one has lived with so long. I saw quite a lot of Prof. Dickinson Miller[3] in Switzerland; he took me on a wonderful mountain excursion and read me at intervals along the way from Matthew Arnold's Obermann Stanzas and Obermann Once More, written about all the familiar places and mountains that we were in the heart of. Well, it was thrilling! The glorious scenery and the poetry and the impressive depth of Miller's voice get fused into a quite un-forgettable picture and feeling. I thought of him just here, because we had a discussion of Erskine, in which I am afraid I damaged a little some ot the ideals held by a colleague who worshipped distantly from afar. I didn't do it maliciously, but I find my tone usually tells the truth that my words are ironically pretending to conceal.

I have had a frivolous summer,—weeks of rapid travel through Belgium, Holland, and Germany, just seeing things, in company with that uncongenial and perverse kid, Swain. Then a week in the Tyrol and northern Italy alone; then three weeks in Lausanne, where I tried to learn French, wrote a lot of letters on my travels to my local paper (the only one I could think of to take them), and excursioned nearly every day with a charming American girl[4] who was chaperoning her younger sister, who in turn chaperoned us on a gorgeous trip, part walking, to Chamonix and Mont Blanc. Then a straight rush to Wales and my amazing experience, and now back here to this old inn on the outskirts of a suburban-country-factory village with which you're probably familiar, and a perfect garden where I mean to do a lot of writing before going to London for the fall. Such a frivolous and unproductive summer, in comparison with you people who are all getting successful and into things while I still dawdle and spectate. By the way, Elsasser sent me Jagy's paper in the International,—sheer joy, throughout! And did you see Dreiser's article on his first European trip, in the "Century"! Perfect drivel; and it infuriates me to think I haven't the nerve to try and capitalize my experiences.

I want to know about what happened to the Paterson strike; have heard only vague rumors that it failed.[5] Also what they did about Alexander Scott.[6] And anything about the I. W. W.; socialistic people over here are keen on it. The great popular hero is Harry Thaw, and even on the near-top of Mont Blanc we had to tell a Swiss gentleman all the latest developments.[7] Gov. Sulzer has dropped out of sight; he shone for a while. I suppose the New Haven is still killing scores. An accident over here brings out a cry for nationalization. I don't even know whom Tammany nominated for Mayor (saw of Gaynor's death).[8] Tell me anything of Socialistic or literary importance. I will try to write something. The Masses did turn down my "poem."[9] You can print it if you want to and think it won't damage my literary career for life. I got such pleasure in writing it that I don't want to see it wasted. Give me some subjects to write about; you once promised to do it, but it never materialized. I will write you once more interestingly from London; I was much pleased with what I saw around Charing Cross between 7 & 11 A.M. last Saturday morning. All Europe is so much more toned-up and prosperous-looking than our American industrial east, that is in the superficial aspects; we are probably much richer than we look and Europe much poorer. I have had so many surprises that I shall have to read up a lot about what I've been looking at to really get to understand. I felt awfully ignorant, most of the time. The only thing I did know was the geography.

As ever,

R. S. B.

[1]*Survey* XXX (August 23, 1913), 645. The review asserts that the center of the collection is "The Philosophy of Handicap." "The Life of Irony," the reviewer claims, is more stoic than Bourne admits. He believes that Bourne shows promise, but, other than these observations, he gives only a cursory analysis.

[2]Slosson became Editor-in-Chief of *Monthly* in December 1913.

[3]Miller taught at Columbia from 1898 to 1919 and was associated with the Theological Seminary.

[4]Louisa James, probably the relative of Mrs. E. H. James, whom Bourne met early in his trip. See the photograph in this volume.

[5]The Paterson textile strike exhausted both sides and did fail in the end, although it is hard to say that either side won. The strike was adopted as a cause by American radicals and leftist intellectuals. In June 1913 there was a pagenat held in Madison Square Garden which dramatized the conflict of the strike. See the note to letter #24.

[6]Scott was the Editor of the Passaic *Weekly Issue*, a socialist paper. In May 1913 he was indicted for advocating hostility toward the United States government. Through his paper Scott had encouraged the Paterson strikers and had attacked the police, whom he accused of being nothing more than strike breakers for the mill owners. His trial lasted only one day and resulted in a conviction. In July he was also accused of libeling a Paterson citizen, but that conviction was subsequently overturned. In June 1914, having lost his editorial position, Scott finally received the opportunity to publicize his beliefs before the Industrial Relations Commission, which was investigating the Paterson strike.

[7]Harry Thaw killed the architect Stanford White in 1906. He never regretted the crime, which he committed before many witnesses in a fashionable restaurant. He was tried and was acquitted due to insanity. He was committed to a mental institution, from which he escaped to Canada on August 17, 1913. During the time in which Bourne was writing, the United States was attempting to gain his extradition. The nature of the crime, Thaw's reputation as a playboy, and the sensation of his escape gained him notoriety.

[8]William Sulzer was elected Governor of New York with Tammany backing. He split with "Boss" Charlie McCarthy, however, and was impeached in 1913 for perjury and improper representation of campaign expenses. He was perceived as being persecuted by

Tammany and became the champion of the anti-Tammany forces. William Gaynor was elected mayor of New York on an anti-Tammany ticket. His election represented an erosion of Tammany power. He died while abroad in late 1913.

[9]Bourne is probably referring to the poem "Sabotage," which was subsequently published in *Monthly.*

43

to Henry W. Elsasser
(Ms Columbia)

Rickmansworth
Herts. [Hertfordshire]
Sept. 17, 1913

Dear H. W. E.,

Your letter and educational clippings gave me a great cheering-up while I was engaged in one of the most piquant and dislocating experiences of my life,— a visit to an English country gentleman whom I had known through his writings and correspondence as an amateur psychologist of most congenial mein. I am still a little bit dazed from my contact with him and his guests, who represented one of the most sophisticated artistic and literary sets in London,—not the big people, but very English little novelists, art-critics, journalists, Tory barristers, etc. My prophetic strain would come out and my Socialism appeared as wild and hair-raising, if not actually mad, in that society of tough British and class-prejudice. Ideals of militarism, imperialism, money-making, conservation of old English snobberies and prejudices, all swept before me in an indescribably valuable and brilliant flood, and I was left, as you may surmise, stranded like a young Hosea or Amos at the court of some wicked worldly king. I got a lot of good advice from the master and an unparalleled insight into the English mind, but I was slightly discouraged in my ambition to make British friends among the intellectual class; in fact the only person with whom I got along was an Austrian boy who was acting as semi-butler. This revealed to me most dramatically my own incorrigibly plebeian nature. London society must be one of the most emancipated (socially) in the world; husband and wife lead quite independent lives, flirting with each other on occasion at the dinner-table in a really charming fashion. Each has their own circle of friends, indiscriminately male and female, married and unmarried, all of whom are called by their first names, and treated with any degree of tender solicitude which is desired. The guests, as they come down from London, to the country house, are partitioned off as they "belong" to the master or mistress of the house, and the latter ride, or fish or shoot & talk with them, quite unhampered by the society or jealousy of the spouse. All relations, arguments, flirtations, are conducted on a plane of absolute urbanity and amenity. Nobody ever gets ruffled or emotional; the talk is even, brilliant, pertinent; everyone participates and contributes. It is society in its perfection; to get such perfection, of course, all factors of conviction, of "caring," must be absent, but it is a life of great artistry that has been worked out, if one of highly sophisticated artistry. Sexual passion and moral indignation are alike absent; proposals are made, I suppose, but if the girl doesn't like you in that way, she doesn't get outraged, but simply doesn't see you again. Londoners are so busy, my host said, they haven't time for moral indignation. My host dines with some stunning girl or other several times a week at a fashionable restaurant during the London season. His wife dines where she likes. Everything moves by inclination; you do not go anywhere you do not want to, and nobody is offended at your refusal. You have such a wide circle that you can pick and choose where you will, and the loss of a friend or two, or their fading away means nothing in the London sea so inexhaustibly full of fish. Cigarettes and liquors are freely indulged in,—one might almost say constantly—by both sexes, but this must be rather to still their cravings arising from their meagre and atrociously plain food than to afford actual stimulation. The talk is very free, spades are called spades, and there is a sort of triumph in coming out with a real shocker. A rather piquant bit in a flirtatious quarrel between my host & hostess at dinner table with several guests was his characterization of her as a "good marital female." It is in general extremely good talk, the sort one rather hungers for in America. As an antidote to my picture of English life, I enclose a clipping to show that Shaw has not lived in vain and that "the heart of England is still around." I have not gotten acquainted with the London papers very much yet, and so have no more at present.

After my visit at Cilmery, which I had anticipated to be longer than it proved, I came down to a country inn here on the chance of meeting an American friend who had been here. She is a worldly-wise, clever, and not unsympathetic person, and I knew I would choke if I didn't have somebody to tell this experience to. She was here and her reactions to my account were so satisfactory that I decided to stay a week, and I have been having a most interesting time. We range from economic theory to the nature of love, on all of which she has subtle ideas; we have our meals together in the cosiest of low, old-fashioned sitting-rooms. I write out in the garden, a charming affair with green turf and old walls and rose bushes and a reedy little river flowing through, or walk through the fields and old villages around here. But time is up, to-morrow and then London and I hope some profitable work.

I received Barr's Monthly and read it with mingled emotions; I say Barr's because I recognized the master-hand behind the disgusting initials of C. F. and G. L. C. &, I think, G. R. L. He has done the rhapsodical business once too often; the Class Poem grazed the edge, but this is too much. It may be the English atmosphere that is perverting me, but really this Litany affair gave me the chills when it didn't make me laugh. And Erskine's! What sort of pidgeon Gallic-English do you call these translations anyway? And Slosson! Let us shake our heads together very mournfully, you and I, over the evil days that have come upon Monthly since we have gone. P[reston] W. S[losson] was one of our pet prejudices, and it is really a wrench to let him go. I see that Buck & Gove have disappeared entirely. One of the guests at Cilmery, a gentleman who "farms in Norfolk" reminded one strikingly of a rather toned-down edition of A[fred] A. K[nopf], and the host himself, of a fusion of Erskine with my uncle, an impressive corporation lawyer of New Jersey. So you see I am the victim of some of my antipathies. Sidney Webb will probably remind me of P. W. S. Here I begin to ramble, so I will close, with that mighty London looming ahead of me, and I so ignorant and without connections. With a new play by Galsworthly, one by Shaw, Masefield's "Nan" running, besides nightly orchestral concerts at Queen's Hall, one ought to find plenty of interest in the artistic world. A new novel by Wells, called "The Passionate Friends" and preaching, as I understand it, the "sister-lover-friend" ideal woman of the future which I have sort of invented myself independently and am very keen for.

Your political news is always interesting. Keep it up. And could you send me a copy of the new Harper's Weekly; I will reciprocate with some London paper which I fancy. The London dailies are certainly stunning.

As ever,

R. S. B.

44

to Sarah Bourne
(Transcript Columbia)

London
Sept. 20, 1913

I am stuck on the top floor of a very mediocre place which I took in desperation. This region is full of boarding houses, not unattractive outside, but horrible inside, with very cheap furniture and awful wall-paper, and meagre, cold monotonous food which everywhere I have been, at Bligh's at the Inn at Rickmansworth and here, is just the same. London itself is attractive with its very gray and stately buildings and its busy streets, but in the manner of comfort, the slump from the Continent is awful, and I shall not begin to find anybody as charming as my Mme. Chollet in Lausanne. To be comfortable here, after I am turned out of Mrs. Schwarz in October will probably cost me more than I expected, much more, and I am trusting to some kind fate to turn up and solve the problem for me.

[no signature]

45

to Carl Zigrosser
(Ms Pennsylvania)

London
23 Sept. 1913

Dear Carl,
        Your letter was so good to get that it should have been answered before this; but I have been hopping around a good deal and didn't get around to it. I am now in the least pleasant land of my travels, and debating anxiously with myself just how long I shall stay here. Conditions of living seem awfully primitive; the nation eats in the most meagre fashion,—as if it were on the verge of famine; the houses, though dignified outside, betray inside all the evidences of mid-Victorian commercial greed and jerry-building; and the people are quite as insular and foreign as if they spoke an unintelligible language. To come from Switzerland and my charming friends to this pale and dull country is an awful slump, and I shall have to drown myself in reading to keep me cheerful. But even then, the public libraries are remarkably primitive, and the British Museum will not allow books to go out. I am just a little downcast now, because my visit to Bligh did not turn out a success. He proved to be very different from the sympathetic, congenial soul that his letters showed, and my formlessness and prophetic strain showed up in startling contrast. He is a wealthy country gentleman with large financial interests, which he is very fond of, and surrounded by a group, not of questing students like ourselves, but of highly sophisticated people of a smart London set, several of whom were at his house when I was there. Have you ever heard of T. Martin Wood, of the Grosvenor Gallery, who writes artbooks and criticisms? He was one of them, and a wonderful specimen of the time-server and the perfectly artificial sophisticated gentleman of the world. I got talking on Socialism and anti-militarism, etc. and they began to treat me as if

I was a harmless lunatic. Even Bligh could hardly conceal his disgust and amazement, and I left long before my two weeks were up. This experience naturally rather shattered my hopes for making friends in London, though it gave me an unparallelled picture of the tough fabric of British prejudice and tradition. My letters of introduction, I fear, will bring me but perfunctory notice, and I shall be without congenial friends, and a winter on my hands. However, I had a glorious summer, not at all the conventionally tourist thing, but quite dazzling. After I left Lausanne, where I think I wrote you last, I went with two delightful friends to Geneva and Chamonix, at the foot of Mt. Blanc, where we took the most amazing walk along a ridge 7500 ft. high, in full view of the great line of needles that are as perfectly formed as cathedral towers, which make up the Mont Blanc chain, with the great snow-covered domes of Mt. Blanc at the end. Lunch on the tough mossy grass far above the tree line, with a glacier below us and the village like a map at our feet, and huge bare mountains across the valley, and this majestic line of snow-dusted peaks rising above us. I should say that we took the railroad up the mountain and walked down, a 3-hrs. walk with the zigzags down this almost precipitous slope which reached a mile high above the village. And the next day we walked down from Chamonix to the Rhone Valley, through a lovely road that ran high above one of the most enchanting valleys in Switzerland, through villages of weather-black chalets and quaint market-places. It was so wonderful that I fear it has discontented me for any other life, and made study a fearful bore. The London School of Economics[1] where I have been working a little has a fair library, but nothing like Columbia, and an ominous and pathetic sign in the reading room which asks students not to crowd around the fireplace. Really Hartley [Hall] has completely spoiled me, and my physical comfort looms up portentiously in my mind.

London *is* nice to look at, with its black palaces and churches and lovely parks, but it isn't much fun sight-seeing alone, though I have done it. A Queen's Hall Beethoven concert; Shaw's new play, "Androcles and the Lion," one of the funniest things ever played and one of the most dramatically impressive; Granville-Barker's "Harlequinade," an amusing presentation of the old Harlequin story in all the ages, from Greek to 20th century American; then evensong at St. Paul's Cathedral, matins at the Catholic Cathedral at Westminster; Sunday morning at Westminster Abbey; afternoon at Hampton Court Palace with beautiful gardens and lawns and picture galleries and the Thames, and—this appealed to me—all public, with thousands of people roaming over the grass and through the stately avenues of beech-trees and through the courts and galleries. The finest thing in London are the 18th century churches, with their slender and delicately tall white towers and their classicly elegant exteriors. And they stand in the centre of open spaces—some of them—so that the whole perfection of their outlines may be seen. I was sorry, but I did not fall for St. Paul's; the dome from outside is impressive, but the interior is too ornate and baroque to please me; the rounded arches seem vulgar after the delicacy of the Gothic. The Catholic cathedral, on the other hand, though quite new, did delight me. It is an indescribable mixture of mosque and basilica—early Byzantine, they call it—with a tremendous campanile of brick, and a lofty sombre interior, beautifully proportioned, and tremendously huge—St. Paul's actually seems stuffy and cramped beside it. And the Mass was not theatrical and offensive as in Italy, but gentle and simple, with heavenly singing by choir-boys, and not six horrible fat old men, as I saw in Milan. Westminster Abbey I knew I should not like; no imagination can make it anything but a rather mediocre Gothic church, and the plaster statues of the great men give me the chills. I would much rather go home and read a living book by one of the poets than see the Poet's Corner. That region, however, is full of noble vistas—the Parliament Houses, Westminster Bridge, Whitehall, Trafalgar Square, with Buckingham Palace not far away,—that are as fine as anything I saw in Europe. But the suburbs are quite awful,—neat enough but offensively dull, with their little brick houses and shops,—and perfectly endless, so that the old villages like Richmond and Kew and Twickenham are completely swamped. Indeed, one sees little of old England; it is melting away before the commercial age, and the thatched roofs and old villages have to be searched for diligently. I have done some walking around the country through the footpaths,—which are amazingly public in this land of property,—and through the beech-woods, but the landscape is very tame and flat and monotonous, few gardens, many sheep, but in general a land of cities with poorly productive fields between them.

Do write me soon. I could not read your German, so please translate. I envy your meetings; wish you were all here.

As ever,

Randolph

[1]The School was founded by radicals allied to the Labor Party and to the Fabian Socialists to promote the study of socialism and social welfare.

46

to Sarah Bourne
(Transcript Columbia)

London
Sept. 27, 1913

I am now completely settled at Mrs. Schwarz' in Gordon St., a place recommended by Cushing of Columbia, and quite the nicest of all I saw in the pilgrimages. I have a big room looking out on a back garden with trees; there is a big double window reaching from the floor, and a big double bed. Mrs. Schwarz, being from the Continent, gives us a much better and more abundant fare than do the frugal English, and so I am content, though I can only have the room for 3 weeks more.

This week I have been very busy sightseeing, studying, and presenting my cards of introduction. I had lunch at the Temple, (a great collection of old buildings and gardens, where the lawyers and law students live) on Wednesday, with an ex-Columbian man, who was just on the point of going back to New York, to help Prof. Monroe at T[eachers] C[ollege] edit the Educational Encyclopedia.[1] I was sorry to have him go, because he was rather congenial though an Englishman, and knew Columbia though didn't like it much. Thursday, I called on Mr. W. Archer,[2] a dramatic critic to whom Prof. Brander Matthews had given me a a card. He was pleasant, but I cannot get that intimacy which I do with younger and less English people. I have another invitation to lunch next Tuesday, and one to tea on Sunday, with invitations to call at two more houses. So you see everybody is being polite, though I do not think I shall be able to form any very permanent connections. Yesterday George Lyon appeared in town (he left to-day for N. Y.), and we made a day of sight-seeing, he spending money on me quite royally. We did the Tower of London and the Guildhall and the Temple church at St. Bartholomew's, the oldest in London; had dinner at Picadilly Circus, and then went to see "Joseph and his Brethren",[3] which was spectacular but hardly worth while. Sunday, I had a bus ride of 15 miles out through Kew, Richmond, and Twickenham to Hampton Court Palace, which had just been reopened, on account of a lull [?] Suffragette storm which had caused most of the palaces to be closed to the public. The old villages are now built up almost solid, and old England is rarely in evidence, though there are some beautiful public parks and commons still kept, with noble beach trees and birches, and graceful feathery trees which make the scene quite different from our own woods at home. Hampton has the loveliest gardens and lawns, bright with flowers of all kinds, and quantities of roses though it was the last of September. And thousands of people strolled over the lawns and through the walks and down the great avenues of beech trees, making it look like a great house party. And in the

Thames there were many boats, and while luxurious house-boats moved along the edge, and the banks covered with people, so that it seemed that all England must be out making holiday. In the morning I went to service at Westminster Abbey, where the congregation sits not in the nave, but between the choir and the altar, the seats facing each other. The tombs and statues both here and in St. Paul's are both vulgar and depressing, and I quite longed for the beautiful churches of the Continent where they have some taste, and their temples of God are not disfigured by bad marble statues of generals and men of war who "fell gloriously" in some raid upon a poor heathen tribe in India or Africa. Westminster, it is true, has some poets, but St. Paul's seems to have nothing but quantities of generals, and is very ornate and shabbily pretentious inside. The most beautiful churches in London are the smaller 18th century ones, with very tall slender and exquisitely graceful spires, and beautifully proportioned and elegant body. Some of them stand out in the middle of the street so that they can be seen in all their beauty. The Parliament buildings, of course, form one of the most stately groups in the world, and with the Abbey seen from the bridges, make a stunning picture. But London is a city of contrasts,—noble streets and mansions and parks and columns juxtaposed to the dingiest and most unattractive little streets of houses and shops, anywhere in the world. Most of the main streets leading to the city (the financial centre), are narrow, so that the traffic is enormous and fearfully congested, and travel is slow unless you take the Underground which is at a tremendous distance below the ground, (with elevators at each station), and besides is so fearfully and wonderfully made that you need a map all the time to get around.

The weather has been very good, unusually warm and a little close, but clear, although even at best, English sunlight is a pale affair. Londoners waste a lot of daylight, because, although it is light now before 6, you can't get breakfast till nearly 9, and nobody gets to work before 9:30 or 10. And it is almost completely dark by 6 P.M. when they are beginning to stop work. It is just their stupid habit, I suppose, which prevents their rationally organizing their day so as to get all the light they can.

[no signature]

[1]Paul Monroe, a Professor at Teachers College, compiled the five volume *Cyclopedia of Education* (1910-1913), which traced the development of pedagogy from ancient to modern times.

[2]William Archer made Ibsen acceptable to English and American audiences. He was a free-thinker and a believer in spiritualism. Bourne did not admire him greatly. Brander Matthews was a famous English Professor at Columbia who specialized in drama criticism.

[3]A play by Louis Parker. It did not receive good reviews, partly because it attempted to blend Biblical language with contemporary speech, and partly because it indulged in spectacle and melodrama rather than in substance.

47

to Sarah Bourne
(Transcript Columbia)

London
Oct 4, 1913

I have been pleasantly occupied this week in visiting people to whom I had cards of introduction, but I find them so stiff and insular, not at all interested in the broad outlook on the world and the curiosity about it and the readiness to discuss any aspect of it, that I and my New York friends are accustomed to. These people, although intellectual and several of them distinguished, are quite provincial in their views, never seem to have let their thoughts stray off their little island except to fear that Germany's going to eat 'em up, and are narrow in their sympathies and quite without imagination. Bligh was a very good specimen, indeed, rather more human than most of them. Mr. Horwill, the London correspondent of the Evening Post was very nice, but he had lived in New York for several years and was broadened out a little. He had me down to tea last Saturday and took me over the beautiful botanical gardens of Kew. His wife's name being Bourne, there appeared another bond of sympathy. Unfortunately he lives far away and is not very young. Sunday I called on the Webbs, who are very great people, Fabian Socialists, and have written books of great influence. Their positiveness and masterful qualities of leadership make them unpopular outside their circle of radical writers and politicians, but they seem to enjoy this unpopularity, and are very influential just the same. You will find in H. G. Wells' novel, "The New Machiavelli", what everybody says is them, in the characters of Mr. and Mrs. Bailey. Mr. Webb talked very informingly and pleasantly to me; Mrs. W. went to sleep. Tuesday I went to lunch at the Alison Phillips'. He is one of the editors of the great London Times, but quite too conservative for me. His wife and her sister were very charming, and I would like to see more of them, but they didn't ask me to call, and I can't make out whether I am supposed to want to and say so, or wait until I am asked. Thursday night I did a stupid thing, which almost queered me with a rather interesting friend, Professor Montague[1] had given me a letter to. This Mr. Kemp wrote me an amusing note saying he would call on me and take me out to dinner. I, who had been calling on so many people all the week, stupidly read it "call on him", so we both went at the appointed hour and sat in each other's halls, waiting vainly for each other. He wrote me a very clever note, (reminded me of Paul), the next day, in which he expressed doubts of my existence and dark suspicions of the Hand of the Evil One in it all, and turned up at noon and took me to a very old and famous Inn, a favorite of Dr. Samuel Johnson's, "The Cheshire Cheese," where we had pidgeon pie and beer and Cheshire cheese. Here I met Walter Lippmann,[2] a young writer whom I saw in New York last spring. He was on his way back to New York. Then we walked along the Embankment down to Chelsea, where we saw Carlyle's House and Whistler's studio, and had tea at a quaint tearoom along the river. He is the only Bohemian I have met, but I am not quite up to his mark. He was not so interesting as his letter would indicate, but I shall cultivate him. He offered to take me to a literary club that meets every Thursday night.

There is a very nice young American artist here at the boarding house now, originally from Chicago, but has studied in Munich and Paris, and seems to have lived all over Europe. If he gets a contract to do some book illustrations that he expects, he will spend the winter in Paris, and that will be very pleasant for me, as Paris will be more formidable than London, where one at least does know in a perfunctory way, some one. I should never want to live in England for any length of time; isn't it tantalizing that where all the books are and the language that you can understand, the physical and spiritual environment should be so uncongenial? Switzerland is still my favorite, gorgeous scenery and air, democratic, well educated, kindly people, and a standard of living these stupid Britishers know nothing about. When a nation lives so meanly and uncomfortably as they do here, it's bound to show in their faces and personalities.

Today I have been through the Parliament Buildings, with the House of Commons and Lords and the galleries, all very fine, but not particularly imposing. Everyone remarks on the small size of the House of Commons; it is a tiny room compared with the great halls of Washington.

[no signature]

---

[1]William Montague, a member of the Philosophy Department at Columbia, was at the beginning of an illustrious career. He believed that students should develop their own creeds and was thus allied to the instrumentalists, but he was also romantic enough to believe in ideals and visions. His lack of reliance on proof and his lack of concern for historical knowledge as a basis for philosophical study did not endear him to John Dewey.

[2]The two men subsequently became colleagues on the *New Republic*. Lippmann's books Bourne admired greatly. The two were sympathetic politically—Lippmann was at that time a Socialist and was impressed by Bergson—and were both young and on the rise in

popularity as essayists.

48

to Henry W. Elsasser
(Ms Columbia)

[London]
10 October [1913]

Dear Henry,
Our letters must have crossed; indeed I wrote about the same day you did; why not use the typewriter while I have it here? I have been doing London up brown since that letter, and finding myself dropping quite into my New York way of life, reading a little and writing a little and calling, and seeing the galleries and sights; the difference is the people, for I do not find anyone who remotely compensates for my New York friends. My first dozen Englishmen were the most frightful old Tories you ever saw, and I began to feel desperate, almost like throwing a bomb at the House of Lords. I made no kind of a hit, and usually found myself tangled up in a long and devastating argument on Socialism. Lately some Liberals have turned up, but their opinions don't hang together in the fabric which I expected and I cannot predict what they are going to think next. The water-tight compartment intellect seems much more common over here. My Liberalism, for instance, would hang Home Rule, Disestablishment, Land Reform, Old Age Pensions, democratic education, woman suffrage, etc. all together, but here you find noble lords like the Cecils[1] out for suffrage, the women themselves coquetting with Ulster, a Secretary of the men's league for woman's suffrage, a classical master violently opposed to the teaching of science in the schools, and a Syndicalist Socialist[2] growing sentimental over the Catholic Church, just to name a few haphazard instances.[3] I will say, however, that the Tories are much more predictable than the Liberals. All agree that the lower classes are of inferior mental capacity, and that they are reasonably happy and contented with their lot. Private property is as strong as it ever was, and England is pretty well off, at least at present. Of course, the Territorials[4] ought to be made obligatory, and the Government is showing too much recklessness and lightheartedness in its dealing with foreign affairs and with the Ulster problem. But England has weathered many a gale and every one believes that her luck is perpetual. I wish we were half so complacent in America. Think of a country where there is no graft, no muckraking, no moral indignation, no prudery, no Senate investigations, no exploitation of the poor by the rich,—a country where

the papers tell you nothing but sober politics, the doings of the nobility, international complications, and occasionally a very genteel crime. The only things wrong that anybody can find are a few patent medicine and fortune-telling swindles, which are duly exposed by a weekly paper called John Bull,[5] sternly but unhysterically. There are only two theories to account for the contrast with our own continual and shrieking exposures; one is that we are much more moral and more sensitive to official corruption and social evils, and the other is that they are here much more moral and consequently don't have such things, and this I very much question. They are never weary of laughing at our Puritanical restrictions, which invite police graft, and of course their own liberality towards drink and prostitution does prevent a lot of corruption. And in the towns municipal ownership abolishes opportunities for franchises [sic] steals and the like, but I am sure that there is an enormous amount of subterranean connection between big business and government which would perfectly scandalize our American conscience, but which here is taken for granted. There is a large class of intelligent men who enjoy administrative work and give their services to their community, and this of course is a great asset, which we have no sign of at home. On the other hand the municipal ownership businesses and city administration do not strike me as much better than our own, and the unfortunate inhabitants have to pay for every bad speculation and error of judgment of their quite fallible councillors. The absence of party government in local affairs aids greatly to draw the veil over corruption, for you have no "political capital" to be made out of the mistakes and crimes of the opposition. And the Englishman has such a surpassing genius for shutting his eyes and annihilating what he does not wish to see. I begin to admire our naive, youthful traits, which make us notice everything and ask pointed and embarrassing questions about our political and social life, an attitude which over here would be distinctly bad form. In fact, we get a very much idealized picture of England from sentimentalists like F. C. Howe[6] with their picture of England advancing to State Socialism by rapid strides, of an honest, wise, capable nation, making itself over in the modern spirit as a model to all nations. As a matter of fact, the Liberals seem to be the most casual collection of divergent views, society is split up into all sorts of fantastic little intellectual groups, who make no attempt to understand each other; a country more than ordinarily destitute of imagination it seems to me. One of my own pet delusions was that a status quo had been worked out with the trades-unions,[7] that they had put themselves in a strong and stable position of collective bargaining and had shown the possibility of the gradual improvement of labor's condition by sound, steady organization and wise leadership. But ever since I have been here, there has been a succession of the most violent and devastating strikes, combinations of masters fighting the unions in the most early nineteenth century spirit, refusing to recognize the unions and using the police quite à la Paterson to bludgeon them into submission. And in the cotton trade itself, the oldest and best organized, local unions are going on strike against the express orders of their own officials, repudiating them altogether as simply allies of the masters. The sympathetic strike is being used more and more with telling effect, and has led to organized sympathetic defense, the masters of Great Britain helping to support the terrible Murphy in Dublin. In short, it pains me to think how we have allowed ourselves to be hypnotized by England; we need to see it as the stupid, blundering, hypocritical beast it is. London is frightfully poor in art; the National Gallery has a few stunning Italian master-pieces, but the ranges of British art—no wonder Ruskin loved Turner,[8] for he was the only passable person they had—with the Pre-Raphaelites[9] and sickish Stevens and Moores and Leightons and Millaises are almost pathetic. Some of them may pass in a black and white reproduction, but in their crude original colors, they are pretty bad. In fact, Rosetti[10] is quite the best of the bunch. And only four Whistlers! All the rest and the Sargents, etc., locked up in Dukes' houses from which they never stir. There is nothing like the social spirit which our millionaires show. One feels everywhere that grudgingness, that insensitive-ness to the social call. And music! No opera, except a few weeks in the Spring! A symphony orchestra with a very unartistic English conductor, Wood, and no-thing heard about town but "Oh, you beautiful Doll!" and all the worst Ameri-can importations. Really an awful place. New York fairly glows by its side. Is it the silly aristocratic glamor and a certain hard intellectuality, really shallow and insular, which hypnotizes so many Americans for England. It is a most uncom-fortable place to live in; the standard of living, even among well-to-do people is amazingly low. What a country!

I read the clippings with great interest. That man Muensterberg[11] is a national disaster; he should have long ago been deported as an undesirable alien. He is so oblivious to every psychological theory but his own, and seems to know nothing of the new doctrines, which show that it is exactly this repression of unwelcome and shameful ideas and aspects of life that cause all sorts of spiritual havoc; that the great need is that life shall become conscious and all its aspects "sublimated" into the main body of the personality. He seems quite ignorant of the fact which I have proved in my own case, that "this instinctive emotion of mysterious respect" can co-exist perfectly in the same mind with the most disturbing and constant erotic emotions and fantasy; his theory would keep them both running in insulated channels, to the immense confusion of life and the loss of energy. He doesn't recognize that most boys and girls are not well-integrated, hardly intellectual, people like himself with well-knit systems of ideas which absorb the attention and keep the mind away from eroticism, but rather unstable, slightly neurasthenic, amateurs, whom the shame and the mystery of sex inflame, but who would often be perfectly capable, particularly at an age when they are most spiritually sensitive, of working the whole subject, if thor-oughly understood, into their personality, and acquiring a conscious control of it, together with a healthy sensitiveness to the enormous part sex plays in life. For I don't at all believe that this "psycho-physiological reverberation in the whole youthful organism" is the bad thing he assumes. It is the basis for instance of most of the sense of beauty, and we need a lot more of it. For if it is really "psycho-physiological", it will mean a sensitiveness to the complete charm of the other sex, both spiritual and physical, and will result in a fine sense of discrimination and appreciation, so that it would seem to be actually the best prophylactic against beastly indiscriminate lust. If a man has a real sensitiveness to feminine charm, I don't see how he can physically bring himself to consort with dirty women. It is only because this Puritanical policy of repression brings everybody up to an idea of the complete divorce of the spiritual and the physical, to a concept of the "nice" girl as all spiritual—as in the romantic novel —and the prostitute as all physical, that the double life is possible. I enclose a sample of what the Suffragettes are doing in England.[12] Christabel [Pankhurst] is certainly a doughty woman! But a thing like this, I think, has more value than almost all the literature on the subject I have ever seen. That a woman should be instructing men in such a matter and in England, the land of "respectability" is certainly piquant. Of course it would be "obscene matter" in the U. S. Also I send a sample of English enlightened cultured opinion on America; it fairly makes you despair. Dickens is immortal!

I am very fond of "Walden" too; glad you like it. It is heroic, but I should think rather mystical for you. I see a thread running through Thoreau, Emerson, Whitman, and William James, of a sense of a background, mystical, inscrutable, but healing and beneficient,—my idea of religion. Have you read Royce's book on "Problems of Christianity"[13]; stupendous, audacious, no one but an American could have written it. And I have been much impressed by Meredith's "One of Our Conquerors"; out of oceans of tortuous irritating irrelevence, emerges a splendid figure of a woman modern. Everything else, as in all Meredith, is fishy, unplausible, but she *glows!* You see I am compensating for lack of my sympathetic friends by debauch of novel-reading. Have found Bennett's "Clayhanger" and "Hilda Lessways" to present beautifully people as I know them; George Moore's "Esther Waters",[14] a ghastly proof of the errors of objective realism; Henry James' "The American", a wonderful study of the rubbing of our American geniality and zest for personal relations up against the stiff, depersonalized life of cultural Europe; I have been feeling the same thing in my own case.

Well, this has been a regular diatribe! I must have forgotten that I wasn't writing an essay. Life probably moves more interestingly and profitably for you. I look at London as an experience that should be done through, as perhaps a necessary part of one's education.

As ever,

Randolph B.

[1]Bourne is referring to Edgar Algernon Robert Cecil, then a Conservative Member of Parliament. He was against most Liberal measures, but supported the Suffragettes. Later he became Lord Robert Cecil. The family had been prominent in English politics for generations.

[2]A syndicalist was one who favored economic over Parliamentary action as a way for working men to attain power. The Syndicalists were in favor of strikes.

[3]Bourne is describing the climate of English politics. Under a new Liberal government formed in 1905 by Asquith, social reforms were being passed, albeit not very swiftly. Because the government depended on the Irish vote as a part of its majority, Home Rule, the ability of Ireland to govern itself, was part of its agenda. Disestablishment, the separation of church and state, was a more radical measure.

[4]The Territorials were a civil defense force.

[5]An English paper which, because of its tendency to try to uncover scandals, went through innumerable libel suits.

[6]Frederic C. Howe, *The British City, The Beginnings of Democracy* (1908).

[7]The trade-unions were attempting to gain political power in England. As late as 1900 they had no rights at all, were even held liable for all damages incurred in strikes. At this time, though, they were organizing what eventually became the Labor Party. The period up to the beginning of the War was marked by violence.

[8]John Ruskin was a famous art critic and essayist. He was undoubtedly familiar to Bourne because of his attack of laissez faire. Ruskin also defended Joseph Turner, a great English painter who mastered many styles. Ruskin called Turner the best landscape painter.

[9]The Pre-Raphealite Society was formed in 1848 as a revolt against the academic, stilted tradition of art they believe started with Raphael. The Pre-Raphealites took subjects from nature and tried to view each scene with a new perspective. Because of this new vision, they commented on the conditions of their times and concentrated on humble scenes. Millais was one of the founders of the movement.

[10]W. M. Rosetti, Dante Gabriel's brother, was a co-founder of the Pre-Raphaelite Society.

[11]Hugo Münsterberg was one of the first to apply psychology to practical situations. He was one of the pioneers of the aptitude test. His orientation, though, was philosophical; he made a barrier between the world of purposes (philosophy) and the world of causes (science). As one of the first men specializing in applied psychology, he was concerned with Freud's theories.

[12]At this time the women were engaging in speeches and disruptive acts—window-breaking, even arson—to dramatize their point. Christabel Pankhurst was a member of the most prominent family of English feminists. She was arrested many times and eventually fled to France to avoid prosecution. She occasionally returned to England to make speeches. In 1913 her mother, Emmeline, visited America.

13Josiah Royce, friend of William James. He preached an absolute truth which went at odds with James' conception of the many possibilities of life.

14George Moore was an Irish novelist and essayist. He was vain and was called vulgar during his career.

49

to Prudence Winterrowd
(Transcript Columbia)

8 Gordon Street
London
11 October 1913

My dear Miss Prudence,

Well, I would hardly know what to make of you, if I had not been through exactly the same experiences here in London, and know exactly how you felt in New York. I could hardly bring myself to stay here the first two or three days; but after a week I was quite at home and those hideous horrors of room-hunting and strange loneliness had faded to a memory. I am really sorry you didn't try it for a week or two at least to hear some lectures and see more of Arthur [Macmahon] and Read [Lewis] ; how envious I am of them and in the Copper Kettle, the scene of so many of my delightful hours, as I suppose they told you—indeed, I tremble a little at what they may have told you about me. Didn't you fall in love with Arthur? He is one of my chiefest of admirations; alas! he doesn't write to me, but I will insist, now that he has seen you. It's quite evident that you didn't like Columbia, and I am sorry, because I think of it as my spiritual home, and I want everybody to love it. You are very good to absolve me for all your trouble, and I do console myself with the thought that you saw New York, and my stray words did not lead you half across the continent for nothing. Of course, the rooms aren't very nice, and must seem horribly shut in to one who hasn't lived in New York, and one should really get into the residence halls to enjoy life. Your college career being ended, I shall be awfully interested to hear what you do now; if it wasn't Shelbyville that caused you to waver in New York, I wonder what it was. Shall you stay in Montreal all winter? It is just the irony of fate that it is this winter of all that they should send me abroad, because I am sure I could have made you like Columbia, and stay at least a term there. I have wished myself back at times, but at this moment I cannot honestly say I am homesick. I am living a little still my gorgeous summer. And then my life here is really becoming very interesting with much reading and a little writing, and calling on people, to whom I have introductions, none of whom I find really congenial, however, because they are mostly able, effective, much older people, and I am a hazy amateur, much affected by the personal aspect of things, which always scares the Englishmen. Then the weather has been most remarkably good, ever since I have been in England, and there have always been sights to see. So England, which I hated at first is growing on me, though I shall never like it as I do my dear Switzerland where I spent such a heavenly month. Here one lives in a Bloomsbury boarding-house, a four-story Queen Anne house with a little garden behind out to which my double windows open. The average English fare, even in the houses of the comfortably off is most meagre in quantity and limited in variety, but fortunately a wise Columbia friend directed me to this Swiss Mrs. Schwarz who retains enough of the Continental flavor to give one fair bounty and quality. And all for about 7 a week, which is less than one would pay in New York, though the difference is worth it in the conveniences, of which they seem quite destitute here. Strange that England in its general standard of living should be so much more primitive than the Continent. You will think that since I have had to travel alone with limited money I have become grossly material, but I am really a very spiritual person, as long as I am not uncomfortable. I dread the cold weather, against which they make only the flimsiest defence of grate fires, and charge you enormously for those; and I shall probably be driven to Paris by December first, if not farther. I have been in correspondence with an American writer, W. M. Salter, author of a beautiful book called "Ethical Religion", who is in Munich, and I think of him as a haven of refuge, and a nucleus in a strange place; then I have friends in Lausanne, where I should love to return, except that there will not be so good libraries or so many fascinating social institutions to find out about. So I am also waiting for something to turn up. I have not tackled the British Museum, with its 4 million books, but am using the very good library at the London School of Economics, and am subscribing to Mudies from which I extract fiction—oh, a regular debauch—and while away many a pleasant evening with the great people whom I have neglected in my youth.

Do write me how it goes with you? If you were very rich, I should like to see you jumping on a Cunarder and dropping into London some fine day; the sudden contrast with poignant New York would be dramatic. I feel still very apologetic for not being in New York, and remorseful for being the means of bringing you to a disappointment at Columbia. I'm sure your Micawberism[1] will be rewarded, and surely your New York experience must have shown you, as my European (which seemed at first so formidable) did me, how easy it is to get around, and what unexpected inner resources one has.

Sincerely yours,

Randolph S. Bourne

[1]Wilkins Micawber, a comic figure from Charles Dickens' *David Copperfield* who lived a hand-to-mouth existence while producing flowery rhetoric. Micawber exposes the villain, Uriah Heap, and emigrates to Australia, where he becomes a magistrate. It is probably to this reward for his virtue and uprightness that Bourne is referring.

50

to Sarah Bourne
(Transcript Columbia)

London
11 October 1913

The weather is getting chilly and autumny, and there is a fire here in the dining room, but no signs of any in the bedrooms. There has been practically no fog as yet, and I hope the good omen will continue. The sun sets about five, but the twilights are very beautiful with reddish sky and a soft mist that makes the buildings and parks look very poetic indeed.

This has been an uneventful week. Sunday, I went down to the Catholic Cathedral of Westminster and saw a very impressive service with a magnificent procession of bishops and clergy, the bishops in their tall pointed yellow hats and magnificent gold and white robes, and Cardinal Bourne himself, the Archbishop, with his gold staff, blessing the people as he walked up the aisle. The Cathedral itself, though quite modern, is very impressive, all of brick, with a very tall bell-tower. The interior is very large, and as yet quite undecorated, with the exception of a few chapels on the side, finished in the most exquisite mosaic work and marble work that I have ever seen. The dim massive interior with the huge brick arches gives an effect of somberness and yet of gentleness which impresses me very much, and the wonderful chapels set it off most artistically. In the afternoon I went to a symphony concert for sixpence at the Royal Albert Hall, a vast circular building which holds thousands. It was a most excellent programme and well played, though London is generally poor for music,—opera only a few weeks in the spring, and a most unmusical conductor named Wood for their biggest orchestra. Really New York is much better provided for both in music [rest of letter lost]

51

to Alyse Gregory
(Ms Yale)

[London]
11 October 1913

Dear Miss Gregory,

Yours was such a beautiful letter; I see your brave and effective spirit so clearly, and cannot tell you how I admire your solution. How I wish I had the power to imitate it! Why were my ambitions, which seem so powerful and poignant to me, destined to be thwarted by outer and inner inhibitions, so that I continue to mark time, year after year, and try feebly to imagine myself, though I do not stir from the spectator's bench, into the swirl and flow of things? You feel and understand; I only imagine. How I regret, though, my presenting myself in the role of silly grovelling despair, as I did when I met you; I wonder that you would stay with me after that. I do not feel like that now. In a country and a world of thought that seems either so unsure of itself or so palpably grotesque as it does, I pluck courage that my own ideas may not be so worthless, and am emboldened to proclaim tham again. And I am so delighted to find unexpected inner resources that I was unaware of, that the dreaded homesickness and feebleness of spirit really hasn't materialized, even in this unimaginative, inartistic country, which at first I heartily despised, and still love to feed my grudge upon.

I don't believe you see my Wales friend very clearly. I wrote you on the innocent eve of the grand catastrophe, which I am yet trying to understand. He really treated me very badly; after inviting me for a fortnight, letting his wife turn me away at the end of four days, on the plea that her old mother and father were coming and they needed the room. The sort of treatment one might give, you know, to a Zulu chieftan who obviously had no feelings and whose utterly alien standards of conduct would make such rough and ready utilitarian treatment quite consort with the honorable traditions of an English country house. My disappointment in him; the transformation from a shy, sympathetic, retiring student of psychology to a greedy, egoistic, unimaginative shallowly thinking, capitalistic country gentleman; the shock of leaving, after the trouble I had taken to come; the chilliness and deplorable shabbiness of London boarding houses; all combined to upset me considerably. Fortunately, between Wales and London, a delightful American friend intervened at Rickmansworth, and I lived a week of the life of irony, and got the world back into its proper order again. The Bligh defection is really a bit of poetic justice meted out to my own grasping selfishness, which saw in him an introduction to a stimulating London world, such as to make a year of exile seem supportable. Well, perhaps his false lure was beneficient in leading me over to a not regrettable succession of experiences.

Englishmen seem to be supremely gifted in running an insulated current of an intellectual hobby quite apart from the main stream of their personality. That was my error,—in assuming that his letters and his books were himself, instead of a quite detachable hobby. I see now why they detest so the personal note in anything,—it seems to indict this dissociation which they practice, and convict their ideas of a blazing insincerity. You know I am glad that I have met you and felt your utter wholeness and genuineness,—else, after this dislocation experience I should suspect any friends whom I knew only in what they wrote. You can see how badly I am off in England, with my zest for the personal; I feel the vivid contrast everywhere, the sanctuaries I invade, the walls I thunder at, the sympathy I put out my hand futilely to grasp. How my crude, naive, genial America glows!

"One of Our Conquerors," which I have just finished, did please me mightily in the heroic Nesta, emerging,—through all that tortuous unplausibility [sic], that wallow of fishiness, which is Meredith at his most characteristic,— serene and shining and prophetic at the end. I got a feeling more intensely than ever before of what women have to struggle against, their hopeless situation in the brute stupidity of "a man's world." Perfect equality is the first indispensable step in making over that world. I like Christabel Pankhurst's campaign—doughty woman—of sex-instruction in "The Suffragette."[1] There is a field that cowardly man will hardly touch, and which must be stirred, in spite of Muensterberg and all the false psychologists.

The Fabians have made Socialism rather respectable here,[2] and I enjoy talking with them, but I am far more desperate than they, and welcome any aggressive blow, any sign of impatience with the salvation of society by our self-appointed leaders of Church and State. England is one succession of fearful strikes, and our fond theory of the triumph of orderly trade-unionism slowly levering up the working class to a position of comfort and influence is daily knocked into a cocked hat. The same raising of the unskilled to demand a share, and the opposition of the aristocracy of the skilled, that we see at home, is taking place here; and the country looks on at starving Dublin quite unmoved, while a ruthless band of employers, assisted by English federations, announce their intention of crushing out unionism in Ireland. We might be in 1813 instead of 1913. It is difficult to see that capitalism has been one whit weakened by all the struggle. If you get a chance, do read Hobson's[3] book on "The Evolution of Modern Capitalism" and "The Industrial System," the most convincing basis for Socialist economics I have seen,—to me, quite unanswerable, and filled with a noble, constructive and far-sighted spirit. I have met the Hobsons and was charmed by her,—was relenting towards Englishwomen, when it turned out she was American, born in New York and lived in New Jersey. Thus I am stamped as the insular mind, responsive only to "people like ourselves."

I enclose a specimen of my friend's handwriting. I should not have told you about him, for then I should have had your interpretation. But, I should want it now anyway. And the other; I should dearly love the impression of personality you get from that. I will help you by telling you that it is of an American girl. Will you give me a masterly character study as you did of your organizer? I should like to know him; I recognize the type perfectly. And what do you do after the fairs[4] are over? More tours and lectures? Please "go on shamelessly." Your letters are one of my chief props in this dingy country.

Sincerely your friend,

Randolph Bourne

[1]Pankhurst's newspaper.

[2]The Fabians, among whom were Shaw and the Webbs, were highly moral Socialists. They believed in individual worth and in the possibility of social reform through government. They favored social welfare programs sponsored by the government. They were considered gradualists by the Syndicalists, who favored more overt action.

[3]Hobson was a leading economist who was coming to back the social welfare programs of the emerging Labor Party.

[4]Gregory was delivering suffrage speeches at small fairs.

52

to Arthur Macmahon
(Transcript Columbia)

London
11 October 1913

Dear Arthur,

I do think you might write to me about the little dinner you had at the Copper Kettle with Miss Winterrowd. It must have been piquant, and I tremble at what could have been said about me and what she said. I have no idea what she is like personally, and it is most extraordinary that she should have found you. And then you maliciously worked in cunning old Read; too bad Harry

Chase wasn't there. Doesn't your pen feel equal to the task of conveying to me the atmosphere just as it appeared to you? Here I am in the position of intellectually luring a girl from her happy home and then deserting her intellect or letting Columbia do it for me, the very first day of our union. Pleasant role to play, isn't it? What I really do want to know—and if you love me you will tell me speedily—is she a helpless girl, who, you think, does find difficulty in taking care of herself, or has she a strong personality, with self-reliance and initiative that one can be friends with and not run the risk of having one's suggestions swallowed whole and put into execution? Because her New York attitude seems rather erratic, and it makes me extremely uncomfortable to feel in a way responsible for her coming, and her disappointment, and to find myself likely to be charged with the burden of further advice. You once advised me in a delicate situation, which I bungled—not, however, permanently. Now I throw myself on your wisdom again.

But make this incidental, if you like, to an account of your teaching experience, which I doubt not is proving both a success and a delight. And also about everybody—Read, Geddes, Harry, how you are being, how your mother and father are, and any loose gossip which you think my ravenous ears would enjoy. Thus making up for your silence all summer. I don't even know what you did then. Is this fair? I ask piteously. And Geddes might be poked a little too. Now that my travels are over, the stream of incident and adventure should be moving Europeward.

As ever,

Randolph

53

to Dorothy Teall
(Transcript Columbia)

London
23 October [1913]

Dear Dorothy,

I was delighted to hear that you are really in Barnard, and immensely flattered at the prominence which you assigned my suggestion in getting you there. That is, I hope you are telling the truth and are really enjoying it as much as you imply and are not just flattering me? For if your felicity now is great, it will surely not grow less; it is the first month that is hard, and lo! you are already finding it delightful. Don't you find it very different from the G[len] R[idge] H[igh] S[chool], quite a more serious atmosphere, where ideas are given consideration, and one is no longer playing at learning things but is in touch with great vital currents of thought? And Columbia appeals to me especially because the teachers are, few of them, the cloistered kind that one finds in some of the older country colleges, but rather men and women of affairs to whom philosophy and science are not mere games, but real aids in understanding the world and living a worthy part of it.

I'm glad to think yourself fortunate in having Professor Baldwin, for I admire him very much. Though I never took a course with him, I know him personally and always thought him one of the most charming of men, and quite the most clear-sighted of the English faculty. He is a fine critic, too, and you may be sure that his approval means something.

All the same, I hope you don't get too immersed in literary studies. Nothing seems to me more deadening than the University study of literature for its own sake, and the "scholarly" research which consists in poring over Chaucer or digging up some obscure poems of facts that the world does not need at all. I find most of the teachers of literature curiously narrow and childish in their philosophy of life and outlook on the world, much more so than any other department, and so I have always kept away from them. I do believe in courses in composition, for they can teach you effective and beautiful writing, if you have any sensitiveness to style and ideas, and one should have a general knowledge of English literary history, but any more academic study than that I consider wasted. It's because, I suppose, I find most of the literature which seems vital to me and moves me to be not included in college literary courses at all, that I am prejudiced against such courses. All this applies equally well to Latin and Greek and modern languages. I am all for philosophy and history and sociology as the true nourishment of the soul.

Dr. Braun I have met and thought very attractive and unpedantic; Miss Thomas, only once or twice, but she knows a very intimate friend of mine named Geddes Smith. I hope you may meet Arthur Macmahon; perhaps you are taking a course with him; I hope you are [. . .] I had the pleasure of playing 500 with (Psyche)[1] one night at Prof. H---'s house, and thought her as you say, very peculiar, but did not know her extraordinary history. Her name is so adorable [. . .] and her appearance is so completely unlike any idea of "Psyche" that ever existed that I smile whenever I think of the poor child.

So you see all your references brought back interesting reminiscences of my Columbia life, which, as I hope, your Barnard year—or years?—will prove to you, was to me quite the most wonderful of my existence. I hope you will write me very often of your impressions and your successes. Are you living at Brooks [Hall] and going home over week-ends? If so, you probably find the comfort and the society very charming. London makes me realize the luxury of Columbia dormitories; here they do not know how to be comfortable; that is, any but the rich. But I have been favored ever since my coming with beautiful and mild weather; so have not suffered from the cold. I am enjoying London very much; the first week was very trying and I thought I should hate it; but I have met many interesting people, and find myself passing the time most profitably and enjoyingly.

Sincerely yours,

Randolph Bourne

My address will be c/o American Express Co., 6 Haymarket, London (2 lbs. postage only)

[1]Teall is protecting the identity of one of Bourne's female friends.

54

to Alyse Gregory
(Ms Yale)

London
1 Nov. 1913

Dear Miss Gregory,
    I hope by this time suffrage people have accepted Mrs. [Emmeline] Pankhurst, and that you had your meeting in Hartford and it was a great success. She seems to have stirred up things in New York and shocked the virtuous papers and citizens with her paper, or rather her daughter's paper, which has been pursuing a courageous and needed campaign of sex-education. London stood it, and I am ashamed at the ridiculous pseudovirtue of New York. I have been trying to get into the W[omen's] S[ocial] and P[olitical] U[nion] [1] meetings over here, but men are fearfully suspect and have to be vouched for by a member. I have finally met one and got a ticket for Monday. I did hear Mrs. Despard of the Woman's Freedom League,[2] a wiry flashing-eyed old lady, grim and militant, who sounded the note of "revolt." She and the other speakers had a most passionate sense of the persecutions of the Government, could hardly refrain from stormy tears, it seemed to me, when they spoke of the brutal arrests and prison tortures. Whoever began the fight, it is certain that they see

themselves now as oppressed victims, members of a sex against whom a coward-ly government is waging relentless war. They are making great capital out of the refusal of the government to arrest the Ulster insurrectionists, while devoting all their energies to hunting down the women, who are arrested at meetings with great brutality and disorder. And it is quite evident to me that in spite of all the talk of democracy and freedom in England, the Government does not hesitate to use autocratic power when it wants to, all covered in the usual British hypo-critical manner by the use of forgotten laws or the forced interpretation of others. Coming from a country where all our dirty political and financial linen is washed in public, I cannot but feel that the perfection of British justice and principles of government, the famous "purity" of public life, the efficiency of government, the absence of corruption, which we hear about so much in Amer-ica, is mostly due to the excessively tolerant view which is taken here as to what constitutes injustice and corruption. Our American conscience is infinitely more sensitive. From the gossip that I hear, it seems certain that great vested interests like the railways are allowed without question to control Parliament and the departments, and that both parties are so deeply implicated that they cannot make party capital out of the situation, even when their extremely blunt con-sciences allow them to recognize it at all. And yet everything is supposed to be actuated by principles, all enunciated with that sickening British unctuousness which makes me wish that Montcalm had won at Quebec and taken the whole coast and we had become tied up with French civilization instead of getting all our ideas from England. However, I suppose Montcalm was too late; the mis-chief had been done so long ago.

This spleen of mine does not mean that I do not like individual English-men; I have met many charming people, luminous and splendid; but it all goes to the support of my sociological theories of the enormous power of institutions, and how little the quality of the *individual* character counts in them. That is why I am a Socialist and want brand-new institutions, and why I think the Webbs and the Fabians with their approval of the Liberal programs are a bit behind the times, and not using their enormous knowledge and ability in the best direction.

London has a soft and gracious charm and there are so many people to see, and things to visit and papers and books to read that I do not do any steady work which will mount up to something. I am soaking in a great deal, but this luxurious diffuseness will keep on disintegrating me, I am afraid. My first suc-cess, if it can be called so, I realize now was too easy, and I shall have to work harder perhaps than I have the moral strength for, to make any kind of a per-manent impression. One thing, however, London has done for me,—immensely strengthened my radicalism. The old institutions, though they may have a glam-or from afar, are so cruel and unlovely on closer acquaintance that I am no long-er assailed with the doubts that did strike me occasionally at home whether I was not assailing the best possible established order of things. But I am hearten-

ed by finding girls and youths here who are going through the same crises that
some of us are in America, though how the social compulsion ever reached them
in their sheltered circles and lives I don't know. Revolt and change are in the air,
and I had such a dramatic picture of the cleavage between the generations when
I took tea with a middle-class family last Sunday. The Clapton villa probably
represented to the white-haired father and the worn, snubbed, sacrificing mother, the climax of spiritual and material success; but the educated daughters
obviously hated the place and the wearing ties of family life, and were moving
with their souls and interests in realms so unintelligible to the Victorian parents
as to make them almost of a different animal species. So many splendid women
to-day seem so much freer than the world they step into; it is like being let out
of prison, in prison garb, with no friends or money on a deserted moor. I am seeing a Welsh girl, (daughter of a country gentleman), come to London to learn of
caring for children, creches, etc. Her sister, with no higher education, and only
21, writes her amazing letters of advice, permeated with a social philosophy and
suggesting so many modern ideas. Where on earth could she have got them?
I believe in the Zeitgeist? don't you?

Your friend as ever,

Randolph S. Bourne

[1]The most militant of the suffrage organizations. They believed in civil disobedience and had waged many battles with the police. Some women had died and many suffragettes spent time in jail, during which they frequently went on hunger strikes. The Pankhurst family headed the W. S. P. U.

[2]Charlotte Despard split from the Pankhursts in 1907 because of their allegedly
autocratic control of the Suffragette movement and formed the Women's Freedom League
which, she thought, was more democratic.

55

to Carl Zigrosser
(Ms Pennsylvania)

London
3 Nov. 1913

Dear Carl,

I got your letter, but the bull was no less successful on that account. My situation has immensely improved since I wrote you; it is now rather that I have too many acquaintances to get much work done. Two of my New York woman friends have been here and that has made it very pleasant, and I have met a number of congenial people through the Sociological Society[1]; the Fabians proving rather disappointing, slightly superior people and for Socialists a little too respectable. Galsworthy is off in Devon, but I think I can get an introduction to Havelock Ellis and mean to do it soon.[2] Many of these great literary reputations fade strangely when you get close to them; Bligh's crowd knew little of Shaw and less of Chesterton and took little heed of Galsworthy or Masefield, and yet they considered themselves highly literary and were indeed one of the smartest sets in London. I can find no friends at all for poor Masefield; break the news gently to K[arl] D. R[obinson]; and all the big men seem to be running dry. There are no heroes at all in London, I'm afraid, literary or otherwise. The idealized picture that one forms of England disintegrates when you come to live here for a while.

I am so glad you are getting on so well at Keppel's[3] and think you have a fine career before you. I felt on the Continent how much life was enriched by a certain natural sensitiveness to art as evidenced in the charming villages and the carefully laid-out towns, and even the modern architecture, and how the complete lack of it here in England brutalizes the people. So if you can do anything towards spreading that sensitiveness at home you have a work before you as important as that of the best social reformer. Any general improvement in taste means a demand for a rise in the standard of living, and this rise is *the* great fulcrum, I am convinced, in social progress. Until people begin to really *hate* ugliness and poverty and disease, instead of merely pitying the poor and the sick, we shall not have, I fear, any great social advance. I am immensely interested in civic art, town-planning and kindred movements over here, and shall use all my opportunities to study them. Architecture, with communal art, landscape gardening, etc., I am almost ready to believe is the King of the arts, because of its completely social nature, and I wish I could see R[oderick] S[eidenberg] to tell him so. He is still architecturing, is he not?

I should like to hear from Anderson & Barr and Hambidge and Chase and

Macmahon, so tell them if you happen to see them. Nothing that you say makes me feel awfully homesick to be back; everything seems to be nicely refrigerating against my return. I find myself dropping into a pretty good imitation of my New York life,—reading at the British Museum, hearing lectures and speeches where I can, calling on people, and reading at home, take up my time, and there is always an interesting walk to be had through old London streets in the soft sunshine. The twilights are indescribably lovely, with a soft bluish mist and a brilliant, slowly fading western sky. The city has a genial charm, but the people lack the charm of the continent, and the institutions are very repellant to me. The whole country seems very old and weary, as if the demands of the twentieth century were proving entirely too much for its powers, and it was waiting half-cynically and apathetically for some great cataclysm. The only live thing is the militant suffrage movement, and that of course is superb, epic; perhaps this indomitable spirit of the women will save the country yet. The power that the men seem impotent to wield may pass to them, although it does look at present as if the Government had outwitted the women by the diabolically clever Cat-and-Mouse Act[4] and a deadlock had ensued, which could not be broken without revolution in earnest. Certainly I do not see how under the Parliamentary party system, suffrage is likely to be granted in a thousand years. The "Liberal" government is complete master of the country and governs in a high-handed and arbitrary manner, to my way of thinking. They have just sent Larkin in Dublin to jail for seven months, for sedition in saying that the masters in the terrible Dublin strike lived off the profits of their employees.[5] It is just what we do in America, but there we have people making a fuss about it, while here there is the most callous indifference to the whole subject, except on the part of a few valiant little Socialist papers.

I heard Shaw the other night and the next night Chesterton, and the contrast was most instructive and impressive. Shaw, clean, straight, keen, fine all the way through,—Chesterton, with the repulsive looks of a glutton, shifty, insincere, as disgusting a figure of a man as Shaw was distinguished. I don't know whether you have read much Shaw or like him, but I read him with ever new admiration and amazement at the clean strokes he makes down through the binding cords of convention and professionalism and hypocrisy and shows the possibilities of fearless, straightforward, personal human intercourse. Read "Captain Brassbound's Conversion" and imagine what the world would be like if we all had the spirit and the manners of Lady Cicely. Would it not be a heaven on earth? Some of us at any rate should try to live that heaven now. I have been luxuriating in fiction and drama lately. Tolstoy's "Resurrection"—do you know it? Henry James' "Princess Cassamassima," a superb novel with wonderful radicals in it; I'm sure you would love it. After a summer of idleness, I am discovering the joys of reading noble books, and I find enough of them that I have not read, to make me vow I will never again read a book that does not interest and delight me. It is a sheer waste of time, reading as a duty what one ought to read.

Yours as ever,

Randolph

[1]The Sociological Society was founded by liberals who supported social reform and investigations into sexual equality.

[2]Ellis was a pioneer of sex-education and of the psychology of sex. His stature rivalled that of Freud.

[3]Zigrosser was then working at Keppel's print gallery.

[4]The Cat-and-Mouse Act was the common name given the McKenna Act of 1913, which allowed suffragettes who were hunger striking in prison to be released in order to recuperate. Upon their return to health they would be rearrested. This not only ridded the jails of fasting women, but it served as a control on protestors, who were always subject to rearrest.

[5]Jim Larkin, the head of the Transit Workers Union of Dublin, led his followers in a bloody strike in 1913 which virtually shut down the city. He was an Englishman who had studied the American laborers' technique of striking while employed as a mill worker in the United States. The efforts of his union were perceived as among the beginning acts of a Labor Party (New York *Times* September 19, 1913, 4:3). Even Irish politicians were opposed to his techniques because he could slow the move toward Home Rule. Larkin was imprisoned for seditious statements and during this time the Liberal government was beseiged by Socialist and Labor members who would howl down Liberal speakers at meetings (*New York Times* November 10, 1913, 4:5). He was quickly released because the government sensed that it was losing votes (November 13, 1913, 4:4).

56

to Prudence Winterrowd
(Transcript Columbia)

London
3 November 1913

My dear Miss Prudence,

The more I think of it, the sorrier I get that you could not persuade yourself to stay at Columbia. There were certainly the things there that you say you "most desire": "knowledge," "stimulating friends," (there were my two friends for a nucleus, and I have a little protégé [Dorothy Teall], a freshman at Barnard that I wanted you to meet), and "an opportunity to justify your existence," (you would surely have been drawn into some social work and met some of the settlement people and have felt the stirrings of the feminist and social movement, and one who does that surely finds existence justified.) Having spurned Columbia for no other reasons that I can see except the horrors of getting settled in a strange place, (I do not minimize these horrors for I know them perfectly and how the imagination pictures the future as just as black as the present and one gets an intolerable sense of not being able to stand it; but a week goes, and those first hours are a dimly remembered dream,) I'm afraid you must wait patiently for the coming of these desirable things in another form. You must forgive me if I preach and even scold a little, because if I do it is only because you do not seem to value the things, to which I give so much importance in the making of my own character, in the way I do. Columbia gave me so completely those very things which you "most desire" that I thought naturally they would be given there too to any questing person who sought them like myself. I realize that it is much harder for a girl to make her way and achieve self-dependence in this world than a man; (it shouldn't be so and the feminist movement is working to change things,) but it is so now. So this excuses your discovered difficulties in New York. At the same time, it is worth a big fight to get finally standing on your own feet spiritually, with a feeling that you are a definite personality with something to say and something to do, and some kind of a career to follow. The feeling of being in control, more or less, of your own personality and career is the ideal to aim at, and until you are in that possession, you will hardly be effective. You certainly will find chances to "disseminate" at home, suffrage, (there must be a strong movement now in Indiana,) charity organization, town improvement, etc. If there is no suffrage club in your town, get acquainted with the State Association and get them to let you form one, and then make speeches, etc. All you need is not knowledge so much as an opportunity to express yourself; I imagine you have a good deal of energy, and it ought to be put to work. Study is, after all, only a sort of substitute for work, a postponement, (as my present year seems to me), of the real duty of life. And I see so many people like myself who are postponing life, when it seems as if they might step right into it. It's on the whole a very bad, maladjusted world for people without an abounding vitality and self-reliance, and the only thing for such people to do is to acquire painfully and slowly that vitality and reliance. I love to hear how people do get started and I often get some sort of clue from them. I got acquainted (in the same way in which I got acquainted with you) with such a splendid girl in Connecticut [Alyse Gregory] who is doing suffrage work speaking at fairs and on street-corners and organizing parades and pageants and, although much of it is evidently very discouraging and laborious, she is finding herself gloriously and learning life by action. I envy her tremendously and tell her so. And she is such a stunning proof that even the most constant participation in the melee of public life doesn't necessarily make women unwomanly; I think it rather tends to make them great. The militant movement here in England is tremendously thrilling; it is a sort of guerilla revolution against the Liberal Government, and the passion and enthusiasm that is excited in hosts of women quite outdoes anything I have seen before. I went to a meeting of the W.S.P.U. this afternoon; the big hall was crowded with women. Miss Annie Kersey [Kenney] [1] who had been hunger-striking and had been released at the point of death, was brought in on a stretcher amidst the most dramatic silence. These heroic women are real martyrs, for the Government treats them with great violence and at the same time refuses to prosecute the Ulster people who are threatening to resist the Home Rule bill. The militant suffrage movement is the only live thing that I can discover in England, and it makes the blood run faster to see what conventions and even laws these finely bred women will shatter to bits in a concerted campaign to make suffrage the livest issue in England. You can hardly go to church without having a woman make a speech in the most solemn part of the proceedings, or, if it is an episcopal church, chant a prayer for the women in prison. You can imagine the horror of the audience at such a breach of propriety and the real courage it takes a woman to defy this sentiment. I believe that these women have worked out a tactic of revolution which ought to win, and is a model for all revolutionary parties the world over. It is a liberal education to watch them at work.

I hope you will find a satisfactory way out of your difficulties, and I am really sorry I can't give any practical suggestions. We are all tackling this extraordinarily complex modern life together and if we don't succeed, at least we shall have had a glorious run for the money.

Sincerely,

Randolph S. Bourne

[1]Annie Kennie was a lieutenant of Christabel Pankhurst, one of the leaders of the
W. S. P. U.

57

to Carl Zigrosser[1]
(Ms Pennsylvania)

London
16 Nov. 1913

Dear Carl:—
    Your letter gave me a welcome whiff of New York life, which I was just
beginning to think I had lost touch with, having heard so sparingly from my old
friends since I have been here. You at least do not fail me, and your analysis of
R[oderick] S[eidenberg] was really a masterly one. The party made me a little
homesick, but the thought of her whom you so appositely call "this Jessie girl"
provided an offset to this momentary feeling; she gives me the cold shudders,
as I suppose she does you. I don't suppose we can add anything to the elucidation of the mystery to what we agreed upon during our all night walk with
Murray—R. S., tormented with the seven devils of sexuality, spends his working
days in the society of a female member of his own race with a business-like
determination to get married to the first attractive professional man she meets.
From this point of view the denoument seems perfectly inevitable. She had her
grip long before these more attractive people appeared on the scene; moreover—
and perhaps you don't realize the subtle compelling force of this—she conveyed
to him with every word and sentiment that she was both possible and probable.
It almost appears now as if he would have been superhuman to escape. I began
to suspect that marriage, beneath all the philosophical trappings in which he
clothed his imaginative life, was really the Leitmotiv of his desire. Now that this
is achieved he can afford to luxuriate in the fantasies of those other ideals which
were really secondary to that one. If you had heard him in the winter before his
marriage discussing marriage, you would have felt, I think, in his tones of rage
and despair a very different attitude from the "exquisite pleasure" which you
say he now finds in discussing the failure of his will to achieve the desire to do
great things. Marriage was a real ideal to be consummated as soon as possible; art
and philosophy were pleasant fantasies which before had got mixed up in the
fiery crucible of his emotions with marriage, but are now analyzed out and seen
at their true value and significance. The mechanical fantasy remains, and the soul
goes on talking about them, but the glow has faded. Of course we are all Ham-

lets; only you and I have the firm conviction that some day our will will begin to operate freely and creatively, when we get orientated in the world and get a certain poise and surety; and our activity is now bent to getting that poise and understanding the chaotic world about us. R. S. seems to lack that ideal, to have no real point of view, and his drifting is not so much that of the learner and experimenter, as yours and mine is, as that of the aesthete who has already begun to feel pleasure in his own decadences. Our decadence is hateful to us; we struggle against it, and in so doing live to a far greater intensity than does the one who sits down and contemplates it, as R. S. seems to do. He really does not want the antidote, I am afraid; it would make life too vividly grim for him; he prefers the slight intoxication that the poison gave him. He used to talk as if only the lack of leisure prevented him from achieving art and culture, and this gave me a guilty conscience, for I have had unlimited leisure, comparatively speaking, for two years, and have not used it productively at all. To make suggestions to him was like a millionaire with an inherited fortune telling a newsboy how to be rich. But now it seems to be something else that is the matter, and it will be absorbingly interesting to discover just what it is. You as the expert on the spot will have to do it.

You may be interested to know that, though I have met many intellectual types here in London, I have not seen anybody remotely resembling Hilary D.,[2] and I begin to suspect that Galsworthy is a very great artist and is weaving his characters straight out of his own personality, which is evidently a highly specialized, sophisticated, reserved one, and is not drawing from life at all. Hilary is Galsworthy, as are all the other characters in his books. The social conscience does not seem to have touched England at all, except in the shape of Christian philanthropy of the type of the poor old Oxford people who are bringing classical education into the slums and attempting to "raise the people" by means of Plato and Burne-Jones[3] and Rossetti [sic]. Toynbee Hall, a reproduction of an Oxford College, with dining-hall decorated in pale Preraphaelite figures, and library and living-room and bed-room copied bodily from the sheltered, quietistic retreats of Oxford, the whole set in the midst of the slum of Whitechapel, is one of the most marvelous[4] demonstrations of the futility of the English mind that I know. But the average intellectual liberal seems to be a very complacent sort of person, quite convinced that England is getting along all right, very impatient with theorists and extremists of all sorts, busy and happy and uncritical just like our American friends. I will say, however, that they have here much better intellectual machines, can turn their minds to almost any subject and write clearly and pertinently, if somewhat superficially, about it. This fluency and articulateness I admire, and I feel we lack it almost completely in America. The middle-class Socialists are many of them hard-headed people, thoroughly saturated with economics and history, and used to addressing working-class audiences without a trace of that patronage which one might expect. These radicals are much superior to our rather childish people, who talk with a bravado as if they were doing the most desperate thing in the world to be Socialists at all. These people over here take the thing much more naturally and cooly, and have much more of a standing. The Socialist speaking and writing seems to me on a much higher plane than at home, much more direct and definite and intellectual. At the same time it is thoroughly seasoned with revolt. Socialism is a word you seldom hear. The "Daily Herald",[5] the livest Socialist paper, speaks only of "rebels", and is making a strong coalition with the militant suffragettes, and each side is deriving tremendous strength from the fusion. Sylvia Pankhurst[6] is leading a great movement in the East End of London in co-operation with George Lansbury,[7] the Syndicalist ex-M.P., and stirring things go on over in Bow and Bromley.[8] Miss Pankhurst has several times been rescued from the hands of the police by the people, and the police seem actually to have become afraid to attempt to try any more. I went to a great meeting of working-class rebels in Shoreditch the other night, where militant suffrage and the co-operative commonwealth fused in perfect harmony. It was really thrilling to hear this audience of grimy working-men, all in the inevitable English cap, and a lot of frowsy women and girls, cheer every reference to suffrage, and to hear their cries of "Shame!" when reference was made to prostitution and venereal disease; these subjects which are so tabooed in America are discussed with the utmost freedom from public platform, at least from radical platforms, here. The suffragette papers are conducting a great campaign of education on the subject; I see that the silly police confiscated them in New York, and the papers are loading Mrs. Pankhurst with insult.[9] Well, I suppose it's a fair fight; she certainly is not gentle in her remarks. Everybody has been greatly excited about Larkin, the Dublin strike-leader, who was put in prison for the usual Paterson thing, and then when the Government found the Socialist votes piling up against them, and even the Liberals protesting, they let him out again, thus giving him an unrivalled prestige, and a sort of free ticket to make all the fuss he wants; which he is doing.

I don't know what is going on at home, except the Mexican trouble and the New York election. You don't know what a relief it is to have all the scandal and mud-throwing and disaster sifted out in coming across the sea, for the English papers print only the most important political news from America and nothing else. Here the press is in a conspiracy to make England appear as Paradise, where no misery, poverty, or corruption ever enters in, so one's nerves are not kept raw by reading the papers, as they are at home.

I am going to Oxford this week, more as a pious duty than with the thought that I will obtain any inspiration there, and about the first of the month I shall burn my bridges and move on to Paris. It will be as bad as leaving home, for I am settled here now, have some very delightful acquaintances, and get invited around and made welcome in quite the same fashion that I did in New York. Mr. Bligh, on whom I counted for my London life, I have almost forgotten; I haven't seen him at all, and he was of absolutely no use. Indeed he was almost insultingly positive that a person of my peculiar temperament and extreme ideas would be quite unable to get along with Londoners at all; his predictions of an absolute vacuum of friends fortunately proved quite unfounded. In Paris there is a most charming young American artist named Bocher; he had two decorative drawings in the Studio for July or August of this year. Look them up and see what you think of them. He is now working on an illustrated edition of "Pelleas". He was here in London for a while, getting contracts, but this drab place soon got too much for his sensibilities, and he moved back to Paris, where I look forward to seeing him again. Mr. Green of the History dept. at Columbia is also studying in Paris, and he will be a link with home. Dana[10] has given me some letters to Frenchmen that he knew when he was lecturing at the Sorbonne, and there is a Madamoiselle who wants to translate my "Philosophy of Handicap"into French; I shall look her up.

I had an interview the other day with Havelock Ellis, but it wasn't very satisfactory, because these Englishmen don't know how to flow genially, and you have to conduct a cross-examination as if you were a newspaper reporter. I asked him some questions, which he answered as if he was afraid his answers would offend me, and he would therefore have to be very guarded, and then I found myself expressing my own views on the subject, and then we stopped. He is a very fine tall figure with bushy grey hair, and a fine white beard; looks very much like Bernard Shaw, but much more retiring and gentle. Do you read much Shaw? The more I read him the greater he becomes to me; he is certainly one of the great prophets of the day, and his prestige and influence here are enormous. He writes to the papers a great deal, and each letter turns England upside down. Most middle-class people, in order to save their faces and make themselves impregnable against his keen thrusts, pretend that he is a jester and a buffoon, and so complacently discount everything he says. But he is undoubtedly the most influential man in England, and there is a sort of earthquake in the prevailing order every time he opens his mouth.

The publisher, Dent, has perpetrated an enormity in the shape of an illustrated edition of "Leaves of Grass". Numberless full-page illustrations by one Margaret Cook, in lurid colors, of naked people with their arms around each other, gazing at a sunset , are supposed to illuminate the divine pages of the divine Walt. Heaven forgive her! Have you seen the book? I warn you thus to spare you pain. The book itself is beautifully printed, an edition de luxe; I think I will write them a letter suggesting the publication of an expurgated edition, it being the pictures that are to be expurgated.

As ever,

Randolph

[1]Part of the manuscript of this letter is lost. I have relied on the Columbia transcription for a portion of this letter.

[2]Hilary Dallison is the protagonist of *Fraternity* (1909). The character, who is an upper middle class writer, is roughly autobiographical.

[3]Sir Edward Burne-Jones was a romantic painter and stained glass artisan. He was influenced by the Pre-Raphaelites. He was most famous for his stained glass windows.

[4]The manuscript letter begins here.

[5]The *Daily Herald* was founded in 1911 by the emerging Labor Party.

[6]Sylvia Pankhurst was the sister of Christabel.

[7]George Lansbury resigned from Parliament because the Liberal Party did not support the suffragettes, joined the struggle, and was imprisoned in July 1913. He was released under the Cat-and-Mouse Act and was widely respected in Labor circles for his honesty. He was a reluctant Syndicalist who believed that the workers should strike since they were not receiving satisfaction. He became Editor of the *Daily Herald* in December 1913.

[8]Bow and Bromley were areas of the East End of London in which labor and suffragette action was prevalent.

[9]In September 1913 the *New York Times* believed that Emmeline Pankhurst would have no effect on the American situation, that she would be shouted off the stage by right-thinking Americans (September 9, 6:3). Upon her arrival in October she was detained and was, at one time, ordered deported (October 19, II, 1:8), but she eventually did go on a lecture campaign.

[10]Henry Wadsworth Dana was a member of the famous American literary family. He taught modern European literature at Columbia but was dismissed during the war because of his pacifism. Bourne travelled with Dana through Germany in the summer of 1914 and returned to the United States with him.

58

to Henry W. Elsasser
(Ms Columbia)

London
21 Nov. [1913]

Dear H. W. E.,

My impressions must not be taken too seriously as permanent and serious views of my environment. I find I write in moods and then come to repent afterwards the extreme bias of what seemed at the time almost axiomatically true. There is a horrible danger in being a philosopher, for one cannot help generalizing on isolated incidents; the more powerfully they affect one, the more obvious seems the truth of the generalization. On the eve of my departure from England I will make a desperate attempt to tell the truth as to what I think of it. First, there comes the impression that I have had an extraordinarily good time, not a lively time, but a full time, during which my social instincts have been periodically, if gently, stimulated. The weather has been wonderful, in fact, they tell me, absolutely unprecedented for Autumn, and this has formed a background for a contentment which would have been rudely shattered by fog and gloom. Several unusually charming people were here at the boarding-house until a couple of weeks ago, and the chatter with them I enjoyed extremely. Last to go was a young German, (the wife of a Hauptmann) who had been with him to China, and most of the German and English colonies. She had an indescribably charming accent, dressed in wonderful colors, which were just on this side of good taste, and withal almost converted me to the old view that a woman is justified in life simply by being superlatively ornamental. When she went with seven large pieces of luggage, I was almost tempted to see her off at the station, but did not wish to offend any Teutonic codes of honor, and have to fight a duel with a German Hauptmann. (I foresee that this effort to give you a perfect scientific account of the background of my satisfactions is going to be attended with difficulties. However, I forge ahead.) Next came the fact that I would meet, either by introduction, or by my own initiative, men who were interested in sociological things who talked to me with the greatest of enthusiasm and kindness. There seems to be a magic in the phrase, "Columbia Fellow", although I always introduce it apologetically through a deep sense of my incapacity in the esoteric world of research and scholarship. What I like best, of course, is to drive them and guide the flow of their thought by an occasional intelligent question or ironic remark, and with some I have had a most thrilling time. There was a morning with Schiller[1] at Oxford; I first heard him lecture on Logic to his class, and then he took me up to his library and talked in the most earth-shaking way,

until most of the philosophic thought and ways of thinking of the centuries lay
in ruins at his feet. As a philosopher he is of course a pariah at Oxford, and perhaps the presence of a sympathetic pragmatist like myself was like wine to his
head, but it certainly was an experience not to be forgotten. He is the most
charming of personalities, slender and dark-bearded, with the brightest and most
expressive of blue eyes. In his lecture he did up the Platonic idealism so delicately and ironically that I wondered if any of the youths, who were faithfully
taking down every word he said, really got what he was driving at. Then there
was Marett,[2] the anthropologist, living in an old Saxon tower at Exeter College,
a thousand years old, who told me about his luck in uncovering Neanderthal
people and wooly rhinoceroses right under his doorstep. I also saw McDougall,[3]
the social psychology man, for a few minutes, and heard him lecture on the sex-
life in childhood. I should like to know what would happen to an American
professor who spoke as plainly as he did in a college lecture. My greatest adventure, however, was the other night here in London with H. G. Wells. On the
eve of my departure I managed to summon enough courage to write to him my
desire to see him. I received in reply a printed document, evidently kept at hand
for such occasions, mentioning the uncertainty of his movements, but extend-
ing a faint hope that if the addressee would ring him up at his flat, he might be
able to arrange an interview. But then there was in his own handwriting the information that he would be at home that evening after 9:30 and that several
interesting people might be there; then came the ominous words, EVENING
DRESS, which my resources, of course, did not include. I thereupon performed
a philosophical exercise of the most approved Benthamite description, balancing
carefully the pleasures likely to be obtained by hearing Wells talk and the pains
likely to be incurred both by myself and the company from my gaucherie in
dress. Needless to say the distastefulness of staying away overcame the thought
of the possible humiliations, and I went. I found a company of a dozen or so,
all grouping themselves around a very distinguished Mohammedan Indian gentleman, here on some important political mission, and hinting of Indian Nationalism and all sorts of undercurrents of great significance. He had with him two
Indian students just finishing their course at Oxford. Then there was William
Archer, who murdered Ibsen into English, and H. W. Nevinson,[4] a famous correspondent and rebel, who has opposed the African slave-trade and got into
trouble in Russia and seen most of the world, and Sir Sidney Olivier,[5] who
recently jeopardized his post in the Government by speaking at a meeting of
protest against armaments. I spent my time in a group of Wells and Indians, and
we went over art, religion, the caste system, East and West, for all of which the
Indians supplied the facts while Wells played around them with his most luminous and beautiful mind. It was a great adventure; there were no discoverable
humiliations, and though I heard later that Wells has a reputation for fierceness,
nothing could have been more genial than his manner towards everybody that
night.

As for the other great men, Shaw has a position which seems absolutely unrivalled; when he lectures, the streets have to be cleared by the police; when he expresses himself on any public question, which he is doing all the time in letters to the "Times", he stirs up a tremendous row; he speaks at labor meetings and puts the Government in a hole by uttering fierce words of sedition, of a much worse nature than those they have just put some poor fellow in prison for uttering. The nonchalant partiality with which this Liberal government applies the laws is an object lesson in the "Civil liberties" and all the rot that Butler[6] talks about in Anglo-Saxon institutions. Larkin goes to prison under a law which forbids the saying of anything which will bring his Majesty's government into disrepute or tend to cause feelings of hostility between classes of his Majesty's subjects! a law which, as Shaw points out, would jail every member of Parliament who voted for the Parliament Act,[7] curtailing the powers of the House of Lords. A man has just been sent to prison for four months hard labor for blaspheming the Christian religion; Gilbert Murray,[8] in a letter to the "Nation", asks that the law be applied consistently and offers to furnish to the Home Secretary ample evidence on which to send to hard labor for a year or so a large number of his learned colleagues, several clergymen and at least two members of HIS MAJESTY'S Government. It is a wonderful country, and all the more wonderful for the nauseating hypocrisy about itself which it has got embedded in literature and in the minds of most of the moulders of public opinion on both sides of the Atlantic.

I enclose some more clippings on America as seen by English poets. And also some letters of Shaw on Gaby[9]; this question is convulsing England now and has been convulsing it in varied forms for scores of years I suppose. They want a censorship on books now as well as plays. Shaw of course sees red whenever the censor is mentioned, and with a Bishop thrown in the whole subject inspires him to his most brilliant flights. Apart from Gaby, woman suffrage is causing havoc in the Church, and Bishops and Deans are belaboring each other in the correspondence columns of the "Times" over the question of militancy and forcible feeding. I only wish we had some such institution at home where our best intellectuals would fight out questions in public as they do here; it is both entertaining and instructive, and necessary if intelligence is ever going to count for much in influencing opinion. There is not the same prejudice here against the most enlightened people getting intellectually excited over an idea or an abuse; they do not leave this here so much to the little fellows like Hutchins Hapgood[10] and Upton Sinclair. Speaking of Hapgood, did I thank you for the Harper's Weeklies; they are as bad as I feared. That silly twaddle about the angelic Administration finishes Hapgood (Norman,[11] I mean) for me. And the whole paper seems so clumsily written, after a diet of English Radicalism. I do not wish to be supercilious, (I'm clumsy enough myself), but this stuff of Harper's seemed curiously infantile and sentimental after the clean robustness of the New Age and the New Statesman and the Clairon.[12] There is a very young woman over here writing under the name of Rebecca West[13] (pace Rosmersholm), who, if she doesn't look out will put all these other fellows like Chesterton et als. out of business. Splendid stuff. I enclose a clipping.

As ever,

R. S. B.

P. S. I find I haven't been able to give the judicial summary I started out to; but this will have to do.

R. S. B.

Address me at Paris after this, Am. Ex. Co., 11 Rue Scribe.

[1]Schiller and Bourne talked on English education. Bourne's notebooks indicate that Schiller remarked that many Oxford graduates went into government service and that they ended up governing India. Bourne reflects that there is a "striking analogy with Chinese system, which produced rather able govt. officials, by preposterous system of education." They also talked about the English philosophical climate, which Schiller characterized as Platonic, and about Schiller's belief in pragmatism.

[2]Marret said that Rhodes Scholars were looked up to by British students as articulate, intelligent, and athletic. The archeological remains to which Bourne refers were located on Marret's home island of Jersey.

[3]Bourne's notebook does not record any results of his meeting with McDougall, who was, evidently, a British Freudian psychologist.

[4]Nevinson, a journalist who was primarily a war correspondent, was nevertheless a pacifist.

[5]Sir Sidney Olivier was a governmental official who had risked his position by denouncing armaments. He was a Fabian Socialist. Later he served on the agricultural board. Olivier had been Governor of Jamaica.

[6]Nicholas Murray Butler, President of Columbia University, whom Bourne disliked. Butler was an Anglophile, whose position as a defender of civil liberties Bourne knew was suspect.

[7]The Parliament Act of 1911 took power away from the House of Lords. It stated that a bill which passed Commons during three different sessions could be sent to the royalty for ratification without the consent of Lords. The part played by the Irish members of Commons in the passage of this Act gave a sense of urgency to the implementation of Home Rule.

[8]Murray was a classicist and translator, and a Liberal. He advocated international understanding, and union, among nations.

[9]Gaby Deslys was a performer at the Palace Theatre who was accused of improprieties by some Anglican clergy. Shaw came to her defense as a method of attacking prudery and censorship.

[10]Hutchins Hapgood was a novelist and essayist. He was a member of the Greenwich Village and Provincetown circles.

[11]Norman Hapgood edited *Harper's* and was a strong supporter of Wilson. He was considered an influential essayist.

[12]All of these were Socialist newspapers.

[13]West's real name was Cecily Isabel Fairfield, but she changed it to that of one of Ibsen's heroines. She was six years younger than Bourne, but had achieved notoriety by the time she was twenty. She was an English feminist, journalist, and novelist. *Romersholm* is the name of the play by Ibsen in which West's namesake appeared.

59

to Alyse Gregory
(Ms Yale)

Paris
11 Dec. 1913

Dear Miss Gregory,
      It seems to me like a long time since I have written to you, and I make reparation now at the end of a long dull day spent in waiting for a friend from America [Harry Chase] who electrified me by a note that he would be in Paris, and then did not appear on this expected day.
      As you see I have moved my Cenates [?] on to France, in the hope that Paris would develop such surprises and interests and insights as London did, with the advantage of the truly foreign atmosphere over the always reminiscent suggestions in London of our ways at home, often sinister suggestions too, which showed the beast in our Anglo-Saxon ancestry and the hard inhumanity which lies beneath the crusted hypocrisy of the face that English institutions expose to the world. I have a tremendous admiration for the French civilization, its intellectual power, its amenity of life, and its capacity for new ideas and for social change, and it is tantalizing not to be able to get into it and feel it here in somewhat the way I felt the English. Just a command of the language, which I should

have taken some pains to acquire if I had known I was coming for so long a stay. I can read easily, but my ear is extraordinarily bad and slow and to be immersed in a sea of unintelligible sound that one is straining to analyze, is a very discouraging experience. And the difficulties of getting settled in this region about the Sorbonne are formidable to one who comes after the season has opened. The University is inspiring, though just as a spectacle,—the big ampitheatres with great mural paintings by Puvis de Chavannes[1]; the crowds of eager people waiting at the doors and rushing in for seats half an hour before the lecture begins; the concourse of students, of all nationalities, men and women, wonderful types, in the courts and corridors; the distinction and elegant diction of the professors; the tremendous list of courses and the strong psychological and sociological bias of the thinking. Paris must be the greatest University in the world. When I think of poor little Oxford, where I spent a week, it seems like an elementary school. And the treasures of libraries and special schools and musées here are colossal; the contrast with London is almost unbelievable. Only the comparison can reveal the poverty and barbarity of the English civilization. I cannot puzzle out the basis for the myth of English greatness. And the fact that most of these treasures here are public and national only emphasizes the contrast. For here is this incomparable University free to everyone, while Oxford, of course, is a luxury, and even the University of London with its poor equipment, is costly to the student.

You will see that my impressions tend to take a large and general manner, and this is very discouraging to my writing, for my mentor of the "Atlantic" [Sedgwick] begs me to be more concrete. I am working on a town planning article now which I don't think even then will please him; because whenever I introduce details, it sounds as if I were writing an advertisement. I am taking such a delight, however, in getting impressions, though I do not know how I shall ever use them. Two things inhibit,—one is, that all these places have been written about ad nauseam, and the other is, that I cannot envisage any clientele of readers, and so do not know just the light in which to present impressions. I enjoyed writing home about my trip to my local New Jersey paper, because there I could be just as naive and superficial as I liked, without feeling that anybody knew it; but I can't do that with my serious friends, can I? Anyway, nobody would print it.

I can't for the life of me remember whether I have already thanked you for your fortune telling. You are either really gifted with clairvoyant power, or knew what comments would please me. The man I don't make out at all; he remains a dead weight on my soul, rather painfully too, for I had made much of him imaginatively; the girl I like, though how she can have any character and write in the atrocious shiftless hand she does is a mystery. How do you sense qualities through such awful handwriting? I was almost willing to believe that it proved some serious spiritual defect. And did I mention my curiosity about the youth, named Miller, you mentioned? I really can't place him at Columbia, unless he is a very amiable, large-eared black-haired young man that I knew slightly in one of the literary societies. I wonder at his competence to judge of my influence. I have just sent off a long defi [sic] to the college paper concerning an impudent attempt to quote my college article in favor of college fraternities and aristocratic feeling. The dangers of irony again! I am quoted by an influential student there, in an article of his, as saying that this snobbishness is inevitable with American youth,—with the assumption that I imply that it is justified! I could not resist a challenge like that, and I only hope "Spectator" will find space for my sermon on democracy.

I am very curious to know the truth about Mrs. Pankhurst's reception in America; the English papers were unanimous in their reports of a "frost." Do you think she created any lasting feuds or breaches in the suffrage associations where she went? Some of my friends who heard her write me they didn't like her. If I don't like English pruderies and bourbonisms, will I be able to endure American when I get back?

Sincerely,

Randolph Bourne

Address: American Express, Paris.

[1]Pierre Puvis de Chavannes, a French painter influenced by Delacroix. The mural he painted in the Pantheon was entitled *Life of St. Genevieve*. His paintings were noted for their serenity. He stood between the neo-classicists and the impressionists.

60

to Carl Zigrosser
(Ms Pennsylvania)

160 rue St. Jacques
Paris
13 Dec. [1913]

Dear Carl,

Three letters from you in four days is a wealth of riches and demands an immediate reply. I had already had a card from Chase on Wed. mailed from the steamer before he left England. I flew to the Am. Exp. Co, and left my address, and have been waiting in the utmost impatience for him ever since. Neither him or a word from him, nor any explanation of his coming, until this afternoon, idly glancing at a paragraph in the Paris N. Y. Herald which I picked up, I encountered the startling information about the disappearance of Miller's brother, whom I met with Miller in Vevey this summer. This makes me all the more impatient and curious, and I shall feel much injured if Chase is carried back home without my seeing him. I do not feel at all homesick to be back in N. Y. but I feel at times a great rush of desire to have my friends right here in the midst of this life; a few days of Harry would be some satisfaction to this appetite. (By the way, is not his wife Olive as charming as R[oderick] S[eidenberg]'s is not? and all the more because though she seems so soft and kittenish, she has real quality and fibre).

I am realising every day how much it means to me to be seeing Europe in this leisurely way, living the foreign life both practically and imaginatively, and soaking in the atmosphere, and converting everything into impressions. Everybody else has done it, of course, and has written it in countless books, but one has to feel it and see it to get any grip of it at all. I do not miss American news, I am ashamed to say; I don't see any of the American papers or magazines. When I was in London I got to feel like a very advanced Liberal and would get so excited in political argument as to forget that I wasn't a native. There was something almost dramatic in the way I pulled down the curtain on England, with a resolve, when I came here, ten days ago, not to look at anything but a French book or newspaper. And though the Dublin strike was still on, and the leaders were jockeying over Ulster, and the Indians were revolting in South Africa, and everything was unsettled, I bravely cut it all off and have read of nothing for the past week but the new French ministry and the Saverne affair in the Reichstag, which France is enjoying to the full, with a quiet and beautiful irony that makes the papers a delight to read. To see the "wackes" of Alsace-Lorraine convulse the German Empire and shake the Constitution is certainly a spectacle calculated to salve many an old wound of 1871.[1]

From my experience with foreign newspapers I am convinced that we Americans are by far the most cosmopolitan people in the world, unless it be the Swiss. We can get from our press a wide view of European affairs that it is impossible to obtain anywhere over here. But the French papers are very delicious; human and ironical, with a running comment on everything. They tell you how the great man looked when he made his speech, the emotions that filled his frame, while the English treat everything human as if it were a block of wood; they must be the least introspective of peoples, for their writing, even their best literature, never gives a hint about how people are feeling inside them. England made me just about ready to renounce the whole of Anglo-Saxon civilization. Henceforth the Irish, the Welsh, the French for me, no Anglo-Saxons. And my judgment is all the more impartial because I was exceptionally well treated in England, after the first experience with Bligh. He was not Welsh, by the way; I was thinking, when I included the Welsh in my non-Anglo-Saxons, of two wonderful girls at Builth, whom he introduced me to, and whom I saw later in London. The prospect of seeing them again on the continent in the spring seems almost too good to be true. For they are beautiful and serious and sympathetic and high-spirited. Their only misfortune is to be daughters of an [sic] country gentleman who does little but hunt foxes, while his wife is a foolish, anti-feminist, would-be society person, who wears big hats and spends her winters in Italy. The elder girl came to London for the autumn to try her hand in social settlement work, and worked so hard in a creche that she got pleurisy, and was last heard of recovering in Brighton, where her mother and sister were. Before this, I had been to a number of Socialist meetings with her, and it was by insisting on going to the big Larkin meeting when she had a cold that she got sick. She is about my age and her sister is about yours, and the miracle is that without any college education or experience of the world, they are both so well-read and so sympathetic and interested in social movements. They can ride to hounds one day and talk on Socialism the next with the most eager interest, and altogether they are the only real *souls* I have met in England. With them I felt thoroughly buoyant, natural, at home; elsewhere, even among radicals, I felt deeply serious,—over-serious; for it is the pride of the Englishman not to display emotion over anything, or take anything seriously. This spiritual frivolity (which is very different from any real buoyancy and lightness of heart, such as the French seem to have, combined with a fundamental profundity and a keen intellectuality which makes all English thinking appear like child's play,) gets on one's nerves in England. And here in Paris, though I cannot get much into the life or talk with people, I have the feeling of breathing a freer, more congenial air. This splendid *free* university, with its great lecture halls, decorated with fine mural paintings of Chavannes and others, crowded with people who wait patiently for an hour before the lecture and make a wild dash for seats; its distinguished-looking professors; its long list of stimulating courses; its crowds of students of all ages and all nationalities; makes Oxford look like a primary school, and even Columbia, which is incomparably superior to any British University, look like an expensive High School. I had no idea of the wealth of free libraries, museums, state-owned theatres and opera-houses, special schools, etc. in Paris. London is a pauper city beside it. Why do we not hear more in America of the incomparable superiority of the French civilization to the English? Our loyalty to the latter is an enormous mistake. I am very glad that Columbia is so Francophile as she is.

I send you my address, so you may direct as many friends as possible there. I have failed to find a pension which is not too cold or too expensive, and so have about decided to stay in this little hotel all winter, where I have a comfortable room on the second floor, with a big window, electric light and steam heat for $15 a month. A full French dinner can be obtained twice a day at excellent restaurants nearby for $.25 per repast, and breakfast of chocolate and rolls costs $.06 - $.10; so I can live for less than in New York, and much cheaper than a pension. I miss, however, the conversation, and must depend for that on two young Frenchmen I have picked up who want to exchange French for English conversation. I miss my exciting life in London, and the substitute in the shape of a couple of small teas in the American artists' colony is hardly a substitute. Of all insipid, mediocre people, they seem to be the worst,—that is, those I have seen. There is one middle-aged Iowa woman named Lucy Scott Bower,[2] who has some charming scenes of French country life, and is not bad personally, but her female young protégées were the limit. The efforts made by good Christian Americans to preserve the Puritan and moral atmosphere of the American home here in wicked Paris are the most amazing things I have ever seen. Of course the effect is to drive any person with any gumption out of the students hostels and students clubs, and make their last state worse than their first.

I have just received a copy of the Columbia Monthly, which I was afraid had died; apart from my poem in the post of honor, I think the number surprisingly good, and find it stirring old fondness and memories. I seem to differ from you in having a great fondness for Barr, and a belief in the power and passion of his writing. I hope he will really arrive some day and justify me. I should like to know your opinion of my own Whitmanesque effort; the Masses were going to print it, shortened down, but I liked it long and so Monthly printed it.

Did I write you about my visit to the Pennells[3]? If not, it will have to wait to be told, for it is too good to write.

Your book I have made unsuccessful efforts to find; will try some more.

As ever,

Randolph

---

[1]This affair became a political battleground between the military, backed by the Kaiser and the Chancellor, von Bethmann-Hollweg, and the Reichstag, which was controlled by the Social Democrats. In Severne, or Zaberne, an Alsatian town, the German garrison had angered the inhabitants—nicknamed "wackes," meaning rowdies—into acts of provocation against the military. Many people were arrested on November 29th and one man was beaten with a sabre. The Parliament protested this action and the garrison was transferred. At the time this was interpreted as a victory for parliamentary process and as a triumph for non-militarism. The real result, however, was different. The lieutenant who had precipitated the arrests was acquitted at his court-martial and, instead, the civil authorities were blamed. Furthermore, the town suffered economically without the garrison.

[2]Lucy Scott Bower was 50 when Bourne met her. She had studied at the Pennsyl-

vania Academy of Fine Arts in Philadelphia and the Academy Julien in Paris. She was a member of the National Society of Women Painters and Sculptors. She died in 1934 of gas poisoning.

[3]Joseph Pennell and Elizabeth Robins Pennell. He was an artist who wrote art appreciation books and especially travel narratives. She was a fiction writer.

61

to Simon Pelham Barr
(Transcript Columbia)

c/o American Express Co.
11 rue Scribe
Paris
14 December, 1913

Dear Barr;

It may not be good form to praise a number in which one's own work is a prominent feature, but I cannot help saying how extraordinarily pleased I am with the number of "Monthly" which I have just received. Though West Hall may be a hole in the ground, our ancient spirit of sincerity and socialism seems to go marching on. To feel the same spirit in the midst of these new names makes me almost think we have founded a tradition. Slosson, I must confess, is a bit of a jarring note, but serves a useful purpose in setting off the goodness of the rest. Your poem appealed to me particularly, since I had been in England and decided from observation of the militant movement there that it was the only live thing in England. One of its most interesting phases is the fertilizing influence it has on the socialist labor groups, so that Lansbury and Sylvia Pankhurst are co-operating in a movement in Bow and Bromley and Shoreditch, whose meetings gave me a tremendous thrill. Feminine emancipation and socialist revolt seem to make there an extraordinarily vital combination, that suggests rather despairingly how far ahead of us they are over here in consciousness of the social movement. Do you know anything of Fred Sumner Boyd?[1] I heard a lot of him in England. When I get back, we must look up some of these people and really get to grips with things.

I don't know why you haven't written me for a long time. I don't know whether you are back in college or on your magazine. I really should think you would prefer the latter. Don't you ever think of getting your verse published in a book? It appeals to me too profoundly to like the idea of having it all buried away in Monthly. I shall be very much disheartened if you do not justify my confidence in the power and passion of your writing by doing something big some day. It really seems to me that these revolutionary poems of yours are already big and gripping enough to make an impression. Why don't you bravely tackle the publishers from Houghton Mifflin down to Mitchell Kennerley? The facility with which I slid through makes me hope for your success. I do think that in England you would be snapped up. The poets have things their own way in London, with special poetry bookshops and anthologies of "Georgian verse" (George V) and revivals of the old chap books, and poetry readings and other interesting expressions. By the way, when in Oxford, I had the pleasure of talking with the Editor of the Hibbert Journal[2]; he spoke of Erskine's article with approval, but quoted Norman Angell's[3] opinion about it that J[ohn] E[rskine] was a very superficial philosopher. Macmahon has sent me Colby's impudent presentation of me in the columns of Spec[tator] as a defender of college aristocracies.[4] Spec is about now receiving a long and eloquent reply from my pen. Do not leave me comfortless from your pen. I hear of you from several people as being much in the society of a beautiful Barnardian. What of this? And tell me who wrote the editorial?

As ever,

R. S. B.

[1]Fred Sumner Boyd was one of the I. W. W. leaders in the Paterson strike. He was convicted in September of advocating the destruction of private property. The New York *Times* saw his conviction as "a vindication of the rights of the people," (October 2, 10:6) because an act of violence was punished.

[2]The *Hibbert Journal* was founded in 1902 by L. P. Jacks to study the philosophical implications of Christianity.

[3]An English economist who was also a peace advocate. He was the winner of the 1933 Nobel Peace Prize. In 1916 he contributed an essay to *Towards an Enduring Peace*, a volume which Bourne edited.

[4]Elbridge Colby was a defender of fraternities and was active in intercollegiate athletics. Although he also participated in some of the literary societies, he was Bourne's opposite on most issues. Colby had claimed that Bourne supported fraternities, whereas Bourne had used an ironic critique to criticize them. Colby entered the Army and eventually retired to become a journalist and a teacher.

62

to Arthur Macmahon
(Transcript Columbia)

Paris
23 December 1913

Dear Arthur,

Your letter was a great surprise and delight, particularly as it came during my first days in Paris when I was having difficulty in getting settled, and needed a touch like yours from home to cheer me up. I shudder to think how near I came to losing some or all of the letter, when you tell me of the adventures it went through in your desk. I must have given an impression of frantic impatience over news of the lady, for your picture, with all its wealth of psychological resources and acute observation, left nothing to be desired, except the fact of my not being there myself [. . . .] I have not heard from her for a long time now, and,—shall I confess to my fickleness and inconstancy? I do not mind in the least, for her incapacity in following the very obvious leads which would have proved her sincerity and determination, began to weary me a little; though, Heaven knows, my own career has been nothing else but a demonstration of the same incapacity [. . . .] The whole thing was an interesting and unconventional adventure, tinged with certain dangers of thin ice, I must admit, on account of the difference in sex, which wore all the more thin because I, as the ostensible hero, not being seen, could, I suppose, be pictured in any sort of personal colors desired [. . . .]I'm afraid I am very hard-hearted, but when these correspondences begun on a highly intellectual plane of apparent understanding of my ideas and a very pleasing radiant sympathy with them, suddenly take a swoop to the personal; it makes me very uncomfortable, and I see the dangers which sensible prudent people feel when they refuse to begin such a correspondence, or rather continue it at all. But my zest for the experimental life—a life lived in conflict with my natural constitutional timidity,—makes me unable to resist interesting episodes of all kinds, correspondences with unknown women among them. Well, we must admit, I think, that Miss W[interrowd] does write very charmingly, and I should have really enjoyed converting her out of Ingersollism[1] into socialism, pragmatism, etc. But she must not call me Randolph before she is fully converted; I think if a line is to be drawn that is a very good place to draw it. What is this feminine intuition that breaks down so lamentably at such a crisis? She should have known better. But I didn't mean to make my letter all about her. Let me pass on to Paris and myself.

I had a letter from Shotwell recently which worries me a little, for he speaks of an "eager and waiting world" which I must "inform before the stimu-

lus wears off." Am I supposed to have a duty to Morningside in sending home a
diary of my adventures, or does he refer to the duty of making some important
sociological investigation, of which I am quite incapable? I wrote a long letter
to Giddings,[2] with a summary of how I had spent my time in London, and felt
that my duty was done. Now comes this portentious responsibility upon me.
You ask about my writing. The several articles I have composed this fall have not
been very successful, only one being accepted—a peace article by Keppel.[3] I
have just sent my impressions of Oxford to the Atlantic, and if they are rejected,
as I am sure they will be, for they are both too ironical and too heavily generalized, they will be available for private consumption. I learned so much in England that I should love to write a book about the English temperament and character, treating them in the purely impersonal and sociological way that one
would discuss the customs and beliefs of the Menanesians [Melanesians?]. For
the whole country does impress me as so entirely alien to my own,—as I flatter
myself—rather Gallic temperament, that I should love to present it as a peculiar
isolated, eccentric socio-psychological phenomenon, working by its own varia-
tions and laws, which are different from those of the bulk of human nature; in
fact, as a sort of evolutionary sport. For a country like our own which makes a
fetish of English law, "Anglo-Saxon institootions," the English literature, (which
more and more impresses itself upon me as exceedingly weird, psychologically
speaking) and which has a strong admiration for what is called English culture,
this point of view regarding England would be exceedingly novel, wouldn't it?
My view would be quite scientific and impersonal, for, as a matter of fact, I
was very well treated in England, barring my first experience with Bligh. I saw
everybody I wanted to, found them agreeable and willing to talk to me, and in
one or two cases almost oppressively anxious to show me things that I wasn't
really interested in. I followed my usual precarious but highly interesting practice of flying around picking up samples of every kind of sociological phenomena I heard of,—socially, four days in a country house; suppers and teas with
a lower middle class family in Clapton; a week at Oxford with a middle middle
class family, Tory and high Anglican; lunch with a Tory leader writer for the
Times, lunches with the bohemians of the New Statesman[4]; an evening at H. G.
Wells with polished radicals; evening with a club of journalists at an old tavern;
suppers at home of Oxford classical professor—a supreme type—; lunch in the
Temple with Jewish barristers, discussing Isaacs[5] and Zionism; tea with the
Webbs in the temple of Fabianism; evening with a psychologically inclined sur-
geon in Harley Street; to mention a few random samples. Besides I had talks
with Graham Wallas, Hobhouse, J. A. Hobson, the economist, William Archer,
dramatic critic, Jane Ellen Harrison, A. E. Zimmern, George Lansbury, the
syndicalist agitator, L. P. Jacks, editor of the Hibbert Journal, MacDougall,
Schiller and Marett at Oxford, and Havelock Ellis. Some of these people I pursued, some I had letters to, some I met naturally. Then as to meetings,—lectures

by W. W. Cunningham, Miss Harrison, Gilbert Murray, Shaw, Chesterton, Wildon Carr, Sidney Webb, Hobson, Driesch, Mrs. Pember Reeves, besides course lectures by Schiller, Marett and MacDougall at Oxford.[6] And political meetings—suffrage meetings, Mrs. Despard and Annie Kenney, (brought in on a stretcher); Ben Tillett[7] and Lansbury at suffrage-socialist meeting in Shoreditch; Winston Churchill at great Liberal demonstration, interrupted constantly by male suffragettes, who were thrown out with the greatest violence[8]; great Larkin meeting at Albert Hall, during which raid was made by medical students, and repulsed by the audience with the wildest excitement I have ever witnessed.[9] Add to this a few theatres and concerts, church at the big places, reading at the British Museum, walks around London seeing the sights, teas and talks with half a dozen much more obscure and humble friends, and a little writing, and you have a summary of my London life from 1-September to 3 December. This summary looks rather impressive, I see; certainly it was highly enjoyable. The weather was delightful, belying all predictions; very little rain, and only three fogs, none of them of the notorious impenetrable kind. Except for the discomforts of a boarding house which ran steadily down hill while I was there, and yet was superior to about a dozen I looked at, and had several delightful people coming and going, I could not have asked for a busier and more interesting time. I collected all the material I could about the operation of the town-planning act, in case I should have to write a report for my Fellowship. But facts and figures are not in my line. I must be interpreting everything in relation to some Utopian ideal, or some vision of perfection which I am so unfortunate as to have, and consequently I hope I shall not have to compile all these dreary details. Yet the idea and the effects are most inspiring, and I have written them up in a literary way for the Atlantic, an article which is still pending,[10] and may be used to show my harsh superiors like Beard and Giddings at Columbia that my intentions are good, and that I have not been entirely frittering my time away. From my last conversation with them, I gathered that they would not really be much harsher with me than I was with myself. Next summer in Germany I want to observe more closely the ideas in town-planning there; I was too green in 1913 to make anything out of it, nor did I attempt anything but a sampling of Germany. I hope when you and your mother come over—and this is positively the best news yet from home; though you do not speak positively I cannot imagine your giving up such a perfect idea; just having seen Europe makes one a different person; it is graduate education of the highest and most profitable kind—you will be inclined to do Germany and Switzerland with me. And do come early, because my money resembles an hour-glass, and I can see the sands all running out about the first of August. So be sure you come over as soon as college stops, and we will have two months. I will not have seen everything; indeed, every American I meet gives me cause to think, in spite of my eight countries, how many things I did not see; and besides, as long as you do not insist on going to England or Holland, (which are the ugliest countries on earth,) and which I have

seen quite enough of, I will be only too glad to see anything over again. Switzerland is divine; I still owe a debt of gratitude to your mother for persuading me to
go to Lausanne, where I had the time of my life with the Deweys. Switzerland
is the paradise for the poor traveller; hotels, wonderfully clean and neat with
enchanting views, for fifty cents a night; pensions for four and a half francs
(90 cts.) a day; and railroad for a cent or so a mile; and better than all, the most
charming and prosperous civilization in Europe.

You will be interested in hearing about — [Swain]. He met me at the
station in Paris, for which I was very grateful, as it was cold and after dark, and
my pension to which I had written for a room betrayed me, so that I had to
spend the night in a murderous old rambing sinister hotel on a back street, in
a room without fire or light except a candle. I found — [Swain] completely
Gallicized, lodged in a charming room, with a vivacious pension-lady, talking
French. My overtures were severely frowned down upon by him; he did not
want any English-speaking persons around his place, corrupting his French. So I
am very comfortably fixed in a hotel near the Sorbonne, and take my meals at
restaurants. This is considerably cheaper than the pensions, with the advantage
of having steam heat and electric light instead of the stoves and kerosene lamps
of the usual pension-apartment. I miss the conversation, but am exchanging
conversation with a couple of French students who come every day. It is tantalizing not to be able to understand the incomparable lectures at the Sorbonne
with all the fascinating sociological and psychological titles, and I envy — [Swain]
who, as a result of his four months in Grenoble, drinks them in avidly at the rate
of fifteen hours a week. He had decided to get a degree here, and talks of never
going home. I must have absorbed the Francophile atmosphere of the history
department at Columbia, for I find I like nearly everything French, whereas
England was always exasperating me and shocking my instincts. Paris is so
charming that it compensates for the not having companions who are congenial
and sympathetic. I have been writing and reading a good deal since I have been
here, and also given myself a debauch of the wonderfully cheap music and opera.
I am waiting most impatiently for Harry Chase, who is flying around Italy with
Prof. Miller. He did not stop in Paris, but a letter the other day says he will
surely be back eventually. Would he would come for Christmas, for which so
far no resources in the way of friends have turned up!

I wish I was home to see you and your mother often. Please give her my
warmest regards. And write me some more about yourself and Columbia.

As ever,

Randolph

[1]Robert Ingersoll was called "the great agnostic." He defended Darwinism in America and was a persuasive lawyer. Winterrowd was a fellow agnostic.

[2]Franklin Giddings, the first full-time Professor of Sociology in the United States, was one of Bourne's teachers at Columbia.

[3]The article is probably *The Tradition of War* (June 1914), but it is certain that the organization he submitted it to was the American Association for International Conciliation, a Carnegie funded body. Dean Frederick Keppel was with the Association.

[4]The *New Statesman* was a weekly founded in 1913. It was generally Liberal, but was iconoclastic enough to attack the government. It was similar in organization, and in political views, to the *New Republic*.

[5]Sir Rufus Isaacs was then Lord Chief Justice.

[6]Here Bourne is running down the list of people whom he saw in London, a list which he kept in his journal. Wallas, Webb, and, of course, Shaw, were Fabian Socialists. Hobson and Hobhouse were Liberal economists who were dissatisfied with the ability of Liberalism to meet the needs of the people and were, consequently, leaning to the new Labor Party, Schiller, MacDougall, and Marett were Oxford academics, as was L. P. Jacks, who, in addition to editing the *Hibbert Journal*, was a philosopher. Jane Ellen Harrison was a sometimes lecturer at colleges. She was an archeologist, but more frequently she spoke on sexual differences. It was her theory, shared by many, that men and women were equal in mental capacity, but different in temperament and aptitude. A. E. Zimmern was a socialist who subsequently contributed to a Peace Symposium which Bourne compiled in 1916. Mrs. Pember Reeves was the wife of the High Commissioner of New Zealand. She spoke on women's issues. She advocated the economic independence of women and argued for the formation of day care centers so that mothers could work. The activities of Lansbury, Murray, and Chesterton have already been described. Some of the identifications are unclear: W. W. Cunningham could be connected with the London School of Economics. Wildon Carr was probably a social psychologist. Hans Driesch was a botonist and philsopher who may have been visiting at Oxford at the time; his home was in Heidelberg. In summary, Bourne relates his encounters with those people with common intellectual interests, with similar educational views, and with like political opinions.

[7]Tillett was Secretary of the Dock, Wharf, Riverside and General Workers' Union of Great Britain. He was a Syndicalist who vigorously supported Larkin's efforts in Dublin.

[8]At a November 15th Liberal Party rally, Churchill was heckled by suffragettes, despite the fact that protestors were put in the rear of the hall and were removed at the slightest sign of disturbance. All but one of those removed were men.

[9]The November 19th incident has already been described.

[10]"An Experiment in Cooperative Living," *Atlantic Monthly*, CXIII (June 1914), 923-31.

63

to Dorothy Teall
(Transcript Columbia)

Paris
23 Dec. 1913

Dear Dorothy,

I don't dare tell Arthur [Macmahon] your journalistic description of him, though it is almost too good to keep, for he has just written me how much he is enjoying teaching Barnard freshmen politics. To know that he got "awfully fussed" would be a bad blow to his pride, wouldn't it?

I'm sorry you didn't meet him at Furnald [Hall]. Your weird account of the perfectly formal and prosaic interior of a college dormitory delighted me greatly. Obviously you didn't meet any of *my* friends. But recognizing your missionary responsibilities, you girls must go over oftener and illumine that benighted male society of the campus.

[no signature]

64

to Mrs. Arthur Macmahon
(Transcript Columbia)

Paris
Christmas, 1913

Dear Mrs. Macmahon,

Your note came to brighten up my Christmas eve, which was spent with much less company than usual. To hear of you and Arthur in New York induces homesickness almost more than any other thought; you must like it so well that you will want to repeat it next winter, when I hope I shall be able to take advantage of it. Arthur writes that he is saving with a view to Europe next summer with you, and if I knew for certain that you were coming, I cannot tell you what a cheer it would give to my whole winter. But the hope is almost as good. How can I persuade you to make the scheme sober reality? It would be such a fine climax to my own tour to be able to travel about with you, and much better than your coming last summer, which I so much wanted you to do, for that would have been all over with now, while this other is a delightful prospect. I found travelling on the continent such a delight with the clean cheap little hotels and comfortable railroad trains, and everything so unexpectedly easy that I want to pass along the good news. There was so much more of charm and interest in the aspects of city and country than I had allowed myself to expect that I soon got over the mood of exile in which I left home, and except for the pangs of getting settled in a new place like London (which has the air of always looking surprised when a traveller appears) and twinges of conscience at not working harder or more systematically, I have scarcely had a dull or painful moment since I left home. New York friends or congenial new acquaintances have been miraculously provided at almost all stages of the journey, and though I miss the quality of my incomparable friends at home, it has been rather that I wish them here than that I wish myself back in New York. But it has all been quite different from the desolation which I imaged before the start. Just now there is a slackening in Paris, for the handicaps of language prevent me from immersing myself as completely into Paris as I tried to do in London. But the batch of good wishes from home this Christmas makes me feel a large compensation for the comparative poverty of my landscape just at present in Paris. And if I knew you were coming over!

And now the happiest of New Years to you and Arthur, and Mr. Macmahon and Harry too, if you will give them my warmest regards.

Sincerely,

Randolph Bourne

65

to Edward Murray
(Transcript Columbia)

160 rue St. Jacques
Paris
26 Dec. 1913

Dear Edward,

There is scarcely any one of my friends in New York with whom I find it pleasanter to people these charming streets and scenes, or to imagine myself getting my myriad impressions. I would have given a great deal to have had you along, with your capacity of appreciation and sensitiveness to the picturesque, on my tour this summer, instead of the curious, bespectacled youth, who thought I was the height of sentiment because I was frankly responsive to everything and went about almost sniffing in my delight. It was a funny tour, unorthodox in that it went unprovided with Baedeker's and took no interest in historical spots and the memorials of aristocratic and political history, and yet thoroughly American in its endeavor to see the maximum in the shortest possible time. I got, however, exactly what I wanted, which was the qualities and superficial aspects of town and countryside of the chief countries of Europe, felt and sensed by actual living contact, by poking about in villages and all the different quarters of towns, which, of course, had to be taken as samples, to be built upon with huge generalizations, but which gave me quite incomparable impressions of the living, breathing social life, such as with all my reading and imagining I could never have obtained. The impression is general over here that Americans regard Europe as a huge Museum; the inhabitants being very much more interested in the busy modern life around them than in the mediaeval relics of the country, naturally resent that attitude, and I do too. For I hate a Museum as much as anything in the world, and am all for the tout ensemble. And one of the chief delights of this modern European life is that it is going on in the old cities with the timeless charm of their ancient architecture, and in the disciplined and composed countryside, which goes on unvariedly producing as it has for so many centuries. Neither in America nor in England does one get either of these charms; there the process is to destroy or alter the old art, vulgarize the cities, and devastate the country, while clinging stupidly to archaic ideas, religious, political, etc. On the Continent the tendency is the reverse,—to conserve the old styles in building the civic art, and to make radical revolutions in ideas and social institutions. Look what France has done to religion in about 10 years; it is almost incredible the thorough way they have abolished religious instruction, disestablished the church, and turned a third of the churches into public halls or monuments. I love France because it has the courage of its convictions,while stupid, hypocritical England blunders along and corrupts America with her literature and so-called religious traditions and legal codes, and standards of morality all of which we were so unfortunate as to inherit from her, and have never had the sense to radically alter yet. Three months of England, during which I tried to immerse myself thoroughly in her atmosphere and get personal first hand impressions of all her institutions and spiritual attitudes, absolutely cured me of everything almost that could come under the head of "Anglo-Saxon civilization." The good things in the American temperament and institutions are not English, I discover, but are the fruit of our far superior cosmopolitanism, which makes one more *en courant* with the world in New York than in the most enlightened circles in London. Paris, of course, is *the* capital of the world; its cosmopolitanism, however, it too bewilderingly various to grasp. One is sad to think how much one misses through one's puny powers of assimilation.

Best of New Years to you and your family! Should like to hear what you are doing, if you will write.

As ever,

R. S. Bourne

66

to Alyse Gregory
(Ms Yale)

Paris
5 Jan. 1914

Dear Miss Gregory,

Surely you must have received a letter from me almost as soon as yours had gone; I seem to be so unlucky in not quite forstalling the well-deserved complaint of corresponding badly. I only wish you would write me all the things you think of; I wish you had my typewriter which I am carrying about with me and which, instead of the books, etc. it was going to write, has only produced three passable articles, two of them about England, and now on their way to the "Atlantic," where I expect their rejection, as being too heavily philosophical for the subjects. I have no lack of ideas now; the thing is to get them into any passable shape that I can imagine people reading sympathetically. I sketch out a whole book every other day, but then the feeling that I ought to be studying sociology takes hold of me and I do not even start to write. I should like to do my impressions of England, but they range themselves on so many levels of the sublime and the infantile, that I do not see any way of getting them homogeneously together. And then my standard of judging things is always so frightfully Utopian that I do not think my criticism of the social institutions and spiritual fabric would be read with any patience anywhere. Just now I am almost in the mood to try, unless another idea comes swooping along and dislodges this one.

I wish Paris was developing the way London did. London was so easy; I came almost to feel that no person or meeting or society was sacred from my invading presence. But here I cannot yet even understand the lectures, and though I go everywhere, it is like hearing opera in an unknown language. And I have the misfortune, when I want to meet radicals who will initiate me into the socialist movement here, to find congenial French friends only among the Catholic and artistocratic. The American art students prove hopelessly insipid. The Americans I met in England charmed me; here they are flat and tasteless. Is it an effect only of contrast? When I think how much it would mean to have one or more of my Columbia friends over here doing the year with me, the appreciation of the difference almost overwhelms me with self-pity that with all the opportunity I should be missing so much through the lack of the electric spark of companionship and sympathetic sharing of it all. The irony of it all is that there is a Columbia boy here—the youth I travelled over with—but he is so stolidly insusceptible, and, with a fine mind, so destitute of imagination, that he rather intensifies the hunger than allays it. Feminine society with which I was so miraculously and prodigiously blessed for my first four or five months is here conspicuously lacking, and the faint hopes of a revival in the Spring do not encourage me very much. I shall take it very unkindly of the Fates if I have to see Italy alone. My best-beloved Arthur Macmahon of Columbia speaks of coming over with his mother in the summer, but that will be just about when I will be ready to go home.

There are so many things I want to read here,—old and new French literature, besides the incomparable work in sociology. I have just finished Rousseau's "Confessions," a genuine event for me, after the rather low opinion I had of him from the English biographers and critics. Morley's book in the light of Rousseau's own story, is certainly a literary curiosity. What arrogance these great English writers have to attempt a biography of men whose inner life they are quite incapable of imagining, or at least sympathising with! But Morley[1] had the Confessions themselves to go by! Well, I despair of the English mind at its best. In reading Rousseau, so frank, human, sensitive, sincere, I found myself feeling so much of him, saying at nearly every page, "Yes, that is what I would have felt, have done, have said!" In all his weaknesses, I found myself so well represented that I fairly caught my breath sometimes at the accuracy of the psychology. And I could not judge him and his work by those standards that the hopelessly moral and complacent English have imposed upon our American mind. It was a sort of moral bath; it cleared up for me a whole new democratic morality, and put the last touch upon the old English way of looking at the world, in which I was brought up, and which I had such a struggle to get rid of. Rousseau, as seen by himself, is a splendid transvaluator of values, and these values of Victorian England certainly need to be transvaluated if we are ever to have any freedom or any life or honesty or sensitiveness of soul.

Another book I read with great feeling of complete understanding was Romain Rolland's[2] "Vie de Tolstoi," short but very illuminating, and written with the verve and glow of a sane hero-worship. I had not realized how I had absorbed Tolstoi, how completely I was seeing the insoluble problems of life in his terms,—sensuality, religion, death, poverty, social inequality, officialdom, etc., or how completely they were my own problems, about which my feeble, ineffectual, so easily discouraged brain was apt to puzzle itself and make itself unhappy. I realized with a start the other day that in all my literary Pantheon there was not a single English writer (England), except perhaps Hazlitt and Lamb,—Hazlitt, because of his artistic sensitiveness and superb psychology and undeviating radicalism, (for while all that traitorous crew Wordsworth & Coleridge turned renegade, Hazlitt stood doggedly faithful to the French Revolution), and Lamb for his irony and exquisite charm. Of all the rest of the English classical canon, I don't think, outside of some poems of Keats and Browning, and some of the Elizabethans, that I ever read a page with real pleasure. Of course there are many smaller writers of the latter half of the 19th century that I delight in, but they never got into the offical canon, as taught by those pernicious high priests of bad morality and bad psychology, the professors of English literature in colleges. I think if I ever get back to Columbia I shall run amuck on this subject. Emerson, Thoreau, Whitman, William James, Henry James, Royce, Santayana, have delighted me infinitely more than all my English official reading. Why can't we get patriotic and recognize our great men? The first six express the American genius and those ideals of adventurous democracy that we are beginning to lose, partly through having filled our heads with admiration of English rubbish, and partly through having formed a stupid canon of our own with Poe & Cooper and lifeless Hawthorne and bourgeois Longfellow and silly Lowell, though he did have his great moments about the wartime. What a great man Holmes would have been if he had had better company than Boston wits and genteel society! He was my first literary love; I almost wept when at 16, I finished the last page of his last book and realized there was nothing more to read. There was nothing American about any of these except the Indians of Cooper and the Salem of Hawthorne. None of them but might have been written, like Washington Irving, in England. But Emerson, Thoreau, Whitman, W. James, could only have been written here; their spirit is really indigenous, utterly unlike that of any other country. And Henry James, too, though it sounds surprising to say so, was perhaps the most thoroughly American, with that wonderful sensitiveness to the spiritual differences between ourselves and the Older World, and the subtle misunderstandings that follow our contact with it. I found him one of the best of guides to Europe. I read him in London with the keenest glow and appreciation, feeling constantly how impossible it would have been for any English person to have seen or felt the things that he pictures so delicately and truthfully. To be sure, where the English writer usually caricatures the American, he always makes the Englishman far too charming; but then his Americans are apt to be too charming too, so I suppose the proportion is kept right.

While in London, I heard a very lovely gossip about him and Edith Wharton, his devout disciple, which I don't think I have retailed to you.[3] It seems that James recently celebrated his seventieth birthday, and his English friends most appropriately got together and presented him with his portrait painted by Sargent, and besides a Golden Bowl. But what did Mrs. Wharton do, but attempt to rally the American friends by means of many letters to subscribe to a purse which was to be presented to the veteran novelist by his compatriots. Unluck-ily he, hearing of the project, and not relishing this form of present, which sug-gested too much a pension for his declining years, peremptorily called upon the horror-stricken Mrs. Wharton, that lady of the matchless froideur and perfec-tion of etiquette, to call the project off. Here the story ends, but it seems to be made almost too good to be true by the fact that this is exactly the sort of in-cident that he would have fastened upon some well-meaning but rather insen-sitive American society leader from the middle West. That the great Mrs. Whar-ton, the cosmopolitan, the irreproachable, should have thought of making a present in a form that one only adopts as a last resort with relatives at Christ-mas time, suggests so many delightful ironies. There is scarcely anything I enjoy more than to see the strict player of the game of etiquette commit some fright-ful blunder, which shows the whole system up, as this does for me.

I don't know how this came to be so literary a letter. It almost sounds as if I was practicing for an essay. But you can imagine the "Atlantic" printing such remarks about its patron saints. As I read your letter I am struck with the artificiality of my life and ideas; I wonder if I shall ever get to grips with things and be really effectual. Writing without the contact of some definite movement, some definite demand, some definite group, must lack real vitality as I feel all mine does. In my loneliness here in Paris I am getting back to my feeling that I had as I left,—the wonder whether I was not making a big mistake to break all my connections, slender as they were, just at the time when I seemed almost within the grip of real movements, and whether I would find my friends just where I had left them and could continue with them as if there had been no break. I realize how little there would be left of me without my New York friends and the warmth of that Columbia and Greenwich Village atmosphere. Everything is so very hazy for next year. This is the jumping-off place for me. I am likely to return home with no money and no prospects of employment. There were vague rumors of future Columbia appointments during my last year there, but I should hate so very badly to be rejected that I almost don't dare to put out any soundings. And my perfect fatality of unsuccess in the past in get-ting any sort of a small editorial position, etc. makes me positively tremble at the prospects. But since everything has been done for me in the past, experience teaches that I sit and wait again. I hope Fate isn't going, by preventing me from earning any regular decent livelihood, [to] force me into the hard and painful labor of writing books. There is only one situation that I have ever found really inspires me to write, and that is a shady garden with a sympathetic friend flitting about to make the atmosphere luminous with personality,—but how is one going to have this to order, (I have only had it twice in my life), and yet how is one going to write without inspiration?

I dare say you are quite bored with all this astonishing fluency that afflicts me to-night, but it seems very easy to talk to you. I only wish I had something bigger to tell you. I get in perfect despair over the sincerity of my revolutionary sentiments when I think of my perfectly humdrum conventional life, my irreproachably bourgeois connections, my lack of real knowledge of the workers, their thoughts, ambitions and feelings, my personal enjoyment of comfort and taste, my interest in art, my [per] sonal[4] complications of character, and the [dis] gusting spectacle of the enormous contras [t be] tween my overweening ambitions and bo [th the] figure I cut in the world and the la [zy way] I am taking to realize my ambitions. [If I had lived in an] age when the personal, the confessional, [were] appreciated I would revel in writing [myself] out remorselessly, not so daintily [or so] Atlantically as I am ashamed to say I have done, but much more truthfully and widely. A great artist would know how to use it in play & poem and novel, but I am only a feeble little artist, and not being allowed by literary taste to pour out autobiography, I shall have to keep on suffering, I am afraid, this indigestion of myself.

Yours as ever,

Randolph Bourne

[1]John Morley was an English statesman and man of letters who wrote a biography of Rousseau. He was a pacifist and was a student of John Stuart Mill.

[2]Rolland was a pacifist and a famous French novelist and playwright. He received the Nobel Prize for literature in 1915. He is considered the pioneer of the psychological novel in France.

[3]This famous incident has become a literary anecdote.

[4]Part of this letter has been damaged.

67

to Frederick P. Keppel
(Ms Columbia)

Paris
9 January 1914

Dear Mr. Keppel.

I was under the impression that I wrote you from London about seeing the Pennells,[1] thanks to your very kind introduction, but lately I have not been so sure, and must apologize if I did not. You predicted, I remember, that Mr. Pennell would be found radical enough for all practical purposes. I can only say that I hope my radicalism does not affect you the same way that his did me. I passed a most exciting evening with Mrs. Pennell and him, an evening that had the adventurousness of a walk in the jungle, for I could never tell what frightful monster of conversation I was going to turn up next. The most innocent subjects would put this artist, who seems most highly endowed with the artistic temperament, into what had all the evidence of a frenzy, until I began to think I was either the most tactless person in the world or had the most painful misfortune of being personally obnoxious to him. But then there were moments of such delightful serenity, when he talked about the Panama Canal and St. Sophia and Westminster Cathedral, that I gave up the second hypothesis and relapsed into puzzled wonder. I left in a torrent of abuse, and was much relieved to hear the next day—and indeed rather flattered—from Mr. Huntington[2] that everybody was received in practically the same way. In my efforts at perfect veracity, I may at one point in our conversation, have seemed to be assaulting Mr. Pennell's firm belief that you were the sole high and lordly directing chief of the University, but since it was evident that he did not believe a word I said about the multiplicity of Deans, no harm was done, and I need not ask your pardon for this treason of mine. I was almost afraid to go again, because, not being able to discover the slightest coherencies in his protests at people and things, I had no rule to guide me in keeping my remarks in inoffensive paths. And then I was going to Oxford and really did not have a chance, although Mrs. Pennell was very charming and asked me to come again.

At Oxford I had a very interesting week, hearing lectures, seeing the buildings, and talking when I could with the dons. The men I wanted to see most—Schiller, the pragmatist philosopher; McDougall, the social psychologist; and Marett, the anthropologist; were all vey accessible and kind, and I had with Schiller a long talk which I shall always rank among the intellectual events of my life. Besides these three men and Gilbert Murray, there did not seem to be anything very vital at Oxford; the atmosphere irritated me, as I expected it would, and I left with a renewed admiration for the American college teaching and system. The students certainly were more dignified than our students, and had often great charm of manner; their speaking was more even and polished, but the ideas were quite childish, and delightfully unorientated with any general knowledge of the world or social sympathies, which even our rawest students possess in some measure. The custom of dictating lectures struck me as rather childish too, and I could not feel the superiority of the knowledge of Greek verses over the smattering of philosophy and Modern history and languages that our students get. My conclusion was that Oxford is less a college, in our sense of the world (not word), than a national institution for turning out members of the governing class, trained by a careful avoidance of the useful and the practical and the veracious in the curriculum, and by a social atmosphere of class-prejudice, to take their places in a rigid social system with an infallible knowledge as to how to treat every person in it, above and below them. If this is true, there is nothing at Oxford that it would be the slightest use for us in America to copy or envy, and to have ninety of our bright American youth sent over there periodically seems a punishment and a disaster rather than a national blessing, unless at the same time ninety young Honorables and "younger sons" are forcibly incarcerated at Columbia at the same time. My view of England made me dread the initiation in America of very many of its ideals and spiritual attitudes. It seemed to me that of all the European countries it had least to teach us. The contrast of this wonderful free University of Paris with the English Universities is very striking. The stately halls, the distinguished professors, the wealth of courses, the eager crowds besieging the doors of the lecture-rooms, the high intellectuality everywhere, seem eloquent of a democratic diffusion of culture which is quite unknown in England. And then the wealth of libraries, and opera, and serious drama, and picture and book-stores, makes poor old London seem barbarous indeed. I had had no idea that the contrasts were so great.

My year, I find, is being much more interesting and profitable than I dared to expect. I had no confidence in my ability to get into the life over here or feel it in the way I wanted to. But I learned a very great deal in England, and, although some of my reactions were quite unorthodox, it was all a very valuable part of my education. Paris, of course, has all been much slower to develop, but now that, after painful and long exposure, I am beginning to understand the language a little, I find interesting lectures and meetings and people on every side. Then the French are such incomparable sociologists that the hours spent in the libraries over their monographs are a great delight in themselves.

France does not seem as militaristic as I expected. Of course there is the new loi de trois ans,[3] but there is a very strong undercurrent against it, and the conservatives seem afraid that the new ministry is going to apply it very half-heartedly. And the row in Germany is very encouraging to all the peace people here, who are raising loud voices in support of the German democrats and socialists.[4] Almost everybody will tell you in Germany and France that militarism is an evil, though a necessary one; I heard none of the jingoistic talk anywhere.

I saw Green occasionally, and he gives me valuable points about the University. Prof. Mason of the Music Dept.[5] (is he still connected with it, I wonder?) is here in Paris for the winter apparently, and I am going to see him on Monday. Swain is deep in the history of religion, and rapidly turning completely into a Frenchman; I am afraid he will marry his pension-keeper and become a naturalized French citizen. I hear of other American students from time to time, but have not come across them, and really would rather meet French or Russians. I have a very charming French law-student, who comes every day and exchanges conversation with me, and a younger boy from the Lycée who reads to me. I can unload, I find, many of my points of view and criticisms on the Frenchman which proved quite unassimilable by my English friends, and this flatters me to think that I am more French than English in temperament, which of course I would rather be.

I am going through my annual wonderment about what I am going to do next year. Family complications make it practically necessary that I find a position with a salary more than enough for myself. I don't know whether there would be any opening at Columbia in sociology or history, or whether I would have any chance for it if there were. I know you will tell me frankly what the prospects are, and so I write you, very mindful and grateful as I am for your suggestions and assistance in the past. If there is no chance of teaching, and I have small hope that there will be, I shall have time, before I return, to try to work some of my magazine connections. Europe has kept my mind working, and given me several ideas for books, but it is a little hard among the distractions of the foreign scene to concentrate systematically on them.

Sincerely yours,

Randolph Bourne

[1]See note 3, letter #60.

[2]Although the identification is uncertain, Huntington was probably a Baronet and barrister. He was a member of the Liberal Party. Bourne may have used his introduction to explore the Inner Temple, of which Huntington was a member.

[3]A law which increased the term of service in the French Army from two to three years. There was sentiment against it from two sides. Conservatives felt that it gave a false sense of how many men were in the Army defending France against Germany, while liberals believed that Germans could feel antagonized and interpret the French action as bellicose. The election of 1914 had this law as its major issue and those who supported it, including Poincaré, were defeated.

⁴This was a reaction to the Saverne affair, and to the increasing militarism in Germany, undertaken without Socialist approval.

⁵Mason was hired in 1909 by President Butler, who was attracted to Mason because of the magazine articles he wrote explaining music to laymen. Mason was reputed to be an excellent lecturer who gave a humanistic approach to the study of music in a department which had been dominated by theory.

68

to Alyse Gregory
(Ms Yale)

Paris
19 Jan 1914

Dear Miss Gregory,

We really must stop envying each other's broader touch with things, for I could not possibly do your splendid work, and this dilettante life of mine, with much feeling, reacting, groping, judging, is, I suppose what I am most fitted for. I feel very buoyant to-night after news of an article accepted by the "Atlantic."¹ It is poor stuff, as I remember it, description without chance of much philosophizing, but it is a symbol that I have not been spiritually exiled from home, and it is honest and true, if uninspired.

Your looking at life in the same general outlines that I do, makes me want to write you so often, makes me want to catch the mood and the reactions that seem truest and transmit them to you, and then when I do get the time, I always have the feeling of disappointment that I have caught myself at a moment which is less typical than it should be. You evidently do just as I do, use people and your personal reactions to them as guide posts to general understandings, and you let small significant impressions light up long vistas of meaning. But I sometimes wonder if I haven't a little the advantage of you, through my enthusiasm for sociology, in getting besides the personal reverberations, certain general social reverberations of types and groups and classes and social milieu.— This sounds so cold, and I wonder if I can make you see what I mean. For these broader reactions are sometimes quite as vivid as the personal, and if they are clear, give me so intense a satisfaction, the scientific one, I suppose, of having sensed a connection, a law,—although one cannot use scientific terms in this connection, for my sociology is not coldly thought by the intellect but warmly felt. Your letters make me feel so many things that I must analyze thoroughly and explain to myself or you or somebody some day, and this is one of them. This attitude gives me some sort of connection between the personal life and the quiet sea of impersonality, though not a complete link, for I struggle with the problem as you do. And it is becoming more difficult for me, because it has been impressed on me this winter of semi-solitude that if I am going to write, and I feel now that I have so much to explain, I must envisage things and people and myself not less clearly but much more personally than I have, assert my own reactions and impressions, and this means a definite choice of solitude against the attempt to mingle brusquely with all sorts of clashing interests and attitudes, as I have been doing. I am so sensitive to social milieus that the mere thought of some of my truest and most convinced ideas rubbing up against the contempt of certain of the little groups, university, family, town, etc. makes me turn pale and momentarily wilts the idea. What a shock to realize that I, the preacher of faith to one's inmost truth, am letting these alien standards and contrasts affect me so savagely! Well, one can pray not to be led into temptation, and if this year abroad does nothing else for me, it will have removed for a time that impossible life which I have been leading in four or five quite alien levels of spiritual attitude. And with the reading of the French, so personal, so seriously emotional, so strong in their belief in the dignity of infinitely varied human experience, a belief that Anglo-Saxondom, it seems to me, wholly lacks,—this has meant an immense fortification of my confidence in my visaging of life. I find in them too the serious consideration of so much of me that is starved in the English culture, and my transvaluation of values begun ten years ago when my Calvinism began to crack, has just about reached its completion.

About the comradeship of men and women, I have a few such wonderful woman friends that I begin to think that perfect play of idea and appreciation is making an ideal real,—when up springs eternal, insatiable desire, the realization of which, inhibited to me, sets the old problem recurring poignantly, and makes me wonder whether Shaw's preface to "Getting Married" is not the profoundest and wisest word on the matter ever written. It is a subject to make one's thoughts, indeed, go round and round without satisfaction, and particularly when one is a man, and a man cruelly blasted by the powers that brought him into the world, in a way that makes him both impossible to be desired and yet— cruel irony that wise Montaigne knew about—doubly endowed with desire. Give him then an extreme fastidiousness of idealism, and you have a soul that should satisfy the most ironical of the Gods. Encase that soul, which is myself, in Puritan morality, and you produce a refined species of spiritual torture, which is relieved only by the demands and appeals, fortunately strong, of philosophy and music, and heaven-sent irony which softens and heals the wounds. But, to complete the job, make him poor and deny him the thorough satisfaction of the higher appeals, deny him steady work and thus make easy the sway of desire, and you force all his self-impelled action, all his thinking and constructive work to be done in hampering struggle with this unrealized desire, which yet—another irony—colors all his appreciations, motivates his love of personality, and fills his life with a sort of smouldering beauty. This is a complete, if perhaps too dark picture. But like many things in life, both it and the other side are true.

So much of the cruelty of human relations seems to me to spring from the unequal endowment of desire and appreciation in men and women, and this arises largely from the inequalities of position and social milieu. That is why my socialism is so democratic and communistic—utterly unlike the English Socialism—and why the feminist movement is so inspiring, for it is going, I hope, to assert the feminine point of view,—the more personal, social, emotional attitude towards things, and so soften the crudities of this hard, hierarchical, over-organized, anarchic—in the sense of split-up into uncomprehending groups—civilization, which masculine domination has created in Anglo-Saxondom. It is significant that the feminist movement is weak in France; for here, though women have not the vote, yet they are "citoyennes," and are taken with extreme seriousness, and are integral part of the civilization, whereas in England one feels they are quite superfluous, and in America occupy a highly artificial position, adored and—despised, at once. Whether we can throw off the evil tentacles of the English civilization in America, and work the feminine into our spirit and life —not the effeminate, as it is usually understood in America, but the personal, the non-official, the naturally human and sensitive, the spirit that Tolstoi preaches in "Resurrection" and Shaw in his best plays. I have had such an illustration of the unstable position of women to-day, their weakness and difficulties, in the romantic history which an American woman here has insisted upon telling me this past week. She was from the South and Southerners, of course, remain infants, intellectually and spiritually all their lives. She is not genuine, and has never been able to meet any crises which her "little-girl" look would not dissolve. The result is that she has evidently been through some of the most remarkable complications and miscomprehensions of which the relations of men and women are capable. She is full of hypocrisies, affectation of tragic realization of her sufferings, remorse, religious faith; just now she is forsaking human relations, (disillusioned, her heart shattered into a thousand pieces,) for the search of philosophy and higher truth. She has never believed anything, though she struggles with moral codes which she tries to fit to herself; she has never cared for anything, apparently; although she thinks she has "loved." She is not even honestly voluptuous. Yet she is "capable," has initiative, the worldly sense of doing as the world does, knows how to spend money to the best advantage, and, without genuine taste, can make all the show of "savoir faire." She has a son of 20, whom she adores as a little girl of 8 would be fond of a baby brother. When I think of thousands of women like her wandering loose about America, or imprisoned precariously in homes, it almost scares me. Men seem to have succumbed to her by the bushel, though she did not really pursue them; they seem rather to have persecuted her, who found them at first amusing and then got weary, like a little girl who wanted to go back to her dolls. A woman utterly without standards, personal attitudes, vivid reactions, tastes, or enthusiasms, yet allowed to circulate in the world and attract men! She gives me a knowledge of the kind of woman we are tending to produce in America to-day. No wonder she is utterly sceptical about the suffrage movement, and believes thoroughly in the helplessness of womankind. To understand the masculine code, and adapt herself to that, seems to be her only code. Her one regret seems to be, not that her husband betrayed her, but that she was not big enough to understand the ordinance of this masucline universe! No hint of revolt, no missionary resolve to wake up womankind and make such things impossible. Very curious and disheartening. Such realities give me a sudden shock of realization of the remoteness of the horizon of one's ideals. But I suppose they should only spur me on to greater struggle towards them.

Your Columbia boy sounds interesting. I know the type, and always wonder how possible it is to make it feel the world as we feel it. That easy command of everything good and prosperous which such a young man would have somehow must make suffering and perplexity and the urgencies of life seem unreal and illusory, try as hard as he may to imagine them.

Your friend,

Randolph Bourne

[1]"In the Mind of the Worker," *Atlantic Monthly* CXIII (March 1914), 375-82.

69

to Simon Pelham Barr
(Transcript Columbia)

160 rue St. Jacques
Paris
19 January, 1914

Dear Simon:

I do hope your other letters are on the way by this time, but I will acknowledge your first, which was quite worth waiting as long as I did for. Its first effect was to give me the most poignant realization of my lack of sympathetic feminine society here in Paris, and to make me envy you most horribly. After a long lecture at the Sorbonne, to which I expose myself rather to accustom my reluctant ear to the language than to learn anything, my flagging spirits crave intolerably the friendly response of a charming girl. I did not know that my year, which had been treating me very well up to Paris, would collapse so lamentably. So I felt every word of your letter. I do remember the girl very clearly, thought her quite charming, and only moved away because I felt my superfluity. There was something hauntingly, placidly mysterious about her face, an expression to which I am extremely susceptible,—a self-reliant passivity, which sets one at work upon the mystery behind it, and the meanings. I'm not surprised that you succumbed,—indeed, thought it was high time you fell in love, because I imagine that your imagination had been busy on the subject and you had many ideas as to your desire and the experience. But what a very objective story you did tell! I would have hoped for a little of the previous imaginations, and a hint of the way they were realized. And you hardly gave an intimation at all as to what must have taken place in your beating tumultuous blood, for you cannot persuade me that you are not highly endowed with the voluptuous. You spoke at times almost in the tone of a scientist making an experiment, and surely you did not take her in your arms simply to set her sex philosophy right. I almost had a feeling that you were writing to the Puritan man-of-straw that the Elsasserian irony has conjured up for me, and not to the person who, made impossible to arouse desire, is, as wise old Montaigne knew, doubly endowed with it, and, moreover, is cursed with an extreme fastidiousness of taste which keeps him from going the easiest masculine way. This purely spiritual ideal of love with which English literature has perverted Anglo-Saxondom I cannot understand. Whitman, whom I believe you don't appreciate, is the glorious prophet of the true and perfect fusion of physical and spiritual comaraderie. It is a very high and perhaps impossible ideal, much higher than either of the separate ones, one of which deludes and tortures, and the other of which satiates and palls. Do read Whitman's glowing lines and write me sometime your real reaction and your real feeling, not the objective side that you think I will appreciate. Of course you can't write about your love; you would have to stand off from it a little. And then, too, forgive me, it is so strikingly unoriginal, except the night walks, which are charming, quite thrilling; they give me the yearning that myths of Greek arcadias do, with fleeing nymphs, etc. I did not know that such beautiful things could happen around cruel New York. You make me feel suddenly very old and bitterly handicapped and foolish to have any dream left of the perfect comrade who is, I suppose, the deepest craving of my soul. It is her I write to, meet casually in strange faces on the street, touch in novels, feel beside me in serene landscapes and city vistas, grasp in my dreams, She wears a thousand different masks, and eludes me ever. In half a dozen warm friends the mask is very thin, but it is always a mask. To touch it chills my blood, and I am touching it constantly when my eager exasperated curiosity about all her goings and comings, my jealous desire to envisage all her life, meets nothing but cool, friendly response. There is a girl now in Italy, with whom I had divine walks and tours this summer in Switzerland, and from whom it is almost as much of a pain as a pleasure to receive a letter, so imperturbable is the reflection of my warmth.

As ever,

R. S. Bourne

P. S. If you have influence with Monthly still and could get a copy of the *first* no. sent to Miss Alyse Gregory, 5 West Ave., Norwalk, Connecticut, whom I want to have see your poem and mine, you will earn the gratitude of your friend.

R. S. B.

70

to Henry W. Elsasser
(Ms Columbia)

160 rue St. Jacques
Paris
20 Jan 1914

Dear H. W. E.,

Yours are the only eyes through which I envisage my native lands and the picture you give of the white slave and medical drama raging through the land, combined with the Wilson myth, does not make me sorry I am here.[1] I get a little scared sometimes when I think of the revulsions of feeling I am likely to have if I ever strike New York again. Here one selects so easily, and so many things are veiled from the barbarian—though many more I am told are unveiled for his particular benefit—that one has a feeling of living in a cleanly civilization, as free from vulgarity as you can expect. I dote so on things French that I find myself making excuses for their rough streets, which are up most of the time, for their disgusting loi de troi ans, for their vices, and their inefficiencies, their ugly women which they themselves find so ravishing. Moved by a vague sense of duty and a real desire to see the French University in action I have taken up my residence in the very heart, opposite the Faculty of Law, with the Sorbonne around the corner, and the College de France down the street. Arctic weather and the high prices of pensions have driven me into a steam heated hotel, where I live for about what I paid at Columbia, but eat incomparably better. I go to lectures every day, and am painfully training my ear; but I cannot

say that I get on very fast, and the soul of France must be felt rather than rub-
bed against in the person of significant types such as I met in England. A really
charming law student comes every day and talks with me; I take him as highly
typical, because he insists on having a philosophical explanation for everything,
talks politics, philosophy, sociology and national characteristics with equal
facility, and altogether works his mind so exactly like mine that we talk way
past our dinner hour. Of course I have gotten to understand him perfectly, but
this does not mean, I find, a general understanding, and my hope of political,
syndicalist meetings, interviews, etc., fades gradually into the realm of dreams.
I miss feminine society rather keenly, and make up for it unprofitably by reading the contemporary romances which I hear mentioned as significant of the
modern woman in France. Put down "La Rebelle" by Marcelle Tinayre,[2] as the
concentrated essence of Paris to-day. And to have these people wandering all
around my quarter in these charming pages gives me a childish but very real
pleasure. Maurice Barres,[3] with his gospel of "Be ardent and skeptical" teaches
me a good deal too, and an analysis of the social system revealed on the Boule-
vard Saint-Michel, where you never see a man accompanied by a woman, is also
instructive. Over my chocolate in the morning I read l'Humanité and sometimes
Le Matin; then go over sociological monographs in the library; after lunch go to
lectures, listen to French read me by a youth from the Lycée, talk to my friend,
have dinner and read novels all the evening in the Biblioteque Sainte-Genevieve,
one of the real social institutions of the world. There can be no place on earth
where such a motley collection of the Parisian proletariat, Russian girl-students,
Poles, Swedes, Arabs, Hungarians, in all stages of prosperity,—soldiers in their
red trousers, young priests, and grisettes,[4] could be found, all reading with an
intensity which is only matched by the precision with which (sans les pretres)
they pair off at the sortie. The library is free and enormous, 400,000 volumes,
most of them on the walls of a long reading room, as big as that of the N. Y.
Library. You get your book in one minute by writing the name and number on
a slip, having it vised, and handing it to one of the perambulatory librarians, who
simply walks to the shelf and hands it out to you. Opposite the library is The
Pantheon, surely one of the most superb buildings in the world, and at night
thrillingly towering and majestic. Chase, (whom I had for one happy evening)
who has just seen St. Peter's, thought my Pantheon could be put inside of it.
I do not believe him, but hope shortly to judge. In front of the Pantheon is
Rodin's Penseur in bronze, and inside are the great mural paintings of Puvis de
Chavannes. I stole in the other day when the sun was shining, but the great
spaces of the building seemed to be imprisoning all the cold that had ever been
in the world, and I soon shivered out again. Down the hill in front, a superb
street stretches away, just long enough to give the most impressive vista possible
of the swelling dome; and, not content with that, these consummate civic artists
have placed a fountain, and, in the adjoining Luxembourg gardens, a long
straight avenue of grass and trees, with a delicious bronze statue of a dancing

faun at each end,—statues, stately greensward, fountain, and splendid rue Souf-
flot, stretching in one straight line up to the stately temple at the head. A vista
that restores one's faith in the intelligence and genius of men. Continuing our
ramble, as the showman says,—I think I would make a good showman—we come
to the Odeon, one of the many national theatres, where I paid 2fr. 50 for a
parquet seat for Loie Fuller's Ecole de Danse,[5] most chaming, exquisitely
youthful and yet individual, and each scene mounted with sumptuous taste,—
Debussy's Sirens, and Children's Corner, Moussorgsky's Thousand and One
Nights, etc.[6] I preferred them infinitely to the Russian offerings, for this was
genuine fresh eternal youth, the Arcadia of nymphs and fauns. I had never
realized the advantages of nationalized culture, and a state department of Beaux-
Arts, as they have in France. I paid 3fr. at the Opera-Comique for a sumptuous
seat for Tosca and Cavalleria and then found the proletariat were getting in
upstairs for 75 centimes. Could New York support an exquisite little theatre
where nothing but classics and a few delicate modern one act plays are given?
I went as an experiment to the Vieux Columbier to a Moliere play, and though I
got not a word, the exquisite music of the language, the seriousness with which
the action—most banal in English—ran, was an artistic treat. And the house was
full. I must see Bernhardt,[7] I think, who is overwhelming the Parisians again in
the role of an old and sorrowful mother. Is there any other city that supports a
daily paper devoted to nothing but plays and music? I was much impressed with
Munich's flaring art, but Parisian advertising kiosks give you nothing but concert-
programs, operas, and theatre repertories. The finding of the Mona Lisa was a
great spree for Paris.[8] Almost every other piece of news fled for a week. How
every paper scintillated with brilliancies; how the whole plot was revealed with
smacking lips! I went to see her on the morning of her first reappearance at the
Louvre, and paid the penalty by finding a crowd which had to be sent through
in single file, as before a bier. She looked infinitely sad and worn, rather than
mocking and inscrutable,—doubtless the effect of her troublous [?] two years.
The sculptures were not open for some reason, so I have not seen the Venus de
Milo, but the winged victory, by whose symbol Wells has immortalized Boston
culture, sailed towards me on the prow of her ship, as I came up the staircase,
with such a splendid sweeping triumphant abandon that one could fairly hear
the rustle of her robes. My democracy for the first time in aristocratic Europe,
went prostrate before the Salle Rubens. As I had never heard of its grandeur,
I entered it unexpectantly and innocently; I traversed it reverently and yet with
delighted eyes, in something like stupor at the sublime audacity, the Olympian
arrogance, of these heroic glowing panels, representing all the cosmic and celes-
tial grandeurs, with indescribable sweep and verve, doing honor to different
incidents in the life of a mere queen. In this superb hall, with rich gilded and
encrusted ceiling and immaculate waxed floor, the walls radiant with splashing
color and warm flesh, I had to admit to myself that Rubens had gotten away
with it. He had made regal power, which my proletarian soul always sneered at

as a sorry myth, seem plausible and dazzling. I found myself liking the early French painters of the 19th century very much. Ingres, Delacroix, etc. and even David, who is so reviled, was for the classic, pretty fine classic, I thought. I have a weakness, too, for Greuze's reiterated girl.⁹ The Dutchmen were disappointing; London is much richer in Rembrandts and Hals and Vermeer, etc. I shall have to take back some of what I said about London; the National Gallery is really superb. The Luxembourg gallery has many beautiful marbles and bronzes, many Rodins, but the pictures do not seem to justify an impression I got somewhere what it was the cream of the Paris galleries. Perhaps it is liked because it is so small and overflows in such rich abandon with its statues into the small courtyard. I hope I haven't retailed any of this gossip before, or that it doesn't bore you. I cannot close without telling about my discovery of the Musée Cluny. I was quite ignorant here too; guidebooks have no soul, and I never believe any more what people tell me about anything in Europe. I also hate museums. Imagine then a delightful seventeenth century chateau with charming courtyard and fine Renaissance facades, picturesquely pointed to the remains of a Roman bath; the chateau,—all its dark-panelled, rich and beautiful rooms, with their leaded glass windows, panelled ceilings and parquet floors, filled with treasures of art, carved chairs and tables, splendid marble mantlepieces, clocks, all the household utensils, but everything arranged discreetly, so that in the gloom of a rainy Sunday morning I saw no museum, but the actual rich artistic life of the middle ages, the home of a great patron noble of the arts. If there were cases they were small and unassuming and were set on the tables as if one had pulled out a drawer of old coins from one of the great chests in the corner. The place was thick with atmosphere; one's head swam with the wealth of delicate treasures. I roamed about purely for the atmosphere, for I have little of the historico-sentimental sense—except that I do enjoy seeing the streets where the barricades of 1848 and the Commune were thrown up—and am unmoved at the sight of the spoon of a queen, but when I came into the last room here at Cluny, and saw in a case swinging by a chain three or four of the golden crowns of Gothic Kings in Spain of the 7th century, I must say I succumbed. Could anything be more packed with romance? And the crowns were oddly beautiful. I can understand now the emotions that sweep the heart strings of the American girl at Stratford in the presence of the relics of the immortal bard. But I prefer my Gothic kings. I am afraid [?] me to Cluny, again for fear it will show itself as a museum and not as an atmosphere; I shall keep the remembrance of one of my richest mornings in Paris.

This gossip destroys all my seriousness; what you say about Wells is very amusing, for with his matrimonial escapades, he is the first man in the world likely to feel the undesirability of jealousy in women, and also to bemoan the impossibility of camaraderie. All his books are said to be perfectly autobiographical, constructed on a different wife. I have not read the last, could not get hold of it in England, and did not want to buy it.

And now good-night! A more profitable letter next time. All our eyes are on Germany, as the enclosed will suggest.

R. S. B.

[1]Bourne is doubtlessly referring to the drive for feminine purity which led to the Mann Act, among other measures. The medical drama to which he alludes is probably connected to dispute in New York over a supposed cure for tuberculosis. The doctor who promoted the cure felt that the medical profession was supressing his information, and the incident turned into a case of the public's right to know. The New York *Times* connected this dispute with other Progressive efforts to gain access to information.

[2]Tinayre was a French writer and feminist. She advocated equal rights for women and said that they should be independent within marriage. At the same time she lauded feminine passion and claimed that women were ruled by their emotions more than men. Thus, while she preached economic independence for women, she said that her sex was more enslaved to emotions.

[3]Barres preached the cultivation of the ego. At the same time he was a nationalist.

[4]A cheerful working girl.

[5]Loie Fuller was a pioneer of the modern dance. Her chief accomplishment was the development of the "serpentine dance."

[6]Both Claude Debussy and Modest Petrovich Moussorgsky were slow to be accepted. In Debussy's case, the reluctance was caused by his impressionistic compositions, while Moussorgsky was "discovered" after his early death. Many of his works were only sketches or fragments and were expanded by other composers into complete, posthumous works.

[7]Sarah Bernhardt, the famous actress.

[8]The painting was returned to the Louvre after a two year absence. The *New York Times* reported that over 100,000 people viewed the painting on the first day of its exhibition; Bourne was a part of this crowd.

[9]Jacques David was a republican at the time of the French Revolution. He was a classical painter. Jean Ingres considered himself a student of David. He continued the classical tradition of painting, but he was also influential with many of the modern painters. Ferdinand Delacroix was a leading Romantic painter and contemporary of Ingres. He was considered a revolutionary artist, although his influence was not as lasting on modern painters as Ingres'. Jean-Baptiste Greuze was a moralistic and melodramatic painter. Many of the subjects of his later paintings were young girls.

71

to Arthur Macmahon
(Transcript Columbia)

160 rue St. Jacques
Paris
30 Jan 1914

Dear Arthur,

With your letter and the clipping came also a letter from Colby and the clippings and a lengthy defense of Alpha Chi Rho from my wanton slanders in "Spectator." Since one of the few occasions when I admire my own genius is the composition of a letter to Colby, I was grateful for the opportunity and sent him a real masterpiece. His reply to my "Spectator" letter sounded just a little as if he had not expected to be caught so quickly, and was sufficiently unintelligible to constitute a skillful defense of himself. If you see anything else that you think demands the attention of C.C.C.C., send it along at once. I was beginning to think that my isolation from academic gossip and my preoccupation with the psychology of nations was beginning to change and elevate my character, but I find that the leopard doesn't change his spots so easily.

I wish it had been Paris instead of Washington that you ran over to at Christmas time. The winter is beginning to tell a little on my spirits, and it was exasperating to see Harry Chase only for one night. I had such wonderful society in Switzerland and England, but Paris has not produced anything half so stimulating. I meet Americans, mostly the art colony people and the idle people with a little money who come to Paris for the winter, and they make me almost blue with their mediocrity. I sometimes almost shudder for my country, that sends such brainless people around the world. They exhibit a fatuous incapacity for ideas, a lack of personal response to what Paris has to offer (except what is starred in the guidebook), an intellectual childishness, which I must say I have been spared from seeing at home. They attend lectures at the American club on "How to see Europe intelligently", and come away stuffed with indigestible historical facts and artists' biographies which represents to them an immersion in the culture of the Old World. They are exactly the sort of Americans you read about in English satires—a sort that I was always patriotic to believe never really existed. It wouldn't be so bad if they were little humble people, but as far as I can judge, they are the cream of the Montparnasse quarter which swarms with them as the East Side of New York does with Jews. Their quarter, by the way, in spite of its poetical name is quite the most banal in Paris, the one quarter which has nothing of picturesqueness in the way of old streets or historical monuments. I am perhaps unduly pessimistic about my countrymen from just having heard a lecture by an M.A. of the University of Pennnsylvania. He is giving a course in American literature in France, and he is listened to by a large number of students of all countries, who are trying to learn English. His subject was Benjamin Franklin, and his treatment was almost exactly what one would present to a class in the fifth grade,—childish, incoherent, flippant, utterly without point or intellectual grasp. Even making excuses for the condescension which an M.A. from the U. of P. must naturally feel in addressing an audience of Russian, Polish and French candidates for degrees at the Sorbonne, how was one to explain such phrases as, "The more educated, better classes," "His paper made a hit," "Franklin was the type of man who knew how to sell you a thing," "He used no literary language, but in spite of that, became a very prominent speaker," "He did not dress too much; not like Rousseau, who went with one pants red, and the other pants green," "He took part in many prominent positions," "Was representative for quite a few years." Do you get the purity and precision of the style, the dignity with which our American literature and the quality of the American mind are being presented to audiences in Paris? If I had not had my notebook—and even then I could not keep pace with him—I should have burned up with humiliation. Fortunately he spoke very indistinctly, and the audience, in spite of its rapt attention, must have lost much of it, and perhaps wouldn't have felt the sticky triteness and banality that I did. Hearing Professor Legouis[1] the next night, who was exchange professor at Harvard last year, lecture on his impressions, which were most unfavorable—I was glad it was not Columbia—made me feel anew,—or rather for the first time, because I did not feel the superiority of the English intellect—how much we have to learn from the unusually minimized Frenchmen who think and feel in such incomparable unity of expression, envisage everything as philosophers and artists, and do not slice their souls up as we Anglo-Saxons do. Legouis found the Harvard professors laborious and detailed, but deficient in imaginative grasp and personal assimilation of their subjects, and generalization and interpretation; too much of the Teuton and not enough of the Latin. He greatly admired the social life of Harvard, the clubs and sports,—a rather doubtful compliment, when he emphasized at the same time the very uneven intellectual preparation of the students.

So you see that this past week, my American intellectual patriotism, which had reached a high pitch after my observation of the University of London and Oxford, has had a fearful slump, and all my own shortcomings are rolling over me to add to the general catastrophe. Add to my miseries the fact that in sheer desperation for feminine society I am thrown much with an adventurous young American widow who is staying at the hotel, and who has a romantic past in a section of middling high society of the Hall Caine—R. W. Chambers sort,[2] which has been quite veiled from my eyes before. Evidently used to mowing down men like a field of wheat, she gets only brusqueries and frank psychological interpretations from me. But she has the bad effect of evoking the desire for feminine response to my ideas and reactions without having any spiritual qualities to satisfy me. She only satisfies my ancient weakness for frivolous bandinage and leaves an aching void elsewhere. What had become of all my glowing American horizon? This is a caricature of what I know. Of course I do resolve to expatriate myself entirely, and do have several French friends (masculine however) and in moments of fatigue at the language and a vivid sense of the peculiar sense of well being which comes to me in spirited conversation with a young woman, I weakly succumb and go to tea to some studio or walk with my widow.

I have accomplished very little since I have been here in Paris,—two articles for the *Atlantic*, one on Oxford being rejected on the ground of being more able than fair—the editor is a master hand at saving one's amour propre; the other on a semi-socialistic experiment in England, the copartnership garden city, being accepted. But it is very dull, and besides, as it is the first time I have attempted to publish any facts, I am very nervous about their accuracy. Besides this I have tried to track down the different sociological schools of thought here in France and get a hint of the method and field. But it is discouraging after finding a fascinating school called "La Science Sociale", with monographs such as Tensey has done at home, to be told by a University friend that they are "*tres mediocre.*" There seems to be small use in matriculating at the University, if, as Ward says, Durkheim and Mauss[3] speak so badly that he can scarcely understand him. I go to the public courses for practice and am getting to understand. Ward has the whole establishment summed up much better than I have and probably writes you his impression. Certainly when it comes to the University teaching and professional idiocyncrasies, you can hardly accuse him of deficiency in first-hand observation and personal impression. Durkheim's latest book on primitive religion seems to be a masterpiece[4]; he is a philosopher as well as a sociologist and makes it very clear that when we get the sociological metaphysics that he suggests by his theories, philosophy will have to become simply a department of sociology.

Do you hear anything about next year at Columbia? I wish I knew how serious was Woodbridge's original suggestion that I go into teaching, and whether they really have any serious intention of finding me a place there. I tried to put out a few feelers to Keppel, but have not heard from him lately. This is the "jumping-off" place for me. My mother's aunt has died, and left her enough property—among it the house—to be an endless vexation, and to eat itself up in taking care of itself. My sister will probably be married shortly, they will try to sell the house and I will return to find myself without a home in the world.

I gather you are surely coming over in the summer with your mother, and this anticipation makes any present dullness bright. And have you thought where you want to travel and if you want to travel with me all the time? It would be simply incomparable to do Germany with you, and I hope you will want me. I have many garden-cities to look up, and Tombs [?] gave me some introductions. Assuming that you do, it would make a little difference in my spring voyaging if I knew when and where you were likely to arrive and how much you wanted to see. For I would put off so many things to see them with you. I think I should do my tour very differently if I had it to do over again, but we live and learn. I have almost forgotten the existence of S. M. Bligh on whom, when I started, my whole year seemed to pivot, and for whom—tragedy— I sacrificed much of Switzerland, though perhaps not so much, as the ignorance of how my money was going to trickle would have made me cautious.

Regards to all your family,

Randolph

[1] Emile Legouis was a famous French professor of English literature.

[2] Hall Caine was an English novelist and playwright. His novels presented a mixture of sentiment and reformism. He was very popular, but did not receive criticial acclaim. Robert William Chambers was an American novelist. His popularity came from the many historical novels he wrote and for the romanticized heroines his works usually featured.

[3] Emile Durkheim was the most famous French sociologist of the time. He was equally interested in value systems and in the relationship between the individual and the group. Marcel Mauss worked closely with Durkheim, testing out his theories through statistics.

[4] *The Elementary Forms of Religious Life* (1912), in which he pointed out that in a primitive system culture is both secular and religious, and that this is not true of advanced systems.

72

to Alyse Gregory
(Ms Yale)

Paris
16 Feb 1914

Dear Miss Gregory,

When I first read your last letter, I had the impression somehow that you were a little vexed with me, and I felt very chill, and regretted so much the indiscretions of my self-analysis that were not necessary. But now I read it again, and it is the same so very good and understanding friend, and I am abashed that I should have seemed to accuse you of not feeling the sociological as keenly as I do, when I am really convinced that you are much profounder than I, and that I only seem articulate because you can always see to the bottom of my thought. I really have little left in me after I have expressed, and to express a thing often means to forget it completely afterwards. I am a firm believer in the therapeutic power, expressed introspection, and wish I could cure all my spiritual pains so easily. Your words, on the other hand, always suggest so many things inexpressible, feelings that I do appreciate but should never be able to find words for myself. You speak so much about your suffrage speaking. I should so much like to have heard you—that is one of the regrets for my untimely snatching away from home—so as to have some image to connect it with. Your life seems to me so ideally what I used to image for myself, though I have gotten very far away from any such realization, and see little chance of realizing it. I sometimes am just on the point of accepting myself, and, instead of building careers, and of feeling that I ought to make prodigious efforts to be somewhere else and be something else, I almost decide to retire and cultivate what I have, regardless of its particular value in the scheme of things, and regardless of its power to move mountains, which I always used to think was the requisite for any action. At the same time, I don't know whether it is good for me to have as much leisure and so much abstraction from the concrete as I have had the last few years, for when I am brought into contact with real people I am always struck with the impossible philosophicalness of my ideas and the really dreadful seriousness of my attitudes. Here in France I admit it much better, but England was very wearing. The French youth will talk pleasantly and sincerely and serious about ideas and is not appalled at isms, when they roll from one's lips in in [sic] floods. But the same sort of "intellectual" in England could only sheepishly jeer at the serious consideration of ideas, even though he might be writing books himself. Yet even here, when last night I had an opportunity to make a speech on the ideals of French and American youth before the students of English (mostly French) at the Sorbonne, a horrid Anglicized middle-aged schoolmaster got up and, almost in the words of the *Evening Post's* review on my book, compared the light-heartedness of his youth with the over-seriousness and deficiency in gaiety of heart of ours, as pictured, I suppose, by me. How uncomfortable and uneasy the world seems to be when one questions any of its standards, and pokes about for new truth! How it does hate to think at all, or experiment or interpret! I seem to have a peculiar genius for meeting people who find general ideas extremely bizarre. The "nice" person I simply cannot negotiate, your "sex talk" I am sure would freeze me perfectly solid. I meet so many cultivated people, knowing just enough to circulate, and having irreproachable manners and ideas,—your provincial club type, (for the women), and the jolly, story-telling professional man (for the men). These people are the most impossible in the world for me; I am always too serious and prophetic, or too mocking and frivolous for them. They cannot stand either any hint of fanatical enthusiasm for a thing, or irreverent playing with a thing, and as I am always doing one or the other with ideas or people, my conversation usually produces a steady descent into nullity. These observations are based on the Americans I meet in Paris, and my remembrance of my family's circle and relations at home. Such a situation is rather tragic for a socially-minded person like myself, who loves to see people. For these people are the professionally social class, who make a speciality of entertaining and creating a smooth and flexible social atmosphere. They are a sort of indispensable social Church by which one must be saved, and yet one always comes away saddened at their limitations. It's rather discouraging here in Paris to find that I prefer my American widow's society, who has very much less soul and a charming ignorance of the world of ideas. But I can say anything I want to, or think of, and she will listen with perfect naivete, having no intellectual sophistication to judge my prophetic strain by, and no sense of intellectual and social proprieties to be staggered at my ironies and irreverencies. She will also accept all my rather cheap wit, and having no rudder of her own, she is spiritually steerable in any direction. She does not really understand very much, but, her attitude towards life being that one thing is just about as interesting as another, she pretends to want to. Then too, not desiring to make any impression, I can turn my resources of psychology on her own situation and history, castigate her to my heart's content, be cruel, gallant, heartless, prophetic, ironical, in turn without caring at all for the impression my words make. A remarkable and, don't you think, a demoralizing experience? And how horrible to talk so much to a woman who has no soul! Why should I be so completely and variegatedly myself with this trivial, rather insincere, and ignorant person, while the pleasant cultivated student of music and art blights me and wilts all my powers? A serious reflection on my personality, if it can only impress the very much less than merely mediocre! Still I will say that the impressions which I bear away from such a conversation are very unsubstantial and frothy; they are quite without quality, and I repeat the conversation simply from the childish desire to tell what one has been doing. What a relief it is to express the trivial. Paris has been very cruel to me in not providing people with whom I could be a much better, if not so versatile, self. Up to Paris my way was rather starred with notable and charming women acquaintances, but everything has gone to pieces here.

There is one sociological English woman, however, who is showing me model tenaments and garden suburbs, and is being extremely kind about telling me of the social institutions of Paris, and taking me to lectures.[1] I have been so occupied in pursuing the mind of the young generation and talking to all the Frenchmen I could meet, that I have rather neglected sociology, and this will recall me to my duties.

Your friend,

Randolph Bourne

P. S. I think I was going to tell you of my wondering what I was to do next year. These fellowship years have been colored by a vague suggestion that there would be a teaching place at Columbia for me, but my gentle hints seem to provoke no response and I am rapidly losing faith in this Utopia. The Atlantic editor, having sought for me last year an editorial or publishing position without success, my resources look very dubious. The life of a hermit philosopher living on a mere pittance does not appeal to me; indeed even the bare pittance is wanting. I have little imagination for the future, and, having been turned away so much, totally lack confidence in my ability to find a post. Some journalistic work, writing a piece every day, like Hutchins Hapgood used to do in the Globe, would appeal to me very much, but I find myself so out of touch with the style of supposedly radical magazines like the new Harper's Weekly, the Outlook, the American Magazine, that I cannot imagine ever suiting them with articles, and the newspapers are hard to persuade, I think.

R. S. B.

---

[1]Bourne's note-book yields the woman's name, Mrs. Austin, but gives no other information.

73

to Carl Zigrosser
(Ms Pennsylvania)

Paris
18 February 1914

Dear Carl,

It seems a long time since I have heard from you, and so I send out a line to pull you back again. I suppose Chase is back by this time; I wish I could have held him, as I wish that all my friends were here. I look with envy on the parks and cafés and benches along the boulevards, such admirable places for interminable talks and walks. Paris on top of Columbia will have absolutely spoiled me for any ordinary New York life.

We have had only one month of real winter, and that was not so appalling to me, though the Parisians seemed to suffer terribly. All this month it has been delightful and springlike, simply calling for strolls and sight-seeing. Though I have made a number of friends, none have the quality of my old ones, or even of some of the English people I met in London. The French mind is very congenial to me, but I do not quite "get" the personality. As others have told me, there is always something withheld, a reserve, which is combined, however, with a frankness of speech and interest of manner. It is very curious, this touch of inscrutability; it is the immortal Latin touch of the Joconde[1] in contact with the Anglo-Saxon.

I have met a number of young professors, highly cultivated and delightful, and as most of the University people seem to speak English, we get along very well, though I try to talk as much French as possible. The professor of English, who has recently returned from Harvard and Columbia, fixed up a soirée for me at a society of French students of English. I held forth from the tribunals of one of the Amphitheatres at the Sorbonne on the ideals of American and French youth, and then in reply to questions, sailed off into expositions of the philosophy of James and the poetry of Whitman. Of course I thoroughly enjoyed the experience, and the audience, of about 40, was very polite and attentive.

I don't know whether I told you about the philosophic Brahmin I went around with here last month. Educated at Edinburgh, he spoke perfect English and knew Western philosophy much better than I did. I expounded American philosophy to him, and we became very enthusiastic about the similarity of Eastern and Western ideas. When he left for India, I presented him with a copy of Whitman to read on his way, so that he could see the rapprochement of thought of the very oldest Eastern country and the newest Western.

I have been so interested in reading the newest schools of French literature—some of them showing and acknowledging the strongest influence of Whitman, by the way—that I have neglected sociology, but lately a very serious and fine spirited English woman [Mrs. Austin] has taken me in hand, and we are seeing model tenements and similar social institutions. I must say I like the English abroad infinitely better than the Americans who are a silly lot. Instead of staying at home and appreciating their own genius, they rush over here, sit at the feet of Old Masters, attend lectures at the Bureau of University Travel by awful illiterates, and expect culture to rub off on them somehow. The French conserve their genius, listen to nothing but French music, fill their galleries with French pictures, erect the most charming statues to every writer and artist of any genius at all, and consequently have a rich and delightful culture which saturates the nation. We have, I am sure, at least one genius in every form of art who is as good—excepting Rodin—as any French genius living, but where are our statues and our praise? Our uninspired millionaires are paying millions for some Italian painting of the 15th century, or presenting priceless sets of armor to some museums. It is enough to make angels weep.

Dolorously,

R. S. B.

[1]A fun-loving lady's man.

74

to Simon Pelham Barr
(Transcript Columbia)

160 rue St. Jacques
Paris
20 February, 1914

O faithless one, where are those letters on "Monthly" that you promised? I see that reaction has triumphed, but wherefore?

R. S. Bourne

75

to Prudence Winterrowd
(Transcript Columbia)

Paris
23 Feb. 1914

Dear Miss Prudence,

I am wondering what solution you found for your winter and what you are doing. I certainly had no intention of making my last letter an abrupt cutting-off of our correspondence, and am very sorry if it seemed to mean that to you. I have been reading Winston Churchill's[1] "The Inside of the Cup" with great interest. If you have not seen it, I think you will find there many suggestions with reference to the religious problems in which you are interested. It is

very significant, I think, that a popular novelist will treat these themes so seriously and profoundly to-day.

Sincerely,

Randolph Bourne

[1]Churchill was an immensely popular American novelist. Although he dealt with
current problems in his novels—was even something of a reformer—his message was usually
buried in sentiment.

76

to Carl Zigrosser
(Ms Pennsylvania)

Paris
6 March [1914]

Dear Carl,
     Your letter came soon after I had written mine, and suggests many things
to say. I had been wondering about Hambidge and Anderson, and am relieved to
hear that they have not departed for Newfoundland and the South Sea Islands,
as they were planning to do when I left. They most urgently do not write me at
all, though I have written them. I do not know why my letters are so uninspira-
tional as not to draw any word at all.
     Slosson's elevation [as the editorial chief of Monthly] I observed with a
slight pang, though the detachment of distance has worked wonders in giving
me a philosophic calm. But Dana insinuates that Barr and I are still held responsible for the degenerate poetry they are printing, surely a caricature on the
stuff we put in. Or is Barr still the power behind the throne and is he responsible
for Babette Deutsch[1] and the "dirty mattress" business? Surely the sole preoccupation of "social" literature need not be prostitution, though I hear that the
white slave drama is raging like a pestilence in America.
     I saw Brieux's[2] latest play the other night, "Le Bourgeois aux Champs,"
a rather cynical comedy of the impossibility of the rich bourgeois' trying to convert the peasants from their favorite vices. The picture drawn of the French
peasant, whom I had always understood to be a rather civilized and admirable

person, was most unflattering. There were no less than eight of them on the stage in one scene, and they were all the very incarnation of stinginess, malice, imbecility, and raggedness. The bourgeois types were deliciously drawn, with their autos and social ambitions and smugness. I lost many of the lines, of course, but gathered that the play touched pretty nearly all the satirical strings of modern French society. After being hastily disillusioned, the bourgeois makes a speech to the peasants full of patriotic nothingness, renounces his Utopias, is wildly acclaimed, and it is understood, as the curtain goes down, that he will be elected deputy. The French people seem to have almost as profound a conviction of the corruption of their government as we have of ours, but they are more ironical about it, and content themselves with vague wishings for the man on horseback. There must however be some virtue in a Government under which the country has emerged to prosperity, with an active effective Socialist Party, a paralyzed church, and an efficient "laique" school system,[3] from a state of utter prostration following the war and the two frightful sieges of Paris.

I have been much interested in a school of writers who call themselves the unanimistes and express in poetry the social feelings and aspirations of the time. Perhaps I mentioned them in my last letter. They are a sort of Gallicized Whitman, whom they revere, and their work is most original and significant. The best of them, Jules Romains,[4] I went to see yesterday, and hope to see again. I wrote an article on his book of poems, "La Vie Unanime," and sent it to the "Atlantic," though I doubt very much whether it will suit; it must strike the normal American as very bizarre, for he is not used to feeling so keenly the social reverberations, the power of the group, and the intoxication of camaraderie. The French writing has the most perfect sociological and psychological interpretations in the world, and my admiration grows with each book I pick up. I am trying very hard to track down the currents of the day, and get some slight orientation in the French mind, but that will be all I can do, for I have certainly fallen down in my amateur attempts at research.

In my hasty tour of Brussels last summer, I saw the fine Meunier bronzes and thought of you. There are some very fine ones, not by him, but in the same spirit, at the Luxembourg here, and every now and then I come upon a charming laboring type in bronze in some little park or square while I am walking. There is a very admirable mother suckling her child, tucked away in the garden of a little old church near my hotel. You would like to see the heroic bronze "Penseur" of Rodin, which stands in front of the Pantheon, and the exquisite "Pensée" at the Luxembourg, as well as his others in marble and bronze. But as far as quantity of Rodins is concerned, New York is better off than any gallery in Paris.

I must read Zola[5]; l'Humanité, which I read every morning, has been publishing "Germinal" serially, but I arrived in Paris after it had begun. We must keep our eyes open for social art of every kind. L'Humanité has a very good literary and artistic department every week with suggestions and critiques of social art. Do you know of Leon Rosenthal, who writes for it. A most interesting autobiography of an Austrian working woman, named Adelheid Popp,[6] has just been translated into French and had a sympathetic review the other day. I mention it because I came across it in the Columbia Library just before I left. I think you would like it. It is the sort of thing that I am always keeping my eyes open for. I should like very much to meet some young Frenchman, who was interested in the sociologico-artistic aspect of things and would show me around, for you have no idea how hard it is to explore alone in a foreign country, and search for ideas and books and attitudes that are not catalogued according to ordinary bourgeois classifications. I am unearthing many interesting Frenchmen, but have been singularly unfortunate as regards the aggressively socialist type. I am now attending a socialist school, which is only a group of lectures on various topics, but very interesting. I may meet somebody there.

I can't remember whether I mentioned my happy falling in with Mrs. Edward H. James,[7] whom I see often. Her husband, you know, is the friend of Mylius, and a sort of Utopist international republican. He is expected back soon from the Orient, and I am anxious to meet him. She is a most distinguished and charming woman, thoroughly radical, with great dramatic talent, which she displays by reciting plays to little groups of friends. She is seeking socially significant plays, and wants to popularize them by reading them before audiences of working-people, etc. when she goes back to America. I told her about the Ferrer School,[8] and she remembered meeting Mr. Abbott.

Speaking of the latter, I wish he wouldn't make a feature of the banal poems of Adolf Wolff, as I see he does in an "International," which I read at Daniel Gregory Mason's the other day. He and Mrs. Mason are here for the winter, and I have been several times to tea; but I fear my sociological taint is too strong for them, and I do not get much musical suggestion from them. I have heard "Thais," which I detested; "Tosca," which I must say I liked extremely well; "Madam Butterfly," and "La Boheme," two old weaknesses of mine; and "Orpheus," given beautifully at the Opera-Comique, and sung by a charming and nobly acting artist, Mlle. Croiza. Schönberg does not seem to strike Paris very often; the French will hear nothing but French music, with the exception of a little Wagner now and then. Just now it is "Parsifal." I have heard almost the whole of the 2nd act, sung by Litvinne at a Colonne concert.[9] I am very fond of "Parsifal,"—the music, that is, for I find the story, like many of Wagner's, preposterous.

As ever,

Randolph

[1]Babette Deutsch was an American poet who was at Columbia at the same time as Bourne, although the two did not become truly acquainted until after Bourne's return from Europe.

[2]Eugene Brieux was a French dramatist. He was largely self-taught, but was a very prolific writer. His productions were didactic—he was very conscious of the plight of the poor—even though they were supposed to be comedies.

[3]A non-denominational school.

[4]Romains was at the beginning of his career. His philosophy subordinated the individual to the group. His followers, called *unamistes*, believed in group life over individual liberties.

[5]Emile Zola was a famous participant in the Dreyfus case. He was a very popular author. Although he died in 1902, his books were still being serialized, particularly in *L'Humanité*, a paper which he founded. *Germinal* was one of a long series of novels written about one French family.

[6]*The Autobiography of a Working Woman*, English edition 1913, dealt with social conditions in Germany and Austria from a socialist viewpoint.

[7]Edward H. James, a nephew of Henry and William James, was then the editor of *The Liberator*, a Socialist magazine published in Paris. In this paper appeared an article by Edward F. Mylius, an English radical, who attacked King George. For saying that the King had been married to a commoner before he became Prince of Wales, Mylius was convicted of libel. Then, when he tried to enter the United States, he was held and subjected to a deportation trial, on the grounds that he had a criminal record. If James was in the Orient at the time that Bourne writes, he could not have spent much time in France, for he had returned to the United States in February to defend Mylius at the deportation trial. James was interned in Germany for the duration of the War and later headed the Unitarian Fellowship for Social Justice. Mrs. Louisa (Cushing) James considered herself a skilled dramatic reader. Bourne kept up his acquaintance with her, visiting her in Boston in 1916.

[8]An experimental school in New York, named after an anarchist leader, which gave the students a very non-formalized, anarchical education. In the evening adult education classes were held at which radicals and avant garde artists spoke.

[9]Claire Croiza was a French mezzo-soprano who had a fine reputation. Arnold Schönberg was a modernist composer. At that time he was composing pieces which led to his formulation of a 12 tone system in the 1920's. During 1914 he was guest conductor with many European symphonies, but his pieces were not well received by the critics. Felia Litvinne was a Russian born soprano who was known for her excellence in Wagnerian operas.

77

to Prudence Winterrowd
(Transcript Columbia)

Paris
11 Mar. 1914

My Dear Miss Prudence,

I don't know whether your letter is an answer to my note, or whether we were both inspired to write simultaneously. At any rate, I was extremely glad to hear how successfully you had solved your problems, and particularly that you were getting after the suffrage question. How I envy you, doing practical organizing work, while I am dawdling worse than ever in Paris! It is very interesting, too, to see you evolve from religion into radicalism the same way that I did, although I imagine that you will be a much more aggressive and practically efficient radical than I, with my academic taints, show any sign of being. So you think that the University life is *in* the world but not *of* the world, do you? and have decided to act rather than to know, or rather learn by acting rather than by studying. I felt the very same thing last year at Columbia, although I do believe that Columbia is in more vital touch with the world than any other American University, though not so much as Paris, where the professors are leaders in political and social movements, and make an integral part of the national life. Our Universities still tend to produce as professors the hardworking patient mediocre scholar, or the clear-sighted skeptical critic, rather than the intellectual leader. This is partly because we are so inarticulate as a nation, and even our university people have none of that incomparable clarity and grace of expression which the French have. Our "intellectuals" will have to sharpen up their knowledge, and stiffen their fibre a good deal, it seems to me, before they can take the commanding place of leadership which they fill in France. I am not accomplishing very much in Paris except orientation, but if I do get some insight into the French mind, I feel that that will be a most useful and valuable education. It is certainly very delightful to meet people here who are interested in the same things you are, and what is more, give about the same values to things, and take things with about the same seriousness that you do. They are not afraid of isms and general ideas, and they revel in interpretations, as I do. In England, all my intellectual and social values were turned upside down. I found almost no congenial attitudes. Here I find them everywhere in the people and books and radical papers. It is very stimulating, and it gives me a great many ideas, which unfortunately the distractions of Paris prevent me from working at very systematically. There is almost too much intellectual wealth; one breaks down in the effort to sample it all.

I hope you will write me the progress of your effort with your suffrage club, and any other ideas, sacred and profane, that you have. You will always have the interest of your friend

Randolph Bourne

78

to Carl Zigrosser
(Ms Pennsylvania)

Paris
13 March 1914

Qu'est-se que vous pensez de ceci? [What do you think of this?] I rather like these sombre pictures of Carriere.[1] I'm sure you would not approve of the Luxembourg generally, which represents all the unreformed French school. It is interesting, however, as sociology,—French types and country scenes. The statues are better. Do you know Roger-Bloche?[2] Poignant working-class types.

[no signature]

[1]This postcard shows a Carriere painting called *La Familie*. Eugene Carriere devoted his early career to domestic scenes, of which this painting is one. His paintings are characterized by very muted, almost non-existent colors.

[2]Paul Roger-Bloche was a French painter, a student of Cavalier and Barrias.

79

to Alyse Gregory
(Ms Yale)

13 Mar [1914]

Dear Miss Gregory,
        O, how did I give you the idea that I spoke in French, or are you teasing
me a little? Of course it was English, for I only chatter in French, and talking
philosophy and politics get into a bad habit of translating words literally. This
works for socialism, etc. but is not infallible. Now that I can handle the language
a little and can understand political meetings, etc. I am enjoying the experience
very much. The simplest ideas sound wonderfully poetical in French; I take a
sort of sensuous delight just in the sound of the language, and like to try to
imitate the inflections and phrases that I hear. Still I have dawdled on the
serious study of the language, as I discover when I sit down to write a letter or
note in it.
        There have been a surprising number of suffrage meetings since I have
been here, for France is supposed to be untouched by feminism, women having
already a practical equality. They are certainly taken much more seriously than
in Anglo-Saxon countries. And the man thinks so little of his vote that it does
not appear as a prize to the women. Still there is a movement for the revision of
the code. The dot system gives the wife economic independance [sic], and
makes her in many cases the business partner of her husband. The effect seems
to be to make the woman of all classes a much more commanding personality
here, a more integral part of the social system than with us, and far more than in
England, where the women had an entirely superfluous air, as being tolerated in
a society which had no real function for them, outside of motherhood, of
course.
        The meetings are interesting, though they say exactly the same things
that they say everywhere else. A big meeting the other night, held in connection
with the "red week" in Germany, had delegates from England, Russia, Germany
and Spain, (socialists all), for in these Continental countries, the feminist movement is hardly distinct from the socialist movement. There is still so much to
acquire in the way of political rights that all radical movements are directed by
the socialists, who have in mind political and economic reform, which they will
have to get all together, I think, if they get either. I wish it was that way in
America, and we didn't have progress blocked by the blind recalcitrancy of
progressives and feminists of the Jane Addams[1] type in the face of the socialist
movement, which, international and proletarian as it is, is the only movement to
made headway against a situation which is international, and from which the
proletariat suffer most, and are therefore the most logical class to end it. It does

one's heart good to see the force that the socialist party is in France,—a little too opportunist perhaps, but still steering with a socialist rudder firmly held against all sorts of opposition.

I'm glad you saw my "poem." I asked the editors, in fact, to send you a copy, but they must have neglected it. They thought it was too "intellectual," not "poetry" really, and most of my poetical friends agreed with them, but I am attracted towards a form which is free and yet gives opportunity for expression a little more elevated than prose. I have not had any ideas, or I should have tried some more in the same style. I am always *going* to write, and it weighs on my conscience like lead; but my ideas never haunt me *quite* enough to demand expression against my will. I must always do considerable ransacking of my mind, and in this process I am always conscious of the different ways in which the idea could be expressed or embodied, and, worse, what this or that type of person will think of it. Then when it is done, I have a feeling of revulsion at the staleness and flatness of it all, which destroys all the pleasure. I am not enough of a genius to know this "joy of creation" of the artist which they talk about, and just enough of a one to revolt at the idea of patient research, and the collection of scientific facts. But your encouragement is very precious to me, and I shall keep on trying, hoping some time to acquire stability and power. I feel my "up-in-the-air-"ness very keenly when I meet some of the efficient people with whom I should really be ranked if I were able to carry out the terms of my Fellowship,—people of dogged facts, experience with organizing, overcoming people and difficulties, whereas I never overcame a difficulty in my life, but wilted at the first rebuff, or sat back and philosophized about it.

I don't see how anybody with a social conscience who has once had his eyes opened to things can ever get adjusted to things, without feeling like an accomplice in great crimes. There is nothing to do but stick it out, I suppose. One can give up a little being the "idealist perpetually disillusioned," and, renouncing that sense of personal offense which I have at times at the muddle of things, look at things realistically and discover what we can do with this world. It isn't any static life to which we must get adjusted, but a lot of moving tendencies, and we can get in with the most hopeful and inspiring and do what we can to accelerate it. That is just what you are doing in the most practical way, and I think that is the best adjustment one ever gets.

I read about the "unemployed" incident in a French paper.[2] Paris takes great interest in the "sans-ari" and writes books about them and their psychology, which rather poignantly appeal to me, for I have experienced all the horrors of unemployment myself, and may very easily again. However, I have never had to sleep in a church; I wonder about the effect of such an incident on stodgy religious New York. And I am wondering whether Wilson will get a hint that there is such a thing as a social problem, before his term is over. Doesn't it take the heart out of writing or thinking or living comfortably, to read of such desperate conditions or to see them? How I hate my smooth writing when such urgencies are about to be dealt with! And what weapons have we?

I must not close without admitting that you are perfectly right about the widow. Unmasking her hypocrisy became a little tiresome, and she did not understand my analyses of her psychology, or my sociological interpretations of her class and condition of life. There is something, I am afraid, hideously American about her. No other nation could produce a person so thoroughly fibreless and yet so harmless. The type seems to be the kind we export to Europe by the quantity. She has passed unwept and unsung, leaving nothing but philosophical reflections on my countrymen behind her.

About the novel and play, you will have to give me the plot some day. I should like very much to write a suffrage play, but cannot see the situations.

Your friend,

Randolph Bourne

[1]Jane Addams was famous for her settlement houses, particularly in Chicago. She was too conservative for Bourne, who wanted to change the social order, not acclimate others to it.

[2]In the middle of a terrible cold spell, Frank Tannenbaum led a large group of un-employed persons into churches for shelter. This was interpreted by the New York *Times* as another effort of the I. W. W. to incite riot. Early in March 200 of these people were fined and Tannenbaum was arrested. Many churches did give the people shelter and food, although the group was classified by the *Times* as a mob of pan-handlers, not unemployed persons.

80

to Arthur Macmahon
(Transcript Columbia)

Paris
15 March 1914

Dear Arthur,

I had originally intended to leave Paris on this date and sojourn the rest of the spring in Italy, but as spring has not arrived here and I am anxious to see it in Paris, I have about decided to stay another month. Then there are some

interesting people that I have met lately, and I want to improve their acquaintance, though I cannot say I have been as fortunate here as I was in London. I
meet no young people to speak of, and miss very much our vivid circle at home.
I hope I shall not return to it old and grey and fossillized. I am just beginning to
realize how very much out of touch I am with things at home; I could get the
news if I wanted it, but for a while it was interesting to plunge into the foreign
atmosphere, and forget all the things that shriek so loud at one at home. But
lately when in course of conversation it was impressed on me that I didn't even
know the names of any of the new Mayor's appointees in New York, I realize
what a hermit I was making of myself. With it came the first touch of homesickness I think I have had. Warmer and clearer weather will cheer me up, I imagine,
and travel will re-intoxicate me again.

[. . .] Here in Paris there have been a surprising number of suffrage
meetings for a country where the women are supposed to be too feminine ever
to demand the vote. At an enormous meeting of the socialist women the other
night, there were delegates from England and Germany and Russia and one got
the distinct international thrill. Of course the arguments are exactly the same as
we hear at home, but as it was practically the first meeting that I have attended
in Paris where I understood everything that was said I enjoyed it hugely. I tried
to get into a socialist meeting last night at which Anatole France, Jaures and
Guesde[1] were scheduled to speak, but as half Paris was trying to get there too,
I had to give up. The crowd, however, was as interesting and educational as
would have been the speakers. The French workingman is a picturesque and
rather distinguished looking person in his corduroy suit, and he talks with an
unquenchable vivacity which makes me envy the intellectual verve that it seems
there must be behind it [. . .]

I am still far from the fulfillment of my desire on inspecting the syndicalist headquarters and institutions, for, try as hard as I could, I have not yet succeeded in finding anybody with the requisite combinations of socialism and
insatiable curiosity to go with me or to initiate me, and I have not felt that I
had enough French to do it alone. I read the literature, but I want to see the
thing in operation. An Englishwoman, interested in social conditions, takes me
around to see model tenements, but I am too Utopian to see in that scheme anything very hopeful for future institutions. The French are not half so keen about
social reform as we are, and have very few of the philanthropic institutions that
our cities have. The state and the church together take charge of most of the
charity, and the poor millionaire must find some other way to smooth his conscience, if he has any. I visited a pitiful attempt to found a settlement house, but
found that the young workman of the neighborhood preferred to go to the
syndicalist headquarters for amusement and companionship. Then the national
theatres and opera-houses provide the best sort of entertainment for almost
nothing, and are liberally patronized by workingmen. Indeed it is cheaper to see
Moliere at the national theatres, and grand opera at the opera houses than it is to

go to a moving picture show. In the first, there are many seats at 15 cts. unreserved, while the cheapest admission I ever saw for a "movie" was 25 cts. So you see there is not the same urgency for the settlement as in benighted New York or Chicago; culture is not here the private property of certain classes, to be brought down to the slums. A most interesting institution too is the popular University, organized in many working class districts, where lectures, concerts, plays, and recitations are given every night by talented people who donate their services generally. Most of these "Universites Populaire" seem to be self-supporting and to have been conducted with great success for several years. They were a result of that wonderful spiritual renaissance which followed the triumph of democracy over the army and church in the Dreyfus affair, but which seems to be slackening down a bit now with the terrified bourgeoisie running to their three years military service, and trying to make up with the church. If France hadn't come out alive from so many stranglements, I should say that the rich bourgeoisie with their militarism, and the peasant with his thrift would between them just about strangle the country this time. These horrible peasants, instead of spending their money, raising their standard of living, and stimulating home industry, pour out their money as capital to develop Russia and other heathen lands. France's famous wealth is the wealth of misers; when you see the dilapidated villages, you understand that this wealth has not been expressed in human terms. This is tragedy, too, for I don't suppose any country ever had so many of the materials of civilization, intellectual and social, ready at hand, if she only knew how to use them!

It is a very delightful experience to read French history, quite the most instructive history in the world, with all the Parisian spots and the types of people and the methods of expression daily unrolling before your eyes. It all takes on an entirely different color. The constant marvel to me is that after so many cataclysms there should be anything, or at least, so much of Paris left. The Tuillieries is gone, and you do not expect to find your Bastille, but the Hotel de Ville was rebuilt practically after the original design, and, with a few exceptions, all the rest of your Paris is intact, after innumerable revolutions, and two sieges. The old Paris is going very fast, but you can still construct it almost from the thirteenth century, from the little old churches and old houses and crooked streets and mouldering hotels. But they are letting the sunlight through very fast, and putting up in their place vulgar white apartment houses, as banal and "New Yorkais" as you could wish. Modern architecture seems to be going to the dogs everywhere, though there are some good things in Germany. The Parisians are certainly working hard to destroy their city. It will be a long time, however, before the lovely silver-grey streets of about Louis Phillipe's time will have disappeared; and as for the very old quarters, far better the vulgarest apartments than the incredible rookeries which are disappearing. I should say that there is much more building going on here than in New York. I expected to find stable, dignified cities, in Europe, and I find Europe almost impassible with building and relaying streets, and making two new subways and changing the trolley system. One wonders if the city hasn't got the barricade habit, or whether the story of the street barricades is not a myth invented to explain this passion for tearing everything up.

And now what about your coming? Dana writes he and several other Columbians will be here early in June. Then I should like to see more of Switzerland, and could meet you and your mother in Germany or there. Don't let anything keep you away; because my whole winter has been sustained by the thought of seeing you. There is a Socialist International Congress at Vienna that we might drop in at on the way home.

Regards to all,

Randolph

[1]Although all three were socialists, they represented the spectrum of opinion. Jean Jaures was a famous Socialist leader. He aimed at social harmony and was not a Marxist. He considered himself a patriot, although he was not a militarist. His assissination in July 1914 dealt a serious blow to both French socialism and the pacifist cause. Anatole France had recently come to Socialism. Earlier in his career he had proclaimed himself a skeptic and was indifferent to politics. After 1900 he became more radical, distrusted government even more, and put an increasing amount of faith in the people. Jules Guesde was a leading Marxist Socialist in France. Although he was a member of the French Parliament, he did not favor compromises between the workers and the ruling classes. Instead, he awaited the revolution he hoped would come. The split between his faction of Socialists, the Guesdists, and the mainstream of French Socialism, who were more gradualist, was mirrored in other countries.

81

to Alyse Gregory
(Ms Yale)

Paris
18 March 1914

Dear Miss Gregory,
        I hasten to repair the fault with which you charge me in the letter that
has just arrived.
        The meeting at Columbia sounds very hopeful; Robinson, Montague[1]
and Beard are all wide-awake people. Couldn't they contribute anything new?
Perhaps there isn't anything new to say. Certainly I hear the identical sentiments
at the meetings over here that I go to. The note of revenge, at once grim and
hysterical, that I heard in London at the W. S. P. U. meetings was new, but I
am not sure we want that note. Mr. Miller sent me a notice of the meeting, and
I saw that my friend, Read Lewis, was to speak too. Do you know him? The
most appalling ability in everything that he chooses to turn his mind to, combined with a most sensitive taste in art and style. One of the few people I allow
myself to be jealous of; represents, it seems to me, every one of my tendencies,
toned up and sharpened to an effective point. A person who can do everything
that I could do or aspire to do, but much better and with infinitely less friction.
Such friends are both nerving and unnerving. I was with him almost constantly
last year, and miss him hugely. Nothing like him or my other friends has appeared on my horizon. Two or three charming people whom I confidently counted
on meeting again this spring have disappointed me, and my looking forward to
some glorious personal climax to my year is fading rapidly. As Lady Gregory[2]
says, "The lack of a conversable person is the abomination of misery." I wish
you were coming to the continent instead of Scotland this summer. It would be
quite charming to see some town with you. My ambitions, with little regard to
my pocket-book, are growing every day, and range from Algiers to Sweden, with
Greece and Sicily on the way. I think, if I can possibly do it, I will take even the
rapidest skim, for the difference between no knowledge at all and a mere
glimpse, is infinitely greater than between the glimpse and the intensive study. I
find myself devoured with curiosity about all these places, particularly since I
am meeting such extremely cosmopolitan people.
        Your mention of Mr. Miller's introduction impresses me anew with our
horrible American inarticulateness. The connection between the thought or the
feeling and the expression seems so tenuous with us, while here in France I am
convinced it is as true and accurate as an electric current. They are much more
intellectually honest than the Anglo-Saxon—if the Anglo-Saxon's dishonesty is
not really an expressional paralysis. If you contradict an American or state your

opinion boldly, you either wound him or you make him sullenly angry with you. If you contradict an Englishman, he will be rather amused, the first time, at your vagaries; but if you repeat the attitude, he will soon cease simply to pay any attention to you. And if you challenge the opinion of the Anglo-Saxon, he has the hardest work rallying his intellectual defenders, and hates you for putting him to the trouble of doing so. Here in France I seem to find it all so different. You can state your opinion with the utmost frankness, and if your friend does not agree, he will contradict you passionately with a dozen "Non, non, non. . . .'s"; and he will, moreover, continue the battle with inexhaustible ardor till some compromise is reached. He can also rally his reasons, and rather enjoys being challenged than left tenderly in possession, as I find myself always leaving Americans. My American friends soon weary of an argument, or insist on making it a personal matter, with slightly ruffled feelings on both sides. The Frenchman's amour-propre somehow does not seem to be situated in his head; his soul is more robust than ours. The newspapers say what they think too, and battle with ideas rather than with characters. Personalities play a great part, but behind the personality is an idea, a group-mind; in America, it is simply the individual, and we have the dimmest notion, unless we are Socialists, what idea he is the incarnation of, or what group stands solidly behind him. The French are incomparable social psychologists in everything they write. It is a sense that we sadly lack. This was impressed on me by reading Winston Churchill's "The Inside of the Cup" recently, after several modern French novels of Bourget,[3] Tinayre, etc. Now Churchill is seriously trying to do just what these writers are, —that is, present in fictional form the crucial social issue of the day. But the treatment was so different, it almost seemed like another world. The French wrote with the deftest, sincerest touch, with a wealth of psychological insight, while Churchill's psychology, though his types were good, was deplorably unreal. The love story, conventional, and the "doing good to people" simply oppressive. It seems cynical to object to so many people being raised from degradation to blessedness simply by kindness, but I am convinced that the world does not run that way—the psychology of Tolstoi's "Resurrection," superb book, is infinitely truer. To seek social salvation in the kind of sentimental mawkishness that runs through Churchill's book, and which Americans seem to drink up with such avidity, is to pervert the whole issue, which is one so largely of class-relations and institutions. From Churchill, one would get the idea that we had only to be infinitely kind to each other to make society a Paradise below. Tolstoi with his pictures of the long extrication from sin, and with his haunting presentation of the blind, irrational grip of institutions, for which no individual is responsible, comes infinitely nearer the realistic view of the world as I see it. The fact is, we Americans have the most incorrigible obstinacy to seeing things as they are, to looking facts in the face. We hystericalize, sentimentalize, and moralize every evil that we see. We need an enormous stiffening up of intellectual fibre, and a lot of scientific cold-bloodedness. We need to see cleanly and

unflinchingly, and establish some direct connection between 1/ our vision, 2/
our intellectual and emotional expression, and 3/ our expression. (All this harrangue to explain Mr. Miller's diffidence.) The English are far better than we.
Their trouble nowadays is rather the will than the vision. My social philosophy is
working around to a paradoxical desire for Tolstoyan ends through Nietzschean
means; socialism, dynamic social religion through the ruthless application of
scientific materialism.

Your friend,

Randolph Bourne

[1]William P. Montague taught in the Philosophy Department at Columbia. He was
more of a Platonic philosopher than most of his colleagues and was a Bergsonian.

[2]Bourne is probably alluding to Lady Isabella Gregory, an Irish dramatist. She was
part of the Celtic literary Renaissance, and was known, in fact, as "the godmother of the
Abbey theatre."

[3]Paul Bourget was a French naturalistic novelist and dramatist.

82

to Prudence Winterrowd
(Transcript Columbia)

Paris
23 Mar 1914

Dear Miss Prudence,
    We are surely a case for the S[ociety for] P[sychical] R[esearch],[1]
though I can't certify the hour of the day. You must allow something for difference in time between S'ville and Paris, you know. I am sure I didn't write in
the morning, and think it actually was mid-afternoon. Your letter is sure enough
dated the 23d., and since your last before that was October 18th., there is something extremely accurate somewhere to make us reappear to each other so
simultaneously. And "The Inside of the Cup"! Well, I give up entirely, and turn
to criticize that brave adventure in social literature. I must say, that after soaking
myself in the direct, sincere, beautifully psychological novels, and plays dealing

with French religious and social life, Churchill's writing struck me as incurably sentimental. The types were good, and the religious argument was extremely well presented, but the love story was "too much," and most of the people talked like no Americans, past or present, ever talked in their lives. Whatever we are as a nation, we are certainly not psychologists, and the result is a truly painful blurring of understanding of people, and a constant confusion of issues. I hope you will not think me a cynic too when I say that there was entirely too much "doing of good" in the book. So many people were being reformed and put on their feet, that the reader is apt to forget in his pious satisfaction that the problem is not so easily resolved as that. There is nothing that our comfortable governing classes would rather have us believe than that all our social ills can be cured by just a little human kindness, while the old inexorable laws, which they will not see, go on grinding all the time, throwing down another into the pit, as soon as one is lifted out of it. Then the whole psychology of the particular Magdalene in this book is too primitively simple. Read Tolstoi's "Resurrection" and get some idea of the real struggles of extrication from the complexities of life. I am frankly much more interested in waking people up to see that the social conditions under which sin and misery are produced are the things to be changed. We weep entirely too many sentimental tears over the repenting, and enjoy too much the luxury of "doing good," to see clearly the stern, hard task of organization and education ahead of us. I am apt to be a little harsh with my country now after this little contact with the lucid, direct, so incomparably understanding French, and to feel her intellectual and spiritual vices now more keenly than I did when I was at home. Certainly sentimentality which is only a disinclination to look the truth in the face, is the chief of them; and springing out of that is our horrible inarticulateness of expression, for obviously if we can't see things as they are, we can't express ourselves clearly and accurately. With the French, there seems to be the directest connection between the inner thought and feeling, and the outer expression in speech, gesture, writing, art; the result is their matchless sincerity. With the Anglo-Saxon, that chain seems to be broken; our inner life makes its connection with action of some kind, and not with direct expression, which is extremely difficult for most of us. When we try to express directly what we feel or think, we are apt to be either cheap or insincere. The Frenchman seems rarely to be either.

But I did not mean to write an essay. I hope to have the pleasure of explaining many of these things to you some day, but you will have to come to Europe if it is to be this summer, for I very much hope to be able to stay over here till September, seeing some more countries that my greedy curiosity lures me towards,—Italy and Austria and Scandinavia, for instance. I am waiting in palpitating hope to see if Arthur Macmahon and his mother are really coming over to travel with me, as he has suggested. That would be almost too good to be true, for I have had some lonely moments in Paris, and have found no one with quite the same quality of my Columbia friends. With the exception of two

young French friends with whom I exchange conversation, all the young people
I talk with are old and settled, a startling change from my Columbia atmosphere,
and one a little too extreme to please me. True to my habits, I am lazy and
dawdling and waste an appalling amount of time. My first concern was to learn
to speak and understand French, which I read without much difficulty. This
campaign I managed very badly, darting around to Sorbonne lectures and lessons, and getting completely discouraged at my denseness, which is very dense.
My student friend, who is a true philosopher and very well informed, and who
comes every day for an hour, has been my salvation, but we are so eager to get
each other's ideas that we neglect the fine points of syntax, so that, although we
promised to correct each other's errors, we really haven't time to be bothered
in our pursuit of interpretations, and "explications." I call on everybody, soc-
iologically or literarily inclined, to whom I can get an introduction, and chatter
on political or socialistic topics with them. Then I read in the library, and go to
political meetings and lectures in the evenings. Considerable opera, and hosts of
museums and promenades stuck in between. I have also formed the bad habit
of taking tea with certain American and English women in the afternoon, who
are interested in social questions and tell me much in their sympathetic way
about Paris. I have also been writing a few articles, and feel I should have written
more, with the opportunities here. Yet it is hard to envisage your audience at
home so far away. I feel guilty too at not keeping a diary of my experiences, but
the generalizing turn which my mind always has makes it hard for me to do the
running commentary. I find myself wanting to look back on things and phil-
osophize about them. I have a record of all my performances and I doubt whether my memory will lose soon many of the essential qualities. The lack of any
definite concrete purpose—one of my old psychological enemies—has beset me
a good deal here. In the welter of impressions, I would give a good deal for a
steadying task. Yet, they would not give it to me when I left Columbia, but left
me perfectly free. Cruel freedom, I think sometimes!

I wonder if you are answering my letters now. It is 11.45 P.M.

Sincerely yours,

Randolph Bourne

[1] Founded in England in 1882, this was one of the most active societies in the field.

83

to Mrs. Arthur Macmahon
(Transcript Columbia)

Paris
6 April 1914

Dear Mrs. Macmahon,

I had hoped to hear from Arthur before this that you and he were really coming over this summer, and that I would have the pleasure of travelling with you in Germany. And now I cannot help writing to make my appeal of persuasion that you will not let anything keep you away. Travelling is so delightfully easy, and one can go such long distances for so little money that it seems strange that anyone should stay home in the summer. I expect to start out now in a week or two for Italy, spend two months there, then a little time in Switzerland again before going to Germany, where it will make all the difference in the world to me if you and Arthur are there. Then there is an International Socialist Congress in Vienna, Aug. 23-29, which I should like to visit. Can't Arthur get himself appointed a delegate to it? America can send 120, I believe, and there ought to be room for him. I am even thinking, too, of going to Sweden and Norway where they have so many advanced social laws and institutions. Of course, I don't know how much I could see there without a command of the language, but one might get a little touch of the spirit of the people. I had rather expected to return to England, but find the continent so much more interesting and suggestive that it hardly seems worth while. And there were really no friends in London so congenial as my Paris friends, although it has taken me longer to acquire the latter.

There is much more interest in feminism here in Paris than one would expect, and I have been to several meetings of great interest. The French women are fine speakers, and the women lawyers, doctors, etc. very fine types. There is an intellectuality here, a grip and clearheadedness, far superior to anything we have in Anglo-Saxondom it seems to me. There is something in the education which gives the student an incomparable facility of self-expression,—a gift which we Americans are notoriously dificient [sic] in. What is said too in newspapers and speeches and private conversation seems to me much franker, directer, and more pointed and pertinent than our style at home. This may be an illusion on my part, but when I read the "Independent" or "Harper's Weekly" after a long period of French reading of magazines and newspapers—I keep purposely from American papers when I can—I seem to be suddenly plunged into a less real and relevent world, a world where ideas and principles are not very clear or well thought out. I hope this will not make me come home a supercillious intellectual snob, but I seem to find so many points on which to lecture my countrymen. Anyway, I am acquiring an almost unreasoning admiration for the French temperament, and am almost ready to believe that, if I had been educated here, my mind would have amounted to something.

Did you see my article in the "Atlantic" for March?[1] I mention it only because it was directly inspired by an evening talk at your house, perhaps you will recall the subject.

And now you will come to Europe, won't you? And early so that we will have two or three good months. Take one of the Italian lines to Genoa and meet me in Switzerland, for instance, the middle of June. I shall hope to hear in a month and will be all impatience.

Sincerely,

Randolph Bourne

[1] "In the Mind of the Worker."

84

to Alyse Gregory
(Ms Yale)

Paris
10 April 1914

Dear Miss Gregory,

Just recovering from a siege with the dentist, I am in a highly disgruntled condition, and can think of nothing but my woes. Every idea has been driven out of my head, and, instead of looking forward to my trip to Italy, which I expect to start next week, I am bemoaning the fact that I must start out alone from my warm circle of Paris, and am cursing the abominable train service of France which will not let me stop off, without endless delays, at all the little places I want to see on the way down. This tyrant of Paris monopolises the country, and everything must radiate from here, and places connect with each other only by way of the capital. The spring has been late, and I have wasted time in the rain here that I might have been enjoying in Italy.

Then there are no signs of encouraging news from home, my good friends ignoring all my delicate suggestions for a humble place at Columbia, and my bad friends telling me—as one of them did—that I had as much chance of obtaining a place in his department as Voltaire would have had of obtaining a bishopric. So altogether I am as disgruntled as can be, and my incorrigible disinclination to playing the Stoic makes me take it all out in a restless discontent, which is as improper for a person enjoying the inestimable benefits of a year abroad, as anything could be. I have the same curious feeling now in Paris that I had in London after a few months,—a sort of feeling of diminishing returns. Not that I have seen anything like what I wanted to, or delved half deeply enough into anything. But there is more resistance, or I am less inclined to put forth effort, or I am getting a little weary of this perpetual poking around and sniffing at things. There is only one ray of light, and that is that I do seem to have learned to talk French, but only after I had given up trying to learn. When I came, I attacked it with the utmost intrepidity, but with no appreciable results. I attended lectures faithfully and despairingly for several weeks, to find myself only in possession of an occasional word which trickled in to me. I gave up the lectures and confined myself to my faithful daily friend, whom I soon came to understand. Then I began going to political meetings, and I could generally understand their measured eloquence. The theatre, however, still absolutely eludes me. But I chatter now with everybody I meet.

The Americans are still a great trial to me. They unanimously denounce the French temperament and all its ways, and none of them seem to see the intellectual and literary side that I admire so much. They are all concerned with the horrible immorality, and the contrast with the purity and beauty of the American home. I can never discover why they all so unanimously leave that American home and come over here to expose themselves to the dangers here, or why so many of them live permanently among a people whose faultlessness they abhor, whose political corruption they shudder at, whose abused femininity they shudder over, whose inefficiency enrages them, and whose literature they would sooner think of burning than reading. They occupy a position something like the Christians in the Roman Empire, in the world, but not of the world, I suppose. And their outraged morality glows to so white a heat that I seem like a perfect cynic when I make any attempt to really appreciate or understand what I see around me. Always ready for a discussion on feminism, I precipitate many a wordy battle, and even people who ought to know better, go to extreme lengths in their defense of the American system. "American husbands are the kindest in the world!" is a remark I often hear,—such an unconscious give away of that attitude of tolerant gallantry, which the American husband seems so often to have towards his wife, as a pleasant child on whom it is a great pleasure to lavish the wealth which his "brains and industry" have "created." That feeling which is so strong amongst the American middle classes, that it is disgraceful for the wife to work, and that it is scarcely honorable for a young man to marry until he can support himself and his wife "in the style to which she has been accustomed," certainly doesn't make for equality, but does make for an economic dependence which has its reflection on the spiritual side. Perhaps the French rather overdo the equality—with the system of the "dot," and the habitual way which the Frenchman has of treating every woman as if she was abundantly able to take care of herself. And women do certainly seem to be a more integral part of the civilization than they are in England and America. After all they are "citoyennes," though without suffrage, and all the professions and occupations are open without prejudice. And as for "respect," there is certainly, in the French papers, none of that patronizing, sniggling tone, which usually accompanies mention of young women in the papers at home. It seems to me that one must look to tones and attitudes and gestures and meanings of words and ways of expressing feelings for the understanding of differences like these, rather than to the formal manners and customs and actions that are so obvious and that everybody sees. And I seem to find many of our American attitudes towards women so belittling still, and so far from the genuine instinctive feeling of equality, which I should think would be the possession of every modern man or woman. And when you get women belittling their own sex, as you find so many American women will do, you are almost ready to give up in despair. This word, "respect," which we all like so much, even seems to me—or am I wrong?—to have some slight aroma of masculine tolerance and benevolent chivalry around it still. It seems to be in that class of virtues with kindness and gratitude, and all those others which the spiritually ruling classes in our moral society got established in the past in order to feed their amour-propre.

I wish there was to be some forum, when I get back to America, from which I could preach some disagreeable truths to my countrymen. I am almost beginning to feel like a man without a country, though I do sometimes see something like the replies to Major Higginson's letter in the "Survey" that makes me very patriotic again.[1] How they did hit him, and with what ill-disguised contempt! Well, he deserved it.

A charming young American artist has just come in and cheered me up by agreeing with me on almost every point I have mentioned above. It has also cheered me up to write to you. I always mean to be concrete, and tell you the things I am doing and seeing, but I find myself inevitably going off into a long harrangue on some subject that is bothering me at the moment. Some day perhaps I can talk my real adventures to you.

As ever your friend,

Randolph Bourne

[1]Henry Lee Higginson was a financier and a philanthropist. Among other things, he founded the Boston Symphony Orchestra. In his letters to *Survey* XXXI (Feb 7 & 21, 1914): 551-3, 656-7, he advocated a common effort for social betterment, while at the same time inveighing against Socialism and extolling the virtues of capitalism and free enterprise as a builder of character and moral strength. Many famous people were asked to respond in the pages of *Survey* to the ideas set out in his letters, entitled "Consider the Other Fellow."

85

to Arthur Macmahon
(Transcript Columbia)

Paris
19 April 1914

Dear Arthur,

It is certainly good news to hear you are really coming. [. . .] Europe is a liberal education, even if you just look at it, as I have been doing, and puzzle your head a little about what it all means. Together we ought to be able to get below the skin a little in Gemany, and find out the nature of a people, so highly civilized and efficient, and yet so politically docile. The contrast with these upstart political, free-speaking Frenchmen must be extreme. Find out all you can from Beard or Mussey [Murray?] about the interesting institutions to see in Germany, will you? I haven't the facilities here, though I brought with me a few names and introductions.

[no signature]

86

to Joseph C. Green
(Ms Columbia)

Pisa
7 May 1914

Dear Green,

To show my gratitude for the inestimable use of your Baedeker I can do
little less than write you a circumstantial account of my travels. I am not as far
along as I had planned, for I found Genoa so interesting that I stayed two
nights, and so got in for the pompous landing of the Kaiser last evening. I did
not see him, but I saw his arrival, which was just as interesting. And then Pisa,
which I planned to do to-day on my way to Florence, turned out to be so wholly charming that I did little else all the afternoon but wander around the streets,
returning every few minutes to look at the Cathedral and Tower, and then I
lingered inside until dark, and hung around to see the glorious ensemble in the
moonlight. It is all quite unspoiled, for all the American eyes that have looked
upon it and the Baedekers that have floated through it. What I admire most
about these Europeans is their excessive slowness in exploiting their natural
resources.

My voyage down through France was the only original part of my tour.
I never saw anybody who had been to Toulouse, except my French friend who
was born near there. After the first few hours, the scenery became as romantic
as one could wish,—Maxfield Parrish[1] valleys and castles. Argenton and its
river Creuse especially charming, & Issoudun. Below Limoges we ran into a terrific thunderstorm, which glowered around for the rest of the day. Near Toulouse, everything was quite Spanish, I should say; certainly highly picturesque,
and the city itself a suggestion of both Italy & Spain, with fine Renaissance
palaces and Romanesque churches. Carcassonne surpassed all my expectations,
though my visit was cut short by thunderstorms again. But the views from the
river and the train are simply superb, and it has very little of the restored look.

Nimes, which I saw under especially favorable auspices,—good hotel,
good dinner, delicious morning after the rain, pleased me immensely. The whole
town seemed almost a work of art, like its incomparable temple, and arena, just
the right size, and just sufficiently ruined to be perfect.

Avignon and Arles disappointed me, perhaps because they were too
touristized and especially Anglicized. I could not extract any attractiveness or
impressiveness from the Palace of the Popes, and the famous view only made me
wish I was across the river at an interesting-looking castle which only just didn't
seem worth while making the trip for. The walls of the city are so horribly restored, too, with that pasteboard box effect which is so ghastly to one in search

of the picturesque. There being only two hotels at Arles and the less expensive being full, I got badly hit. The Roman Theatre in the twilight was memorable, but the town as a whole struck me as unnecessarily primitive and prosaic, and I much preferred Aix, where I went on your suggestion. Marseilles being very crowded and dusty, I stepped on a boat, as soon as I reached the Old Port, which was going to Chateau d'If. As I stepped off on my return, the first thing to catch my eye was a trolley about to start for Aix. I could not resist this, and had a most interesting ride along the wharves, through a vast factory district and out over a charming Provencal countryside, dotted with prosperous-looking farm houses. From Marseilles I came along the coast to Monaco, having a glorious day, with the Riviera in the superbest of form, but very much deserted. Monaco delighted me so much that I should have been there yet, but for a showery day which drove me out of the gardens and excited me to come to Genoa. My naive truthfulness kept me out of a visit to the Monte Carlo Casino, (no students or professional men admitted, apparently) but I did six miles along the Grand Corniche road, meeting only half a dozen autos and one pedestrian, so completely was the "season" over. I forgot at Monaco that I was a sociologist but remembered it again on the way to Genoa, when the charms of Riviera di Ponente had to yield to the extraordinary interest of the new industrial Italy, and the long string of prosperous modern towns and villages that stretch along to the coast of Savona. I was quite unprepared for such impressive evidences of this industrial Renaissance; although I had read about it, it is one of those things that must be seen to be appreciated; Genoa was so stunning in its handsomeness and prosperity and so almost painfully clean, that I wonder how it was that I had expected Italy to be backward and dirty.

Sincerely,

Randolph Bourne

My address will be Am. Ex. Co. Paris

[1]Parrish painted dream-like landscapes, and was influenced by his time in Italy.

87

to Henry W. Elsasser
(Ms Columbia)

Rome
19 May 1914

Dear H. W. E.,

I utilize the hospitality of this friend of the wandering American to write a short note to you. Three weeks of rapid travelling have sufficiently divorced me from my Parisian life, and I almost forgot that life isn't all third-class railway cars, antique ruins, old churches, rolling valleys, mouldy villages, and looking for cheap restaurants and hotels. I took in Provence and the Riviera on the way down, and found them quite equal to reputation, though the only place I should care to live is Monaco, with the most delicious gardens overhanging the blue Mediterranean. I could not get into Monte Carlo, which is perhaps just as well.

Italy is very much alive with new factories and bright pink and green suburbs, and new political parties, and little polemical intellectual papers and magazines, even more heterogeneous than the French. The Cinema, with Aeschylus, d'Annunzio and Dumas presented indiscriminately,[1] seems to have almost abolished the orthodox theatre. A Futurist[2] girl of 20 I met in Florence (American) quite converted me with her extraordinary pictures of moving machinery, and I am looking forward to the show here. You can understand all this business better when you see the barbaric forms that Italian modern taste assumes. It must have started with the Reformation, for all those baroque churches which sprang up in the 16th century are unbelievably gorgeous and theatrical. St. Peter's interior is quite spoiled for me by the wilderness of gold and white and flying marble legs, and gruesome canopies and flaming shields. This was one of the times in Europe that I was emphatically not impressed, though even Henry James, whom I suspected of a more austere taste, speaks of it as the most beautiful place in the world. You get a much huger conception of the size when you have to walk around it, as I did with a sore foot, en route to the Vatican galleries. The frescoes of Michelangelo are wholly divine, and the sculpture halls of the gallery one long procession of delightful things, of which, with that perversity which I find haunting me through Europe, I like the double-starred things much less than certain obscure but lovely things that I see.

Rome itself is such a charming gallery with its warm orange-tinted houses and its little piazzas and fountains and palms and firs, and high palace gardens seem quite inacessibly above your head in the street. Ruins are quite monotonous, and I much prefer the ensemble of the Roman Forum, with its chaos of brick and marble columns and little christian churches audaciously built right into some old Roman ruin, to picking my way about down below and trying to identify some shapeless wall or courtyard. And there are quite stunning ensembles from the Capitoline hill, with the really colossal Colosseum, and arches of Titus and Constantine in the background. On the hill of the Capitol, you can see the very shewolf of Rom[ulus] & Rem[us] walking about in a cage, and if you are religiously inclined, you may see in the churches practically every object mentioned in the Gospels, and many others like the altar where St. Peter first said mass. A familiar sign in the churches I know would delight your scientific sense,—"In the name of God and in the interest of hygiene, you are requested not to spit on the floor." This, at [least is my t] translation, and I am sure it is cor[rect————si] mouve [?], this world of ours, even in [——s]ign did not prevent an old priest at St. Peter's from [———] [3] infernal din, which he was making with about twenty others, long enough to use the floor as a cuspidor. I doubt whether he believes in hygiene, and judging from the way they yawn, and nudge each other during service, I don't think they believe much in the name of God either. I advise the person who still believes in the aesthetic value of Catholicism not to come to Italy. France perhaps; but here everything that is not displeasing in the services, etc. is amusing. The mutual duckings and genuflections, and the ceremony of shaking incense in the face of all the officiating canons [?] upsets my gravity so that I leave with a broad smile. The music is thoroughly nasal and quite un-Gregorian. You get at Rome the Christian religion revealed with all its primitive naked origins, and it is not a pleasing sight.

As ever,

R. S. B.

---

[1] Here Bourne tries to show the range of the Cinema's selections, from the classical to the modern, florid, eccentric plays of Gabriele d'Annunzio.

[2] Futurism was Italian in origin. Its manifesto was published in 1909 and its demise came during the First World War. It rejected tradition and lauded the present through a glorification of power, dynamism, and machinery. Bourne's notebook indicates that the Futurist girl's name was Miss Stevens, but no other information could be found.

[3] The letter has been damaged.

88

to Alyse Gregory
(Ms Yale)

Rome
May 20, 1914

Dear Miss Gregory,
      And you make me realize so wistfully what I have lost in not having a
friend to have seen all these lovely and exciting foreign scenes with me. I find it
a little hard to forgive my luck which has sent me alone through Europe, with
only tantalizing glimpses, when I have had a week or two of friends or congenial
people with whom to walk, of what it would mean to have had all these impressions reverberate with another, some incomparable person of light and comprehension and charm. I dallied along in Paris, hating to leave the warm and stable
milieu that had grown up there and believing impossibly that somebody would
appear to travel with me. But nobody did, and I stepped out, just three weeks
ago to-day into the cold world. I have been much happier than I expected, and
have kept up a really furious revel of sight-seeing in order not to be tempted to
think how much more radiant the world would be with that other with me. I
did have luck in breaking my journey at Monaco and Florence, with introductions to some charming people, though at Florence this was almost counter-
balanced by a depressing pension of old ladies and "Americans" and a bright
young American architect, both charming and shuddering, for he had a hobby
of militarism and talked guns and war against my revolting spirit. In Rome, a
couple of introductions and the discovery of the Deweys, whom I saw last summer in Lausanne, make me feel very much at home, and I have enjoyed my few
days here thoroughly. I only wish you were to be over here somewhere this
summer, where I could drop in on you some fine morning and many fine mornings and walk with you. I think we should find much to say, and I hope you
would find me more confident and a little more integrated than you must have
when we walked in the Park, and all I can remember doing is wallowing in a
foolish pessimism, which I wonder did not quite disgust you.
      I am very glad your mother came in, for I have been very curious about
all those things which you wrote me, and which I see and feel so very clearly.
This sacred institution of the family has a sort of blind jealousy towards any
assertion of individual ideals, hasn't it? And the suffering which it causes in the
name of loyalty and self-sacrifice and unselfishness and all those other ideas that,
for all the beauty of their sound, seem so peculiarly fitted for instruments of
tyranny, has, I suppose, an exquisite poignancy that no other kind of suffering
has. (Perhaps that is one reason why I am so lenient towards these wicked
Latins, whose perfidies so shook us). Personally, I have had none of this sort of

suffering, and was always allowed to be quite as I liked, though treated as a rare and incomprehensible species of person. But these advantages I attribute entirely to my sex; I can see quite clearly my lot, had I happened to have been a girl. But really, what does all this idea of selfishness and self-centredness amount to? To be excellently unselfish and correct, you would be remaining at home, playing some sort of a social role which your mother would deem adequate to the social position of the family? And all this to the glory of whom? Not to yourself, for you would obviously despise it. Not to your mother, for it would obviously be most *selfish* of her to constrain you to do things displeasing to you in order that she might derive some sort of satisfaction from the result. It must be then a sacrifice to some blind, abstract concept of propriety, of the fitting, that idol that lurks behind every conventional person's door, and to whom all the virtues are burned in interminable incense. I should like to have this question of "self-ishness" threshed out sometime. In your case, I don't see how you could confer any imaginable benefits upon your family by being unselfish and as long as they don't feel that your public work is in any way dishonoring to them, it seems to me the wildest confusion of ideals to hamper it at all. (Please excuse any misconceptions, because I am just guessing and may be ignorant of the real issue.) But a story like this makes me so angry; it seems to uncover such a tangle of perverted ideals, such an unhealthy tangle, that our American mind hasn't the courage or the intellect to straighten out. I come across the same attitudes of my own family, towards other people, girlfriends of my own, for instance, and shudder to think of my sufferings if it had been myself instead of them. But I have long ago given up any attempt to find congeniality, or even a spark of understanding in literally a single one of my relatives, and, going my way as much as possible, leave them to their amiabilities and perplexities of a world that doesn't interest me in the least. But I see how very much harder this would be for a woman, though I think she would find a great relief in working out some sort of stable truce, giving up all attempt to live in two incompatible worlds or make them understand each other; live in the real larger world spirit-ually, and physically in the other when necessary, conducting all relations with it with a diplomatic, unruffled urbanity that I think with most conventional people will pass for real devotion. Since I have given up caring what my relatives thought of me,—the formidable phalanxes of uncles and aunts, who, in our semi-fatherless state, exercised a sort of guardianship over us,—I have taken a positive delight in our smooth, superficial intercourse, which so resolutely declines ever to touch reality. I am very fond of my mother and sisters, but their world is quite different from mine, and, although they coddle me a little, it always depresses me to be with them at home. Any attempt to inject my world only produces intense sufferings, and I find it much simpler to be interested in their world momentarily than to soothe those sufferings. Every now and then I survey myself from the standpoint of my old Puritanism, and see what a monstrously undutiful son I am, how little of the warm love and devotion I pay back for what has been given to me, how entirely ignorant I am of the heart-burnings and griefs and disappointments and ambitions my mother has had for me, or how her heart may be craving for something that I cannot give. But I have decided that it is much more virtuous to accept courageously the situation, act up to the affection I feel, and not torment myself into duties and attitudes which can never be mine. I know so many families who wear each other's lives out by trying to act up to a standard of loyalty and love that none of them feel, that I have come almost to shudder at the word "home," which Americans roll on their tongue so unctuously. Thus far, you see, has progressed my perversion. In the family you see you have touched one of my most sensitive spots, but I only hope that these reflections of mine have not added confusion to your horizon.

I meant to tell you something of the charm of Rome, but undoubtedly you know it, and it will not be necessary. The suffrage clipping was immensely interesting. I will send it to my friend, Mrs. E. H. James, in Paris, who is such a fine radical, and interested in Massachusetts suffrage.

Your friend,

Randolph Bourne

89

to Carl Zigrosser
(Ms Pennsylvania)

Rome
May 20, 1914

Dear Carl,

I have been on such a rush for the last three weeks that I have hardly had time to write letters. But now that I have quieted down a little, I can take advantage of a cloudy day and a sore foot to write you some of my impressions of the tour. It was very hard to leave Paris, and I dallied along, making so many farewells to my friends as to weary them a little and make them taunt me about my cowardice in setting out from the warm milieu I had formed there into the cold world. I have so little time to give to Italy than [sic] I can do little more than see the sights in that professional tourist fashion that I hate so much, though the first time there is almost incumbent upon one, isn't there? a duty to see the chief things of fame, and get them over with, so that on the second trip one can really choose and follow one's personal taste. There are so many intellectual leads that I should like to follow up here, little intellectual papers and currents and political movements, and I buy every paper I see and make an attempt to read it. But the intellectual life is so much less significant than in Paris, that I am not sorry to have stayed so long there, though my first intention was to come to Italy sooner. I really haven't the sight-seer's instinct, for I much prefer to go sauntering about the streets, looking at all sorts of charming and obscure scenes, than to dash madly about from one celebrated monument to another, and I enjoy poking about a lifeless, hidden little village often as much as some busy city square. One of the tragedies of travelling is that one can't spend, without infinite trouble and cost, more time in the countryside, but must forever have cities and more cities, with the countryside,—as lovely in Italy as anywhere in the world, I suppose,—as something to be whisked longingly through, on the way to a new city.

My journey down from Paris was as strikingly picturesque as anything could well be imagined. First a long day's journey to Toulouse, through rolling country of silver rivers and grey towns and ruined castles, making pictures at times that almost vied with Maxfield Parrish. Towards the end of the day a most romantically foreign, Spanish-looking country with low houses and brown corrugated roofs and curious open barns. Then Toulouse, a city with a character all its own,—fine old Renaissance palaces and Romanesque churches with fine arcaded towers. Then through a delicious vineyard country to Carcassonne, the famous theatrical mediaeval walled town on a hill. The imagination could not ask anything more satisfying than these fifty towers and splendid ramparts, grey and worn, yet perfectly sullen and intact, and without that hideous pasteboard-box restored look that so many churches and walls in France have where Viollet-le-Duc[1] put his healing yet destroying hand. Carcassonne was quite worth my anticipation, though the new town at its feet was prosy and dusty. Next Nimes, all of white-grey stone with red roofs and yellowish facades, quite modern, yet as charming a town as you could wish, with its quiet provincial life and French mellowness and culture. A Roman arena and the exquisite Roman temple called the Maison Carree, both just sufficiently ruined, and and [sic] yet with a curious virgin-like innocence and freshness in their lovely lines and proportions. My early morning tour of Nimes and its terraced environs with their olives and vineyards under the deepest of blue skies, represents the high-water mark of my tour, I think, for charm and satisfaction with life. Daudet's Beaucaire and Tarascon,[2] whitish-grey and dusty, with their castles, looked very charming, but I went on to Avignon, where everybody goes, and which really is not worth the trouble. The Popes were satisfied with a blank, bare, mounting fortress for a palace, but my more exacting eye looked in vain for anything picturesque. The rest of the town was either evilly squalid or blaringly commercial, and the restored town walls unusually shiny and artificial. Arles, besieged by English and Americans, was also a disappointment. One could be glad that the inhabitants were obviously so much more civilized than their funny yellow little houses. I was almost persuaded to wait for a bullfight in the Arena, and am almost sorry I didn't, for

the Arena is splendidly Roman, and the scene would have been most picturesque. But instead on to Marseilles through the beautiful plain of Provence, luxuriant olive groves and green fields and cypresses and distant blue mountains
with white patches of villages. Marseilles is a very crowded and dusty hole, with
a most picturesque oriental-looking port, and fierce Moors and Arabs coming
suddenly out at you from side-streets. A trip to the islands in the bay gave me a
view of the really grandiose bay, with the long line of white bare cliffs running
out on one side, and the huge Riviera mountains stretching away on the other,
and an unbelievable and almost chrome-like blue sea. Then all along the Riviera
to Monaco. Everything quite as painted, the colors exaggeratedly red and blue,
palms and roses and firs and olives in abundance, one succession of delicious sea
and mountain-views. In the perfect sunlight, everything had a cleanness and intensity of outline that I have seen nowhere else. Baedeker added a touch of unconscious humor by saying at the point where the train leaves Antibes and
comes suddenly out on the bay of Nice, to one of the really greatest views in
the world,—"The country now becomes more beautiful."[3] All these towns are
quite spoiled, of course, by popularity, and have become very large and crowded, but Monaco is an unbelievably model little city set on a high rock, jutting
out into the Mediterranean, with the neatest little comic-opera palace at one
end, and a square with a view of the coast so beautiful that one had to pinch
oneself to believe it was really R. S. B. who was enjoying such beauty. And at
the seaward side, spreading down over the side of the cliff, are the loveliest gardens of geraniums and cacti and roses that I have ever seen, with all sorts of
walks and nooks overlooking the blue sea. Wholly enchanting. As I sat in those
gardens, nothing that was not altogether lovely seemed to have any reality, and
the world and all its complications seemed a bad and fantastic dream. And while
the stupid crowd was at Monte Carlo across the bay, this perfect place was
almost deserted all the enchanting afternoon.

   To Genoa then on a sullen afternoon, in which I missed the radiance of
the Riviera di Ponente, but saw the striking evidences of the great Italian industrial Renaissance in a long chain of striking villages and towns, with prosperous
market-gardens and fine new tenement-houses, and great factories,—a great
impression of the throbbing life that is making the Socialist Party strong and
powerful, and also inducing that blatant capitalistic nationalism that made the
Tripolitan War.[4] Genoa is a very splendid city,—finely-built and incredibly prosperous-looking, quite putting Marseilles in the shade. I had expected something
old and swarming and unhealthy, and found a modern town, apparently admin-
istered with almost a German cleanliness and efficiency. As in every large city, I
tried to see samples of every kind of quarter, and I am still amazed at my inability to ferret out real squalor.

   Even after seeing Florence and Rome, I still think of Pisa, where I stopped a day, as one of the most charming towns I have ever seen. Touristically it
seems not to be a la mode at present; the Leaning Tower, I presume, having be-

come so hackneyed. But for all the eyes that have looked on it, it is still quite
unspoiled; the group of Tower, Cathedral, and Baptistry, in their soft mellowed
marble and exquisite forms, standing in their meadow by the old city walls,
remains one of the supremely lovely creations of the human soul, and the view
from the Tower still one of the loveliest in the world. There is no jarring note in
Pisa. Nobody has learned how to exploit the natural resources of the place; there
are no cafés in the cathedral square, (one must walk half a mile to get lunch, as
I found); there are no new buildings or hotels around the famous Tower; everything is at least a century old. The town has a saturating quality, a quiet, prosperous, sweet, highly civilized and genial life. Florence was hard and grim after
it, and ruined by the incredible number of most objectionable tourists,—mother
and the girls, well-fed, worldly, and vacant-brained, "doing" Europe, while
father stays home and earns the money,—a social situation which the Europeans
seem to be unanimous in regarding as highly immoral. (I should say "makes"
the money, for he is usually, I presume, a highly predatory capitalist). They
have driven me to Rome, of whose manifold charms and intricacies I will write
later. Having lost my note-book in Florence, in which I had my jottings of my
tour, I am trying to get up courage to reconstruct it and send some letters to
the Newark News, or, if they won't take them, to the Bloomfield paper. I don't
think I would stand any chance with any other paper. And speaking of this,
K. D. Robinson had recently the pleasure of rejecting an article I wrote for
"Harper's Weekly," which he did with genuine grace and charm.

I hope you have been participating in the demonstrations against Rockefeller in New York. I read the most blood-curdling stories of the Colorado strike
in the foreign papers, and those from home that I see.[5] When one has realized
the strong and unquestioned position that the syndicates hold in France and
Italy, one feels the hopelessly mediaeval point of view that still exists in America
on all these questions. Rockefeller has the psychology of a twelfth century
baron whose serf might revolt against his cruelty, not of a modern industrial
entrepeneur co-operating and bargaining on fairly equivalent terms with a
solidly recognized and cohesive body of workmen. A strike in America is still
considered as a species of rebellion, apparently. These incidents give point to
the universal European opinion that we are a nation ruled by ruthless industrial
barons who know no law or mercy in the maintenance of their powers and
privileges. Over here the greater stability and comprehension is both cause and
effect of the powerful and efficient Socialist representation in Parliament, who
exercise a constant missionary influence on the country and a protecting force
towards the workman. With an adequate Socialist representation in Congress, for
instance, these bloody wars could not exist in America, for the howl alone that
they could raise would be enough to keep the facts before the public, and the
constant pressure would slowly modify general public opinion. I should say that
the imperative need of America at the present moment was a score of Socialists
in Congress. My observations over here lead me to the belief that, if, as I see it,

the path of progress is *away* from a Christian civilization and all it implies, *towards* a Socialistic civilization and all it implies,—then France and Italy are the most advanced countries to-day, with less complications and impediments to the forward march. England and Germany are headed in the same direction, but with a thousand thwarting traditions and strongly tenacious aristocratic bonds to make the progress slow and hesitating. While America lags woefully behind, hardly yet conscious of the situation, as they are so clearly conscious here. And with our deep-seated distrust of social equality, our incapacity for political life, our genius for race-prejudice, our inarticulateness and short-sightedness, it seems highly probable that we shall evolve *away* from democracy instead of towards it.

On your recommendation I read "Germinal,"—with mingled emotions. The picture of working-class life is incomparable, moving, and—for what do you or I know of the realities?—genuinely plausible, and, as far as I can see, realistic. But the flood of theatrical horrors at the end rather spoils the art of it all, I think. The combination of tragedies is put on with so lavish a hand as to become both nauseating and incredible. But it is very great as a book, with many splendid and unforgettable moments. I am wondering if you read it in English, and whether the English edition can have all the numberless and unparallelled grossnesses that occur in the original. Much of that might have been spared, I think, with no loss to the total impression.

As ever,

Randolph

[1]Eugene-Emanuel Viollet-le-Duc was the leading restorer of medieval monuments. In addition to this, he was important as a reformer in architectural education.

[2]Alphonse Daudet wrote a satirical romance about Tarascon. Bourne could well have gotten this information from his Baedeker.

[3]Karl Baedeker, *South-Eastern France* (Leipzig, 1898), p. 245.

[4]In 1911 Italy waged war with Turkey over Tripolitania (Lybia), then a Turkish possession. Italy invaded that territory, with the backing of all the Italian people except the socialists. Italy won against the Turks, but had to contend with a guerilla warfare with the indigenous Berbers. The war imbalanced the Italian budget. Still, despite these troubles, the war was seen as a triumph for militarism and as a blow to liberal democracy.

[5]In 1914 there were great battles between the Colorado coal mine owners, among whom John D. Rockefeller was quite conspicuous, and the coal miners, who had been organized by the I. W. W. The demonstration to which Bourne refers was held on April 28th. It was led by Upton Sinclair and featured Fred Sumner Boyd, of Paterson fame.

90

to Alyse Gregory
(Ms Yale)

Zermatt
5 July 1914

Dear Miss Gregory,
Here we are in the midst of the Alpine mountains, revelling in the air and sunshine and mountain views. While my friend climbs the Gornergrat and I wait for the train to take me up, I will write a short letter to you. This will be my one wild spree in the Alps, and I am anxious to see how I feel at 10,000 feet. I took a long walk at 7500 at Chamonix last summer, without evil effects and trust I shall survive this one. My friend [Macmahon] is very ambitious and talks of twenty-five miles a day, so that I am a very poor walking companion, heroic on the descent, but painfully puffing on the up-grades. We walked, however, a good part of the way up from the Rhone valley, stopping a night at Stalden, a most charming chalet village, on a little height at the meeting-point of three lovely valleys. Yesterday we left in the rain, only to have the clouds begin to break and reveal gradually all the afternoon one wonderful mountain or glacier after another, until finally we came in sight of the peak of the Matterhorn shining in the sunlight at an incredible height over the ridge of another mountain. And we were fortunate enough to have an almost cloudless twilight.

This cold air is very different from the sweltering heat in Venice, but we need some of it to blow through us after our three days in that somewhat odorous place. Its magnificence, (when you didn't penetrate behind the palaces), was quite amazing, and it delighted me, contrary to my expectations, more than any of the other Italian cities, though I did have such a very good time in Rome. Florence I could not warm up to, and thereby commit, I find, an Anglo-Saxon heresy which is almost unpardonable. I saw it twice, (the second time on my return with my friend, whom I met at the steamer in Naples), and found it again the same grim, overtouristized, inconvenient city, that had hopelessly artificialized and exploited its ancient life and had no genuine throbbing modern life of its own. Rome had a peculiar fascination for me, because it was so intensely alive in a modern way, and yet had all the materials for an imaginative reconstruction of the successive layers of its ancient life. And I would give one little orange-colored street or piazza in Rome for most of the dark brown streets of Florence.

Siena, where we spent a day, pleased me much more, though it is Florentine in style. But it seemed to me richer and more imaginative, and the delightful way in which the Tuscan countryside washes right up to the walls of the city would itself make Siena one of the loveliest of Italian cities. The annoying thing about the big cities is that you cannot get the country without passing through miles of straggling outskirts, quite as hopeless, I think, as anything we have in America. But at Siena we could step straight off into it and have a long sunset walk that will be one of the most charming of my Italian memories.

On the way from Venice to Milan we had a whole day on Lake Garda with its shimmering opal water and its magnificent cliffs. At Riva, I tried hard to miss the boat, but my stupid friend spoiled it all by yelling so that they held it for us. Half a day in Milan and a record-breaking stop at Baveno to visit the lovely gardens on Isola Bella, one of the things I had most looked forward to seeing in Europe; then to Iselle that same evening, where we took the diligence over the Simplon next morning. Here again, starting in gloomy rain, we had a magical clearing, so that the summit at noon was glorious, and we could hardly bring ourselves to leave. My friend had his picture taken sitting in a snow bank in the most orthodox fashion; we had our lunch of warm milk and cheese and bread in the intoxicating air and sunlight, and then rolled swiftly down to Brie.

The fascinations of Switzerland, I am afraid, will encroach seriously on our study of German town-planning, (which is the ostensible purpose of our trip, for my friend is instructor in politics at Columbia, just finishing his first year of teaching; he was my room-mate in 1912, you know), and if I am to carry out my audacious plan of whirling through Scandinavia and then coming down to Vienna for the Socialist Congress, I shall have to make some rapid movements. If all this happens, then I plan to sail from Trieste about the middle of September. I don't know exactly what I am coming home to, though there is an interesting prospect, in the way of a new radical paper dangling tantalizingly before my eyes.[1] My intransigeant [sic] reputation, though, is going to damage, I think, my chances of getting any very permanent position, and since I have boasted the glories of spiritual free-lancing, and acted some of my maxims at Columbia, it looks as if the world would take me at my word and let me free-lance at my will. While I, a little weary of directing myself, would really like some tight little niche to work around in for a while

As ever, you friend,

Randolph Bourne

[1]The paper is, of course, the *New Republic*

91

to Carl Zigrosser
(Ms Pennsylvania)

Kandersteg, Switzerland
7 July 1914

Dear Carl,

If my hand seems to tremble it is because I am shivering with the cold, after sitting around all day, waiting for it to clear off, so that Macmahon and I can continue our walk. This Swiss weather is most treacherous, and, since everything depends on its being clear, when you come for walks and scenery, most disappointing. Still we have perhaps no right to complain, for two days have miraculously cleared up for us,—one, when we came over the Simplon Pass from Italy (this I rode while Mac walked up) and the other when we started up the Visp valley toward Zermatt. And then we had there an almost cloudless day for our excursion to the Gornergrat, where the whole sublime panorama of snow-mountains were visible in the clear sunlight, something that happens, I suppose, only once or twice a month. Mac insisted on walking up, while I rode in the train and then walked down with him, or rather the last two-thirds of the way, for the upper part was covered with snow, and the slushy path went at times through banks three feet deep. I was prepared for cold and giddiness at 10,300 ft., but neither of us felt it at all, and the air was even warmer than down in the valley. The walk over the bare slopes with the incredibly huge Matterhorn, (which Mac says looks to him like a great hand rearing up with a torch, a sort of colossal cosmic monument to the I. W. W., I suppose), looming ahead, was splendid. It was the nearest thing to flying, I suppose, that I shall ever experience. We found so many varieties of Alpine flowers in a little space of a few feet way up above the tree line that we filled our Baedeker with them to bulging and then had to stop counting. We have had a great tour through Italy; I don't know whether I wrote you after I met Mac at Naples. I wanted to meet him and so dallied longer in Rome than I had intended to, and this meant seeing both Rome and Florence over again on the way North with him. But I do not consider my month in Rome wasted, for besides seeing all the sights, which are themselves an education, I picked up a good deal of Italian, and succeeded in getting through several books, besides small oceans of newspapers and journals. I met some interesting people, among them a modernist priest, and might have met more if I could have talked Italian more fluently. As Paris contributed to my experience a Parliamentary election, so Rome enlightened me with a general strike, which had enough elements of a revolution to give me a very good idea of the beginnings of one. The suddenness and completeness with which Rome shut up shop, (in a few hours all trams and cabs disappeared, every store put up its

boards, factories closed down, and the only thing left in operation was the telephone, and the railroads, though haltingly), spoke volumes for the solidarity of
the working-classes, and for the reaction against the militarism of the African
war. For almost a week the whole country was more or less upset, and it was not
until the proletariat had vented their anger by smashing things and rioting generally that the country resumed its normal condition. I must admit that on the
third day in Rome, as the streets became more and more littered with garbage
and the people more and more uneasy and demoralized, and the most alarming
reports began to circulate of a complete railway tie-up and the powerlessness of
the government to handle the situation, I began to wonder whether I liked being
in the midst of a foreign revolution. It was as good as a siege. There were no
newspapers, except a little red bulletin that came out each morning and contained only the news of the riots the day before. One of the interesting features
was the hysterical demonstration of the bourgeoisie on the third day of the
strike, when they formed a procession that marched down the principal business
street and cheered frantically as from one balcony after another the Italian flag
was somewhat tremblingly unfurled. This, unfortunately, was the only excitement I saw, as the real riots were always in some inaccessible quarter. But I did
see the squares and open places heavily guarded by soldiers and the people
walking aimlessly and excitedly up and down, wondering what would happen
next. The Government did not seem to be in any too strong position, and it was
lucky for them that the excitement simmered down. In some provinces there
was practically a revolution, the Republic was proclaimed and organized for a
few days, and the papers were full of the most interesting stories that took me
back to the atmosphere of the French Revolutions. Nobody knew at first who
was at the bottom of it all, but the final conclusions were that it was a rather
well-organized anarchist and republican revolt, with the moral support of the
socialists and labor federations, who jumped at the idea of a general strike to
show their power and strike terror into the heart of the bourgeoisie. The anarchists and republicans seem really to have believed that they could overthrow
the state, and touching tales were told of the disappointment of some commun-
ities when communications were restored, and they found that Victor Em-
manuel still reigned Italy. I arrived in Naples just in time for the last kick of the
strike there, was greeted with pistol shots, found the station heavily guarded by
troops and a small riot going on in front, and when that was over, we come out
to find the town barricaded as if for a siege. The city was said to be terrorized,
but next day things were running again, and Naples seemed as vivacious and
rapacious and unpleasant as its reputation usually has it. We found all that region
rather depressing, on account of the contrast of the beauty of the scenery and
the luxuriance of the vegetation with the brutishness of the people, who seemed
really a different sort of race from the northern Italians. Capri was quite delightful, but the Sorrento coast we were glad to get away from. Heaven knows Venice
is evil-smelling and dilapidated enough behind the gorgeous palaces, but at

least the people looked human and genial, and did not growl hoarsely at you or whine and beg from you. I hope I have not written you all this before.

Your letter with the pictures arrived the other day, and were both charming. I hope Mr. Burroughs has not forgotten me, and that I shall see him again when I come back. Wish you were with us.

As ever,

Randolph

92

to Sarah Bourne
(Transcript Columbia)

Dresden
July 28, 1914

We have managed to see many interesting things, though hampered by the weather. We spent a day and a half in Nuremberg, but found it so big and bustling and spoiled by ugly modern buildings as to be little like the quaint old town that we had imagined. We stopped at Bamberg, a pleasant small city with an old castle and a big Cathedral, and then went to Coburg, one of the most splendid of the mediaeval castles, though unfortunately for us the interior was being restored, and we could not get inside. We saw, however, the interior of the Wartburg at Eisenach where Luther translated the Bible, but our little walk in the Thuringian Forest was sadly marred by rain. Weimar and Jena proved interesting, though we landed at Weimar in the middle of a big gymnastic festival and had some difficulty in securing a room. We went through Goethe's house, which has been restored as much as possible in the manner of his life there, and visited all the classic haunts of his friends. We stopped in Leipzig for a day, though a less interesting city it would be impossible to find in Europe. Dresden is simply New York transferred to Germany, and, as Arthur said, we showed our usual philosophic wisdom by coming straight to the Hotel New York. Berlin, from all accounts, will be worse, and I am a little sorry that I shall not have something really picturesque and European for a last remembrance of Europe. Last night the streets were filled with crowds until 2 in the morning, singing patriotic songs and cheering for Austria, which had just declared war on Serbia.[1] The situation looks very dubious, and I am afraid these belligerent Germans will start a conflict that might easily become one of the most disastrous the world has ever seen. The whole German atmosphere is most unsympathetic to me, and while I am glad to have seen this part of the world, I doubt if I should ever be tempted to come here again. The towns and countryside in Southern Germany are very charming, and the people much more genial, but above Rothenberg, everything seemed to change, and you got the modern, pushing, pleasure-loving German at his worst.

[no signature]

[1]The demonstration to which Bourne refers was held that day.

93

to Alyse Gregory
(Ms Yale)

Dresden
30 July 1914

Dear Miss Gregory,

I am beginning to look homeward already and find it very pleasant, though I should never have anticipated, when I left Paris in the Spring that I should ever really be enthusiastic about coming home. But being in Paris and being in Germany are two different things, and as these northern big cities get drabber and drabber, I begin to think even of New York as rather picturesque, and to imagine living there again as interesting. My family thinks I ought to be home with them, and, while it does not cheer me to think of living again in the dull house and town where I have so many thwartings to remember, it looks as if I should have to do it at least till I try to consolidate some work for myself that will let me live nearer my friends. The weather, which has been abominable except for the three little mediaeval towns of Nördlingen, Dinkelsbühl, and Rothenberg, which we took in on our way up from Munich,—undoubtedly has been a factor in my distaste for Germany, but there's the language, which— though I have really studied, in contrast to French and Italian, which I just picked up—I cannot handle, and the realization that I would have to stay here longer than I possibly could to get anything out of the country. And there's the threatened war, which has already damaged the Socialist Congress that I anticipated attending at Vienna, and which seems about to set the whole world crazy. It made me very blue to see the crowds of youths parading the streets long after midnight the other night, cheering for Austria and the War and singing "Die Wacht am Rhein." It will give these statesmen who will play their military pawns against each other such a splendid excuse for their folly, for they can say that they were pushed into it by the enthusiastic demands of the people. So war, weather, and everything conspire to make me think that, if I can possibly secure passage, I will be home before the first of September, and be starting to tackle some real problems of livelihood, which after a year of almost mythical ease and liberty, loom up threateningly ahead of me. When I think how I always longed for Europe, and then had this unexpected and impossible chance of luxuriating with a year of time, going about where I wanted, and being left perfectly free to choose out what I should see and do, I begin to regret that I came away with so little knowledge and so many illusions, and to be sorry that I haven't economized my resources better and gotten more at the heart of the congenial things. And I am rather annoyed at myself for getting so blasé towards the end of the trip, though this perhaps isn't bad preparation for the homecoming of an over critical person like myself. There is one thing that I do hug myself about rather, and that is that I stayed in Paris as long as I did, and didn't fly off, as I thought of doing, to one of these German cities or universities, where I know I shouldn't have been content at all. I do like very much the clean and massive lines of the new German architecture and the boldness and versatility of the household art and decorative work; and I am enthusiastic about their municipal science, and their sense of efficiency and their instinct for machinery which makes their factories and workshops look almost like laboratories or hospitals, so clean and professional are they. But there are too many traces left of that horrible age of materialism and barbarous taste that must have followed the French war, and it will be a long time before that truly glorious Germany, towards which every-thing seems to be converging, will be perfect. But then there is something in the soul of the people which I can't make articulate, but which I know I don't like,— a sort of thickness and sentimentality and a lack of critical sense, which puts them poles apart from the ever-delightful and expressive and introspective French.

I have been travelling with my friend now almost constantly for six weeks. It will be good to settle down for a little while in Berlin. I only hope I have not spoiled his trip, by having seen so much of Europe before him. He put great store on it as a necessary part of his education, and should have grasped it all enthusiastically. I started in most unfortunately by not liking the flies and human wretches of Naples and environs, in whose presence I had been living for some days before he came. I often wonder how different his impressions would have been. But we had a happy time in Venice and Switzerland and Bavaria, and it is only this soaking in Central Germany that has really brought out all my latent weariness with the European scene.

As ever,

Your friend,

Randolph Bourne

94

to Sarah Bourne
(Transcript Columbia)

Copenhagen
August 4, 1914

We got away from Germany on the last boat for Sweden, having a most adventurous trip, and going with out sleep for two nights. We were in Berlin right at the height of the crisis, and saw all the excitement. There must be hundreds of scared Americans marooned there now, and we count ourselves fortunate to have gotten away just in time. We want to see more of these countries, but are afraid that the unsettled state of things will make travelling about inadvisable. We had one delightful day in Sweden at Malmo, and then came yesterday evening here.

[no signature]

95

to Sarah Bourne
(Transcript Columbia)

Copenhagen
August 6, 1914

I have engaged passage on the "Oscar II" of the Scandinavian American Line, due to sail from here on the 13th.[1] Of course nobody knows whether it may not be held back owing to hostilities between the fleets in the North Sea, but it seems reasonable to suppose that the boat will get away sometime.

We read of an American cruiser being sent over to bring Americans home and are wondering whether it would not be cheaper to let ourselves be brought home as refugees than pay good passage money. I hope you have not all been worrying about us, for we do not know what alarming reports may have gotten into the American newspapers about the stranded Americans. As for ourselves, we have so far been as comfortable and easy as we could wish. Yesterday we had a little run out to an old Danish town and a long walk along the water in the breeze and sunlight. We hoped also to take a trip up through Sweden and Norway and perhaps I will wait and take the boat at Christiana, where it stops on the way from Copenhagen to New York. Of course all mail is cut off, so I shall remain quite out of touch with my home until I reach New York.

Do not worry about me, for I am at least booked for home, and this is one port in Europe where perhaps there are the best chances of getting away.

[no signature]

---

[1]The Oscar II carried 1,104 passengers on that voyage, with many riding in steerage. It is unclear how Bourne and Dana, his companion, managed to secure first-class passages. All that month the papers were flooded with news of stranded tourists.

96

to Alyse Gregory
(Ms Yale)

Scandinavian American Line
SS. Oscar II
25 August 1914

Dear Miss Gregory
It is taking us a long while to get home, and I don't like these great gulfs between my European experience and New York life again. I want to step back with everything fresh in my soul, but these eleven days will be blurring it all a little, and I am wondering whether I shall have the genius to retain many of my golden moments when I get back in unchanged and unchanging Bloomfield. I never expected to be so glad to come back to America, for, although I don't feel at all like a refugee, having fallen into an amazingly lucky chain of circumstances which allowed me to get in my leisurely Scandinavian trip and

then get first-class passage on a boat just where and when I wanted it, the wheels
of the clock have so completely stopped in Europe, and this civilization that I
have been admiring so much seems so palpably about to be torn to shreds that I
do not even want to think about Europe until the war is over and life is running
again. I wish now I could find some way to see America as extensively as I have
been seeing Europe, and feel its currents as sympathetically as I have been trying
to feel those abroad. Do you think perhaps that I have been almost too snob-
bishly Utopian with regard to things American, and so have missed many good
things and people that I really should have admired if I hadn't suspected their
"bourgeois" label? I am beginning to wonder whether the utter defalliance [?]
of the Socialists in Europe under the war situation will not give me an excuse for
a little holiday, when I can try to understand more sympathetically what other
kinds of people are doing. I am hoping that a lead that I have been given in
connection with a new radical paper to be started soon, may turn out well, and
I may be able to do some useful work for them. I expect you, too, to give me a
lot of good advice about what to try and write about. I want so much to turn
my experience to some useful purpose, but have always the demons of choice
and feebleness of spirit to fight. New York always scared and confused me a
little. I wonder why it was that I found the atmosphere of the foreign cities so
much more friendly and sympathetic, even though I didn't know any people.
Well, to-morrow I shall see New York again, and, trying to treat it like a tourist
city, I shall make the experiment of seeing how gently it receives me.

I wonder if you are having a vacation or are by any chance still around
New York. If so, cannot we have an afternoon together in the near future, either
there—for I can come in very easily from Bloomfield—or wherever you say?
I hope I have not been away so long as to lose touch with my friends, for I think
of them as the real home to which I am returning.

As ever, your friend,

Randolph Bourne

290 Belleville Avenue Bloomfield, New Jersey

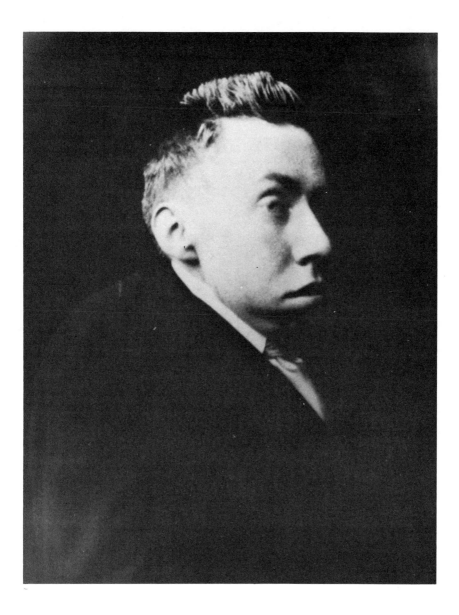

Figure 7. Randolph Bourne (1916). Photograph courtesy of the Randolph Bourne Collection, Columbia University Library.

The *New Republic* (1914-1915):

The Search for a Profession

Any division of Bourne's letters after his return from Europe can be considered arbitrary. From October 1914 until his death Bourne lived in New York, wrote for three different magazines, and, except for the estrangement from Carl Zigrosser, kept a stable circle of friends. However, it is true that his association with the *New Republic* dominated his professional life through the end of 1915, after which his association with *The Dial*, and then the *Seven Arts*, began. This introduction, therefore, will deal with Bourne and the *New Republic*; a discussion of Bourne in relation to the other two magazines will precede the last chapter.

From Europe Bourne had hoped for a suitable position on the newly-formed radical weekly, but, by the end of 1915 he had decided that the magazine, while it could afford him a living, would never be close to him. Bourne quickly became enmeshed in the politics of the early *New Republic*, a struggle which became increasingly complex as American intervention in World War I approached. Herbert Croly organized the *New Republic*, the first issue of which appeared in the Fall of 1914, to extend the program of Progressive social engineering he had elucidated in *The Promise of American Life*, a very influential 1909 volume. With the backing of Willard Straight, a wealthy financier of the house of J. P. Morgan, Croly brought together Walter Weyl and Walter Lippmann to form a magazine which, they anticipated, would represent the apogee of progressivism.[1] Originally, the *New Republic* backed the Bull Moose Progressivism of Theodore Roosevelt. In 1914 editors even met with the ex-president to plan the 1916 campaign. However, in late 1914 there was a falling-out and the magazine was cast adrift from the programs of the Bull Moosers and chose to formulate an independent editorial policy.[2] There was a contrast between the stated progressivism of the editorial board and the inability of the publication to back radical social action. In short, "the editors talked of mastery but they acted in terms of drift."[3] This dichotomy between a bold general policy which preached social change and a timid platform of specific measures which would lead to this betterment plagued the domestic view of the *New Republic* from the start, but, as the European war slowly entangled the United States in a mesh of diplomatic complexities, the lack of a consistent foreign policy on the part of the magazine proved to be disastrous.

At the beginning of 1915 the policies of the *New Republic* could be summarized as "activism, internationalism, conscious control, cooperation, and the use of just force."[4] Three forces caused the magazine to move within a year from this position to the support of Woodrow Wilson and his "peace without victory" policy. For one, isolation was unthinkable to the editors:

> the sources of their new liberalism in the imperialism of Theodore Roosevelt, the dependence of their magazine upon the bounty of the Anglophile interventionist Willard Straight, and their own intimacy with the largely pro-Allied educated classes of the Northeast—all made for militant internationalism rather than isolation.[5]

Also, the publication was formed on the premise that neutrality was political impotence, that action was the key to needed social reform[6]; therefore, during 1915, when American foreign policy was trying to find a consistent principle upon which to base itself, the *New Republic* enunciated different conceptions of American reaction to the European situation in an effort to influence these policies. Finally, the figure of Wilson himself drew the magazine to the administration. The culmination of this attraction was the election of 1916, in which the magazine backed the incumbent, but already in 1915 the editors were reformulating their original assessment of Wilson's indecisiveness. What they wanted, above all, was a man with administrative talent, a leader; increasingly Wilson fitted that description.

The resumption of submarine warfare by the Germans in April 1915 brought the *New Republic* out into the open; the editors no longer concealed their support for the Allies. All during 1916, therefore, they built up the logic of intervention, until, by the end of the year, they were advocating "a new kind of war"—limited warfare.[7] By the end of 1916 the magazine claimed that the Allies were fighting against the German government and not against the German people; the war furthered the cause of democracy and liberation. In other words, the *New Republic* came to adopt the logic of the administration, so much so that it is unclear whether the President or the publication coined the phrase "peace without victory." While advocating pragmatism, the magazine had adopted a new logic:

> this was not war; this was the making of the good society. The conditions of war had greatly accelerated the transition the world was undergoing; they had greatly increased the fluidity of society; they had made man's environment plastic and capable of being remolded into a new and better form. Mankind, standing on the edge of something approaching the millenium, could not help seizing the opportunity.[8]

From the end of 1916, then, the *New Republic* favored intervention at least as much as Wilson did. In fact, one scholar asserts that interventionist intellectuals, such as the editors, made Wilson hesitate in his response to the German peace proposal of late 1916.[9] The war had called into question the international cultural awakening; American intervention would set things right again.[10]

The *New Republic* was hampered from the start because it professed to speak for a movement which was losing its force—progressivism—and was immediately faced with the greatest challenge to its policies—the First World War. Through the influence of Croly, the editors tried to retain the synthesis of cultural and political nationalism, but the strains on this quintessentially progressive program were too great. From an original policy of guarded neutrality, the *New Republic* emerged in 1917 as a mouthpiece for a wartime administration, a publication which was proud of the role it had played in leading America toward war. While the magazine was impressed with its influence over specific policies, it had developed a war-logic backing up these specific measures which was, in the editors' opinion, founded on the original pragmatic tenets of the publication.

I

Bourne contributed to the *New Republic* on three subjects: education, politics, and the arts. In 1915 it is clear that Bourne's area of specialization was education. Throughout the year he published articles which were the foundation for his 1916 volume, *The Gary Schools*. He lauded the inclusion of vocational education as an element of elementary education equal to traditional academic subjects, promoted the platoon system of classroom management which was laid out by the educational reformer William Wirt in the Gary school system, and expounded on the idea of John Dewey that education should not be limited to structured classroom segments. According to Bourne, the school should not remain divorced from life, but should, as closely as possible, model itself on the community. The influence of the school, like that of the community, should not be limited to a specific segment of the day and should not be confined to a particular activity. Education could take place in the shop, on the playground, and after hours, as well as in the classroom; lessons could be taught by peers, and by resource persons from the surrounding community, as well as by professionally trained teachers. Few of Bourne's ideas had not been put forth by Progressive educational theorists—indeed, it is largely because of these articles that Bourne became known as a student of John Dewey, a professor he had had relatively little to do with at Columbia—but his position on the influential new magazine brought him national attention.

Bourne's contributions in the area of education were never controversial to the editorial board members of the *New Republic*; because of their progressive beliefs, Croly, Weyl, and Lippmann worked toward educating the electorate. Nor was Bourne heavily challenged by them when he wrote articles and reviews advocating cultural nationalism. When he spoke of adopting the concept of town planning put forward by Europeans, or when he analyzed conditions in an Italian slum in Bloomfield, he was working within a strong Progressive tradition of domestic reform. Similarly, his championing of Theodore Dreiser, and, through him, of the realist movement in fiction, or his criticism of Paul Elmer More and H. L. Mencken, could find little opposition among true Progressives. Even his demand, expressed in a late *New Republic* article, "Sociologic Fiction," that realistic novels not bend sociological truth to conform to novelistic conventions, did not arouse ire. It was his opposition to the war that caused his estrangement from the *New Republic*.

At the beginning of the European war, Bourne's writings were consonant with the stated neutrality of the magazine. In an early review, for example, he criticized Hugo Münsterberg for trying to swing American opinion to the side of Germany. Bourne even echoed the opinion of the editors that, perhaps, the war, could accomplish a liberation of spirit in Europe. After the war, he felt, the various important national cultures on the Continent could co-exist in peace, both their stability and their self-consciousness heightened by the brief skirmish. After the resumption of submarine warfare, however, the magazine and Bourne began to drift apart. Instead of using events as a rationale for entering into the war, Bourne stated that American interventionism should be considered an indication of a lack of education. The younger generation had believed that the world was working toward a better society, a belief which the war had now shattered. This attack of history on the Progressive ideal should be analyzed: "We simply have to change our ideals; it's the pragmatic thing to do. We should try to find out what kind of world we really live in; this should be a time of education. . . . If we desire that new world where all can live, we must first thoroughly understand how all want to live."[11]

In a 1915 essay, Bourne paid homage to the German influence on American thought.[12] He retained his neutrality in the conflict by saying that, while the United States was tied by tradition to England, in many respects, to be modern was to admit to a German influence. It is clear from his letters that this article received an unfavorable reaction. Increasingly, Bourne was given little chance to comment on the progress of the war, or on possible American involvement in it. In an occasional review he could blast a facile interpretation of the causes of the war, its progress, or prospective American intervention in it, but, most often, he was relegated to reviewing books which could be approached from a more orthodox, and less controversial, Progressive perspective. His letters corroborate the restlessness of his position on the *New Republic* staff, in the general debate over the war, and over the direction of American cultural development. Throughout the period Bourne tried without success to find an environment which would allow him to speak clearly and would protect him in a stable universe.

Ironically, though, Bourne did enter such an environment during the summer of 1915, which he spent at the fashionable colony of intellectuals in Dublin, New Hampshire. Here there was stimulating conversation and ample opportunity for Bourne and Edward Murray, his companion, to demonstrate their proficiency at piano and violin. Yet the reasons why Bourne could not stay in Dublin are symptomatic of his restlessness during this period. Such a rarified, isolated atmosphere did not allow for social responsibility. "I am becoming a kind of Lotus-eater, very much reconciled to life, forgetting that I am poor, or that anybody is poor or ever has been," Bourne lamented. "A society that is rich and also cultivated is a very demoralizing thing." (9/10/15) Bourne felt torn between the aesthetic pleasures of living in such an idyllic environment, and the participation in social reformation which his principles demanded. The example of George de Forest Brush also hung over him—an intellectual radical who nonetheless painted over-romanticized copies of Titian.

The second reason for Bourne's dissatisfaction with Dublin became more important as the year progressed—the approaching war. Abbott Thayer, with whom he had had so many delightful talks, was preparing for the Army a tretise on camouflaging which had started as a matter of artistic and naturalistic curiosity in a study of the protective coloration of animals. Had Bourne not left Dublin, war sentiment would have isolated him from even this congenial group of artists; indeed, Bourne found it difficult to gain an invitation back to Dublin in subsequent years, due, in part, to his unpopular views.

This period was therefore characterized by a restlessness which was manifested in his estrangement from the liberalism of the *New Republic* and his intellectual isolation from even such a delightful enclave of artists as at Dublin. Indeed, he felt both forces of this tension most strongly within himself, between his willingness to proceed in his essays along his own course of action despite the resistance of the *New Republic* and his tendency to observe society from intellectual isolation. He strove to achieve the vital, and yet paradoxical, position of the active observer.

Notes

[1]See David Noble, *The Paradox of Progressive Thought*, (Minneapolis, 1958), p. 34 and Henry F. May, *The End of American Innocence*, (New York, 1959), p. 322.

[2]Charles Forcey, *The Crossroads of Liberalism*, (New York City, 1955), pp. 187-93 describes the early politics of the *New Republic*.

[3]Noble, *op. cit.*, p. 36.

[4]*Ibid.*, p. 38.

[5]Forcey, *op. cit.*, p. 227.

[6]Christopher Lasch, *The New Radicalism in America, 1889-1963*, (New York City, 1965), p. 191.

[7]Forcey, *op. cit.*, p. 240.

[8]Noble, *op. cit.*, p. 48.

[9]*Ibid.*, p. 271.

[10]Lasch, *op. cit.*, p. 196.

[11]"Mental Unpreparedness," *New Republic*, IV (September 11, 1915), p. 144.

[12]"American Use for German Ideals," *New Republic*, IV (September 4, 1915).

97

to Alyse Gregory
(Ms Yale)

Bloomfield, N. J.
28 Sept. 1914

Dear Miss Gregory,

It is good news that you are back again, after such an unhappy voyage. I had such good weather both ways that I had become skeptical about these tales of the sea. But my friend Macmahon seems to have had a dreadful time your same week.

I have been home a month now, getting "adjusted," and, though I have not accomplished what I should have, I have done rather more than I feared was possible. What with taking up the threads with my friends and worrying about my mother's and sister's winter, and writing some of the adventures and philosophy of the war, the time has passed pleasantly and encouragingly enough. I am looking forward to a connection with a new radical weekly [*New Republic*] in November, about which you may have heard something. It seems like just the opportunity that I have wanted to get myself expressed, and I am only hoping to be really big enough for the opportunity.

I quite understand how you shudder a little at taking up your struggle against sordidness and indifference, trying to convert people who are too miserable to know how miserable they are. What little I saw of Connecticut town-life from the train on my way to Danbury last week seemed almost too grotesquely squalid and frowzy to be true,—the unkempt station surroundings and unhealthy factories, and dingy workmen's houses. All this after Germany rather hit me like a sharp blow. I have been trying ever since to explain to myself our hideous objective, if not subjective or actual, poverty. The reaction almost makes me want to renounce all ideals of individualistic freedom, if the German scheme will produce a civilization so superior. I am learning to do what I suppose all Americans do, that is, pass through streets and cities without seeing anything, or allowing anything at least to sink in. Whereas on the Continent I was always absorbing and assimilating, here I find myself constantly rejecting, denying the admission of the squalor and vulgarity that presses on every side. This sounds like an awfully egocentric sentiment, doesn't it? But I don't see what can be done but slowly sting people into new ideals and tastes, and meanwhile certainly not let one's own soul be poisoned by the hostile environment. I find myself bracing against the war in much the same fashion, using my energy not in despair or recrimination, but only in an attempt to understand. While the clock of the world has stopped, we can learn many useful things, and at least look forward to the momentous readjustment.

I hope you will feel more courageous and less self-deprecatory. And I wish you would live nearer so I could talk some of these things with you. Do make an engagement with me for a New York afternoon, tea and walk? Will you?

Your friend,

Randolph Bourne

98

to Alyse Gregory
(Ms Yale)

335 East 31st St.
New York
15 Nov. 1914

Dear Miss Gregory,

I'm afraid you are offended with me for not responding to your telephone message last Sunday. I wrote you a short note explaining my defection, but you remain implacable. Or are you very busy, and have not had time to write? For you do understand, don't you, how annoyed and chagrined with myself I was when I found I had missed you, after all the false alarms and expectations? I had somehow counted on seeing you so soon after I should return from Europe, and here it is nearly three months, and you are quite as elusive as ever, and bad luck seems to dog our attempts. I have forgotten many of the things I was going to tell you, and you have come now to seem a sort of interesting but indefinitely distant promise, possible but not expected. I should like very much to know that you are not vexed with me and that you will really let me know the next time you are in New York. After writing me about the fire, you can't blame me for feeling a little bit cheated.

I feel very much myself to-night, but I have had a quite horrible week of stupid idleness, and a curious sort of loneliness. It is bad enough to be lonely away from your friends, but what are you to do when you find yourself lonely in the midst of them? They used to satisfy me so wonderfully, but now I find myself listening for responses that do not come, and feeling a sort of hunger that my old excitement of friendship doesn't appease. I envy so much my big blond friend Carl, with whom I am living. He is all-sufficient to himself, loves Nature and books, and his own slow-moving thoughts and quiet unperturbing reactions. And he is deliberately schooling himself to live, if necessary, absolutely alone, where he can look after himself, and be happy forever. It must be a glorious power to feel one's self having. And he has a deep-down, unconscious disdain for women, and is not attracted by them in any way. Oh, he is such a splendid Teutonic boy, able to drink in all the goodness of refinement and civilization, and not troubled at all by the other complexities and inhibitions that make one feel at times like a tortured animal in a cage! I wish I could have grown up so seriously and simply undisturbedly, or else I wish I could beat into some sort of expression my frictions and rebounds from the world. I almost think, if I could do that, I should find it all worth while. I haven't begun to scratch the surface.

As ever

Your friend

Randolph Bourne

99

to Alyse Gregory
(Ms Yale)

335 E. 31st St.
1 Dec 1914

It was so pleasant to see you and so tantalizing to have you go so soon. I suspect you went because I said something about a concert, but I really didn't mean to go, and had a decidedly lost feeling when you went away leaving so many things to talk about.

You cannot think how I envy you with all your hustle and adventure of work, your crowds of interesting friends, and your ostensibly—though you do so often hint differently—so easy command of life. I do almost despair at the puniness of my outlook, and activity, which is at present sitting around this pathetic apartment, and attempting to hammer out with great pain ideas for the "New Republic", most of which never see the light. I don't want to drift into peevishness, as I seem often to find myself doing, but it would be so glorious to be "in" something, or making something go, or at least connected up with something or somebody to whom you were important and even necessary. At college I had some such illusory feeling with my silly activities and my friends, and then Europe was so compensating and nourishing in itself that I didn't mind my isolation. And now back here in New York, I begin to feel it. Carl takes very good care of me and he is charming and soothing, but so unresponsive to many of the things that delight or "rile" me. Friends in quantity seem less attractive than they used to be. I seem always to be pursuing them and this grows monotonous. Is this what the world becomes? Am I really growing old? Must one look forward to a gradually shrinking horizon of stimulating pretences, a gradual drying up of this "outside" which has seemed so wonderful and glowing to me? For this outside, I suppose, gets broken up into individual units, each of whom is more and more absorbed in his work and, if he marries, somebody else, and thus passes out of that free, inexhaustible, spendthrift atmosphere that we used to know. And so anybody who has no work grip him except what he will initiate laboriously himself, and finds no one to take and marry him, gets slowly beached high and dry, out of touch of everything but the amiable conventionalities of his old de-inspired friends, and the new conventional people he meets in the world. Isn't this a quite horrible thought, and how does one fortify one's self, do you think, against such a doom of isolation? My friend Carl is cultivating isolation as a fine art which he loves, but suppose your artistic appreciations run in other channels? What are you to do? All this is rather a new and menacing discovery for me. Life sweeps you into it, and you cannot extricate yourself. I imagine you have quite settled all these things by this time yourself, or have found hard work quite a narcotic for such useless worries. I may be reduced to calling upon you in despair to endow me wholesale with some of your friends.

Meanwhile it is very consoling to have you to write to—though it does seem intolerable that it should always be writing instead of talking—for you seem to understand so much. To see you now I am absolutely dependent upon your charity in calling me up when you are in town, and upon the bad fates that break the connection. I have a horrid fear that now this long delayed occasion has come off, you will not try again to reach me. Remember and have pity on my helplessness!

As ever,

Your friend,

Randolph Bourne

100

to Dorothy Teall[1]
(Transcript Columbia)

New York
December 9, 1914

I don't know whether you enjoyed yourself very much yesterday, and if you didn't this would be a pity, since you were the fountain of all the social blessings that gilded my tea-table in such feminine abundance. The adventures of Miss K. (Freda Kirschway)[2] *did* allow themselves to monopolize almost too much of the situation, but then, on the other hand, was not a rare bird like her a sort of guest of honor? The irruption of Mr. B. was most unfortunate, for I made a special trip to ward him off, even to the extent of a lie, and then missed him, so that he infallibly came, and showed me some of the perils of being too democratic in one's social endeavors. He often amuses me privately, but there was something quite ghastly in his flounderings. My friend Carl, whom I don't know whether you recognized as my living-companion, was quite sternly right-eously indignant with him; I shall see that Mr. B. does not occur again.

I should like to track down your dissatisfaction with Miss. S. (Lillian Soskin, later Lillian Soskin Rogers, a novelist).[3] She seems to me quite harmless and of naive good-will, and would probably be a very good friend of yours if you were not the most terribly proud and aristocratic personality I know. One of the characteristics of proud and aristocratic personalities is an over-estimation of other people's greatness. The remarks you dropped on leaving—the most interesting remarks are always made just as you can't follow them up—seemed to imply this. If you wish to continue this conversation, or introduce any other, I will hereby invite you to a special tea at the Copper Kettle, Friday afternoon. I will be in the Periodical Room of the Columbia Library about four if you will look me up. If you do not come, I hope that will mean simply a postponement.

Sincerely,

Randolph Bourne

[1]Parenthetic material was added by Dorothy Teall when she transcribed this letter for the Columbia collection.

[2]Kirchway was then at the *New Republic*, but later worked for *Nation*.

[3]Soskin had been the Barnard representative for the *Monthly* editorial board during 1913, the year that Bourne was in Europe. Her first novel, *The Royal Cravatts*, was published in 1927. It concerned a family of Russian Jewish immigrants.

101

to Simon Pelham Barr
(Transcript Columbia)

13 December 1914

Dear Barr:

I showed your poem to the editors of the "New Republic" but they side-stepped. They are too busy interpreting America to each other and to America to care about efficiency.

Alas [or also] there aren't going to be any more Tuesday public afternoon teas.

As ever,

R. S. Bourne

102

to Alyse Gregory
(Ms Yale)

335 E. 31st St.
Monday [Dec. 1914?]

I am thinking that I am very glad I got a note from you, and, as for what I am doing, I am writing as speedy a reply as I can. I am wondering if you were in New York yesterday, and I am wishing I could write like Walter Lippmann. I am being amazed at the stodginess or the lack of grip of the things of mine they print in the "New Republic", and I am wondering if I will have the nerve some day soon to sit down and try to begin to write a book.

I have been shamefully neglecting the account of my European trip which Professor Shotwell at Columbia urged two months ago, in an excessive burst of confidence in my ability, and which has made the thing go round and round in my head ever since without striking any tone on which I could even begin. Yet it must be done, if only for his benefit, for I have conceived a large and heroic admiration for him. And then there is a novel with which I coquette, and many things which I want to explain to myself, and the interfering joy of reading Dostoievsky and Zola, and educational psychology, and the hunger that pulls me out to talk and gossip with my friends and the pleasure of sleeping late and sitting before a fire, and all sorts of feelings for my friends and castles and attempts to understand and recoils from their neglect, and a vague yearning for a wider horizon, and a disgust at feeling so very much "out" of the circle of the "New Republic", and my tempting and demoralizing piano,—in short, the incurable life of a dilettante, equally amorous and intellectual, who takes life with an almost priggish seriousness, and finds the world almost despairingly wrong.

I went out to dinner with Schapiro[1] the other night and found he had an astonishing number of my ideas. His reactions to Europe came out almost in my very words, and he is writing articles on them which are the veriest plagiarisms. I like him very much.

I was a little angry at myself for giving you such an inartistic evening last Saturday, but not angry enough to spoil the pleasure of having you for so long. I was in Brooklyn on Sunday and the terrors of the sloshy streets sent me home instead of to the Liberal Club.[2] Luckily the Macs never got my card.

Won't you tell me when you are coming to New York?

Randolph Bourne

[1] Jacob Schapiro wrote, for example, "War of the European Cultures" for the April 1915 number of *Forum*.

[2] The Liberal Club was founded by Rev. Percy Grant to promote reform and liberal discussion. The club split over the radicalism of Henrietta Rodman, a prominent member, who then took the more radical members with her to Greenwich Village, where a new Liberal Club thrived. The Club was known as the gathering place for young radicals; it helped to foster such significant organizations as the Provincetown Players.

103

to Alyse Gregory
(Ms Yale)

New York [?]
Monday
January, 1915 [?]

I was out in New Jersey yesterday, doing up a list of friends, relatives and disciples, and got back this morning to find that you had been here. I am deeply disgusted to have missed you, and to have spent instead such a silly day. It began nicely enough, and I could have stayed on talking with my friends in Glen Ridge, if I hadn't had to go to Orange to see an old poet-woman who pesters me and who took me to her nephews and nieces, such conventional, would-be cultured types, with an enchanting baby, whom they insisted on banishing. I will *not* go through this performance again. And then the evening dragged away with cousins, old habits of mine (uninspiring and not even very gossipy) dim ghosts of old gossips coming up occasionally. How annoying to whistle at people who won't follow! My first friends are a haven of comfort. There is the most remarkable girl of 16, a Sophomore at Barnard   [Dorothy Teall], who introspects and disillusions herself beyond anything I have ever seen. She is not attractive, has a brooding, dark face, but loads of humor, and a rather sharp irony too. Her helpless family, solidly built and with an intellectual heritage of dictionary-makers, treat her as an infant prodigy and infuriate her beyond words! She is very pugnacious intellectually, and lays them all out by her unanswerable arguments. When she is angry, she simply keeps still. I conduct rapid-fire duels with her, and prove her a good deal, but am always unintentionally striking something which throws her into a glowering glumness, when she seems on the verge of tears. Our extremely personal conversation about people's ideals and sincerities, and the use of our limited common Barnard acquaintances as dummies on which to hang our generalizations, alarms her mother, and the girl is duly warned against me. I feel as if I was just about to touch the raw, sensitive flesh of a soul of youth, but some reticence springs up, and away from her family I am the big professional man and she is the little girl. I imagine she is incredibly unhappy. What in the world do you do with such people? She has the most facile musical and artistic talent, tosses off little wax models and plays the violin; her school record made her an intellectual outcast of perfection, and she is eating up her college work. She writes with such sublety and sensitiveness, and has an insane dread of letting anybody see it when it is written. Unlike any youthful intellectual that I ever saw, she has remarkable taste in clothes, and follows the fashions with commanding touch, makes her own costumes to do all that is conceivable with her tall and not at all gracious body. Her facial expressions are really unpleasant, a sort of grimace of "Well, you make me out a little girl, and I will spite you and the Universe by acting like one." She talks about people's real selves, but apart from that she is astonishingly free from cant, and rages with a sort of Swiftian *saeva indignatio* [savage disdain] at the shams and imperfections of the world. She is so exactly what I was not strong enough to be at 16, that I am much moved by her. Why are you not around to go on some of these personal enterprises with me? I have a long grievance against you for having discovered yourself and then not put yourself where I could work you into my schemes of things. Please don't leave me in the lurch, and make me feel like a precarious incident. Too many of my friends make me feel that way, and I have horrible moments of littleness and panic, when it seems as if all my friendship with them was merely a constant asserting of myself upon their good-humored tolerance. My pressure relieved, they would not follow. I need them, but they would light-heartedly never feel the need of me. All their personal urgencies, so largely disguised in college, and forgotten abroad, come back to me now with almost too much force, certainly with demoralizing frequency. Yet as a hermit, I should die.

You asked me about Mrs. Macmahon. I will ask her about Mrs. O. [?]

As ever,

Randolph Bourne

104

to Dorothy Teall
(Transcript Columbia)

New York
January 9, 1915

Do you need a special invitation to come to tea again? I begin to fear so. And don't let L[illian] S[oskin] feel neglected, either, however distasteful it may be to you to have allowed yourself to like her once. I must not forget that she presented me with candlesticks and sent me a New Year's card.

I have lately been misanthropic, wondering how soon any of my friends would look me up here, if I ceased to pursue them. I have about decided to introduce a passive regime and wait for attention, which, I suppose, is more nourishing to my soul than I am ever prepared to admit. I could do a lot more work without it, though. If I continue in this melancholy state, this may be the last invitation anybody gets, you see, so I want you not to neglect me.

R. S. Bourne

105

to Alyse Gregory
(Ms Yale)

New York [?]
January 13, 1915

I went down to the Liberal Club Saturday, but neither you nor Miss S[ergeant] [1] were there to protect me, and if it had not been for Miss Rodman, I should have been lost in that wilderness of people, all of whom must be interiorly interesting, but whose exterior appeal is certainly not excessive. They are a type, but a type that does not make me think I want to meet them, does not draw me. There was one young woman I warmed up to, but she froze me and began to run over a catalogue of her college friends with a neighboring man. Most of the people look as if life had knocked them around a bit, and they were trying to forget it; it took so much of their energy to be radical that they had no time left for the life of irony. I am always looking for the one perfect person or the one perfect group, and always being disillusioned when I think I've found them. H[enrietta] R[odman] I like very much and Miss S. too, but they don't make a group. And my old Columbia group is slashed to pieces, all the heterogeneity appearing in aggravated form as soon as we left college. They were all little people perhaps, but they were all expressive and leisurely. The big people that you meet are all so busy that they can never permit themselves those long hours of talk which are necessary if you are really to know them. I must have a much greater capacity than most people for other people, for a whole day is scarcely long enough for a real conversation. These miserable little snatches that one gets in the city, these funny prejudices about sitting up over the fire till morning, all speak of a fussy sophistication and old-maidishness that I dispise. Or else my people are getting old, or else I am an awful bore. Spring and summer we used to lie about the Columbia campus till two or three, but we were men, and perhaps no women have a real talent for this sort of thing. Sleep is always better than ideals, their restlessness requires constant change, and long stretches of monotonous experience are distasteful to them. I imagine women are very bad travelers, and have no appreciation of the sensuous bliss of a ten-hour railroad ride, or the leisurely day-long scouring of a foreign city. Even a day's excursion usually brings them home cross and hungry, their minds worn out and filled only with thoughts of supper and escape to dreamlessness. I am moved to this outburst of philosophy by an experience of the other night, which I take to be deeply typical. We were a little party at the delightful apartment of a girl who has some sort of office suffrage job. We were alternating a little music on her baby grand, and talk, and were just sinking into that evening comfort about the glowing fire, preparing to be ruminative and delightful when at ten o'clock we were smartly turned out, graciously but finally, on the ground that this was her closing hour, for she had to be at work at 9 the next morning. When you realize that she is usually grumbling a little about her wage-slavery and envying the untrammeled ones, her incapacity to extract enjoyment from the slow Debussy-accompanied passage of time before a grate-fire, stealing pleasure in the very face of encroaching night, is almost inexplicable. The thing is a personal outrage from which I shall not soon recover. I can only ascribe it to some profound, incorrigible perversity of woman. It becomes more malign when you realize that the girl pretends to be not only anti-man but anti-woman too. The vivacity of her defenders convinces me that she is not alone, that we are in the helpless grip of an inexplicable feminine philosophy of life, a sort of spiritual callousness which almost gives point to the claim of my German friends that women have no souls. Can you throw any light on this disaster which has so shaken my faith in womankind? It will be a long time before I take up again the threads of intuitive understanding which I have deluded myself into feeling. I shall watch the clock for the striking of that mechanical hour; when the executioner arrives to end the conversation, I shall click my heels and depart in the middle of a sentence to the scaffold. I shall recognize myself as a filler-in of certain tightly-compressed moments, a stop-gap between 8.30 and 10 P.M., a sort of dull vaudeville act. Is it possible that women regard all men with whom they are not in love as mere more or less interesting vaudeville acts? No wonder the N. Y. Journal and Anatole France are sceptical of Platonic friendship.

Your friend,

R. S. Bourne

[1]Sergeant was then a writer for the *New Republic*. Later she was a biographer of Frost and Cather. At this time she was also writing a series of articles for *New Republic* on French life.

106

to Prudence Winterrowd
(Transcript Columbia)

335 E. 31st St.
New York City
19 Jan 1915

The only thing that precluded my not answering your last two letters was the fact that I never received them. If you sent any letters to Europe after July 1, they are entombed somewhere on the Continent, and there also seem to be hiatuses between Bloomfield and New York. I have come, since the fateful experience of the war, to look upon letters as a gift of divine grace, rather than anything to be expected or predicted.

I am glad not to have been forgotten and glad there is a chance of meeting you soon. You will probably like me better if you don't see me. There have been one or two people to whom I gave much pain by appearing in my uninspiring reality after apparently a much nicer person had been created out of the "Atlantic". So I warn you. I had just been thinking of you and wondering whether I should happen to see you out of a car-window on my contemplated trip to Gary etc. next month. There are so many places I want to stop at on this my first trip west of Pittsburg, and I don't know how much time I shall have. I think I did tell them to send you the N[ew] R[epublic]. You'd better subscribe, so that wisdom will be justified of her children. I get in an occasional article and editorial and more frequent book-reviews. I spend almost my whole time writing for them, but produce much more than they use. I feel as if I were attending an incomparable school of journalism. I hope, if you come to New York you will like it better than you did. I really despise it, after Paris and Rome, and am trying to decide where and under what circumstances I could be happy. People here are too industrious or sophisticated to go deeply into that rather ruminative, searching, personal life that I got more and more immersed in when I was abroad. I have a great deal of trouble with my writing, but am a little more callous towards it than I used to be. One of my correspondents claims to have seen articles in the "Atlantic" and N. R. purporting to have come from my pen, but utterly lacking in the quality of my personality. Have you followed me, by any chance, closely enough to notice this spiritual degeneration? Just now my ideas are very chaotic. I seem to be able to believe diametrically opposite things. All I hate now is not opposing ideas but muddiness of thinking. I am glad Shelbyville is picking up.

Sincerely yours,

Randolph Bourne

107

to Dorothy Teall
(Transcript Columbia)

New York
February 6, 1915

I wish I could get you to come to tea Lincoln's Birthday. This is to be a really big party. I am trying to get Mary Antin[1] and Louise Paine, and some less celebrated though equally charming people. I hope the Chases will come, and you can meet the lovely Jane Olivia.

Your not condescending to come any more to my lesser affairs, at which there is always somebody, does not discourage me, you see, and I trust you will find these bribes big enough to induce you. It seems evident that I like to talk to you much better than you do to me, or you would not have thus turned down what I thought was rather a pathetic appeal. I wish you were interested enough to justify yourself. You must know that I am hardly enough to stand any form of truth, and if you are to be that fine, free, and unscrupulous person that I take it you are going to be, you must begin by treating the world in a more open-handed manner as if everybody was your friend and you were all equals and understood each other perfectly. You do do this a great deal, but then you have sudden panics which I don't quite understand, and make me think I've stepped on something and hurt it, and I am sorry and don't know just what to do about it. If, as you imply, you are not overburdened with people you can trust, I shall take it very badly if you don't trust me. Or are you going to be a lonely Zarathustra, wandering in the mountains with your eagle and your serpent? You see I haven't the slightest inkling whether you despise the chattering world because you don't need friends, or because you do. Come on, clear this up, and commit yourself.

Very much your friend,

Randolph Bourne

[1]Mary Antin was the author of *Promised Land* which was serialized in *The Atlantic* in 1912. She preached the value of immigrants in American life, although she was in favor of their assimilation into the American scene.

108

to Dorothy Teall
(Transcript Columbia)

335 E. 31st St.
Sunday [Feb 21, 1915]

It was not any unfaithfulness of yours, but the appeal of worldly matters weightier than myself that spoiled my Thursday evening. A charming note of somewhat confused candor explaining why our lady [Beulah] [1] could not be found at Brooks [Hall] when I discretely appeared as predicted by myself. My trip is postponed again, and this leaves a Tuesday next, 23rd., when I charge you, if any human means are possible, to corral her and bring her down on that day. I have written her, but I have no assurance that this alone will ensure this act of grace. So I rely on your valiant aid. A certain note of remorse both at having betrayed me, and at having put you in the role of an unfaithful (apparently) messenger, might be struck. Or the fact that two other parties yawned for her unavailingly might draw her. On the other hand, one would not want to annoy her by too arduous pursuit. I can trust you to know just the delicate thing.

Your own note, apparently wrung rather cruelly from you, told me some things, and also chagrinned me a little that it was dutiful daughter responding to family's counsels that got me my first and only London letter. I'm sorry I failed so dismally in the role I was supposed to play. Your complaint that I did not keep my remote impersonal father-confessoriness doesn't go with you accusing me of regarding you as a sociological specimen. But this latter I do to myself as much as to anybody. Why it is partly because it seems to me that a lot of this human kindness business is sheer sentimentality and a result of quite a wrong way of cutting-up the world. All this moral and religious and social trying to find out what people expect you to do and then doing it, instead of being your very best, most expressive, most controlling self, makes me tired. Yet the first is what the older generation is trying to make us do, and it is in the conflicts between the two attitudes that so many of us get lacerated and torn. When you distinguish my roles, as you did in your letter, you are simply talking the old language. What I am is your very good and interested friend, and if these other things are there they are all mixed up, I certainly never analyzed them out. What I like about you is that you have come up against the world with the same sort of recoil and rebound that I do myself, and what's more you seem to be going to settle yourself in a couple of years with issues that have taken me then, and not at all settled yet. I am really not at all older than you, and probably shall not be any older than I am now. I hope you won't let yourself be inhibited by anything from your fullest expression. Let those brambles turn into the weeds on the

roadside, which do not obscure the distant mountains. Don't be afraid of brush-
ing through. Chase the fine, the true, expressive people and let the rest slide to
perdition. Chase them indefatigably and find yourself in them. They will never
completely satisfy, but perhaps you won't satisfy them. And don't wonder
whether people "like" you or are only "intellectually interested" in you (of
course, you may not be wondering this at all), but anyway, this contrast is only
one of those confounded intellectual stunts that we do all the time, dividing
things that are really just one complete whole. See how many problems dis-
appear when you realize that the terms in which you have set them are quite
artificial; and you find the world simpler.

Your very good friend,

Randolph Bourne

[1]Beulah Amidon, a North Dakota girl, was then at Barnard. She then went to law
school at Southern California. In the twenties she became associated with *Survey*, and remained with that magazine until its demise in the early fifties.

109

to John Erskine
(Ms Columbia)

New York
February 22, 1915

Dear Professor Erskine,
    We are all very much interested in Mr. Kilmer's article in yesterday's
"Times" about the literary spirit at Columbia. If you are quoted correctly, you
seem to imply that the now unhappily defunct Monthly somehow did not represent the best literary spirit on the campus, and had to die, because it could
enlist only second-best material. Surely you must know that it is the men who
took the leading part in editing and writing the paper from 1911 to the end,—
Hambidge, Barr, Robinson, Henle, Anderson, Slosson, and myself, who have
been selling our stuff in that outside way that you speak so proudly of, and not
the people outside of our Monthly group. I know personally of editorials,
articles and verse from the pen of these seven men that have appeared in the

Atlantic Monthly, the *Unpopular Review*, the *Independent*, the *Century*, the *North American Review, Harper's Weekly*, the *New Republic, Travel Magazine, Lippincott's*, the *Masses*, and the supplements of the *N. Y. Evening Post* and the *Brooklyn Eagle*. Two of us have now published books, one has a book in press, and five are now connected editorially with New York magazines or papers. If there is a single undergraduate of Columbia of those years 1911-1915 (outside of our Columbia Monthly group) who has so much as contributed to any of these magazines I have mentioned, or to any others of *equal* standing, I should be very glad to hear about him. I honestly cannot think of any now. If it was exactly those persons who edited the college literary magazine who have this creditable literary record, and rather surprisingly prompt recognition, and if no persons outside of this group have anything resembling this record or this recognition, don't you think the spirit and training of the Monthly deserves greater emphasis than you were pleased to give it in your interview? The Monthly appears to me as so amusing and profitable a literary school that I naturally tend perhaps to overvalue it. So I ask you merely to consider it in this objective way, and judge its spirit and value by these results. The Harvard Monthly has the same story to tell. It proves, too, the incomparable value of a little group of self-conscious, interested undergraduate writers who are trying to produce a magazine as expressive as possible of their mutual spirit and enthusiasms. Our record, I think, is rather extraordinary, considering how entirely independent and indeed unpopular our activities were.

I shall be much interested in the literary undergraduate output developed without the stimulation of the Monthly, and the prompt recognition of this new literary spirit by the better magazines of the literary world. The lighter verse of Mr. Archie Austin Coates does indeed strike me as a promising beginning.[1]

Sincerely yours,

Randolph Bourne

[1]Erskine was pointing out in this article (February 21, V, 21:1) that college no longer shuts students out from the world. They too are a part of the cultural reawakening. Bourne was cited as an example of a student who had succeeded in writing to more than a college audience. A college literary magazine, Erskine said, was then unnecessary, receiving only second-rate stuff that students could not sell to publishers. In fact Bourne had relatively little to stand on in this argument. None of the colleagues he cited had published more than two articles as of February 1915. Then again, Archie Austin Coates, whom Erskine lauds, had succeeded in publishing a small collection of poetry through the Boar's Head, a Columbia literary and dramatic group, and had had only two of his poems published by a magazine, *The Delineator*, as of the date of this letter.

110

to Alyse Gregory
(Ms Yale)

16 March [1915]

It was your leaving me that was my undoing. Left with a hopeless hour to put in, I dropped on my Christian Science friend [Mary Messer] ,[1] and found so many dragons to slay, and so much interesting combat of Nietzsche and Christ and Americanism that I simply didn't come. She is perfectly mad, all her style and subtlety destroyed—she used to write charming verse—so that she writes now worse than Mrs. Eddy.[2] But she retains more real comprehension of the personal issues of life than almost anybody I know. She is sublimating suffrage to the spiritual plane in an atrocious work, and living and talking most delightfully and humanly a dual life I don't attempt to fathom.

We are going to have a party Sunday for Mrs. E. H. James, who was the bright spot of my Paris sojourn. Her husband is a visionary international Socialist, founding red republics in various countries when he isn't libelling King George. He represents the last degenerate flare-out of the old James stock. She is very fine, best of Boston idealists combined with cosmopolitan radicalism. She likes to read plays, and is going to do Synge and H. V. Lindsay.[3] Will you come? I quite worshipped her in her Paris drawing-room. I don't know how it will look in Phipps Houses. In a confiding moment I invited Schapiro, and immediately afterwards heard a savage feminine reaction to him which curdled my blood. He won't spoil my party, will he? There is a certain large pervadingness about him which, set in my small room, does kindle my vivid imagination to anticipate. You will come and neutralize him, won't you?

R. S. B.

[1]Mary Messer was introduced to Bourne by Read Lewis, who worked at the Charity Organization Society with her. She soon devoted most of her time to Christian Science and Bourne (and Lewis) lost interest in her.

[2]Mary Baker Eddy was the founder of Christian Science.

[3]Synge was an Irish dramatist most famous for *Playboy of the Western World.* H. Vachel Lindsay was an American poet who was then being discovered. Many of his poems appeared in *Poetry.* His poetry contained many populist themes.

111

to Dorothy Teall[1]
(Transcript Columbia)

New York
March 20, 1915

Did I answer your letter? I have been back over a week, and all the glories of Wisconsin spirit and Gary schools have faded in the chilling light of New York. As misfortune would have it, Dr. (Ernest Sutherland) Bates[2] came one Tuesday when I was away, and is preserving strong silence against my remorse and renewed invitations. Beulah (Amidon) has not been seen again, is very coy, and is probably raving *at* me rather than about me, if I can believe your flattering implications that she ever did that. It seems she inspired me to some rather extraordinary flights. I may have been dashed to earth by now.

I saw your sister, already matronly and protecting in Pittsburg, arrived, in fact, in time for breakfast, and stayed to dinner and supper. There is nothing to report, except a perfectly orthodox happiness on both sides, an atmosphere of calm content, which slightly chills the bachelor who returns home to no such adoring trustfulness.

Can't you come Tuesday? With somebody or alone. There will be somebody here.

Randolph Bourne

---

[1]Parenthetic material is Teall's addition.

[2]Bates was an historian on the faculty of the University of Arizona. Religion was his major interest. He became the literary editor of the *Dictionary of American Biography* in the '20's. He wrote the original entry for Bourne in the *DAB*.

112

to Dorothy Teall
(Transcript Columbia)

New York
March 26, 1915

Would you not like to go Wednesday and see Isadora Duncan dance?[1] Say yes, and I will get the tickets, and you can meet me at two o'clock at the Century Theatre, Central Park West and 62nd St., in the vestibule, near the ticket-office.

Beulah came to a party Sunday. I thought your mother would not approve of Sunday tea-parties so I did not dare ask you.

Hope you can come Wednesday.

Randolph

[1]Duncan was a dancer who revolutionized her field through her improvisational techniques. She was in the United States only briefly in 1915, but did give a month of performances at the Century.

113

to Dorothy Teall[1]
(Transcript Columbia)

7 April [1915]

1. Mon Amie[2] pretended to read my book. I suspect her English apperceptiveness.

2. As my article indicated (in the Atlantic, reprinted in the Literary Radical), we discussed both of the "forbidden things" (sex and death).

3. Do I rule out these two bugaboos?

4. Is it *my* fortress that's barred?

5. The A. of Y. (Apostle of Youth) has not changed sides.

6. I have not noticed any sorties on your part.

7. Formula for Youth;—1. general *desire*—for achievement, ideal person

of both sexes, expression, attention: 2. warm sensuous reactions to beauty, inspiring causes, desirable persons; 3. disgust at mediocre people and cant, disgust at the past; 4. sense that the world has just begun with you, that it is in a dreadful condition, but will speedily be set right, mostly through your own efforts; 5. susceptibility to large ideals; 6. intolerance of the control of older, graver, and more judicial persons; 7. inexhaustible daydreaming, rosy fantasies of love and fame; 8. a rich conscious life that bursts inhibitions and makes itself felt over any barriers.

1, 2, and 3 are necessary; others not, but useful.

8. I think we have unmasked the fair Lillian. Would you have anticipated finding a Tolstoyan Christian?

9. Would you like to do the art-shops Friday afternoon? I am going to be uptown for lunch and could meet you at 2.30? by the 116 Subway station. Don't bother to write if you can't.

R. S. B.

[1]The parenthetic remarks are Teall's addition to her transcription.

[2]"Mon Amie" appeared in the March 1915 number of *The Atlantic* and proved to be one of his most popular essays at the time.

114

to Prudence Winterrowd
(Transcript Columbia)

335 E. 31st St.
9 April 1915

When is that Spring tour coming off? Didn't I answer your letter, and say that I would be very glad to see you in New York? I passed through your State last month, and spent several fascinated days at Gary. I got also to Milwaukee and Madison and am all for the West, barring the inferno named Chicago.

Sincerely,

Randolph Bourne

115

to Dorothy Teall
(Transcript Columbia)

11 April [1915]

I see you have played the same trick my friend Colby[1] did last year in another connection—put in an "ought" where I had only an "is". I described a situation and lamented it; you interpreted my description as an ideal. I said these subjects (sex and death) were tabooed; but I also said that some day I hoped there would be wise and sane people who would neither taboo nor debauch them. No American girls that I know under 25 seem to possess this wisdom and sanity. I am perfectly consistent, therefore, am I not? I looked up the passage (in *Youth and Life*) and was surprised to find how much there was of it, and how clear it was. All I said was that the present orthodox American social situation made calm thinking and talking difficult on these subjects, but I do not consider myself a factor in the present orthodox American social situation, and I discuss these subjects with anybody else who is not a factor in it.

I don't follow all the convolutions of your thought, but I wish you would say any "terrible things" you may happen to think. I am not easily shocked, and have, I think, an unusually objective attitude towards a great many things. You are perfectly safe in being unsafe. And why were you cut up? L[illian] S[oskin]'s cold water plays far too big a role in your consciousness. She is so delightfully naive, and so strikingly inferior to you in ironic sense, that I shouldn't think she could possibly damage you. However, I can understand your not wanting to confess before her.

I wish you would be a little more daring and send me these scareful notes; and this "fearful impoliteness," etc., really escapes my memory entirely. And what *was* the fearful blunder? I have an intuition that you think I am sensitive to blunders, etc. Actually I am thick as a stone. You aren't likely to do anything to damage yourself in my estimation, no matter how hard you try. You see you have a good many of those qualities I put into my formula, although you may not think so. That's why I like you. I can see though where some of those qualities don't fit into Westminster church society, but I don't know about this role of mine as conspirator in your household. As I sat at your supper-table the other night, I had a real sense of danger, as my ideas collided with the older generation in the person of your mother. It was rather thrilling. I played on and on fearfully and adventurously. I waited for the heavens to fall, while you did up Thackeray and Dickens, and analyzed old-fashionedness. Nothing particular happened, but I feel that I should be forcibly prevented from tempting you to expose the modernness of your soul.

You really ought to write your autobiography and fling it nakedly on the world. Get some of my serene objectivity and look at yourself as an interesting stranger to be interpreted. Don't implicate yourself in anything you do, and you won't need to go through the chrysalis-butterfly stage.

I still don't see why L. S. should scathe you, and I can't remember being cruelly sarcastic, but since one of my best friends told me last night that I went around looking for defects in people, I am willing to believe almost anything reprehensible about myself. If her philosophy is an index to her socialism, you know quite as much about it as L. S. does.

I have tried to answer your letter, but if you have forgotten what you wrote, you may find this difficult.

Can't you come Tuesday, and we will have more of this and that, as Pepys would say.[2]

R. S. B.

[1]The incident involving Bourne and Elbridge Colby has already been referred to.

[2]Samuel Pepys was a famous 17th century diarist. His extraordinary diary was frequently quoted, often out of context.

116

to Dorothy Teall
(Transcript Columbia)

[April 29, 1915]

I certainly do [thank you]. The day was so much more glorious than I dared to expect. You could hardly feel all the innumerable little touches by which B[eulah] soothed and delighted my soul. There were moments under the tree—Do you remember how she laughed when I threw acorns at her? How she hugged the brown ground? There were unpropitious moments in that unlucky corner where we halted and saw the lovers, but things flowed again when we started to walk, and even the nightmare of the trolley ride could not dissipate the high mood of the afternoon. And then the after-dinner discussion! Except that I could not look at her; you had all that pleasure. And how she dramatized her whole generation, and how hotly distressed she was as she gazed into her future, so passionate and yet so intellectual! Ah, a great mood, and a great day. You were lovely to share her with me; I'm afraid I monopolized her too much, and bored her with my quantity. I wonder if she liked me any better after it. I think she did like me for stretches that day. I wish I had not caused any lapses from her radiance, as I did when I probed her so deeply on the bank. She seemed all the more daringly lovely because I had had that week a letter of really excoriating savagery, ending in a page of sentimental slang. I still marvel. It could not be the same B., it seemed. She was so much bigger and lovelier than that letter, though that did have a fine prophetic ring. It was not you that were cynical and bitter, but myself, and pouring it upon others. This was her charge, and she feared for you [. . . .] And there was no "unkind thing" said about you; you are mixed up there.

You are right about Mon Amie; she is eclipsed, abolished. Her only superiority lay in her availability. B. is so elusive, so busy, and time rushes so. Can you believe that there will be only a month more of her? I lament to heaven! Is there nothing we can do? And would we see her again in such golden moments? Can't you catch her for another walk? Couldn't you get her Saturday afternoon for the Palisades? That would be a glorious excursion. Write me, if you can.

R. S. B.

117

to Dorothy Teall
(Transcript Columbia)

[May 2, 1915]

If you are going to see B[eulah] on Tuesday, why don't you bring her down to tea? Please do. That will be the test of your scheme, which shows a high power of novelistic imagination. Don't you think, however, that it's rather old-fashioned for me to marry her? Why don't you get *her* to marry *me*? That would be truly delightful, and it would save me so much spiritual trepidation. You should come to tea whenever you liked.

Ask her to show you a poem I sent her, which must have been unconsciously written about her, for it so exactly describes her very self. It is called "Prairie Spring" and speaks of

Evening and the flat land,
Rich and sombre and always silent,
The miles of fresh-plowed soil—

. . . .
Against all this, Youth,
Flaming like the wild roses,
Singing like the larks over the plowed fields,
Flashing like a star out of the twilight—[1]

I wish I had written it myself.

    I shall be disappointed if you don't come Tuesday.

R. S. B.

[1]The poem appears at the beginning of *O Pioneers*, a 1913 novel by Willa Cather.

118

to Dorothy Teall
(Transcript Columbia)

335 E. 31st St.
5 May [1915]

    I don't understand why you didn't come, if you said "Well then, come along!" I am vexed at you both. I had to put away my things sadly. I don't imagine anybody will come, so I choose Tuesday, as I play trios Thursday afternoon. However, if it is impossible for either of you, I will break the trio. But Tuesday it shall be until further notice. Of course you will *not* have any foolish engagement; you are necessary for the combination. And if you can both get away at two, make it two. Write me whether it shall be Tuesday, two or three, P. M. Manhattan St. subway station, downstairs, is a good place to meet, if we go to the Palisades.

    You are a scientist and an artist to have arranged this occasion. I can say no more. I hope you will be proud of your handiwork. If the weather is bad, we still have Thursday to fall back upon.

R. S. B.

119

to Dorothy Teall
(Transcript Columbia)

335 E. 31st St.
[May 12, 1915]

Well, I was disappointed. I did not get your letter until I got home at night, rather sore and wondering. Why did you not come yourself and tell me? We could have had an amusing excursion, instead of getting me to go over alone and sit on a high rock and look at the stately line of battle-ships, and read a fascinating novel. You were excessively modest to stay away, or perhaps you had a headache too. I don't at all like that reference to "week after next." That seems to put it at the very brink of her going, and imply that a walk with me is the least important of events in her life. She will actually make me fall in love with her if she does things like this, creating empty voids in my days, and making me spend a whole frustrated evening in thinking how much I would like to see her. I suppose there is no chance now until that week after next. There will be the excuse of examinations, and after that of Commencement. You have a stern duty upon you now of seeing that she goes out of our lives with much splendor. Don't let her trail off like this. There must be one supreme and final occasion.

R. S. B.

120

to Dorothy Teall
(Transcript Columbia)

[May 27, 1915]

I'm sorry you are so disappointed in me. I hope B[eulah] E. A[midon] can't come. I could have gone walking with her last evening if I hadn't invited somebody here. Isn't that heartrending? But I have another chance Saturday. This will be the *very last*, unless she brings her father down to tea! *If* he comes to N. Y., which he won't, and then she will have had the immense joy of flattering myself at no cost to herself. She is becoming Mephistophelian and Machiavellian.

Thank you very much for the ticket, hurled with such scorn!

R. S. B.

121

to Elizabeth Shepley Sergeant
(Ms Yale)

335 E. 31st St.
New York
9 June [1915]

Dear Miss Sergeant,

I threaten to be as bad a correspondent as I thought you said you were going to be. And my only excuse for not answering your letter sooner is my distraught situation, with friends going away at end of college year, and some literary plans buzzing, and wondering where I shall go for the summer, and a general restlessness at the city, and an inability to seize the work that I am constantly thinking I might do. You never can tell how ideas are going to turn out, and you will work away at a world-shaking one only to have it get itself expressed in the most conventional way, while an utterly unimportant one turns itself off in the easiest and serenest manner. I have yet to discover a method of stimulating inspiration, or of bringing yourself up to a luminous and God-like control of your ideas, when you feel like a helpless nobody.

It always seems as if one could be inspired somewhere else—"dort wo du nicht bist" [there where you are not]. Just now it is the country that appeals to me. The city is incredibly dusty and acts like a huge sounding board for all the din and children's cries. I have a home out in New Jersey in what used to be a country town, but is now surrounded by a thick blanket of cities. We have an old, dull and very uncomfortable house, and every summer I have spent there I have vowed would be my last. I don't want to be forced back now, but no other chance seems to offer itself to get away from New York. I seem very queer out there and all my friends seem very queer. My family conveniently puts the corruption to the account of Europe. I am constantly confronted there by the immeasurable gulf between my outlook and theirs, and I feel a constant criticism of my futile high browism and Godless pursuit of strange philosophies. My young sister is almost a passionate vulgarian, and takes with really virtuous indignation any deviation from the norm of popular music, the movies, Chambers' novels,[1] Billy Sunday,[2] Presbyterian dogma, automobile parties, musical comedy, tennis, anti-suffragism, and the rest of the combination that makes up the healthy, hearty, happy young normal person of the well-brought-up family of the day of the middle-middle-class. I find her an index to current America, but we scarcely get along. I envy you your being as firmly and happily placed in a stimulating family, with backgrounds and connections and responsibilities and a place in things. My relatives are quite hopeless, and I feel at times like a home-sick wanderer, not even knowing where my true home is.

Sincerely yours,

Randolph Bourne

[1]Robert Chambers, an American novelist, wrote primarily historical, sometimes overly-sentimental fiction.

[2]Billy Sunday was a famous Presbyterian revivalist minister who was attracting large crowds.

122

to Dorothy Teall
(Transcript Columbia)

June 14, [1915]

It was very lovely of you to write me your appreciation, and it came at a time after the Beulah shipwreck when I had begun to feel that I was no more than an incident in anybody's life and to wonder if I could stand that sort of thing for the rest of my days. Nobody does feel more than I at times this hunger, this *besoin d'etre aime* [need of friends], and I annoy my friends, I think, by asking so much. They seem to feel all sorts of spiritual defects in me, which come down finally to a rude and grasping selfishness, which must look very different from the outside from what it does within. But your first intuition about the lack of something, supported as it was by public opinion, was much truer than your final conclusion. I wish you had said more about how you interpreted those first impressions and just what made you think I was any better after Sunday. As I recall it, I was rather cross at times, and not at all shining. You mustn't, you know, have absurd notions about me. In spite of all the time I have spent thinking about myself, I don't really know my real self very well. I only know that some people are very different and rasp upon my soul, and others sort of caress it and set a golden glow about life. But there is always the poignancy of not satisfying them, and never getting your boundless desires of them. You mustn't make me into the kind of a person you want me to be, in the way that Beulah says I idealize her. She knows, for instance, that although she may give a very good picture of that ideal person when she is with you or me, when she is away she is very different and much less attractive and noble—very complicated and shot with all kinds of different-colored streaks. So you know very well that with me, though I find your mind and outlook so sympathetic—not always but very often—that I give out good parts of myself that other people wouldn't take, life is always setting off malice and envy and low spirits and blindness that make me altogether not at all the kind of genius that you want to admire. I won't deny that I like your admiration and that it warmed my heart, but it would make me uncomfortable if I didn't think you understood all this darker background. *Youth and Life* is a good deal of a fraud if it is taken as *me* instead of what I would like to be, or to have been. This last year has so unsettled me that some of it isn't even what I find I could possibly be. The great problem now is, as Lippmann says in his great book, *Drift and Mastery*—have you read it? If not, you must do it at once, *There* is a book one would have given one's soul to have written—to know what to do with your emancipation after you have got it. You fortunately don't need a great deal, and your only danger is in getting a little off the drift of things and dragging some pettinesses after you. Otherwise you ought to fly much higher than I, who will always struggle. Don't allow yourself inhibitions like I did. Soar, but be sure it is your very you that is soaring.

You are a good and understanding friend, or were until you began to idealize me. But perhaps you are yet and see all around me, just as I see around B. and yet feel that her passing is a sore mutilation of my very best life. Please do see around me—and thank you for liking me.

R. S. B.

123

to Dorothy Teall
(Transcript Columbia)

June 14 [1915]

    I should certainly like to see B[abette] Deutsch, but I have invited a couple of people to tea, and will go from there up the Hudson for a day or two. B. D. will keep, won't she? She will have to take Beulah's place next year. I thought, by the way, you were reconciled with B. by this time. As I said, she has a great soul, even if she has forgotten me now, and will never write to me again. Don't pull down so ruthlessly your goddesses from their seats. As for me, though she slay men, yet will I trust in her.

    I am rather silly when I talk about girls, and I thought the other afternoon would impress you with its and my futility. So I was a little surprised at your third. You make yourself very interesting by scampering away by postal again, and not very intelligible. I will try not to be a problem, if you will doggedly and with set teeth go at this "confession," or this talk intentionally aimed at these things. How long would you like to have to think about it beforehand? Please don't excite my violent curiosity. I wonder if you are adroitly trying to tantalize me. I will be very good and quiet and let you talk. Why do you want to be eternally springing to the rescue of your threatened "self-respect"? My own amuses me so, that I quite understand and maliciously enjoy a little seeing you wriggle. You must learn a certain immobility of countenance before you can be sure of rescuing yourself! At present, your expression, like that of Mon Amie, speaks quite as loudly as your words. However, I don't mean to tease you. Your letters weren't at all horrid—in fact, I haven't the faintest idea what you mean by "horrid." They were neither "terrible, frightful, rough or bristling," but very comfortable and good. They couldn't be answered, however, as I found when I tried the other day in person.

R. S. B.

124

to Elizabeth Shepley Sergeant
(Ms Yale)

335 E. 31st St.
New York
25 June [1915]

Dear Miss Sergeant,

It is very good of you to take thought for my summer. I must have unconsciously made it seem more important than it really is, I hope I didn't really fool you as I fool myself about that inspiration. It gets to be an excuse that one makes to one's self when one can't get on top of the situation and feel really in command of one's soul. I drift so horribly, pulling myself up with a start, only to slip the oar again somehow. Place I think would help, but it would have to be people too and then some smashing victory, which just to think of would give me a feeling of power. Those people who want to create things oughtn't to have too much critical power, ought they?

What I really have been hoping for the summer was to find some slightly furnished cottage near New York, on the Sound or anywhere, that I could go to with a friend or two and live mostly outdoors. Mr. Croly[1] suggests dimly coming into editorial conferences once a week, and there is just enough advantageous in the sound to make me think I had better do it for a while instead of going far away from New York. I had almost decided, since I knew no way of finding what I wanted, to stay in New York all summer, but I know a few warm days will make me miserable. Mrs. Fernandez suggested Mrs. McRae's at Cos Cob,[2] and it must be very pleasant, but, for me, expensive. I cannot think of being contented anywhere without friends, and I put no trust in American hotels or cheap boarding-houses. I am really grateful to you for thinking of the house in Woodstock. It sounds most appealing, but would be too far away, wouldn't it? I wish I had had your long letter, or was it all about the house. Do you know attractive and inexpensive places in New England where one might go with the expectation of meeting somebody interesting? The horror of getting with uncongenial people who freeze one up is, as you guess, what would keep me from making adventures of my own. If it was Europe one could start and travel endlessly and always be amused and caressed, with scenery and towns for companions.

As I reread your letter, it disquiets me again. If you did find me *the* place and if my ideas didn't sprout, and I am not confident that they would, then I should have most desperately deluded you, and the working of your wits would have been worse than in vain. However, it would perhaps be a challenge that I would have to meet. You are absolutely the first friend who has given my case thought, and I am really grateful.

I have spent a week trying to make a book out of my Gary articles,[3] floundering most dreadfully and getting myself surrounded by a mass of loosely connected notes and reflections in all stages of importance. Houghton Mifflin have agreed to look at it, but I think they will demand something less impressionistic than my articles. I find it almost impossible to say anything without assuming that my reader knows all the details of the organization I am supposed to be explaining. Some of my friends even had trouble with the articles. Is it really possible to combine facts and figures and the tone that you feel the thing in? If I let go of my tone for a moment I drop into something worse than flatness. I am really having a difficult time, and I can hardly feel that labor will help me out. Even an orderly outline won't do much, for in this school idea, which I really believe is the biggest thing in the country to-day, everything is significant of everything else, and won't be cut off into pieces and still live. I know I will seem too poetical for the publisher, and will have wasted a summer in working at the futile thing. I admire order and precision immensely and it makes me angry not to achieve it in a subject about which I am so enthusiastic. And there is every motive to do the book,—that of spreading a good news, and the sordid one of making a book that will appeal.

I cannot think what I have done with my winter. It is discouraging to look at one's self objectively. All I can find is my having written 31,000 words for the "New Republic" that got printed, and about half as much more that didn't; two or three long articles that either weren't paid for or didn't see the light; and some scattering shots of dubious value. My Western trip was a brightness, though I was scarcely responsible for it myself. And besides this there is scarcely anything worth remembering. And there is nothing at all of permanence. There was much reading of Nietzsche with a high fervor and a sense of illumination—(would there have been in any winter but the war)?—and a tracking-down of Dostoevsky, and a discovery of Sanine and "Sons and Lovers" and "Sister Carrie", and a sampling, with many wry faces, of Robert Herrick and Henry Snydor Harrison and Mrs. Watts.[4] And I should not forget "O Pioneers!"[5] which you recommended and which was so sincere and wistful. Do you remember the poem "Prairie Spring" at the beginning? There was a girl from North Dakota up at Barnard who was exactly *that* poem, so glowing and sort of earthy and passionately intelligent, one of the most beautiful persons I have ever looked upon. Disentangling such people from one's emotions, and playing the piano and sleeping and dropping in on people, and adjusting one's self to a startling change of levels and circles, and feeling very amateurish and unconnected, made up the rest of the winter. I say to myself that my next one must be very different, but I wonder how I shall discover the way to make it so. The girl at least is tragically gone home for good, and Nietzsche is read, though not

assimilated enough to issue in ideas. But the piano and the people and the am-
ateurishness are still here to tempt me, and I remain, and Miss Rudyard said,
"a promising young author."

Yours sincerely,

Randolph Bourne

[1]Herbert Croly, Editor of the *New Republic* and the person instrumental in the
hiring of Bourne.

[2]Cos Cob, Connecticut was an artists' colony. It is described in Lincoln Steffens'
Autobiography. Steffens also reports that Elmer McRae was an artist who lived there.
Perhaps Bourne is talking about the same family.

[3]Later published as *The Gary Schools*.

[4]Herrick, an American novelist, was also a teacher at the University of Chicago.
Although his realistic novels were never immensely popular, they received critical acclaim.
H. L. Mencken called Harrison a "merchant of mush." Mary Watts wrote mostly realistic
historical novels. *Sanine* was a novel by Artzybaschev.

[5]See letter #116 for another reference.

125

to Dorothy Teall
(Transcript Columbia)

335 E. 31st St.
1 July 1915

Dear Dorothy,
        Why don't you have that picnic that Ray[1] speaks about? I am coming
out Monday, and unless she has planned some other spree, which she probably
has, I should be very amenable to a suggestion of a day in the fields or woods.
If nothing of this sort happens, will you anyway take a walk with me Sunday or
Monday?
        I had a short letter from B[eulah] E. A[midon] looking me up, and
offering to let me let her "drop out of her life." Would you let her do it? There

is much to be said on both sides. More later.

R. S. B.

¹Perhaps John Ray, a commercial artist, at whose house in Caldwell, New Jersey Bourne stayed during the summer of 1916.

126

to Dorothy Teall
(Transcript Columbia)

Thursday
[July 9, 1915]

Dear Dorothy,

I had been hoping to hear from you something that would make me think I hadn't wounded you as much Sunday as I was afraid I had. It seems as if I understood too well what you are thinking about college and the world to do you much good by talking about it. I have been through it all myself at a later age than you. I wasted two good years trying to justify my existence by getting a job—two years that I might have spent in learning something and growing. Instead I wore myself thin against an immovable wall, got into habits of despair and futility that are riveting me still, and all to no purpose. Nothing that I planned and made for did I get, but gradually my own seemed to find me. My labor to settle myself in the world was really worse than wasted. If I had merely sat down calmly and read and written and thought as best I could, and made the most of what was lying around me, I would be infinitely better off now in the world that finally found me. In spite of all my desperate efforts to renounce college, to be content with my poverty, to get a good routine position, to work hard and support myself and help my family, to give up all thought of writing or ambition, I now find myself exactly where a few years ago I should have considered it Quixotic even to pose as an ideal. I really believe your destiny pursues you, and you can't evade it, even though you may postpone it very much by your own well-meant efforts; and thwart it, even do it infinite damage. But if *you* have a destiny, you don't want to damage it, and that's why it worries me when you talk the way you did. What one needs always is to grow, and you need it particularly now. College is, in spite of everything, an incomparable place to grow, and you play fast and loose with yourself when you let yourself even speculate about dropping it. It's like stirring up the ground around your roots all the time. You can't expect to grow unless you serenely drink up the sunlight and air, and soak yourself in this environment. You do a good deal of thinking and you will do a lot more, and you ought to have the solidest background of ideas. College does give the frame-work, and it isn't very safe to trust to picking it up elsewhere when you have the chance there. If you fritter away your energy, and lacerate your soul with speculations what you might be doing or ought to be doing elsewhere, you are simply conspiring to stunt yourself, and nobody will want to answer for the result. Of course, I myself spent a large part of my first two years in college planning my future, which didn't turn out at all as I had planned. Such intellectual exercises seem to me now about as valuable as a picture-puzzle, and that is why I must seem so unsympathetic and dense to you. It's a very painful role, though, for a prophet of youth to be preaching on the basis of experience, so I shall leave you with the comforting conviction that however much you struggle to mangle your destiny, it will probably get you yet.

R. S. B.

127

to Dorothy Teall[1]
(Transcript Columbia)

[13 July 1915]

Since your interesting fact is not a hint and not even an invitation, you will not be surprised not to see me. I should like, however, to meet B. Deutsch and Elsie W [?] Couldn't you get up some sort of roof-garden party in the near future? Bring them in to tea some afternoon, that is, if you should happen to be in N. Y. or could arrange it. Life is not very interesting just now. I don't seem to like America in the summer. Europe has ruined me.

Of course, I knew you had no idea of leaving college, but I couldn't be blamed for thinking from your talk that you would be staying on with a fine bravado, a sort of noble desperation, rather than a real serene meeting of the situation. Or doesn't your talk correspond to your real ideas? It was the tolerance of college that I was talking against, and pleading for a whole-hearted jumping at it. It's not my fault that I'm fatherly, but quite your own. But you have me at your mercy, for it is quite against my philosophy to plead experience as an excuse for anything.

Was B[eulah] E. A[midon]'s letter "vile," or is that just a cryptic word that I don't get?

R. S. B.

[1]Material in brackets is contributed by Miss Teall. If her reading of "Elsie W." is correct, Bourne could be referring to Elsie de Wetter, the daughter of an industrial engineer and inhabitant of Cos Cob, Connecticut.

128

to Dorothy Teall
(Transcript Columbia)

Ulster Park, N. Y.
21 July 1915

Dear Dorothy,
Probably next week I shall be back in New York and amenable to that tea-party you spoke of. The summer should not be allowed to drift away without some sort of social spree. I had almost decided to give a large roof-garden party myself, with Chinese lanterns, etc. I am up at Carl's farm for a few days, but the country does not seem to agree with me. A winter in the effete city has enervated me, and I cannot breathe the strong air and feel the sunshine without having all sorts of things happen to me. This summer will have to be written down as a failure. There is obviously nothing but Europe. If you can't go there, it is New York you must stay in. This is really a charming place, however, with rocky Norwegian-looking country, a comfortable old house, beautiful woods. Mrs. Z. gives us wonderful food and there is a piano and lots of books. It is a little annoying to have to work, and I am rather behind. This letter, for instance, takes the edge off a morning that I shudder a little to begin. I have not got over my old feeling that every piece I write is my last, and approach each new one with the same trepidation, as if it were breaking entirely new paths. There is nothing in this experience and practice business. I never learn to write, no matter how much I do.

Yours,

R. S. B.

129

to Alyse Gregory
(Ms Yale)

Ulster Park, N. Y.
24 July 1915

I have been up here on Carl's farm for a week, enjoying the calm country, and the freedom from noise and distractions. I think I ought to live in the
country, for I work very well, there seems to be plenty of time, and I delight in
the colors of the hills and meadows and the passage of the summer day. I was up
here three years ago most of the summer, and finished my book [*Youth and
Life*]. With a summer at my disposal, I almost feel as if I could write another
one. But Carl will be going back to New York in a few days and then it will be
wondering again where to go. It was really less trouble when I worked all summer long at my job, and had a week only of vacation. It takes a strong soul to
handle one's own freedom. Miss Sergeant, who has been devoting herself to de-
vising a vacation for me, writes of a camp in Dublin, N. H. The problem then becomes to get somebody to go with me to feed me, and as all my friends are industrious and ground to their jobs, this will not be easy. I wrote and telephoned
to your Miss Duncan but could not get her. Why didn't N. S. [?] tell me about
her cottage, when she heard me desiring a summer place?

I don't like to hear your tales of overwork and discouraging drudgery
any more than you like to hear about my sickness. I am well again, but your
labor goes on. People must pay the penalty of their efficiency by overwork, I
suppose. You ought not to envy me who no sooner got into a movement or
group than I am thrown off by the roadside, by irresistible centrifugal [written
centripfugal] motion. I shall give up clamoring to be "in" things and "do"
things, and accept my fate as a lonely spectator, reserved from action for con-
templation. It used really to worry me, to be filled with so much reforming spirit, and to be so detached from any machinery of change. I felt very useless and
treacherous, and envied those who were in the heat of the fray. But after the
desperate attempts I have made this last year, only to be shouldered out almost
before I knew it, I am convinced that some deep destiny presides over it all, and
that I have unsuspected powers of incompatability with the real world. It isn't
altogether good for me, either, for it makes me narrow and selfish and peevish
and not very human, and this always comes out in what I write, becoming worse
and worse. Still I think the country would cure me, if it was filled with congenial
presence. The New Republic has just come, and irritates me frightfully by printing a lot of articles on the end of the first year of the war, thus cutting out the
chance for two of mine on the same subject, that I had been working on and was

getting quite proud of. Its coming also always gives my proud spirit the awareness that I am having nothing to say about its policy, and that I am a very insig-
nificant retainer of its staff. I haven't done anything to deserve the high place I
would like, but this only makes the cut all the deeper. However this is an old
sore, which doesn't go well with smiling July. I wonder when I'll see you again.

R. S. B.

130

to Elizabeth Shepley Sergeant
(Ms Yale)

Ulster Park
24 July 1915

Dear Miss Sergeant,
   I have been up here for a week on the farm of my friend Carl Zigrosser
with whom I live in New York, and only received your kind letter yesterday.
You have done yeoman work, in my behalf, and I am very grateful for what you
have done to get me a summer. Of course the Dublin[1] appeals to me most, and
would be exactly what I have dreamed about. The only considerations would be
how closely the New Republic wants me, and whom I could get to go away with
me. Most of my friends are busy, but I shall work on them as soon as I get back
to New York next week. All the people sound delightful, and the whole setting
very rare. I had thought of the Macdowell colony,[2] but gave it up because I
seemed to be needed nearer New York. Boarding-houses would not appeal to me
even with the careful character-analysis of your friend's letter. Because I have an
unhappy knack of finding myself dumb with the most excellent people.
   I should like very much to see you at Medfield, and will probably take a
New England trip anyway later in the summer, whatever happens. I cannot think
why you devote so much time to me, and can only be devoutly grateful for my
blessings. Could we go suddenly to the Dublin camp, or will your friends want to
know definitely in case of other deserving or undeserving people who might like
it? Will you thank them very much for me? I will let you know as soon as I can
what I can manufacture out of this rich material of possibilities you offer me.
   Hastily for the R. F. D.

Randolph Bourne

[1]Dublin, New Hampshire has for its site one of the highest elevations of any town in the state and, because of its prime location, was a watering-hole for many literary and artistic figures.

[2]The Macdowell Colony was formed by Mrs. Macdowell after the death of her husband, the composer Edward, in 1908. The Colony was situated on the Macdowell farm and featured secluded cabins in which artists, sculptors, and writers, could create.

131

to Elizabeth Shepley Sergeant
(Ms Yale)

335 E. 31st St.
New York
30 July [1915]

Dear Miss Sergeant,

Mr Greene[1] kindly telegraphed me saying that the small house at Dublin was at my disposal, and I have sent him word that I would come next week. I have found a friend to go with me who can cook a little, and there seems to be no reason why we should not get along, although I am not used to pioneer life. The people who have been there tell me the region is enchanting, and I can scarcely wait for the pines and the high air. I want to leave Monday or Tuesday on the night boat to Boston, see my friends and then go to Dublin next morning. If you were free, I would run down to Medfield in the afternoon for a call, and take my chances of finding you.

I can hardly thank you enough for working out a summer for me. I am sure it will be the happiest I could have found. My friend is the original of Fergus by the way.[2]

I have asked Mr. Greene for directions, but perhaps you can give me some too. Your letter makes me very well acquainted with the sociology of Dublin. I hope I can meet some of the delightful people you mention.

Sincerely,

Randolph Bourne

[1]A Mrs. J. S. C. Greene built the first summer cottage at Dublin in 1871. Perhaps

Mr Greene is a relative.

2"Fergus—a portrait," *New Republic* II (May 22, 1915), 62-64 was based on Edward Murray.

132

to Van Wyck Brooks
(Ms Pennsylvania)

New York
July 31, 1915

Dear Mr. Brooks,

Your suggestion does interest me, and I thank you very much for the idea. I shall set about it and see what I can make out of it, and whether my reaction is at all similar to the editor's.

I hope I may have chances for talks with you when I come back from my vacation.

Sincerely yours,

Randolph Bourne

133

to Elizabeth Shepley Sergeant
(Ms Yale)

Dublin [N. H.]
5 August 1915

Dear Miss Sergeant,

We have been here about two hours, and already feel much at home. We have seen Mr. Brush[1] in the barn, and somebody has dumped a fine load of wood in the stable. It is still raining and very gloomy, but I'm sure we shall be very happy when the sun comes out. The intricacies of a patent stove confined our lunch to eggs and bacon, but Edward [Murray] is studying the situation now and will doubtless evolve a technique. He was marooned yesterday in the Museum until they turned him out at five o'clock. I found him peacefully sleeping when I returned, and to-day are both none the worse for the hardship of weather. My train was very promptly late, and I found the Boston downpour as indefatigable as I had left it. I had such a delightful time at your house that I wince when I think that I almost let the weather scare me from coming. If you don't like to be thanked, you must at least know how much I appreciate coming to see you in perfect old houses, and becoming endowed with cottages.

It looks as if we were more secluded and in the woods than I expected. But we shall not mind that, and I hope the air will inspire me to much work. The school business doesn't seem exactly appropriate, but it must be done. Perhaps I will find time for other things too.

Sincerely,

Randolph Bourne

[1]George de Forest Brush was a painter best known for his studies of family groups and for his portraits of Indians. He was a sentimental painter.

134

to Elizabeth Shepley Sergeant
(Ms Yale)

Dublin, N. H.
9 Aug 1915

Dear Miss Sergeant,

I hope that you are not worrying about us any more, for we are quite settled and happy. The weather is annoying, but a great aid to staying indoors and working. It has turned warm, and there is so much moisture in the air that our matches won't strike, and our salt and sugar are almost liquid. Friday afternoon tried to clear, and we walked around the lake, but almost before we reached home, it had closed in again with another deluge which lasted all night. Yesterday was lovely, however, with soft sky and clouds, and we spent the morning on the little dock where I found I could write, though not spread my Gary things. Gerald Thayer[1] and his wife called Friday, and we went to see them yesterday afternoon. He is a pleasing, simple soul, and she, I think, is quite charming. The little boy is very sturdy, but the baby a sad, thin little thing with such deep, wistful eyes. There was quite a deluge of visitors, some Misses Taber and a Mr. Sumner and a gigantic thunderstorm coming straight over Monadnock caught us all there at supper time. Dublin will perhaps learn that Fergus and I never refuse a meal. Everybody stayed, and Mr. Thayer showed us all his color diagrams and demonstrations, and told a great many stories, and everybody was delightful. Gladys Thayer was steadily sociable, and we were all very much at home. After supper, they unearthed an antique piano, brought over from Germany after 1848, and a fiddle, and Fergus and I played Schubert songs for an hour out of an old Liederbuch. Mr Thayer's appreciation was almost embarrassingly ecstatic, and he proffered sketches and dinners and thanks if we would come often and do it again. I liked his simple emotional ways and his telling us we had "watered his soul." We are to go again Wednesday. He took us down to the road with the quaintest of lanterns, and spoke constantly of the music. Fergus' gallantry took us to the village with the young women, through oceans of mud, but he talked a great deal and enjoyed himself. He likes to walk better than to practice, and is thoroughly pleased with the place. His slight cooking prestige soon disappeared, and canned things have been our salvation. After three hours on breakfast the first morning, he was ready to go home, but I suggested improvements in the technique. The stove is perfect, but there seems to be no way of accelerating wood-fires. One merely feeds their voracious jaws with wood for half-an-hour and then has a stove that will cook anything.

Miss Monroe[2] came in to see if we were all right, and I went up to see Mrs. Upham Saturday afternoon. She was a delightful experience, talking in long, polished sentences and remembering much about old Dublin and her neighbors. The house is perfect with the view of the mountain through the pines, and the big open rooms and porch. I looked at the encampment, and decided that we were much more comfortable here, though we have none of that delightful view.

Mr. Brush I have seen several times on the road. He is living very near, but I have not decided to drop in on him. He seems a little dry and unadvancing, though one of his daughters was very pleasant. The Smiths are away. Mr. Greenslet has solemnly conjured me to deliver a letter to Miss Lowell,[3] which I shall, though one hears much here of her enormities. We shall have plenty of society, and all of it so far very congenial. The place has the atmosphere that I "get along" in, and that is all I ask.

By the way, how do you pronounce your name? If I say "Sirjent", then they say, "Oh, you mean Miss Sarjent," and if I say "Sarjent", then they say, "I think they call it Sirjent."

Another thunder shower is coming. Gerald Thayer ascribes the weather to the cannonading in Europe.

Sincerely,

Randolph Bourne

[1]Thayer was a painter best known for his natural scenes and portraits. He was working then on camoflage techniques, a study which came out of a book, *Concealing Coloration in the Animal Kingdom* (1909), on which he and his son Gerald Thayer collaborated. Gladys Thayer, Abbott's daughter, also helped illustrate this volume.

[2]Harriet Monroe was then Editor of *Poetry*.

[3]Ferris Greenslet was Editor-in-Chief of Houghton Mifflin and was a close friend of Amy Lowell, an American poet and an eccentric member of the famous Lowell family.

135

to Alyse Gregory
(Ms Yale)

Dublin, N. H.
12 Aug 1915

Have I written you since I came up here? I have been living very comfortably and happily here for several days with my friend Murray. Just now I am in a little state of trepidation about him, as he started off for a walk before I got up, and it is now the middle of the afternoon. He may have taken it into his mind to climb Monadnock. At six I shall set the town on his trail. Our house is well furnished and comfortable, near the lake. The people are both distinguished and interesting, and I experience the pleasing sensation of arriving with some slight prestige. I am, of course, not working as much as I meant to, but expected far more solitude than we have already had. Only the turbulent weather has marred the perfection, but we have had two delicious days. The woods are unusually lovely, with many pines and birches, and the lake is said to be the highest in New England.

We have substituted out of cans and the butcher's wagon (infrequent), for our original culinary experiments have been uniformly disastrous. We have lots of room; I wish more of my friends could be here.

R. S. B.

136

to Dorothy Teall
(Transcript Columbia)

Dublin, N. H.
13 Aug 1915

Dear Dorothy,

Fergus and I are trying to keep house and feed ourselves in this most delightful cottage on the lake. What was offered to me as a "mere shack" turns out to be a house with electric lights and competent furnishings, where one can be as comfortable as anywhere. We have most distinguished society. George de Forest Brush uses our barn for a studio and the Abbott Thayers are very near. Fergus brought his violin and has made Mr. Thayer so ecstatic that he offered us sketches and dinners and anything if we would come and play for them two or three times a week. His daughter Gladys is a very good artist, and is the most curious sort of glorified Paul Heyden to look at. Our social entourage almost prevents work. Miss Bertha Haven Putnam, who is professor of history, I think at Mt. Holyoke, had us to tea the other day. Miss Amy Lowell in a house on a high hill had me to dinner. Do you know her verse? She is very witty, a wonderful gossip, and a smoker of big black cigars. She is the fairy godmother of young poets, American, English, and French. Her picturesqueness, against her solemn brother and president of Harvard, is the scandal, not only of Dublin, but also of all New England.

I wish our summer camp had come to something. If we could lay our hands on an unimpeachable chaperone, I would invite you up. We have plenty of room, but the social atmosphere seems a bit thick. Nothing is hidden here that might be revealed. I know the family histories of everybody in the place, and my own past seems to be public property.

What intellectual and spiritual adventures are you pursuing this summer? Write me a letter worthy of the 300 miles between us.

R. S. B.

137

to Elizabeth Shepley Sergeant
(Ms Yale)

Dublin, N. H.
17 Aug 1915

I must send you a bulletin, and try to anticipate your reply to my last letter. The warm weather, I imagine, is all gone, with a rousing wind to-day and an autumnal-looking sky. We still have our daily deluge, and Fergus was caught on Sunday with Gerald Thayer on the first ridge of Monadnock. I started with them for the "high pastures," but some intuition warned me, and I came back to spend the afternoon with "The Tragic Comedians" of Meredith. I liked it very much too, though it is far too simple, and not sticky and fishy and pretentious enough for the true Meredithean, I believe. The Thayers have been too good to us; they will be tired of seeing us again. Saturday, an afternoon of music on Mrs. Gerald's piano, in deference to my modest but probably noticeable reluctance at the relic of 1848. I'm afraid there were sundry subterranean interfamily complications, in consequence, but not very dangerous, I guess. The music was flanked on both sides by a meal, and the Geralds had us up Sunday again. We really should decline some of these, but I tell them the peril is theirs.

Other social adventures last week were a call on Miss Eugenica Frothingham, whom I liked, and dinner with Miss Amy Lowell, who seems to share with the Germans the faculty of setting off dynamite bombs in peaceful social groups. Mrs. Gerald came home from Miss Lowell's talk at the club Saturday, quite beside herself with fury, and a mild Harvard professor was stirred to warmth in recounting her atrocities on ship board. She slips into every conversation, and spreads havoc. I went to her house in considerable trepidation expecting to be pummelled and overawed. Instead, I spent a wholly delightful evening. She walked right at me as one of the oldest of friends, and we had a truly grand gossip. I found her immensely witty and keen, and willing to spread out the contents of her mind before you. Surprisingly fair, and a friendly lover of all sorts of queer and little people, whom she touches off inimitably. She has a delightful zest of life, and would be a much greater person without her money and position, which apparently give people these extraordinary reactions and breed unpopularity for her. She seems quite innocent of this, however.

I also had tea with Miss Putnam and her sister, with both of whom I'm sure I should disagree on almost every subject. But we found much to talk about that didn't involve agreements and got along very pleasantly. Mr. Brush stopped yesterday morning, probably astounded to see us up so early, and talked long and charmingly on violins and violinists. Mr. Thayer took us out in his boat one peculiarly heavenly morning, and, having got us to the middle of the lake, discoursed on Art and Religion. He is a very charming friendly harbor to have, and his house grows so on me. That jumble of studios, and that study of Gerald's with the wide view of the mountains, where one would *have* to be inspired if one were not overcome by the loneliness! We amuse ourselves already with building a house in Dublin, and coming here always to live, so you see how much captivated we are.

Your own summer sounds a little disconsolate, in spite of so delicious a house. Do your varied consciences hound you along like mine do? So that nothing is ever a real vacation, and nothing ever a real normal drudge of work? My only solution is to get so somehow proud of myself that I cannot bear to have the world deprived of what I could tell them. Unfortunately, I am still far from that condition, and I suppose you are too. I wish we might see you up here.

Sincerely,

R. B.

138

to Dorothy Teall
(Transcript Columbia)

Dublin, N. H.
19 August 1915

I have no objection to being the G. Washington I am not. B[eulah] E A[midon] once said, I remember distinctly, after a little discussion of the evil influences of my cynicism upon your young mind,—"I don't know but what she's half in love with you now." (This may not be the weird conception that you referred to. If it is not, please forgive me.) B's romantic phraseology probably meant that you seemed to understand and appreciate some of my best moods. However, since it seems so weird to you, even this interpretation may be only a deplorable exhibition of my complacency at your seeming to tell me of this appreciation in one or two of your letters. "Being in love" is so much more fierce and brutal a thing than B. herself seems to even care to imagine, that every one should be warned against it. I don't find that it corresponds to anything that is said about it in books. I am surprised to find that so much is written and said about it when it is scarcely a subject that, as things go to-day, can be mentioned in polite society. I am a complete Shavian on the subject.

What B. really meant only a mid-Victorian, I suppose, could explain. She is a good deal of one herself, and has just sent me the most school-girlish letter, which almost finishes her.

I like very much your phrase of "sacrificing truthfulness to comfort." Exactly the thing to do. Let butterfly self grow up in chrysalis family and burst with the emancipating years. Family itself, I gather, veiledly looks to a terminus to the span of conformity. Why object to being a parasite at seventeen? Family brought you into the world, knowing perfectly well what they were doing. Don't you know that it's cruel to deprive people of the pleasure of serving you? if they like to serve? We are all parasites, none more than I, and it hurts my feelings to have you despise them. Of course, it is very nice to earn a little money to lubricate your way along, and that is probably why you are tutoring this summer. But sometimes a lordly idleness is better than an uncounting job. If your only ideal in life is to be fiercely unparasitic, like a New Hampshire farmer, then by all means bury yourself in any old kind of a job, perfectly uncritical whether it is worth while doing, or whether anybody else can do it. But if you want to have an interesting, rounded, and luminous life, and do work that other people don't do, or with a tone that only you can give, then you certainly don't want to hurry time and nag and irritate fortune, and sap your vitality drop by drop. It's all a question of the goals you envisage. And it seems to me a very clear issue between them.

R. S. B.

As a futurist, you probably despire our friends the Thayers and the Brushes.

139

to Alyse Gregory
(Ms Yale)

Dublin
30 Aug. 1915

· I don't forget that you talked in your last letter about going to Europe, and about thinking of death, and I meant to write at once and ask you please not to think about either. But you will probably go just the same, and it won't do any good to argue with you. I can only tell you about the neighbors who reproached a friend of mine who went to Russia last May to join her husband.

They thought it very heartless of her to wilfully add to the cares of our dear overburdened President. I should never forgive you if you were the cause of war with Germany. That seems to me the last calamity to which this teetering world of ours could come. And I can't make out whether the President is wobbling innocently towards it, like a child playing with fire, or is running a high and daringly successful course, which will bring us out with prestige. But this doesn't excuse your putting yourself in danger. So please don't.

This place is seductive, and we are getting all wrapped into the fortunes of an artist family which lives in the woods, in a romantic warren of studios and charming big low rooms, with great fireplaces, and windows that frame delicious pictures of pine trees or mountain and sunset. The old father has a hobby of protective coloration, to which he has, in a way, sacrificed his son and daughter. She is intense and repressed and a little sombre, but very kindly and genuine, and is on the point of making a wild intolerant burst for a winter of freedom, painting in New York. The son, having painted interminable birds for his father's book, hates painting, wants to write, and lives along giving lectures and classes in nature-study. He married a delightful model, who came to pose for his father, and has two babies, who take their whole time. They are all such charming, simple, wistful, unworldly people, with whom you can sit silently before the fire, and know you understand them. Two or three times a week my friend takes his violin and we go to play for them, being rewarded with a supper, and the most unaffected gratitude. I could serenely live up here all winter, I think. I wish I was not so helpless and alone and poor. I would do it. There is nothing enticing about going back to the cross-currents of the city, and the assaults of alien people, and the ache for friends and their inaccessibility. Carl has been here for ten days, and though we were grateful for his culinary art, he suddenly seemed to me somehow forbidding and as if we didn't know each other, and I felt the wistfulness for a much greater response and vivid congenial life than we had together last winter. He has a certain hard interior pride of individuality, which I must have unconsciously been assaulting constantly with some of my little arrogances, and I had a queer fancy that the accumulations of a winter suddenly burst out back at me up here. He seemed almost a stranger. We made a pilgrimage to the Macdowell place, and he thought so much more and so irritatingly about feeding the horse than about seeing the log-cabin in the pines where the subtlest music yet thought in America was written. Going back to live with him would be much mollified by the union with our friend Greene—Irish, and unfortunately a little woman-minimizing—whom we have adopted and who has our apartment this summer. The few weeks we were all together there he blended a very pleasing atmosphere, so undoubtedly I shall return and we will look for a larger apartment for the three of us.

R. S. B.

140

to Elizabeth Shepley Sergeant
(Ms Yale)

Dublin [N. H.]
August 30, 1915

I began to think I would have to be cold and miserable, or have you think we were uncomfortable in Dublin before you would write me again. I can assure you that to-day is most unpleasant, cold and so damp that we can scarcely light our matches and papers and books are limp and moist. The good days have been delicious, however, and I'm sure they will come again. The climate must have been queer this summer, for I have been very sleepy, and not at all exhilirated, except for one or two bouncing days when it seemed a crime to work, and I had to drown in a drink my disappointment that I couldn't climb mountains or fly. One day—did I tell you?—we drove to Petersboro to the Macdowell colony, which I very much wanted to see. Ridgley Torrence[1] and his wife were there, and after a long search which took us all over the woods and fields, we found them in their studio about lunch-time. I wanted to stay and roam around, but my friends—rural Marthas—had the burden of the unfed horses on their minds, and we had to make for the tavern in the village. While the horse was being tenderly cared for, we met Torrence again, and took him home, he telling us his usual marvellous tales all along the way. He showed us Macdowell's grave, and the log-cabin, and for me it was a real pilgrimage, though my friends— Carl and Fergus—seemed strangely bored. The log-cabin looking out over the pines "towards the westering sun," has all the atmosphere of a holy place, silent and undisturbed. In it was composed the noblest music yet thought in this country. Very noble too is the great rock in the little hedge-close that marks the grave. There is a high plateau with meadows that remind me of Switzerland, and a background of forest, with a great sweep of mountains. It is all quite different from Dublin, but very distinctive. The artists are few, but real ones, working in the semi-solitude that seems to me the high, heroic test of personality.

My friend Carl with whom I live in New York, has been here, and we have lived ten days on his culinary art. Now it seems harder than ever to cook, and as Fergus has acquired prejudices against canned things and meats, I am facing a starvation which can only be allayed by some merciful boarding-house, I fear. My enticements are not sufficient to bring other friends from New York. I shall want to stay several weeks, however, if I find that the "New Republic" does not forget my existence.

We still live half our time at the Thayers though we have gradually shifted to the Geralds'. Mr. T's head is so full of piebald warships and the conversion of college presidents to protective coloration that he cannot any longer let his emotional nature be stirred by our Schubert and Bach. But Mrs. Gerald and Gladys and Dorothea Taber, who has been there, and a neighbor or two, provide an audience, and, as we are always ready for endless music, we play there, several times a week. Mrs. Gerald is very charming, with a strangely-colored life, and their literary ambitions among the moil of constantly-demanding babies are rather touching. G. reads me snatches of his book on the West Indies, and talks vaguely about publishers, though several have rejected him. His father, for all his charm, is, I'm afraid, a choice parental tyrant, and used up his children's youth in his hobby. The great book seems to have taken a lot of grudging but uncomplaining starch out of G. and he doesn't know just where he is now, except that he hates painting. Warfare is now raging about Gladys' going to New York the coming winter alone, with her flying tragically to the upper house from her father's cloudy remonstrances, and me feeling very wise as the champion of the younger generation. She seems so very genuine and serious and obscure and repressed, and says startling things sometimes that seem to come up from a hidden life. She has evidently been minimized always by both father and brother, and is now ripe for some intolerant burst of freedom. Her savageries seem to be rather enforced than desired.

We had a glorious picnic one cold moonlit evening on a knoll back through the woods. The Geralds, Gladys, Miss T., Miss Redfield, an artist here, Carl, Fergus, and myself. Supper, and then a fine skirmishing quarrel about a fire, Gladys in almost a priestly attitude of insistence against her brother. Finally he went and telephoned for permission, while the lusty ones did heroic feats of birch-springing and swinging, and we watched the great moon. We had our fire, and stayed till eleven, coming back through the woods without a lantern, the pine floor splashed with white moonlight and the trunks standing solemnly around.

There have been so many delightful hours that I cannot tell of them all. The people you and Mr. Greenslet recommended me to, with their friends, still remain the congenial. I have ruined my reputation by going three times to the club. Very thin pablum indeed. Professor Richard Burton,[2] a monologist, & Major Putnam were the speakers. The Dublin you know certainly has an unpardonable fringe of fashionableness.

Miss Lowell jumped up and walloped Mr. Burton after his speech. This was one of her unfavorable manifestations. If you don't know her, I'm sure you wouldn't like her. My introduction was under the happiest auspices, and my impressions most favorable. Perhaps she has had two phases, the Lowell-arrogant one, and the Imagist-kindly Shavian one. I got her only in the last, without any memories of the other. She even looked almost handsome at dinner in her own charming house, and reminded me strangely of a gay and heroic young woman

The New Republic (1914-1915):

friend of mine who has just died.

Thanks for the offer of French! You haven't any of the Unanimistes to loan, have you? or the novels of de Regnier, or Peguy's "Eve"?[3] I'm reading Emerson & Nietzsche.

R. S. B.

[1]Torrence was the Editor of *Cosmopolitan*. In the '20's he became poetry editor of *New Republic*. He was also a playwright who attempted to write serious material about—and acted by—blacks.

[2]Burton was a Professor of English at the University of Minnesota. He was President of the Drama League of America from 1914 to 1915.

[3]Charles-Pierre Peguy was a French poet. He started out an athiest but converted to Catholicism. Throughout his life he retained his socialism and his love for the figure of Joan of Arc, about whom he wrote one of his most confusing poems. "Eve" was his last long poem. De Regnier was a prominent poet of the early 1900's. He used mostly Classical and Renaissance themes.

141

to Elizabeth Shepley Sergeant
(Ms Yale)

Dublin, N. H.
7 Sept [1915]

I do hope you did not decide last night on your plans, for I should like very much to persuade you to come to Dublin. I write in great haste, wondering if it would make just the deciding difference if I telegraphed you. The boarding-house is Mrs. Preston's, and it is situated next to the Library not far from the stores and the church (towards the lake). The situation is not ideal, but you will remember it is not far to the lake, and her rooms look very clean and pleasant to me. A couple of friends of Gladys Thayer, Miss Taber and Miss Redfield, have been there for several weeks, and speak very well of it, good table they say. Mrs. Preston told me last week that all her people were going by the 15th, so there would be plenty of room. She has a room for $8, or $10, or $12, according to size. When I talked with her last week, I was playing with the idea of staying

many weeks there. My friend leaves Monday or Tuesday next, and then I intended to move there probably, unless Mrs. Thayer discovered another house she had
hinted at. Since then Dublin has given me too much society, but that will rapidly pass. It would be delightful to have you here in Dublin, and you would quite
clinch my decision to stay. The big front room *here* would give you an admirable place to write. Of course Mr. Greene would lend it to you. Mr. Brush is in
the barn, and is living only a short distance away. We went to see him the other
evening and had a delightful talk. What can I do to induce you to come to Dublin? Remind you of the gorgeous foliage and the lake and Monadnock, which my
friend Carl, a connoisseur in mountains, calls "a most delightful mountain"?
Mr. Brush, unusually available just now. The Thayers mellowed and familiar
from our music, and open for many delightful talks and suppers and before their
great fireplace. Can't you think of the Adirondacks and the Green Mts. as pale
and dreary like your house-cleaning Brookline, and so come to Dublin? Can I
get any more information to you? The Russo-German lady runs only a tea-room,
I believe, and is very expensive. Has made an ultra-fashionable sensation.

    Excuse my haste and uncontentedness

R. S. Bourne

142

to Prudence Winterrowd
(Transcript Columbia)

Dublin, N. H.
8 Sept. 1915

    Well, I hope you will find New York more pleasing this time, and really
come to know Columbia. You have at least taken the strange and dreary edge off
of it by your first visit, and will know how to place yourself more cheeringly.
I wish I could suggest possible accommodations, but probably you have settled
that. 118th St. between Amsterdam and Morningside is popular, much prefer-
able to lower down the hill.

    I may be here for several weeks more, and if so I shall be sorry not to
meet you when you come to New York. But when I return, I shall have to invite you to tea, if my way of life this winter reproduces last year's and I give tea-
parties in my very diminutive apartment. I did not get away from New York
until after the First of August, waiting for my [?] to come to me. Which it finally did in the shape of a cottage in this delightful place, near a lake and Mt.

Monadnock, with unusually lovely woods of pine and white birch. With a violinist friend I am keeping house, and trying to write. But the society is very attractive here, and the outdoors alluring, and I get little done. I want to stay as long as possible, certainly until all chances of hot weather have vanished in New York.

Sincerely,

Randolph Bourne

143

to Alyse Gregory
(Ms Yale)

Dublin, N. H.
10 Sept. 1915

Dear Alyse,

Your adventures thrill me. Our mosquitoes are very few and apologetic. I shudder to think what New York must be suffering with its heat, too. It is even uncomfortably warm here, but bright and lovely, and I am becoming a kind of Lotus-eater, very much reconciled to life, forgetting that I am poor, or that anybody is poor or ever has been. A society that is rich and also cultivated is a very demoralizing thing. I have never come across this kind of people. Perhaps they don't exist outside of New England. But people here get things off with such taste and simplicity, and pose so little, that one is fairly seduced to such an aristocracy. There are a few nouveaux from St. Louis and Baltimore, just to furnish the dark background, but the general atmosphere here is most charming. Look around you as you will, you will not find a false or ugly note in the place, woods, houses, roads, lake. The occasional flashy houses are hidden in the trees. The wood-road winds unspoiled around the lake close to its shore. You may wander through private woods and estates at will. The mountain looms grandly from many points, and all my best friends seem to have appropriated the most charming houses and the best views. Autos pick you up on the road, and a friend or two comes around and takes you out. You get invited to dinners and teas, where you do not feel your lack of clothes, and you don't care whether you make a hit or not. The electric lights on the wood road are symbolic of this quite unusual mixture of beautiful wild nature and a serene and informal, yet pleasantly ordered life. There may be other American summer places with such a tone, but I have never seen them. Our house is plain weathered boards inside, rough and woodsy, and furnished with just everything you want. We are in a broad meadow by the lake, bursting with golden-rod and asters and dotted with pine-trees, private, yet near the road and just the right distance from the village.

Our best friends, the Abbott Thayers, live in a delightful nest of studios and unfinished rooms, in the woods, and are such serious, impractical, unworldly people. George de Forest Brush, the painter, who uses our barn for a studio, is a most charming person, full of socialistic ideas, and the raciest tangiest talk and expression.

I shall probably stay some time. When my friend goes, I expect an old man, an artist I met recently in New York, to come to stay with me. I have not told you about my present friend, because there is a complete description of him —of which he knows nothing—in the New Republic for about May 15 or 22, entitled "Fergus—A Portrait." He was unemployed, and the only available friend to carry off with me. Congenial, but reserved. We go our comfortable ways. He plays the violin, and has a few pupils in New York. He returned from his walk all right; I'm sorry to have kept you in suspense.

A charming letter from Carl makes me remorseful for my ill-humor, which was a curious precipitation from the new and untested chemical combination of the three of us, I'm afraid.

If you must go to Europe, don't get blown up. Why don't you take a vacation and run up to the boarding-house here for a week? That would be a very jolly, and more sensible thing than going to Europe.

Nina sounds most scandalous.

R. S. B.

144

to Carl Zigrosser
(Ms Pennsylvania)

Dublin, N. H.
12 Sept. 1915

Dear Carl,

Your two letters recount enviable adventures, social as well as nature-all. You will be doing the Sierra Nevadas next, though I'm glad you still retain your admiration for Monadnock.

Our life has scarcely changed a hair's breadth since you left. Murray has advanced to muffins and strange vegetable combinations, but this week we have had a long run of five consecutive dinner invitations. One morning I found him packing to go next day, but he called it off until I should make arrangements for myself somewhere. Eastman Chase[1] writes he will come, but I don't know just when. Murray may leave this week if he comes. I tried to get the Fernandez' on their way back from Canada, but they were already in New York. The boarding-house which held Miss T[aber] and Miss R[edfield] now stands empty to receive me at any time, if I am left deserted. Miss Sergeant talks vaguely of coming some time, and I think now of staying on indefinitely. The weather has been delightful though warm, and the stars superb beyond anything I ever remember to have seen. Social events include Miss Frothingham's musicale, with Lilla Ormond singing. Weakly pretty and undistinguished voice. Pleasant company and wonderful view. Some slight sensation of my German article which had just arrived that day.[2]

Then there was a musicale at the Pumpellys' studio;[3] Herman Sandby, a Danish cellist, with interesting personality and ravishing tone. An artist, and said to have one of the finest 'cellos in the world. Tea later on a grassy terrace bounded by a stone wall, overlooking the mountain and the sunset. Girls in bright Italian costumes. Most delightful picture.

Then I had another dinner at Miss Amy Lowell's, at which was also Edwin Arlington Robinson,[4] whom we got a look at from Torrence's piazza. He read us his latest poem in "Poetry" (September issue),[5] and Miss L. read us "Lead Soldiers" in the same issue. Both pretty good, I think. Look up "Patterns" in the "Little Review" for September. She is always interesting and has both beauty—I mean her verse has—and intellectual pithiness.

Much of the Thayers. Can you do anything about a studio for Gladys? Have you looked at those 14th St. places at all? And are you and W. G[reene?] contemplating a larger apartment with me this winter? If you find any precious jewel, available to Public Lib., Greenwich Village, Russell Sage,[6] and New Republic,—the four boundaries of my intellectual world, apparently—why not move at once? However, don't be rash.

R. S. B.

[1] According to Van Wyck Brooks, Eastman Chase was an old Yankee painter, formerly of Boston, who then had a studio in MacDougall Alley in New York City.

[2] "Americn Use for German Ideals" appeared in the September 4th issue of *New Republic*.

[3] Raphael Pumpellys was, according to Van Wyck Brooks, an artist.

[4] Robinson lived at the Macdowell Colony, where he made his reputation in the 'teens. In fact, he was the most famous of the residents of the Colony.

5"Bokardo."

6The Russell Sage Foundation was created in 1907 to better social conditions in the United States. The Foundation funded studies which attempted to apply new theories of social science to social problems.

145

to Arthur Macmahon
(Ms Mrs. Arthur Macmahon)

Dublin, N. H.
13 Sept. 1915

Dear Arthur,

I'm still sorry that you and your mother weren't induced to come up here. You could have come at any time, and I'm sure you would have enjoyed it. A mountain, Monadnock, which Carl [Zigrosser], with his long experience in the Catskills calls "a most delightful mountain;" all sorts of forest walks, a charming little lake, and an informal rough house where you can have all the pleasures of camping out and being comfortable at the same time. Murray and I have tried housekeeping, and have been fortunately prevented from doing our worst. Carl was here for ten days, and applied his culinary art, and since then we have been invited out repeatedly by various kind people who like our music. There are some very congenial artistic and literary people here, and I find myself leading a small edition of my New York life,—not small either, because really more interesting, with the outdoors and the more leisurely and unworldly people.

Murray is talking of going soon and then I shall have to move to the boarding-house, unless an old man named Eastman Chase, an artist & charming, comes to stay with me. I wish you could be induced to come up for a week before college opens. I don't think you'd regret it. It is not so inaccessible. There is a through day-train from N. Y. in six hours to Keene, and then a drive. Fare is about $5 each way. If you will come I will meet you any day you say. College is late this year, isn't it? I want to stay as long as possible, and shall, if the "New Republic" does not cast me off. By the way, express no opinions as to the authorship of "One of Our Conquerors" in a recent issue of the N. R. and if you hear any comments, register them devoutly for my ears.

Another item of news is the coming to Columbia again of Miss Prudence Winterrowd of Shelbyville, Indiana.

Wish you had come and hope you may see your way yet.

R. S. B.

146

To Dorothy Teall
(Transcript Columbia)

Dublin, N. H.
14 Sept [1915]

If I had your mother and you at my beck and call, I should certainly have summoned you up here to take the place of my friend Fergus, who has been feeling it his duty to go for some time, and seems actually leaving to-morrow. I am awaiting an old gentleman, an artist, to come and stay with me until we get frozen out. The woods are very slow about putting on their promised glory, and it may be really October before I have had enough of Dublin. I don't work very much, but as much as in New York, I suppose, and the summery freedom and the nice unworldly people we see so much of make New York most dispensable. The Thayers like us and our music so much that I seem to find myself always at their hospitable board, so that our housekeeping, which might be fatal, had no serious consequences. We speculate about the country-house I am going to build up here. I realize that I must have it here or elsewhere sometime. A clear day in the country seems to make me quite contented, and smooths out all the knots of the city and the hectic people one chases there. You must meet Gladys Thayer in New York next winter. She is a pretty good painter, grave and strong and naive, a creature of the woods, but very wistful for experience and freedom from her painter-father, who is an unconscious tyrant, I fear, though a winsome and Emersonian old person.

How can I tell you anything about B[eatrice] T[eall]? I understood that you and she were so exactly alike that you understood her better than she understood herself. Of course you are not at all alike, but I can't contribute much to an elucidation of the difference. B. served a most useful purpose in my life for about three years by keeping me from falling in love with anybody. She had a way of allowing you to bask in her appreciations, and shedding a certain pleasing glow over the scene, and her own struggles and final extrication were very interesting. She had some kind of a curious conscience that hounded her into doing things that she really, in her heart of hearts, had no talent or love for. She did have a talent for personal relations, and I imagine cared more about getting those right than about being musical. Mr. B. offered a focus, not absolutely perfect, but one that permitted the play of a good deal of her talent, and so she converged on him. There is a beauty about being worshipped, and, if she could not herself worship, she was at least not insensitive to that other beauty. I speak of her in the past tense, only because she has passed, with much interest and no regret on my part, out of my world forever.

R. S. B.

147

to Elizabeth Shepley Sergeant
(Ms Yale)

Dublin [N. H.]
14 Sept [1915]

You *are* a gay deceiver, deciding against Dublin before I had even read your letter, and making all my persuasiveness vain. And now you must, in compensation, make the October trip, for longer than four days, I hope. I shall probably be here, and would surely wait if there was a certainty of your coming. Mr. Brush has just finished a portrait of his daughter Nancy, Titian-like, with rich draperies and classic calm, and all the world comes to see it, filling our meadow with motors and chatter. Everybody says it is the best thing he has done. How amazing that so radical a mind should make his art so imitative! He seems completely untouched by the art-tendencies of the day, living only with the Italian masters and working devoutly after their principles.

I read your dialogue with pleasure and some unexpected reactions. I haven't read the stories, but you make it unnecessary, and have probably saved me much irritation. If these people, like Mrs. Gerould,[1] prefer the timid decencies of academic life and all the harmony of a life that reduces emotion and personality and robust irony to the minimum, why aren't they willing to pay the price, and not be always wistfully looking over the hedge at passion and freedom and frankness? They are not really protesting prisoners, nor are their characters, but they like to appear as if they could really live in the open air, at the same time that they would not think of surrendering their luxurious jails. I am a little mixed perhaps, and I haven't read Mrs. G[erould], but I seem to detect the same note here that one finds in Galsworthy, that of people cultivated outside of the humanly animal sphere, yet in no genuine new angelic sphere. Much good art is wasted in trying to touch you with the infinite pathos of such lives, when they are merely dull. The theme is usually the renunciation of individual desire in obedience to some higher immemorial social law which transcends the petty willfulness of the one person. But such a law ought to transfigure those who obey it, and the hollowness of it all is shown by the fact that it never does, at least in English fiction and in the Puritan life I see around me. These great laws of obligation which constrain people to loyalties ought to make their lives epic, and it seems never to do anything but make them dull. Won't you write up the New England conscience sometime all by itself? I don't get a chance to read you on anybody but these fearfully sophisticated writers who don't seem a bit like you as a friendly, human person. But then you usually sit heavily on them, so that is all right.

Why were you so cowardly about the French family?[2] And with my impudent example before you? You make me feel very impudent indeed.

R. S. Bourne

[1]Katherine Gerould was a popular writer of short stories and novels.

[2]Sergeant's articles were later collected into *French Perspectives*.

148

to Elizabeth Shepley Sergeant
(Ms Yale)

Dublin [N. H.]
23 September [1915]

I hope you will tell me you are coming to Dublin next week. For otherwise I shall probably find myself driven away. Things seem to be disintegrating rapidly, and I do not want to be left with ashes in my hands. Fergus has gone, and now my old Mr. Chase who has been keeping house for me since with such skill and companionly charm is called back to New York just as I had begun to contemplate long October weeks living along in this house. I chafe at my bad luck. Gladys Thayer suddenly goes away for two weeks. I quarrel with the Geralds over Meredith. Various people drift away. The boarding-house does not seem inviting for loneliness. Do come and save Dublin for me. These are glorious cool days. We got up to the high pasture yesterday but could not stay long for the wind.

I meant to answer your kind inquiries about the Gary manuscript. I finished it in a wild burst of speed on Saturday, and had to pay with a lame back which has kept me sitting around with pillows ever since, and a cleaned-out vacuum at the New Republic staring me in the face. It is an awful thing to be told that there are no more things of yours down there, and you not feeling at all like sitting up and writing, and without an idea in your head. Each day makes the delay worse. I do not want to be chidden, and if I am not I shall think they do not miss me.

The Gary work is a fearful thing. I tried to be official and descriptive and to quench all unqualified enthusiasm, with the result that I am duller than the most cautious schoolman. And now an agent has, by some miracle, put over a Gary article of mine on Scribner's,[1] which is utterly characterless. Can one do these things without blushing. I shall never touch Gary again, Mrs. A. B. F.—who summons me back to the New York fray—notwithstanding. I am rather a precarious aid to her, anyway, in her Nepoleonic campaign, for I usually get my facts wrong and put my foot in it. She seems to like the explosions, however, that I sometimes get off, and believes in publicity, good or bad. I hope she gets some reward for her supernatural energy in this enterprise. She has put in enough to stand any ordinary school-system on its head. She is a great general and could scarcely have a better cause.

I hope you manage to come to Dublin. Is not life long enough to crowd it also in?

R. S. Bourne

[1]"Gary Public Schools" was published in September 1916.

149

to Alyse Gregory
(Ms Yale)

Dublin, N. H.
25 Sept 1915

At last my housekeeping has collapsed, and I am left stranded. My first friend was followed by a delightful old man, a Bohemian New Englander who has a little studio in Macdougall Alley and comes up here when he hasn't any work in New York. He cooked for me, and we spent hours walking, or talking poets and music and pictures before the fire. He used to have a picture gallery in Boston, and knows everybody and everything interesting. A rare old character, 74 years old and quite untouched! Emphatically not of the older generation! But work calls him back to New York. He started out this morning to walk to Petersboro, eight miles, to get his train. I walked a couple of miles with him down the delightful Dublin hill with its little old houses and pleasant meadows. It was almost like June, so green and fresh and not a touch of autumn color yet. There were rounded hills in the distance that looked like Wales, and here and there lively old flower-gardens, bright with purples and yellows. Now I am back, quite desolate before the fire, doomed to a week at the boarding-house, in a faint hope of a friend's coming for a few days. Then surely a few days in Boston, and New York again. I shudder a little at the thought of 31st St., and still more at the fear that we may not be able to find or afford anything better. Given better weather than a New England winter provides, and an able-bodied and charming companion, and I can think of nothing I should like better to do than stay here for a long time. And I think it would do me much good, be better for me than coming back to be tossed about in New York, with the dissatisfactions and frustrations of last winter and avoid some of the personal and official rocks on which I battered myself before. I hope you get something quieter to do, or, better still, nothing at all. I don't see how a woman can help wearing herself out with such a fiercely objective and active life as you have been leading. I must say you stand it extremely well. I always expect to see that something has happened to you, that some of the indifference and bluntness of the stupid world you face has been forced into you. But you always seem quite as fine and sensitive as ever, and come through it all unscathed. Occasionally you do seem to hear the mill-whistle in your ears, and to be thinking of to-morrow rather than to-day, but your general resiliency is quite amazing. How do you really do it? You don't seem to miss anything in spite of your grind, and you manage never to get that lean and harrowed look of so many of the hectic Villagers.

I have been away from so many of the Heretics[1] meetings that I suppose

H. D. will bounce me. You won't go to Europe before I get back, will you?

R. S. B.

---

[1]The Heretics was possibly one of the clubs which sprang up in Greenwich Village as an off-shoot of the Liberal Club.

150

to Carl Zigrosser
(Ms Pennsylvania)

Dublin, N. H.
28 Sept [1915]

Dear Carl,

The discomforts, as depicted by your eloquent pen, seem far to outweigh the advantages. When Dublin has steam heat and electric lights, why should one camp out in N. Y.? I'm sure we can do better for $35. I expect to be back next week, probably Thursday or Friday, and I can devote my leisure time to house-hunting. If there are any of those studio affairs in the Phipps to rent, why, I should favor them. I will consult my Greenwich Village cronies too. Kinglet's place is more charming to visit than to manage. I gather *you* must be seeing quite a little of her. Is W. G[reene?] taken by her or L.? Your new infant prodigy evidently needs my master-hand. You sound much wrought up about her oppression and spiritual struggles. Don't let her get away before I come.

Everything combines to draw me back. Chase has gone, called most unfortunately back to do some work; Gladys T. is away on a visit; the weather is suddenly very cold, so that I have moved to the boarding-house to which we had so many midnight rambles with our be-bicycled lady. Last night, I had one myself, coming from the Geralds.

Last week Chase and I gave a dinner party to the Geralds and Gladys. We drove to Keene for our provisions, and Chase did up a fine banquet of chops, sweet potatoes, peas, baked apples. He had a quart of whiskey, too, which was imposed on us all, and we sat for hours gossiping about the littered board, Chase in fine form, recalling all the artists and Boston notables of bygone days. He is a Mr. Roberts but the real stuff, perfectly genuine, with an amazing knowledge and taste in pictures and music and verse. He recited some of the fine things of

Edward Arlington Robinson, and castigated Geo. de Forest Brush, to the horror
of the young Thayers. He thinks Thayer will last, as a real artist, but Brush, with
his imitation Titians, he consigns to limbo, even calling him a fake. Chase was a
great delight and we must see him in N. Y.

My Dublin days are over, and I am merely hanging on in the hope of Miss
Sergeant's coming this week for a few days, and then taking me to Brookline for
a night on my way to New York. If she doesn't come, I shall be swindled.

R.S. B.

151

to William Wirt
(Ms Indiana)

Dublin, N. H.
29 Sept. 1915

Dear Mr. Wirt,[1]

I have been working on a manuscript descriptive of the Gary School
System, with the thought of getting it published in book form. I assume that
you would personally have no objection to its publication, providing, of course,
that it told the truth. Houghton Mifflin Company are now considering the manuscript for publication in their educational department, but desire that it meet
your approval before their final decision is made. May I send you the manuscript
for perusal? And will you tell me frankly whether you consider it adequate for
publication? Of course, I should not think of publishing it if you did not think
it would aid the public in getting a clear idea of your remarkable school.

I was delighted to see in the paper that Mayor Mitchell had come out in
favor of the complete reorganization of the New York elementary schools.[2]
This is great news, and should mean speedy success.

I expect to be back in New York next week, and perhaps you could then
give me time to show you the manuscript.

Very sincerely,

Randolph Bourne

[1]William Wirt was the Superintendent of the Gary school system whom Bourne visited earlier in 1915. Wirt's ideas were being introduced into the New York City public school system.

[2]The *New York Times* of September 28th (9:8) carried news of Mitchell's support. Wirt's plan had been instituted on an experimental basis in the Bronx, but full implementation was meeting with some resistance. Bourne supported Wirt enthusiastically and wrote two letters to the *Times*—on June 15th (12:8) and December 11th (12:7)—advocating Wirt's plan.

152

to Alyse Gregory
(Ms Yale)

Dublin, N. H.
1 Oct 1915

Your letter is full of the most horrible portents,—getting married, earning your living in Europe, things I have never heard you even mention before. And why should you have to attend policemen's conventions? What do you expect to find them doing, listening to Brahms sonatas and reading Amy Lowell? I should say, You poor distraught thing, if I did not know how infinitely capable you were of standing almost anything and bounding up again into serenity. But you ought to have a rest, and I suppose your European trip will do it. I don't think you were serious about getting married (I hope not, that is) but were you serious about earning your living in Europe? I should think New Jersey, taken at a leisurely pace, would be more profitable. For you really could do it in a leisurely way, couldn't you? And then you would be near enough to be often seen, which is the main thing, and seen perhaps in a more leisurely way. I wonder if I will get to N. J. in time to register for the vote on the amendment.[1] This is the first time I have had a chance on the question, and, though I have lost interest in voting lately, this would be something I would do with real satisfaction and a sense of accomplishing something. Have you calculated the possibility of the antis or indifferent staying home? A special election ought to favor you. If N. J. is as indifferent as the recent N. Y. Times editorial (vile sheet) says it is, you ought to have a very good chance of winning.

I'm glad to hear that Dora is making herself useful. She is a very old friend of mine, the useful older sister of a girl with whom every boy in town was in love twelve years ago; now the girl is married to my oldest boy friend. Dora suddenly married a middle-aged theatrical agent, who died and left her with a little girl. I thought she was hinting towards marriage again. She was meant for better things, has a lot of unfocused intelligence and spunk, but never just found her circle or niche. She needs to be much better looking, but has had a miserable time living around and trying to earn money. How did I happen to come into the conversation? And how did she happen to come into the work?

My last week up here has really been an unusual debauch of laziness; work staring you in the face, which you deliberately leave and go and roam vacant-mindedly about the country. Four of the most perfect days that God ever made. Brightest of yellow sunlight, brightest of white moonlight, and the woods and hills nobler than ever. But there has been nobody to enjoy them with. The first cold weather drove everything away. I have eaten in solitary grandeur here at the boarding-house, and felt alone except for my good friends, the Thayers. But Gladys, strange political, repressed girl, living all her life in their enchanting warren in the woods, is away in Vermont visiting the inspired country and the charming niece of a genius, of whom I had never heard, but had only to look in his book to see it. Did you ever hear of Edward Martin Taber of *Stowe Notes?*[2] G. is to be in New York this winter painting, and you must meet her and make her talk. At home, her father talks all the time, and she has had 29 years of male spiritual domination. I am very curious to see what life in New York will do for her.

The father, besides being a real artist, is a winsome old person, and an evening in front of their fire is a delightful experience. Thus Monday evening with a long walk through the moonstruck woods at the end. Tuesday I discovered a new road and walked along it, with tantalizing views through the trees, until I came to the fairest meadow with the view which is like nothing so much as that across the Roman Campagna from the Janiculum, the same valley, the same contours of hills, even jagged Mt. Soracte, called in New Hampshire Crotched Mountain. Only the city and St. Peter's were absent. Instead to the left some hills that looked like Wales. I lay in the warm grass for hours, dreaming, and hearing the foxes barking in the woods behind me. Wednesday there was another ride around the lake and to Jaffrey, through the woods where sun and shade through the leaves fairly intoxicated the senses in the rapid kaleidoscopic movement as we spun along. Yesterday morning I lay in bed and saw the most glorious orange dawn—deep orange springing from the deepest of blue hills, with the picturesque village church silhouetted black against it. To lie warmly in bed and see this amazing glory of color and form was the rarest of experiences. Then in the afternoon to my field again, warmer and even lovelier, and then to the Thayers. An hour watching the mountain turn purple in the sunset, and the golden clouds through the western pines, and then a talk by the fire about country houses and Dublin views, supper and some Schubert on the piano, and a walk under the belated moon along the lake wood-road, with mysterious shadows and sudden white forms of birches and queer luminous patches in the forest and the calm outline of the hills under the stars. My conscience tells me of some retribution due for these stolen delights. Articles not written, books not read, thoughts not achieved. I shall rush back to the city to get some rough massage of life that will make me angry or comical again. I mean to leave Monday, and stop a few days in Boston. Will you be in New York the following Sunday? If so, let me try to see you somewhere. Don't put the responsibility on me by coming to see me and finding me out. Tell me where you are and I will come to see you.

R. S. B.

[1]A suffrage amendment came up for the vote in New Jersey on the 19th of October. The *Times* was against giving women the franchise and urged the antis to get out the vote. Suffrage was, in fact, defeated in what was considered to be a crucial battle; New Jersey was the first Eastern state in which a suffrage vote was taken.

[2]Published in 1913. Taber was a landscape painter who had died before the turn of the century. The naturalistic reflections of this volume were accompanied by sketches. The book was thought of as being in the Thoreauvian mold.

153

to Elizabeth Shepley Sergeant
(Ms Yale)

335 E. 31st St.
10 Oct. 1915

New York was not really as bad as I had expected it, not even East 31st St. and our tiny rooms. I had remembered it all smothered in July dust and heat, and was surprised to find October here too. The New Republic had killed my woman suffrage paper, perhaps happily for me, but took the other things I had sent from Dublin, so that I am relieved for a few days of their urgencies. I should have lingered on in Boston, I think, if I had known they were to be so gracious. You seem to be appearing with great regularity and interest. Tinck admired "The Merciers", and had not known who wrote it. Your guess about the married article was right, but don't tell anybody you know.

A. B. F. was right; I had missed the epic of Gary,—Wirt's trial before the Board of Education, Tinck leading the claque in the gallery.[1] She was quite mollified by my paragraph in the N. R. and is now reading my manuscript.

Denunciations of my recent articles continue to come in. I have become an impious, ungrateful, pro-German, venomous viper.[2] This sums up my college, Atlantic and German articles, and gives me a Byronic reputation that I shall have work living down, even if I wanted to. I am, I confess, a little bashful about visiting Columbia in the daytime. Mine ancient enemy, "The Professor", is on the warpath, I fear, and "Juvenis" scarcely conceals me with Thayerian protectiveness.[3] Fergus is still unscathed, however. My next portrait is permitted, but will probably lose me the lady's friendship just the same.[4] It is even more dangerous when you get permission, for then things are read into your most innocent phrases.

I have been house-hunting to no purpose. It is quite as you say. And my friends are saving money to go to Europe next year. I did hope for a room in which more than four people could congregate at one time, but it is evidently not so to be. I hope you have better luck, and will stay. Will I see you before your tour?

Please excuse my paper. It is Sunday and I am out of everything.

R. S. B.

[1]Bourne could be referring to the assessments of the Gary system—some favorable, but more critical—or to the political issues which resulted from the New York experiment.

[2]Among the articles Bourne could be referring to are "American Use for German Ideals," which appeared on September 4th, and "Mental Unpreparedness," which was published one week later.

[3]Bourne's portrait of Erskine, "The Professor," which appeared in *New Republic* in July 1915, was not complimentary. Bourne sometimes used the pseudonym "Juvenis."

[4]Bourne wrote only two sketches of his women friends. One, "Sophronisba," was modeled after Sergeant; the other, "Karen, a portrait," was not published until September 23, 1916. It was based perhaps on Frances Lundquist, or on Lucille Deming.

154

to Dorothy Teall
(Transcript Columbia)

335 E. 31st St.

25 Oct [1915]

When are you going to bring Babette [Deutsch] to tea? You have been quite neglecting me for a long time, don't even take the trouble to come down when I call at your house. It's sad to be so soon forgotten. One has only to go away for a few weeks and lose all one's friends, apparently. But perhaps if I invite you very particularly you will come with Babette, whom you must admit it is necessary for me to meet. I'm afraid Palazzo Phipps will see no such brilliant social life this winter at least. What seemed amusing then in our squalor has ceased to be a joke, and only the company and the cheapness and the contemplated horrors of moving keep me to my orbit here. The ideal must be postponed still another year. How do you like college this year?

R. S. B.

155

to Elizabeth Shepley Sergeant
(Ms Yale)

335 E. 31st St.

9 Nov. 1915

One look at your "Dean of Women" was enough, and only a threat from F[rancis] H[acket] [?] will make me read it. My "Feminism in America" got away with Dr. Shaw's book alone, and I am wondering whether it will be printed with its belated suffrage stuff. Dreiser and Miss Cather were also finished just in time,[1] and I shudder to think what misunderstandings may arise from them, that is, if they ever get past the censor. I am taking a whack at the college through Canby's book and a Princetonian creation called "Through College on Nothing a Year," which makes me positively see red.[2] So you'd better have your college articles ready to restore the balance.

I stopped at Mrs. Stockton's last Friday afternoon, but did not find her and have not had a chance to try since then. I think I shall like them both, and have every intention of "Turning up." You are a wonderful expander of my horizons.

Gladys Thayer is in town, but I have not seen her. She looked up Carl, but tactlessly neglected to write me or look me up, so my feelings are hurt. I had an unexpected telephone talk Sat. with Mr. T., who was in town for some reason and departing—somebody said for Europe!

A friend of mine [Alyse Gregory] is leaving soon for a vacation after her suffrage campaign in two states. All this talk of passports and routes makes one very restless too, but it will be long before I see another country, I suppose.

Sorry you are so disgusted with N[ew] Y[ork]. Would you want to double up? My two friends at 28 Grove are apparently about to separate for the winter. One goes to the country; the other stays. The staying one works for the C[harity] O[rganization] S[ociety] [3] and is away all day. She is very charming. I have no idea whether she wants a "paying guest", but think it likely. I mention it to be of service. Probably it is not even discussable.

Randolph Bourne

[1]"Desire as Hero," *New Republic* V (November 20, 1915), 5-6, was a review of *The "Genius"*. No Cather article was published until late 1918.

[2]"What is College For?" appeared on December 4th. Bourne reviewed *College Sons and College Fathers* by Henry Seidel Canby and *Through College on Nothing a Year* by Christian Gauss.

[3]The Charity Organization Society was founded by Columbia Professor Edward Devine as a social welfare agency. It later became the Community Service Society, which is still in existence. The woman in the employ of the C. O. S. was Mary Messer.

156

to Van Wyck Brooks
(Ms Pennsylvania)

New York
November 12, 1915

Dear Mr. Brooks,

Only my usual shiftlessness prevented me from following your suggestion of that article for the "Century". I had an idea of working in my favorite "scientific curve of distribution," and of showing that from the modern point-of-view all classifications into black and white were inaccurate, because things graded off into each other by degrees. I was then going to take up some of our social institutions and show how they were organized on the "black and white" plan, and suggest how a popular appreciation of the new idea would put us in a receptive mood for social changes. If you think that this idea, worked out in not too heavy a way, would make a good paper, I will drive myself to it again.

In regard to the educational article, I had not felt that the "Century" would look at any more since they turned down my one on the Gary schools, which was later taken by "Scribner's". I have in mind now a paper on the "Work-Study-and-Play" plan, as embodied in more progressive schools, both public and private. This seems to be the "school of to-morrow," and could be treated in a broader way. Then there is the very interesting subject of psychological tests for intelligence, manual skills, etc. with which some schools are experimenting. These subjects might meet your suggestions, and I shall likely try them any way, for I should really like very much to have a chance at the "Century" again.[1]

Sincerely yours,

Randolph Bourne

[1] Bourne never wrote for *The Century.*

157

to Elizabeth Shepley Sergeant
(Ms Yale)

335 E. 31st St.
15 Nov 1915

I was delighted to hear that the great meeting had come off. Mrs. Stockton added some more thrilling details, such as your not being able to sleep after it for poetic excitement. I was never put quite into this stage of exaltation, but I have rarely spent more interesting evenings than those with your new friend in Dublin. Don't you thank me a little for preparing your mind?

Mrs. Stockton, again thanks to you, seems likely to be a very good friend. I went up to tea the other day and had a long discussion on the noble life and the way to bring up children. I had been reading "The Research Magnificent",[1] and the spell was still upon me. You object to my personal classifications, but I am getting new ones all the time. I like particularly that one of Wells' between those who still expect to lead the noble life some day and those who have given up the idea as priggish and unnatural. I am irresistibly led to put P[aul] L[ittell] [2] in this latter class, both from his writing and from that suave and discreet disapproval which I feel him to be shedding around the more fervent things which I send to the office of the N[ew] R[epublic]. I thank God every day for Croly, and wonder how soon the burdens of his office will make him lay down the septre in favor of P. L.

I am very lazy to-day after a whole day in the woods in the gray and bitter November air around a camp fire with two very unworldly girls and my still more unworldly Carl. One of them is a blond Norwegian[3] from Wisconsin, and she says things like this, "My mother keeps writing and asking if I know any young men, so she will know how much money to send me for clothes." Do you like such little flashes of primitive sociology? There was also a special ceremonial trip of a prosperous Norwegian farmer half across the State to get her for a wife. But she was agonizing over social problems at the University, and she could only store him up for deliciously naive tales of Norwegian manners and life.

Did I tell you about my reminiscence of Dublin in the shape of a weekend at Lenox. I was almost wheedled from Dublin by these open hills and windswept moors. And my hostess, Elsie Clews Parsons,[4] has severely ousted Miss Lowell from my bright foreground. After all I *am* an ethnologist, and she is a so clever and stimulating one that she sets one's thoughts tumbling all over each other. And such a fine adventurousness and command of life as she radiates! Do you know her? If you are interested in rare persons, there she is.

I hope Brookline will not prove too seductive.

Randolph Bourne

Did you see my Ezekiel paragraph in the N. R.? I *am* proud of that.

[1] A work by George Bernard Shaw.

[2] Littell was then an editor of *New Republic* who also contributed the column "Books and Things."

[3] Perhaps Frances Lundquist, or Lucille Deming (see letter # 161).

[4] Elsie Clews Parsons wrote for *The Dial.* She was an ethnologist who later worked with many of the tribes in the Southwest.

158

to Elizabeth Shepley Sergeant
(Ms Yale)

335 E. 31st St.
Wednesday [November?] 1915

Gladys Thayer's address is 124 E. 25th St. (studio that is), and her room, I think, is at 113 E. 18. I have been unable to find her at her studio lately, and am guiltily conscious that I must write her about not going to Dublin for Christmas. I shall have to spend it instead drearily at home as always, except for the time that I spent it even more drearily in Paris.

Your fortitude of search sounds heroic. You will of course be eventually rewarded by finding exactly the ideal, I wish, if you find any very limitedly good places which you spurn, you will tell me about them. I must leave here in a week or two, and the uncertainty preys on my mind. O, for a settledness, which should not be so complete, however, as to make one restless!

There is a new apartment-house at Sixth Avenue and Eleventh, probably not very good or quiet, two rooms $30, and audacious price, for me. I have the encumbrance of a piano, and long for space.

Randolph Bourne

159

to Elizabeth Shepley Sergeant
(Ms Yale)

335 E. 31st St.
Dec. 23, 1915

I tried to reach you several times the other day, and now conclude that you must have gone home for Christmas. I was indeed sorry not to see you again and find whether your endless search had been successful. I walked half heartedly through Ninth and Tenth and Eleventh yesterday morning and found the houses positively forbidding. I am up against a blank wall, and see no solution but to pack my piano off home and ignominiously follow. I cannot make out whether Carl is waiting for me, not wanting to turn me out on the street. Apparently plans for the country house go in his mind, with the confident assumption not only that I am going to live with them but the fair Norwegian too. I find myself in the most extraordinary complication conceivable, with the alternative of going into a most dubiously successful menage, or wrecking the plans of three of my friends. The modern non-exclusive feeling is a little bewildering. I feel the most determined efforts being made to throw the chains around the four of us. Admitting its logical aesthetic effectiveness, wouldn't you be deterred by propriety? Here is a problem indeed to put up to your New England conscience. Won't you think less well of me for getting in with such an unconscionable set? I feel singularly detached, but my aloofness is getting me a reputation with Carl and his protective mate of the most hideous obstinacy and selfishness. I have to find all sorts of reasons for my reluctance, and I begin to appreciate the hollowness of reasons. At the same time I cannot analyze my intuitions, and drift in a foggy state that prevents work and keeps me talking constantly of the thing. What a dreadful fate is mine to be unable to remain self-sufficient, and yet to be immersed too deeply in personal relationships when they do arise! I almost haven't the courage to run away now, I feel I would miss so much. And yet if I don't run away I may get horribly tangled and mangled. I feel as if I was living in a different order of society where people don't do such things. I was a little surprised that you were even sympathetic to my tale. You gave me great comfort, but I couldn't have been very intelligible since you didn't know the people. How wonderful it must be to be settled and confident, fixed in some stable order, where people took you for granted, and weren't constantly discouraging your life with demands and seductions? And yet the curse of it is that I know I should find stability very dull, and should crave to be upset emotionally again.

Just now I am for the stability, though the intricacies and cross-currents of our present situation are frightfully interesting. I am the only one who attempts to decide things, and when I do, it seems like tearing apart living flesh. Of course people oughtn't to marry if they don't want to be fiercely exclusive, and break other affections. But here they are doing it in defiance of all normal psychology, and of course it *is* a modern world. Won't you tell me what I should do? What would you do with us if you were making a novel of us? I get a sense of how well we would go into a novel, but I get a sense too of the remoteness of some conventional categories.[1]

Haven't I written a word about anything else?

R. S. B.

[1]Carl Zigrosser's marriage to Florence King unsettled Bourne's life for several months in early 1916, and strained a developing friendship with Lucille Deming.

Figure 8. Bourne and the three women with whom he shared a house in Caldwell, New Jersey in the summer of 1916. From left to right: Frances Anderson, Agnes de Lima, Esther Cornell, Bourne. Photograph courtesy of the Randolph Bourne Collection, Columbia University Library.

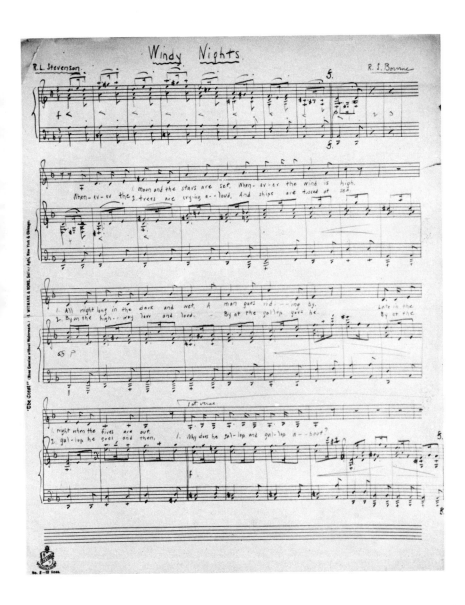

Figure 9. A song, music by Bourne. Courtesy of the Carl Zigrosser Collection, University of Pennsylvania Library.

The Dial and the *Seven Arts* (1916-1918):

The Opposition to the War

After two years of increasingly uncomfortable association with the *New Republic*, Bourne found two magazines which more closely matched his beliefs—*The Dial* and the *Seven Arts*. *The Dial* both preceded and, in a revitalized format, survived him, while Bourne witnessed both the birth and the death of the *Seven Arts*. It was in these two magazines that Bourne was able to air his cultural nationalism and his pacifism.

By the time that Bourne started contributing to *The Dial* in late 1916, the magazine had changed considerably from the sedate publication it had been since its founding in the 1880's. In 1915 the Chicago-based magazine reflected the cosmopolitanism of its new Editor, Waldo Browne. Unlike the *New Republic*, however, this international spirit was reflected in pacifism and socialism rather than in interventionism. On the other hand, the implications of this world view for *The Dial*'s depiction of American literature were not as satisfying as the *New Republic*'s cultural nationalism, for *The Dial* remained respectful of the Anglo-Saxon tradition advocated by genteel critics. When the war began to intrude on the magazine's consciousness, *The Dial*, unlike the *New Republic*, retreated from involvement in international politics to literary subjects. Indeed, its format of many book reviews, preceded by a few short essays, was conducive to this position.

It was under the editorship of Martyn Johnson, who succeeded Browne in late 1916, that Bourne first contributed to *The Dial*. During this period the magazine was attempting to address the problematical connection between its view of literature and its assessment of the world situation.[1] Slowly, the publication was coming to endorse the social conception of literature which Bourne advocated. In this evolution Bourne was significant as an influence, although he never took part in the policy-making sessions of the editorial board. His advocacy of the youth movement, his contempt for the Anglo-Saxon tradition, and his outspoken political views reflected one of the directions in which *The Dial* could go.[2]

1918 was a transitional year for *The Dial*. The magazine changed Editors again; Harold Stearns took over at the beginning of the year. Financial pressures forced a move to New York which was completed by September. A Reconstruction Board, including John Dewey and Thorstein Veblen, was appointed to reform the objectives and the policies of *The Dial*. Also, Scofield Thayer, a Harvard friend of Stearns', became interested in the publication. It was his financial support of *The Dial* which allowed Bourne his prominent position outside the circle of the editorial board, and it was his developing control of the magazine which moulded *The Dial* into one of the most influential avant garde publications of the 1920's.

During this time of changing policies and of battles within the editorial board over the direction of the magazine, Bourne found himself increasingly at odds with a portion of the board, and especially with Johnson and Dewey, both of whom supported the American intervention in the war.[3] Bourne's relationship with Dewey was especially painful. An historian of *The Dial* has asserted that it was chiefly due to the objections of Dewey that Bourne was not admitted to the editorial board after the move of the publication to New York.[4] In fact, Bourne was probably correct in his impression that it was chiefly due to Scofield Thayer's respect for him and the money which Thayer contributed that he retained his influence. Although Bourne contributed few political essays under Johnson's editorship, he did write many reviews which put forth his views on literature and on the interaction between imaginative writing and the social situation. After Bourne's death Thayer withdrew his support from *The Dial* and the magazine was doomed financially. When Thayer resurrected *The Dial* in 1919, the legacy of Bourne was more predominant. Bourne has been considered the inspiration of *The Dial* of the 1920's.[5]

It is more difficult to classify Bourne's contributions to *The Dial* than it is to the *New Republic*, beyond the statement that he wrote mostly book reviews. Fewer of his essays dealt directly with educational theory; the Gary book behind him, and his appreciation of Dewey destroyed by war sentiment, he confined himself to only a few articles on education. Similarly, his overtly political articles were few; the energies he expended in furnishing the *Seven Arts* with political essays left little for *The Dial*. Mostly, his essays were based loosely on literature and the arts, but in *The Dial* he was able to draw more clearly the connections he saw between the life of the mind and social action. Bourne defended Dreiser again, and reviewed new books by Wells and Bennett, old favorites of his whom he believed had now become passé. These reviews show Bourne's developing ability to work within, and yet to revolutionize, the book review. All his reviews emphasized the interrelationships between literature and life, thought and action. Both for the subjects Bourne discussed and for the ways in which he placed his books in a larger context these reviews are significant.

A good example of the richness of these reviews can be found in his assessment of Friedrich Nietzsche, which was contained most obviously in "Denatured Nietzsche,"[6] a review of two books on the German author, but which ran throughout many of his essays. Bourne gave close attention to the literary value of these two studies. Both books came under fire because their language was inferior to the excerpts from Nietzsche's writings, rendered into English in a good translation. More important, however, Bourne defended Nietzsche against the charge that he was the epitome of German militarism. The Nietzschean doctrine that life is the will-to-power was being wrenched out of context, Bourne pointed out. The will-to-power, once it is recognized, could be sublimated into the service of good causes. Nietzsche's attack on Christianity Bourne interpreted as diagnostic rather than ethical; Nietzsche did not condone the immorality which Americans were attributing to the German war effort, but the German philosopher was urging a realistic assessment of human capabilities. The will-to-power, if properly understood, could liberate modern man: "Fact and ideal must play freely back and forth, conspiring against the staleness, the mechanicalness, of modern culture and morals and theories of knowledge."[7]

Bourne had three uses for Nietzsche throughout this period,

all of which are present in this review. Most important is his feeling that the will-to-power could annihilate the suffocating influence of Puritanism in America, a force which was strangling personality and which was enforcing an oppressive social control over creativity. When Bourne spoke of his transvaluation of values, he was referring to this vision of the power of the individual over iron-clad systems, among which he classified Calvinism. In another review Bourne brought out more explicitly a second important aspect of the will-to-power which linked Nietzschean philosophy to Bourne's educational ideas: to classify is to control.[8] Once the individual knows his or her own boundaries, what can be mastered and what must be obeyed, a personal universe can be constructed. Not only does this liberate ideas from normative, social control, but it corresponds to the self-centered educational ideas of what Bourne referred to as the modern school. Finally, Bourne endorsed Nietzsche as an antidote to the influence of Anglo-Saxondom on American culture. In his view there was a war going on, one undertaken on a cultural level, between American ideas and British intellectual control. In this battle the Germans could be allies. On this subject Bourne was more explicit in the *Seven Arts*. His reviews for *The Dial*, then, were rich in their cultural implications and broad in scope. In addition, they frequently referred to political issues which were more explicitly discussed in the *Seven Arts*.

I

The history of the *Seven Arts* is brief. The magazine was founded in 1916 by James Oppenheim with money given by a wealthy client of Dr. Beatrice Hinkle, a Jungian psychologist who suggested the gift as a method of therapy. The first issue of the journal was brought out in November 1916 and, unfortunately, the operation collapsed by the end of the following year. The key figures of the editorial board were the poet James Oppenheim, Editor, and Waldo Frank, Van Wyck Brooks, and Paul Rosenfeld, Associate Editors. Although Bourne was not a member of the board, he wielded a significant amount of influence;[9] in fact, his first article in the *Seven Arts*, which appeared in April 1917, was hailed as a great triumph for the publication. Two theories have accounted for the collapse of the venture. According to the more popular account, the benefactor of the magazine, Mrs. Rankine, withdrew her money, primarily because she did not agree with the pacifistic essays in the magazine. Robert Frost is said to have remarked that the *Seven Arts* died "a-Bourning," referring to the prominent essays which aroused Mrs. Rankine's ire. It appears, though, that other financing was made available to the magazine—a wealthy friend of Paul Rosenfeld's was willing to assume Mrs. Rankine's subsidy—but, that the members of the board could not agree on a specific organization, so the magazine failed. In fact, Waldo Frank asserted that the demise of the *Seven Arts* was due more to the personalities of the Editors than to the lack of funds: "The organ's disappearance after one year is not due to the War, as commonly supposed, but to the war between the individuals of the group—to their mutual distrusts and spiritual failures."[10] This assessment may be closer to the truth, for, other than in their wish for a strong national culture, the interests of the Editors were varied.

Nevertheless, while the magazine was in circulation, it was a very invigorating outlet for people like Bourne who believed in the promise of the rising generation, in social realism in fiction, in the power of the personality, and in the development of an independent, self-conscious, national culture purged of both its bellicosity and of its subservience to British taste. In the first issue the Editors issued a call which must have appealed to Bourne:

> It is our faith and the faith of many, that we are living in the first days of a renascent period, a time which means for America the coming of that national self-consciousness which is the beginning of greatness. In all such epochs the arts cease to be private matters; they become not only the expression of the national life but a means to its enhancement. . . . It is the aim of *The Seven Arts* to become a channel for the flow of these tendencies; an expression of our American arts which shall be fundamentally an expression of our American life. We have no tradition to continue; we have no school of style to build up. What we ask of the writer is simply self-expression. . . . In short, *The Seven Arts* is not a magazine for artists, but an expression of artists for the community.[11]

Here was the sort of haven that Bourne had been searching for ever since he returned from Europe. Furthermore, the magazine encompassed the ambiguities that Bourne felt between the urge to speak for the people, for the national culture, and his sense of alienation from it. While the magazine functioned, Bourne gave it some of his best essays.

The message which Bourne put forth in the *Seven Arts* remained consistent throughout his essays: pragmatic intellectuals, who had prided themselves on their ability to control circumstances through the application of reason, had abandoned their principles for the expediency of war. In doing so, they had sacrificed principles to technique; they had abandoned the American position of neutrality which gave this country the opportunity to become a peaceful leader in the world.

Bourne found distressing "the relative ease with which the pragmatic intellectuals, with Professor Dewey at the head, have moved out their philosophy, bag and baggage, from education to war."[12] In supporting the war the intellectuals had allied themselves with the most illiberal elements of American society; only a world devoid of irony could create such a situation.[13] Whereas during the days of American neutrality, the United States could force both Germany and the Allies to compromise on their terms and to approach a negotiated settlement, once America entered into the war logic the only solution was to wage "war to exhaustion for the sake of military decision."[14] Not only had pragmatism moved into the war camp cheerfully, but there was not even a recognition on the part of these intellectuals that they had compromised themselves.

Bourne's objections were two-fold. On the one hand, he found incomprehensible the capitulation of the pragmatists to the war logic. In his view, the intellectual should be stronger than that. The war offered the best opportunity for pragmatic action through neutrality, but this opportunity had been lost. Secondly, Bourne felt that the youthful vigor of American promise was being sullied as the United States became mired in the morass of European petty rivalries. "The war—or American promise; one must choose," he warned. "One cannot be interested in both. For the effect of the war will be to impoverish American promise."[15] This was the more threatening result of the war. In his wish for peace, Bourne united his pacifism and belief in the idealism of youth with the basic tenets of the *Seven Arts* and issued a warning against the alienation of the younger generation:

> If the country submissively pours month after month its wealth of life and resources into the work of annihilation, that bitterness will spread out like a stain over the younger American generation. If the enterprise goes on endlessly, the work, so blithely undertaken for the defence of democracy, will have crushed out the only genuinely precious thing in the nation, the hope and ardent idealism of its youth.[16]

Aside from the tender letters written to Esther Cornell, Bourne's letters become much more perfunctory during this period. One incident deserves special notice. In December 1916 Bourne visited his sister Natalie at Hampton Institute, where her husband Lawrence was chaplain. Bourne looked upon vocational schools with favor, although he called the Black students slaves. He never wrote an essay on Blacks, or on the vocational system of education for Blacks advocated by Booker T. Washington, but it is clear that Bourne felt that this sort of limitation of Black potential was grossly unfair. How could the White race, which had lived beside Black people for generations, consign them to a inferior position, he asked. In answer to this question he translated his social theories into a racial critique which spoke directly to the equality of Blacks and Whites: "It seems to be nothing more than a crude enjoyment of caste-power, and the unpleasantness of having a social group that was once your property become now potentially your equal." (12/21/16) It was not vocational education for Blacks that was wrong; rather, it was the implicit exclusion of Blacks from academic and professional pursuits which was reprehensible. "The thing is full of ghastly ironies, and I shall unburden myself of it some day." Had he been able to do so, he probably would have sided with W. E. B. DuBois over Booker T. Washington.

Bourne rose to intellectual maturity in *The Dial* and the *Seven Arts*. Both the form of his essays and the subject matter he addressed demonstrate a sophisticated, perceptive vision of the world. At the same time, his letters indicate that he was unable to find a stable personal life. The war, which is mentioned only infrequently in the letters, nevertheless underlies all of his actions. It diverts his energies from writing letters to the formulation of his many essays. It also increases his feeling of homelessness and his alienation from society. At the same time, it heightens his sense of the responsibility of the intellectual to attempt to lead the country from this disaster. These feelings were finally expressed in his last surviving letter when he exclaimed to his mother: "Now that the war is over people can speak freely again and we can dare to think. It's like coming out of a nightmare."

Notes

[1]Nicholas Joost, *Years of Transition: The Dial, 1912-1920*, (Barre, Mass., 1967), p. 77.

[2]*Ibid.*, p. 130.

[3]Nicholas Joost, *Scofield Thayer and The Dial*, (Carbondale, Ill., 1969), p. 10.

[4]Joost, *Transition*, pp. 184-85.

[5]*Ibid.*, p. 158.

[6]"Denatured Nietzsche," *The Dial* LXIII (December 20, 1917), 389-91.

[7]*Ibid.*, p. 390.

[8]"A Modern Mind," *The Dial* LXII (March 22, 1917), p. 239.

[9]Frank A. Wertheim, *The New York Little Renaissance* (New York, 1976), pp. 178-79.

[10]Quoted in Claire Sacks, "The 'Seven Arts' Critics: A Study of Cultural Nationalism in America, 1910-1930," unpublished Ph.D. dissertation, (Madison, Wisc., 1955), pp. 150-1.

11"Editorial," *Seven Arts* I (November 1916), 52-3.

12"Twilight of Idols," in *War and the Intellectuals*, Carl Resek, ed., (New York, 1968), p. 56.

13"War and the Intellectuals," in *Ibid.*, p. 5.

14"The Collapse of American Strategy," in *Ibid.*, p. 31.

15"A War Diary," in *Ibid.*, p. 46.

16"Below the Battle," in *Ibid.*, p. 21.

160

to Alyse Gregory
(Ms Yale)

January 3, 1916

The only reason I haven't written is that, since you left, my domestic affairs have been so entangled that I haven't even kept up my work. Carl has married Florence King[1] and the process of detaching their mutual mates and planning for the future has been devastating. A psychological web of the utmost intricacy has been woven, possibly aided by my gift for intrigue. Now I am left, a homeless, helpless waif, about to desert my empty Phipps apartment, but not able to find any even decent room that I can afford. Bloomfield, to which they want me to return, stares me in the face. I have to give so much psychic energy to the mere problem of getting a place to live that I haven't any left for work. It is hideous, and I wish I could go straight to Nassau or Honolulu for the rest of the winter, and leave everything behind. Carl has acted with dignity and decency, but his new mate is a truly formidable and devastating person, impossible to agree with and impossible to avoid. She has succeeded in destroying a month of three persons' lives, while wearing her own nerves to a thin edge. Oh, women! Particularly the pseudo-emancipated, the pseudo-idealist, who disguises a will to power under a fierce claim of loyalty.

Yesterday at the Ridgley Torrence's I heard the most charming thing about you from a most charmingly graceful person named Miss Gladys Cromwell. She had heard you speak in Bernardsville and seen you personally, I think, and was quite overcome by your qualities. It gave me quite a glow to hear you so much appreciated, for she seemed to have gotten much the same impression of your spirit that I have, even though I may be cross and perverse at times. Your thinking of Poland and Servia is quite like you. I wish I had a tenth of your courage and energy and endurance which doesn't harden you. You can't be blamed for not liking Scotland in winter, I suppose. Isn't Norway better? And apparently you didn't go to Denmark. If you have plenty of money I should think you could travel a little and write? If you get to London, look up my friend Mabel Robinson[2] at 1 Holmburg View, Clapton, N. E. A militant lower middle-class young woman, remarkable type of college-trained intellectual out of her element, a victim of taste, it seems to me.

Your letter only came this morning, opened by the Censor. What it must be to read some letters. The other one I enjoyed, very much, and this last had a great tone to it. Christmas I spent dully in Bloomfield with my family, resisting Carl's invitation to the farm. Pray for me in my troubles. O, for that calm stability of comfort, place and mood, which I keep looking forward to, where I can work and really live! Do you think it will ever come?

R. S. B.

[1]Florence King was a suffrage worker at that time.

[2]Robinson could be the Miss M. Robinson the London *Times* reported as having co-founded the Social Psychology group within the Sociological Society.

161

to Elizabeth Shepley Sergeant
(Ms Yale)

[New York]
January 4, 1916

You have probably received a ribald telegram in which my name stood startlingly prominent. I hasten to betray my accomplices and ascribe every word of the composition to them. I shared, however, all the annoyance at your non-appearance for dinner. New York will evidently not see much of you this winter, and I am sorry. I guess at going to France for your exciting project. I wish I was going most anywhere. My affairs are in a hopeless tangle. I must move in a few days, and looked for advice from you at dinner Tuesday. I see two beautiful and expensive rooms on 12th St. and have almost decided to take one of them and then work hard enough to pay for it. This is a good economic principle,— to force up your wage-level by raising your standard of living, and it is one that I have rarely tried. The country proposal is wrecked. I emerge as the head devil, a Shavian contending with romantic principles of loyalty, which seems to me to disguise thinly an inordinate will-to-power. The fair Norwegian [Lucille Deming[1]] is expelled as unworthy and treasonable, for having betrayed confidence, and now, in an effort to build up character, has amputated me. I am still struggling to right my values, and wonder if all might not have been clear if I had not tried to save her soul from the subjugation of her friend. I don't like your distinction between living and working. It is one that she seems to have made, and I am desolate. The poor girl represents herself as having been torn to pieces in the mighty struggle between her friend and myself. My victory was doubly abortive. The friend took the initiative, became frightfully wounded, and dragged me to perdition in the melee. I am the victim, lonely and scorned.

R. S. B.

[1]Very little is known about Lucille Deming. She had been Florence King's roommate prior to the argument. Later she returned to Wisconsin.

162

to Alyse Gregory
(Ms Yale)

New York
January 21, 1916

Your letter was very comforting, for it reached me in the same mail with one which removed from me my last hope of friendship on earth and relegated my character to the scrap-heap. Your seeming confidence restored my balance, and made me feel there were still friendships left in life for me. My domestic affairs have been unutterably entangled. My work has suffered, and entirely too much time has been devoted to a feud with the neurotic woman who happens to be Carl's beloved. The process of separating her friend from her, and me from Carl proved a creator of psychological complications, and we are still far from the end. I emerge as the head devil who has wrecked all the beautiful relations which were to have been. Greene was in it too, making a pentagon. A difference of Weltanschauungen has developed, my Shavian and ironical attitude towards life not suiting an emotional feminist, who has the misfortune to be only a rebel and not a freewoman. The mid-Victorian attitudes which she developed, the insufferable will-to-power over the innocent younger girl and even myself, tempted me to precipitate crises which have now buried me in waves of opprobrium. The worst part of it is that I have only the dimmest idea of the nature of my own infamy, and defend myself therefore somewhat maladroitly. But I cannot convey the fury, ingenuity, resource and intensity with which the affair has been waged. Really, I have the most extraordinary data, and my feminism reels under the strain. The mere knowledge that women can be so is unnerving. Only my psychologic sense has saved me from bitterness and wounds. And the worst of it is that the thing cannot be thrown off. There are rumors of the departure of the couple to the country on February first. I cannot believe it, but if it happens I shall be a rejuvenated man. I am living alone in a "front parlor." Excepting Europe, it is the first time I have lived alone for four years. I miss certain warm contentment of companionship, the knowing that there is a friend to come in to. I have really no good excuse for not packing myself off home, where they would enjoy my piano and take care of me. But the old stifling house and my insufferably chattering sister fill me with dismay at the thought. I had hoped I would be so much inspired here that I should earn enough to pay for my larger and grander habitation, but the maddening irritation of this personal controversy has devastated my time pretty much. I must allow perhaps a year to recover my poise. I sometimes think I shall never really do anything until I get a stable and satisfactory way of living, with the right golden and protecting person. But this sounds awfully parasitic and tastes of the clinging vine. These last few weeks, however, I have felt very much like being served and cared for and coddled. All my friends this winter seem to be living in the most charming apartments in a most admirably married way. I flit around from one to the other, a homeless, helpless waif, eternally passing out into the cold from their warm and confident firesides. And I seem to face a long future of such waifness.

Having given you this most lurid picture of my envies and despairs, I will talk of more cosmic things. My Gary book is in the press; it saddens me with its banality, but then I tried to make it colorless and inoffensive to the teacher.[1] I long to redeem it now by some slashing work, but have a miserable Peace Symposium to prepare for my old friends of the International Conciliation.[2] The New Republic keeps me busy, either eating my stuff or rejecting it, so that I have an impression of working most of the time for them. Then the business of qualifying as an educational expert keeps me at the libraries. And the Atlantic would take some articles if I could only get around to the business of writing them. 24 hours a day and the strength of ten wouldn't achieve the work I want to do. And I spend my time drinking tea, talking about my woes, or psychologizing privately about my domestic complications. I have given this letter enough analytical attention and interpretation to make a Henry James novel. If I am finally cast adrift, I shall certainly take my revenge by writing it.

Your question of America's shame does not disturb me. The Allies' attitude, which I imagine is played up for political reasons, seems to me the sheerest impudence. If Wilson has kept out of trouble through sheer luck rather than statesmanship, he has at least kept out, which was the one thing he should have done. I am still a determined pacifist, and look upon Roosevelt and the other preparednessers as madmen. We get the impression here that it is the expatriated Americans who are most bitter against us,—a sort of reverse Freudian twist of a guilty conscience of theirs. The hyphenated English-Americans in the East are the ones who do the loudest ranting here. I'm sorry if the Allies' virtuous indignation prevents you from serving them, but you may decide that your own country needs you more and come home to us. You do not sound at all happy in your Scottish mists, and I wonder why you linger all winter there. Last month I had a debauch of concerts but this month I am living a village life. A few interesting friends and a little reading and writing make up my days. I feel no great push of life and am rather sidetracked as far as big issues go. The little busy people repel me and I am not distinguished enough for the great. Yet I am too gregarious to bury myself and work out my own salvation. I sit in my room and think, but not very creatively or concentratedly, and cannot get the thrill and color out of writing that I do out of talk and companionship. This is really a tragic thing, and I had expected long ago to change my leopard's spots. But perhaps people never do change, and I must count on my little increments of work to get me somewhere. I wish I were going to see those manuscripts you charged to me. Won't you show them to me anyway when you come home? I am quite sure you could get no more appreciation of them from anybody than you would from me. I think of you as very interesting, and wish you were here to talk to. Shall you not be coming home?

Yours,

R. S. B.

Do you hear anything of the New Republic or Lippmann's new book? Or Rebecca West?

[1]*The Gary Schools* was published in 1916.

[2]The Symposium was published as *Toward an Enduring Peace* in 1916.

163

to Dorothy Teall
(Transcript Columbia)

New York
March 8, 1916

I have yet to hear why you didn't come to my party (to hear Mrs. James read Trojan Women).[1] I can only say that you missed seeing my conception of a noble woman, and of hearing her read the noblest of plays. Most of my friends came Friday night, only your family, strangely enough, turning up Wednesday.

Your letter, which purported to be an objective view of my case, seemed mostly a subjective exposition of your own. You seem to have imbibed much wisdom and experience—a little vague to my curiosity, it is true—and to have reacted to it with a kind of Henry James subtelty. My outlines, alas, are very simple and crude. I am still in the drama, which drags on endlessly, my indomitable will beating at the bars. The Persephone mythology[2] is surprisingly accurate. I am too often loved—and that quite perfectly and paganly—but so might the god of darkness be when he carried the daughter of Ceres away in his arms. Of course, I prefer to think of myself as Ceres, the fruitful mother, creating all sorts of expressiveness and glows. But I am not wholly allowed to do this. Always steps in the virtuous, disinterested motherly friend, pointing out my lighthearted infamies, calling *her* to the high ideals of character and action and will. It is a clash of philosophies as well as wills, and my victories are only temporary. I rack my brains to find a means of destroying the fallacious image which Persephone has formed of this mine enemy and her evil genius. Doubtless mine enemy is engaged in a similar cogitation. Meanwhile Persephone wrestles to keep both images and reconcile a perfect friendship with two people whose philosophies spit at each other. In this struggle to be black and white at the same time I can only dimly surmise what is happening to Persephone's soul. Sheer weariness sometimes suggests that I give up the struggle. And then the utter greyness of any other personal enterprise, the futility of living with any other quality than what has been shown me, stiffens my will, and I determine never to compromise with this hateful force against me. The cards, however, are stacked against me. Five years of idolatrous worship of mine enemy by Persephone, a subborn conviction that the surrounding world shares this idolatry, and a belief that these strong qualities of decision and virtuous omniscience are what make women successful in the modern world—combine to hold her back from my Shavianism. And yet she is wholly Shavian, and was stifled by her year with this neurotic Puritan feminist [. . .] who has married my poor friend. I am handicapped by my lack of morality. A good cause to mine enemy hallows every war. So that the urgency of virtue brings her to drop malicious innuendoes about me, and communicate to her circle her version of the whole case. Having no such virtue or omniscience, I am a little squeamish, and have to keep to myself the mounting evidence of the contempt with which mine enemy's truculence is greeted by her circle [. . .] and the sordid motives which they impute to her sudden marriage. I do lose my temper sometimes to Persephone, but otherwise I have to leave her in blissful ignorance of the fall of her idol. The moving of the idol to the country is now unhappily postponed, and only a complete removal of Persephone from the sphere of influence can even hope to solve matters. My unfortunate finding of a job for her prevents that removal, and the battle is destined to sway back and forth endlessly until we are all broken to pieces. Can you suggest any way of defeating this illusion of Persephone's about her evil genius without telling tales and being malicious? This is now the major object of my life. If I don't succeed, summer will have to take my shattered spirit far from the scene. I am thinking of moving again into a small apartment and then I shall have some tea parties to cheer my gloom.

R. S. B.

[1]This is probably the play by Euripedes. The parenthetic material is Teall's addition.

[2]How far the Persephone mythology should be taken is questionable. Persephone was taken from her mother, Ceres, but was allowed to return from the underworld each year. This myth explains the seasons in terms of Persephone's return (summer) and her absence in the underworld (winter). In this analogy Florence King is the lord of the underworld, while Bourne thinks himself as Ceres. He is trying to explain his feeling of loss, and, perhaps, to account for the suddenness with which the catastrophic argument occurred (the rape of Prosperine/Persephone).

164

to Dorothy Teall
(Transcript Columbia)

42 Bank Street
Friday [April 21, 1916]

Your proposal appeals to me. But will it appeal to the others? Am I not proscribed at Barnard? However, I'll come if I'm asked. I should like to talk on Morality. I have several ideas which I should like to experiment with, just to see the reactions. Is it to be Apr. 28? And what time? And not a big room, for my voice is very small? And how many minutes?

Walking in the Park this noon on the way to have lunch with Elsie Clews Parsons, who should I see but L[illian] S[oskin]? Elsie C. P. had been shooting them up morally at Bryn Mawr, so I got L. S.'s impressions, and immediately retailed them to E. C. P. L. S. was with her young man, I regret that she is engaged to him. She is too young to allow her wandering libido to fasten itself on any one, certainly not one so gently colored a blank wall as he. She should be challenged to higher personal aspirations. She invited herself to tea on Tuesday. I'm afraid she will bring him.

I didn't get that sympathetic alignment with Babette [Deutsch]. I thought she was austerely disapproving of my persiflage on B[eulah] E. A[midon]. She was a little haughty, with a haughtiness that always puts me at my ease and gives me a flow of conversation.

E. C. P. told me a good story about a Barnard girl who has asked her to speak there on the need of discussion in graduate schools. The poor girl thirsted for intellectual discussion, and would accost young men in her courses with an opening "Lovely weather we're having!" or something like that. The man would reply with a "Yes. MY WIFE thinks it charming!" or some other crusher; showing the non-existence of any conception of social freedom in graduate schools. My own observation bears her out. A big reform is needed. What E. C. P. calls the "Tagging-on spouse problem" should be handled without mercy.

R. S. B.

165

to John Erskine
(Ms Columbia)

New York
April 25, 1916

Dear Professor Erskine,

Mr. Strunsky[1] in the "Evening Post" last Saturday seems to have gotten the same impression of Dr. Flexner's "Modern School"[2] that you did in your verse on Jim Reilly. Having read Dr. Flexner's pamphlet with much care and enthusiasm, I am interested in discovering how it could be interpreted as advocating any kind of specialized narrow training "and nothing more." If it is anything, it is an exposition of a rounded, organic, education on principles which are as sound for the college as for the elementary school. This manifesto is too important to be misinterpreted. I should really like to know where you found in its twenty-three pages the remotest implication that would give relevance to your "ode." You leave one in the very painful dilemma of believing either that you have not read the pamphlet, or that you dislike the educational ideas contained in it enough to misrepresent them. I hope you and Mr. Strunsky will somehow clear my mind.

Sincerely yours,

Randolph S. Bourne

[1]Simeon Strunsky was an editorial writer for the New York *Evening Post*.

[2]Abraham Flexner wrote on all facets of education. He traveled widely while researching a study of medical schools under the auspices of the Rockefeller Foundation. He was a critic of the Gary System, who said that the ideas of Wirt's system had not been fully carried out. *A Modern School* was published in 1916. The book was influential enough to foster an experimental school, the Lincoln School, at Columbia Teachers College.

166

to John Erskine
(Ms Columbia)

New York
April 29, 1916

Dear Professor Erskine,

Your letter makes it plain that you meant no misinterpretation. The point seems to lie in your taking "now" to mean "at the moment only." Dr. Flexner says, "Modern education will include nothing simply because tradition recommends it or because its inutility has not been conclusively established. It includes nothing for which an affirmative case cannot *now* be made out." I took the "now" of course to refer to the general social situation, as I think the context clearly implies. The whole spirit of the pamphlet is against any implication that the affirmative case would mean a "well-established need at any one moment." It would mean a well-established need, rather, as determined by the general modern uses of intelligence and information. In regard to the curriculum, Dr. Flexner says, "The Modern School would from the first undertake the cultivation of contacts and cross-connections. Every exercise would be a spelling-lesson; science, industry and mathematics would be inseparable; science, industry, history, civics, literature and geography would to some extent utilize the same material.— The man educated in the modern sense will be trained to know, to care about and to understand the world he lives in, both the physical and the social world. A firm grasp of the physical world means the capacity to note and to interpret phenomena; a firm grasp of the social world means a comprehension of any sympathy with current industry, current science and current politics. The extent to which the history and literature of the past are utilized depends, not on what we call the historic value of this or that performance or classic, but on its actual pertinancy to genuine need, interest or capacity. In any case, the object in view would be to give children the knowledge they need, and to develop in them the power to handle themselves in our own world.—The realistic education we propose must eventuate in intellectual power. We must not only cultivate the child's interests, sense, and practical skill, but we must train him to interpret what he thus gets to the end that he may not only be able to perceive and to do, but that he may know in intellectual terms the significance of what he has perceived and done."[1]

In the light of these statements, you must perceive that your skit on Jim Reilly was really a quite remarkable piece of unconscious misrepresentation. Jim Reilly would have gotten at college only a very imperfect feeling for the world he lived in. This broad intelligence would have been his only indirectly, and not because the college had any definite intellectual ideal such as this one of the Modern School. And surely, if you have assimilated Professor Dewey's philosophy you must have appreciated the fact that there is no possible way of providing for a child's probable needs in the future except by satisfying the student's needs at the moment. This is the way we are educated, no matter what our schools try to do, and it is because of the failure of educators to realize this that education is so wasteful and imperfect.

In regard to manners and morals, I am not unconscious of the way I destroy the amenities of life when I have any bearing towards you. But this is only because of my need for a personal symbol for my intellectual betes noires. It is much more dramatic to pack them all into one symbol than scatter them loosely through the world. I am quite sure that I perform this same office in a limited way for you, so that I feel less remorseful than I otherwise would about giving you pain. Since education is to me a philosophy of life, your success in misunderstanding the Modern School convinces me that I have not been unjustified in waiving manners and morals. I may have misinterpreted you at times, but I evidently haven't misinterpreted your philosophy, and that is what really counts, as Professor Woodbridge told us the other night.

Sincerely Yours,

Randolph S. Bourne

[1]Bourne's excerpts from Flexner's book can be found on pages 117-18, 97-8, and 102.

167

to Dorothy Teall
(Transcript Columbia)

42 Bank Street
3 May 1916

Your woe was quite needless. I enjoyed myself very much, and found the audience quite adequate in quality and quantity. Where was Babette? I don't understand your cryptic reference to her address, and Leo Ornstein.[1] Of course I'd like to hear him, but how?

The explanation of my parting was simply that the aggrieved young Jewess appealed to me even less than a sundae at that moment, and, having a date with Macmahon for dinner, I walked with your two friends to the gate of the South Field. Why don't you bring them down to tea some day before the 15th when I am resolved to move, either to Blfd. or for a visit to my sister in Va.

I'm sure your mind was so filled with the cares of Martha that you had no thought for my speech. I have no idea of its intelligence or effect, but it won't do to tell me now that I have finished. Thank you for inviting me. I am sorry it caused you so much woe. My calm was merely a reflection of my innocence that any woe was involved.

R. S. B.

[1]Ornstein was a young Russian composer and a frequent contributor to the *Seven Arts.*

168

to Herbert J. Seligman
(Ms Columbia)

Grand Central Station
June 10, 1916

Your card seemed to be missing when I returned your book. Can I stay with you until Wednesday?

R. S. Bourne

169

to Herbert J. Seligman
(Ms Columbia)

Cos Cob, Conn.
Thursday [late June 1916]

Dear Herbert,

Why don't you call on my friend Alyse Gregory? You said you were going to, and I have told her you were coming, and said enough to make her think you are an "interesting young man." She is at **8** Patchin Place, just off Sixth Avenue and Tenth St. and is usually in at six or six-thirty. If you are reluctant to go alone, perhaps Lawrence[1] will escort you. His opinion is not worth anything about her, for her intellectuality has given him a godly fear of her. But it would be amusing to take him.

I am living peacefully in a beautiful house, from which I have not stirred for days. I seem destined to go to Caldwell next week for the rest of the summer.

R. S. Bourne

[1]Probably Lawrence K. Frank, a college friend at Columbia.

170

to Van Wyck Brooks
(Ms Pennsylvania)

Caldwell, N. J.
13 July [1916]

Dear Brooks:

I left Cos Cob last week and am sorry not to have seen you. I had a chance to come with some friends to an unusually charming house out here, and so here I am. I wish we might have the pleasure of entertaining you over a night or a week-end. If you could come any time, won't you let me know? Caldwell is only about an hour from New York. I rather envy you at Sound

Beach, for I like to have the water to look at.

Sincerely yours,

Randolph Bourne

171

to Elizabeth Shepley Sergeant
(Ms Yale)

Caldwell, N. J.
6 Aug 1916

Have you completely disappeared out of my line of vision, or is it that I owe you a letter, or that I have been forgotten? It has been most ungrateful of me, after the wonderful summer you conjured up for me last year, not to write and tell you the queer arrangement that has been ordained for me this time. Feeling most lonely and deserted in the Spring, with all my particular imaginations shot to pieces, I played with the idea of taking a house for the summer near New York with a few people including Miss Anderson[1] and two of her friends. The coalition suddenly became real, and for a month now I have found myself living in a most charming bungalow with the three girls, and numerous visitors over week-ends and nights. Everything is quite luxurious, but we lack everything that summer should have,—water, mountains, views, bracing air. The occasion is almost the exact reverse of Dublin last year. All the advantages we didn't have at Dublin, and all the disadvantages. But I think Dublin was far more exhilirating. The weather has been tropical, heat and rain. I have scarcely been out of the house except for a couple of trips to the N[ew] R[epublic]. The girls are excellent company, but a little demoralizing. Two of them go into New York every day, and the other tempts one to talk. Gloom and masculine austerity are the best moods for writing, though my winter has so demoralized me that I get frightened sometimes at the idea that I shall never recover my poise or be able to command my thoughts again. It is horrible to think that the only chance one has of writing or accomplishing anything will be through resolutely excluding from imagination everything that has made life beautiful and that one still wildly hopes will make it perhaps some time again. But perhaps all this is mere excuse for natural indolence. If one could only be disembodied spirit!

I have no idea where you are. You may have gone to France for all I know. I hope fate will bring you to New York next winter. I spent three weeks in June at a house in Cos Cob that you should know about. Near enough N. Y. to go in often, and everything charming. You pay $15 a week, and are like the guests of the MacRaes, who are interesting and leave you alone. It is a perfect retreat, of the desired kind we have spoken about.

My friends are talking of a coalition house, but I should like to go round the world, or to California or something remote.

Please let me know where you are. If you are near N. Y. won't you visit us?

R. S. B.

[1] Frances Anderson was then a staff person at the *New Republic*. In 1917 she married and went with her husband to Brazil. See the illustration in this volume.

172

to Elizabeth Shepley Sergeant
(Ms Yale)

The New Republic
421 West 21st Street
New York City
24 August 1916

Does your postal mean that you are going to Wyoming, and, if so, how exciting? It sounds like a long way from France. Meanwhile I envy you your New Hampshire. New Jersey was an idiotic place to come, especially for so tropical a summer. I have been quite limp and hopeless most of the time. I sometimes wonder if I shall ever do anything worth while. I have so little inspiration or industry that my personal complications upset my balance constantly. I meant to write a book, and here I am living just as intensely and imaginatively as ever in the muddle of my last winter's life. It all gets more and more bewildering, and everything else seems so pallid and unimportant in comparison. And really honest work that would hold me to routine would perhaps cure me, but the New Republic continues to sidetrack me, and I haven't a show anywhere else. There is a new wizard down there named Merz[1] who can do everything from writing advertisements, running the business department, editing the magazine to doing articles far cleverer than any of us can do. However, he has no bashfulness in him, and we tremble for our futures. I become more and more negligible, and if I attempted to advertise myself would only succeed in being foolish. All this is very faint-hearted of me, I know, but I feel more or less caught in a trap and do not yet see my way out. I do not like to think of going back to New York to live and there is nowhere else to go. On New Republic starvation wages one can scarcely afford to live there, and one has no friends anywhere else. I look back with amazement on last year's Dublin summer when I felt so strong and confident and serene. I am banished from Dublin this year because it is feared that I will be too exciting for Mr. Thayer. He needs rest and I talk too much; otherwise I would be invited to Thayerdom. This I gather from a long letter from Gladys, with a thousand reasons and apologies why her original invitation can't be ratified. I should very much like to go for a short time, and might if I promised to be very quiet.

I hope you are well and happy. I should very much like to see you. Won't you be back in New York?

R. S. B.

[1]Charles Merz was then a recent graduate of Yale who was beginning a long career in journalism on the staff of the *New Republic*. He served on many magazines and became the Editor of the *New York Times* in 1938.

173

to Elizabeth Shepley Sergeant
(Ms Yale)

20 Sept 1916

I don't know if this will reach you, but I must write anyway to thank you for your letter, which was quite a crisis for me. All the advice I really knew, but needed it said to me sharp. My summer has been a great mistake and all the more because it was so cunningly devised to be delightful that I can't regret it. I haven't been happy, but I have been luxurious, and a good deal of the time exhilirated. And now I am going to pay. The N[ew] R[epublic] which never knew just what to do with me is getting restive under the burden of paying me a hundred dollars a month—mere living wage—for work they can't find space for. So my "job" is trembling and that "gloom and solitude" you urge upon me will probably come in an ignominious swallowing up of me by my doleful home, with its strident lowbrow sister, and depressed mother. If I was in Europe, there are a thousand little hotels where I could go peacefully and live alone. But in this country, is there one single place where I could go that I could afford and where I wouldn't die of sheer nervousness? This is the first unalterable barrier to "gloom and solitude." And the second is the wonder that anybody should think my talent worth making all this fuss about. I really thirst for fame, but the minute I begin taking steps for it, it seems so absurd to imagine that I am likely to do much more than I've done. And then I'm still in the mad career of thinking that solitude a deux is the only solitude that is supportable. It would not only be supportable but I conceive it as heaven, and see myself as such a victim. I suppose it's cowardly to think that passion must be satisfied before gods can be worshipped. Life is always tugging at my moorings and calling my adventurousness out to sea. I just get reconciled to riding safely at anchor when something happens. And my last swift thrilling run before the glowering storm leaves me hopelessly desiring, I'm afraid. What I shall probably have to do, however, is to return to Greenwich Village, but take myself austerely in hand, live a Spartan life alone, deprive myself of my piano, turn myself into a journalist trying to cling to the N. R. by my wits. I think I can do this, but it will be hard. I have too many friends too much like myself. I have been besieging Alvin Johnson[1] and others to get me a teaching job, but I never get anything I apply for. I seem to be permanently side-tracked from activity, and not quite able to make my private side-tracked career.

You are coming back to N. Y.? Your account of the West stirs me, makes me wish I'd gone with my mother to California. I am coquetting with the idea of going out to bring her home as she has a round trip ticket till Oct. 31. I think I would if there were a chance of meeting you somewhere on the way. I am homeless Oct 1, and so are all my friends. But the community house is killed for me.

Randolph Bourne

Your work article was fine. I so envy you your easy, understanding, sympathetic flow.

---

[1]Alvin Johnson was business manager of the *New Republic*. Later he headed the New School and, in the 1930's, the University in Exile.

174

to Alyse Gregory
(Ms Yale)

[early] October 1916

If I had known you were going Sunday, I should have come in to see you, but you said Monday morning and I was in early only to find you gone.[1] It was good of you to think of my need of a home, and I am still waiting anxiously for my bed, and floating between Bloomfield and Milligan's. But I did [?] avoid my lowbrow sister, reaching home at midnight and staying in bed till she had left in the morning. Two cousins are with us, mother and daughter, whom I like. The mother has just been thrown on the world by the death of her second husband, who like modern men, did not expect to die and left all his money tied up in a 1000-acre Virginia farm. They are available, and we spend our time concocting schemes for the future. I retire with them to the farm and lead a life of austere literary endeavor, or we spend the winter at Nassau living royally in a tent on the beach. Or they come to N. Y. and run a community house in Greenwich Village, thus giving our little Estherian circle the benefit of a housekeeper and chaperone. Agnes claims to be still working on the idea, but E. has consigned me, for my own good, to gloom and solitude. I am accused of having sacrificed my gods to my passions long enough, and I am seriously resolving to renounce philandering, and turn to Stoicism. But when I resolve this, it comes over me how impossible that is for my temperament and how my spirit will be torn, torn until I decide that the pursuit is quite hopeless, and then I do not know but what I would let down my perfectionism and snatch at what I can get. If the serious women will not marry you then they cannot quite acquit themselves of the responsibility of your turning into a genuine pursuer of ephemeral loves. Strange how the American spirit cannot see anything between the eternally and sentimentality of bourgeois alliance and the cheapness and vulgarity with which the Washington Square Players poisoned my evening last night through their caricatures of love. L[ucille] is the only Pagan and passionate thing that has ever crossed my horizon, and she was soon submerged in the general unreality—efficiency and cheapness managing to do their deadly work upon her idealism. I pray that some time I shall meet people who have some kind of high seriousness about personal relations which is not metallic and which fuses the sensuous with it. Probably America doesn't produce it, or at least pure America. (L. was a hyphenate.) Then I pray that something will get me to the continent. Or perhaps its all just as impossible there too. I'm all at sea. The poignant thing is to have glimmered it and lost it. Something really has been taken out of me. I have lost faith in something, and I am too impatient and greedy to expect I shall find it again.

I am thinking of writing an article on "The Menace of the Washington Square Players." Their full horror only dawned on me last night. We had all gotten into the habit of thinking that the mere fact of their doing the thing and succeeding put them beyond criticism. Nobody now seems to be attending to the quality of their work. That bill of smart European comedy last winter was bad enough, when Lopokova was the only "lady" on the stage. None of the rest either had the manners or the temperament of smart comedy, or, what was worse, could imagine remotely what such manners were like. This year they start with "The Sugar-House," a New England spinster's conception of passionate love. The light lady, immured by the lusty young farmer in the cabin, is visited in tears and despair by the young wife whom he is deserting. But when some villagers arrive with tar and feathers to ride the hussy on a rail, she bravely faces them down, protects the hussy, appeals to their better nature by wanting her unborn child to be born into a noble community, shakes hands all round and falls into her husband's arms while the Scarlet Woman sneaks away. The spectacle of the college-boy type of villagers, reduced in a moment from aboriginal Puritans to sheepish sophomores is so unintentionally funny that you almost break up the play with your mirth. But the play is Alice Brown and quite serious; a touch here and good acting would carry it through I think.

They have the nerve to do a French comedy with the unspeakable H[elen] W[estley], their vulgarest whom they have made their star.[2] Love is a game and should go with snapping lightness. None of the actors has the faintest imagination for such Gallic play of irony, and their lines drag like the veriest village farce.

Then a dreadful farce by the same author of "Helena's Husband."[3] The gorgeousness of the scene really makes the puniness of the acting and humor pathetic. One leaves with all sorts of bad tastes in the mouth, and nobody particularly caring.

They are far inferior to the Neighborhood Players[4] down on Grand St. Isn't it discouraging? Is there no effective, serious talent, or the enterprise to organize it?

I can't write any more now. Nina is going to have A[rthur] W M[acmahon] and Mary C come to tea tomorrow.

R. S. B.

---

[1]Gregory went to Colorado to visit a sick relative. In the meantime Bourne stayed in her new rooms in Milligan Place. James Larkin, the hero of the 1913 Dublin strike about whom Bourne had so much to say, lived downstairs in the same building.

[2]Although Bourne was critical of both Westley and Brown, the New York *Times* reviewed their efforts favorably.

[3]"Sisters of Suzanna," by Philip Moeller, was not well received. The play parodied Prussians and featured a lot of slapstick humor. The French play he is referring to could be "Lover's Luck," by Georges de Porto-Riche.

[4]The Neighborhood Players evolved from an effort to get inhabitants of one section of Greenwich Village to realize their own creativity. First there were pageants and festivals, after which more organized productions were organized. Still, the Players were considered less professional than either the Provincetown Players or the Washington Square Players.

175

to Herbert J. Seligman
(Ms Columbia)

Stonover Farm
Lenox, Massachusetts
Thursday [mid October 1916]

Dear Herbert,
Reading about "The Living Corpse"[1] in the "Tribune" smites me with the horrid and sudden remembrance of your note. I got it just as I was leaving for here, and my subsequent excitement drove it clean out of my head. A few minutes before the train went a miserable horde of militia decided to march down Fifth Avenue with a band, streets cleared for action, cheering spectators. I was engulfed in the crowd, and cut off from Grand Central. I braved their guns, dashed across their line of march and caught my train, but never thought of the Living Corpse again. I hope you'll forgive me. I will look you up on my return next week.

Randolph Bourne

[1]A play by Tolstoy.

176

to Alyse Gregory
(Ms Yale)

Friday
[October 1916]

A detective is on your trail, and if you don't return this book to the Public Library you will probably be arrested on your return. "The Life of Jesus"[1] too, an infidel book which doubtless has perverted your morals, and made you act in this irresponsible way. I have looked through your books, but cannot find it. You must have it with you.

I am back at Milligan's, having lent the place to Gladys Glaspell while I was away. My reposeful week at Lenox made me quite serene again, and I am trying to enjoy the present and not look ahead into my futureless future. I must always expect to be poor and unloved and obscure. I shall probably have enough to be thankful for if I am warm and fed, and may creep into the Public Library now and then to read with the other forlorn poor, unloved and obscure.

I sent you a telegram about my mother, scarcely thinking that you would not recognize each other and that she would not be looking for you.[2] If you met her, it was awfully kind of you, and if you found her, it was a miracle. I knew it would mean a good deal to her to meet a friend in a strange land. I am annoyed at her for insisting on coming home when she might have had a comfortable winter in California. She is dominated by Puritanism, and wants to suffer for her daughter's sake. The daughter's philosophy also includes the idea that it is her mother's duty to make a home for her, and the combination brings her home, in spite of my expostulations and reasonings, to spend a cold and dismal winter in Bloomfield. I can do nothing with a family that is both helpless and stubborn. Then are determined not to be happy, and all my little schemes go for nought. Then if I try to be happy, I am open to the criticism of neglecting my family. Such entanglements does the Nay-saying philosophy of life lead to.

When are you coming home? E[sther] and A[gnes] are my only social resources.

R. S. B.

---

[1]It is unclear whether Bourne is referring to one of the many orthodox "biographies" or to the more critical studies of Schleiermacher, Strauss, or Renan.

[2]Bourne attempted to set up a rendezvous between Gregory and his mother in

Colorado.

177

to Elizabeth Shepley Sergeant
(Ms Yale)

New York
31 Oct. 1916

Your postal from the Canyon makes me think you are on your way home. I wonder if you are to be in Brookline next week. I will call you up, for I am coming to Boston on Wednesday for a few days.

I have just finished your book. How wise and tender you are! And how you make the humble soul of French people live! It is all so true and refreshing after the bombast of French war spirit retailed by patrician Americans. I should give almost anything to write like that, which means to see things and people so humanly and sympathetically. You keep yourself so modestly out of the picture, and yet what wonderful people and unforgettable occasions were in your intimacy.

I have been camping out for a few weeks in the half-furnished rooms of a friend of Milligan Place who is away. The cost of living is mounting, so that it doesn't look as if I should ever have a home, even by myself. There is a certain relief, however, in the calmness of despair, and most of my friends are in a like unlucky state. I shudder to think what your search for perfection would be like this year, if you came to New York this winter. But probably you have wonderful plans.

Hope I may see you next week.

R. S. B.

178

to Alyse Gregory
(Ms Yale)

Stonover Farm
Lenox, Mass
Saturday
[late October 1916]

It's really a shame that you have been made nervous about the furniture. It really hasn't mattered. There had to be a bill of lading which didn't come, and it was impossible to get the railroad people to look up the stuff without it. It was very easy to go home, and use your room as a study in the daytime. It is delightful here, the real "great good place." But I should like to be walking about in Colorado with you too. Here I forget all my troubles, write serenely, and endow myself with a mood which I always think is going to carry over permanently when I get back.

I can see nothing better ahead of me than to go to Bloomfield when I return, coming into New York every day or so and returning in the evening after my disturbing sister has retired. I am to speak before a Jewish society at Harvard on the 8th and might stay in Boston for a week or two. Then there is a long postponed visit to my sister in Virginia, and one in Washington which might take me up to Christmas. In January I have an invitation to speak at the Association of American Colleges in Chicago,[1] and wonder if I will have the courage to continue on to the southwest and California for the rest of the winter. If my life is to be spanning of time in short loops, this program seems as good as any other. But don't bewail my desertion, for it is as purely tentative as all my life. What was that workable philosophy which I had when you came back from Europe? I have quite forgotten it. My perturbations since then have all been so needlessly chaotic. I wonder if the time will ever come when they will please me to have remembered. But one learns from one's own experience if never from other people's.

Of course you are being feted. Why in the world do you (and I) fiddle around hectic and unperceptive Greenwich Village? The world must be full of possible and appealing people. But you imply that you like to suffer in New York. I don't, but I don't know how to liberate myself. Strength and money would do it, I always think, and I let the lack of them inhibit me. It is so terrifying to plunge out alone. It would be all right except for the evenings. Mon Dieu, the evenings! No wonder the human race invented alcohol as an antidote from breakfast-time. This is the real horror of living alone.

R. S. B.

[1]Bourne spoke on "The Chief Weaknesses of the American College and How They May Best Be Met" in a symposium with President Blaisdell of Pomona College at the third annual convention of the Association. The Association was founded to promote and refine the education of the whole man, a form of education which the organizers of the Association felt the college could accomplish best. While Bourne doubtlessly agreed with this effort, the Christian definition of "the whole man" probably displeased him. Unfortunately, as the 1917 *Bulletin* of the Association reported, Bourne's manuscript was lost by the printer.

179

to Alyse Gregory
(Ms Yale)

49 Russell St.
Milton, Mass.
10 Nov [1916]

I suppose you are very angry with me for deserting you, and for leaving myself so much in possession of your place. But I did not tell you of my chance to come to Boston and make a speech before the Harvard Menorah Society,[1] all expenses paid? I was introduced in the most cosmic terms; never have I ever conceived myself such an international figure, and the reverential awe which surrounded me was thickly oppressive. My Atlantic article was the basis of the invitation, and I find it still reverberating around these parts.[2] I am enjoying myself so much that I think of coming to Cambridge for the winter. (Just now Mrs. James is entertaining me.) I really must have a complex on New York, for when I get away, I have an entirely new sense of freedom and command of my own resources. I pick up new acquaintances, and converse with ease. Here I am seeing some of the N[ew] R[epublic]'s friends, who terrify me when I see them in N. Y. but who are wholly buoyant to me here. Felix Frankfurter, for instance, who teaches law at Harvard; Harold Laski, an Oxford Jew, now teaching history at Harvard (often in the NR as H. J. L.), an incredibly brilliant specimin of the young English radical school. These two with W[alter] L[ippmann] make up a Jewish trinity which is the wonder of the world, or, at least, of my world.[3] Yesterday I got hold of "Seymour Deming," of "A Message to the Middle Class" and other things in the Atlantic, a delightful young, clean, radical journalist. Boston seems so smiling and restful and yet modernly intelligent. I lose all that hectic, anxious note of New York. People have much more time. One feels so much more of a person. And then the eye is constantly charmed by noble old houses and gracious expanses and wonderful white steeples. Milton is the last word in patrician dignity and gets away with it without seeming stodgy.

Mrs. James you should know,—bluest Boston blood, serious almost tragic feeling, socialistic, cosmopolitan, with little of the intellectual training to carry it all off, yet with a sheer nobility of emotion really doing it. She is starting a socialistic salon, to discuss the Industrial Relations Report. My relatively greater acquaintance with concrete things, the placing of people and books, etc., make me a little fountain of light.

R. S. B.

[1]Subsequently published as "The Jew and Trans-National America," *Menorah Journal*, II (December 1916), 277-84.

[2]"Trans-National America" appeared in the July 1916 number.

[3]Frankfurter, an Austrian by birth, later was a legal adviser to Wilson at the Versailles Conference, a participant in the founding of the American Civil Liberties Union, and a member of the United States Supreme Court (1939). Harold Laski returned to England in 1920 and entered the faculty of both the London School of Economics and the University of London. He was an astute student of the United States and was a Socialist.

180

to Dorothy Teall
(Transcript Columbia)

Milton, Mass.
November 14, 1916

Dear Dorothy,
My New York social life is held up indefinitely, both for the reason that I have no home there, and that I am sojourning in these parts. I came to Boston last Wednesday to read a paper before the Harvard Menorah Society, and have since been visiting my friend Mrs. [E. H.] James here in Milton and seeing Boston. It is so delightful to get out of the hectic atmosphere of New York, and people up here seem so much more genuine and human, that I am persuaded to stay as long as I can possible hang on. Later I may go to my sister's in Virginia, and to a friend's in Washington. The parasitic life appeals to me for the winter. In January I am due in Chicago to make another speech, and why shouldn't

I then take a flying trip to the Southwest? Life seems to ordain for me a long course of impersonality and I might as well get into training now while I have no home and nothing to hold me.

You suggest interesting gossip. Why do you resign from the Bear?[1] Were you not expected to be editor-in-chief? And what makes you think I would like Mirsky or Thirsky? Have you not observed when you confront me with your valued friends that I have a weakness for charm, yes, even beauty. A mere mind is apt to chill me. I hate to be crude, but I was rather shocked at the way I did not rise to the mental lure of your last brilliant galaxy. I thought you were far more interesting than the sacred E[sther?]. But probably you now have a new idol. I still like Lillian Soskin best, and Babette interests me. When I come back, they must both be seen somewhere. And if you will introduce me one at a time to your other lights, I may be serener and more agreeable than I was last time. Won't you be glad when college is over and you shake them all, except the tried and true?

R. S. B.

[1]The Barnard student newspaper.

181

to Alyse Gregory
(Ms Yale)

Milton, Mass
19 Nov 1916

Your soulless letter chilled me so that I was glad to get a familiar plaint again. I began to think that you were becoming reconciled to life, and my last link with comprehension was gone. I am not in New York, as you see, and will not be until the 17th. Then I shall probably go to Virginia on the 4th for a couple of weeks. But quo faire? Il faut vivre. New York will not let me live the way I wish to live, so I must try elsewhere. My first Boston buoyancy has already worn off. I find I have dragged, of course, the same unsatisfied soul up here, and the same yawning and uncomplicated life. I merely fled my problems, but they came after me by slow freight, and are now comfortably unpacked and settled around me. They are so very clear, and they almost begin to appeal to me through their sheer aesthetic brilliancy. Having led the experimental life, and sifted and sorted, I feel that I know now exactly what I want. It is all as far away as ever, with only samples to tantalize my memory and impede my clean delivery of myself over to the present. Love, fame, joy in work, would bring, perhaps, the resources for the freedom that I want to move about and yet have a centre and a hearth. All my problems are interwoven; if I had one solved, it seems as if they should all be solved. Of course, it seems to me that the key to all of them is love, and the deprivation the one impediment to blossoming. At least, I should give anything in the world for an opportunity to test this theory. Is it Greenwich Village that is the poison, or is it the times that produce the type of fair and serious and life-denying woman, who in the name of a career and her pride and the sacred independence of woman destroys not only you but herself. The philosophy that you are not a man but Man, and therefore, in spite of your sympathy, personal quality, and contribution, really only a lustful Being who wants you to cook for him,—this is the philosophy that has succeeded in poisoning all my days and my work. Probably I shall not be revenged till Patchin's and King-dom[1] are blotted out and not one stone left on another. I am inclined to doubt whether Man's wrongs to women are so much greater than woman's wrongs to man. We certainly have a peculiarly acute mechanism for suffering.

R. S. B.

[1] Florence King's nickname was Kinglet. Bourne's modification shows his appreciation of her.

182

to Esther Cornell
(Ms Columbia)

Milton, Mass.
20 Nov 1916

The expected trip between Boston and New York has come. Mrs. James wars with my invitation to you for Sunday. It seems she has been planning a "preparedness" soirée for Monday evening, and counts on me to make a speech. I murmured about concerts and friends, and then it was, You want to get back to New York! Now how can I be so ungrateful as to break up her soirée? And what more delightful way of showing one's gratitude for being invited this long than by staying longer? Will you be gracious and overlook my offense? Anyway, the concert the next week is a much better program, and I shall stay over for it. I shall surely come down Tuesday the 28th. Will you have your new house by that time? Your fate continues to haunt me. Really such disaster is wholly romantic. Something will have to happen that will make you thankful all your life that you didn't fall in the thirteenth chair. Of course nothing about the thing suited you. You were made for a different world. So that some presiding genius of art snatched you away in sheer indignation at the waste. I wish that you could run amuck through the W[ashington] S[quare] P[layers]. Show them for once what beauty and spirit and intelligence will do for play. I'm glad to see the papers are getting a little less complacent about their acting.

Here is my latest portrait, my vicarious self.[1] The Menorah Journal pestered me so for a photograph to put with my article. I like it; it makes me look so serious and well-intentioned. Do you like it?

R. S. B.

[1]The photograph was taken on November 18, 1916 and is included in this volume.

183

to Alyse Gregory
(Ms Yale)

Milton
Sunday [November 26, 1916]

I expect to come down Tuesday. Will you be in for tea in the afternoon? I will try to find you. I must go first to the N[ew] R[epublic] and find out why they don't print me when I am away. Is your despondency due to the lack of a job, or just general living? Greenwich Village, I decide, is enough to make anyone despondent. There is nothing of the kind, apparently, in Boston. Don't say I'm smug when I return, or that I have an other-worldly look as of superior regions visited. It is almost two months since I have really seen you, and I doubt whether all your Rocky Mountain tang will have worn away. My mother wishes me to invite you out for Thanksgiving dinner, and I wish you would come. But I suppose, of course, you go to Northfield. You can tell me Tuesday.

You are a great one to talk of forsaking New York when you left me at the most critical moment when I was to be turned out of Caldwell on a homeless world. You did serve me by lending me a home, but you took away your spiritual support. You and Leo seem to agree in being more concerned about my stopping in New York. Other friends are almost too sure that it is the best thing for me. One does acquire a certain vacuum of the imagination when one is away from the familiar people and incidents that touch old wounds and complexes. My first days here were remarkable, a fixed serene glare of intellectual poise, not very brilliant but vary calm. Lately I have been more restless. You are right. Poverty is a hideous thing. Not to have enough to command the resources of mere getting around, of having what you need, is appalling. And still worse to have the slender minimum resource that you have, so uncertain. One takes a certain satisfaction, I suppose, in the discovery that one's problems are hopeless. When one has decided that, then they become interesting as problems, as intricate designs which one can study out and comprehend, though one can't take them to pieces.

As ever, but a little more sardonically.

R.

184

to Elizabeth Shepley Sergeant
(Ms Columbia)

Hampton Institute, Va.
6 Dec 1916

My long postponed visit to my sister is now taking place, with great satisfaction to myself. Her model house, husband, child, environment, purpose make me feel very idle and wasteful, but I like the momentary sensation of being a part of it all. It is nice to see one member of my unhappy family come admirably out, and she the most deserving one too. And all done just not too late. I must try to find some articles here, though my journalistic sense, never very strong, does not seem to grow stronger. The N[ew] R[epublic] suggests my becoming an authority on prohibition for them (doleful subject) and Virginia would be a good place to study it, while people still know what they think they are doing. Do you still think I ought to write stories, a novel? I always meant to find out from you on what you based your opinion. I have a sort of general, if quite unfounded, intuition of confidence these days, and I feel that my winter, even in New York, will be very different from my hectic life of last year. That was experience, heavily paid for in suffering, but wonderful and necessary. Now I see that there are other things to express and work out. I wish I was artist enough to use my experience without tangling myself up too much again in my imagination. The reformer got such a terrific start in my youth over the artist that I'm afraid the latter is handicapped for life. The reformer with an amour-propre is a temperament pretty quenching for any upflow of art in one, isn't it? I wish I had stayed to have another talk with you.

R. S. B.

185

to Esther Cornell
(Ms Columbia)

Hampton Institute[1]
Friday [December 8, 1916]

Such weather I have never been able to dream of, soft cloudless skies, the temperature exactly neither too warm or too cool, a hint of sea air. I could not ask for anything better. Autos here are plentiful and the people leisurely. The other day we had a pleasant ride in the sunset, white straggling roads with negroes going home from work, flat ploughed country dotted with cedar clumps against the broom. The shining magnolias and live oaks give a fine greenness to the landscape and make winter seem only a temporary doze. I am very sleepy here and cannot talk to the teachers who drop in to see a mild celebrity. One rather gay lady who looks a little like you was much interested in what she conceived I hadn't said about "Mon Amie." On this evidently rests most of my fame. She is rather embarrassing for there is nothing more to tell, and strangers seem almost too willing to believe that I am not a Don Juan. How well you know better, I hear you say! My sister is so very much literalized and democratized that I hardly know her. She is not as exotic as I am, but there is a certain triumph for me in finding our attitudes upon which we used to split coming up now and again to agreement, and to her giving me a sort of authority. I was so encouraged that I sounded her a little about you, and was delighted to find that she did not seem at all displeased or even critical of my design. She says marriage has much expanded her and her perspectives are different. What are you doing and why don't you write to me? Do I have to send you another picture? And if yours are good why aren't you sending me one?

I am wanting to see you very much today. I don't know whether to enjoy the full implications of what you told me Sunday. It would be so easy for me to delude myself into thinking that you cared for me more constantly than you do, and really even imagined marrying me. When I come to my senses it seems grotesque of me to imagine your being willing. You are so radiantly adequate for any fortune. There is nothing I would not wish for you. But there is also nothing I would not wish for myself. And I go right on having delusions of grandeur that you could love me and be happy with me. All my life I have alternated delusions of greatness with the most cowering and abject feeling of worthlessness. I turn cold when I think that someday you might find me out and drive me into the latter state again. But sometimes my society seems to keep you in a low-lying state. Oh, what an adventure it would be to try to get the most out of life together! We could be very wise, and we are already so very intelligent and so very reasonable. Your reasonableness is divine, there is nothing like seeing it squelch your impulse. And I really get a physical sensation from your intelligence, your attested glowing inquiring look that makes one feel a flexible, poised instrument within. For you do understand—when you will—and that is what counts. I loathe boggy knowledge, but your quality means light and air to me. My own reasonableness is far less calculable, but my intelligence is good if a little too analytical. Or perhaps you don't really think it is good? I don't wish to be smug.

R.

[1]Hampton Institute was the most famous of the early attempts at establishing higher education for Blacks in the post Civil War South. The Institute was organized around vocational education; its philosophy was best articulated by its most famous alumnus, Booker T. Washington.

186

to Esther Cornell
(Ms Columbia)

Hampton Institute, Va.
[December 1916]

I am determined that you shall not forget me. If necessary, I will write to you all the time. It is far more uncomfortable to be away from you this time, and my Boston apathy does not come over me at all. I take a far less fatalistic attitude towards your fading away out of my life. When I was in Boston, it seemed too much to expect that you wouldn't keep out of it. It was safer to hold my breath. But when I got back I found you so very much more caring than I had dared to hope. And now I find I can't hold my breath this time. I'm becoming horribly afraid of boring you. I have pictures of you gradually receding from me, gently and tenderly, perhaps, but still receding, when you find that the qualities you have imagined in me aren't there, and my wickedness seems all predominant. Do you really feel my wickedness, or is that only your little joke? I don't feel wicked when I'm with you, only rather completely and exhiliratedly human. I'm never so emotional that I can't bring out the high lights, even the intellectual. Indeed, there's nothing in me that I feel you don't understand or wouldn't if you want to. If I emphasize my wickedness it is only because my special circumstances make me more suspicious of being understood and responded to in that way. Other people would take things for granted, but I have always to be convinced anew. I don't think my spirit is naturally roaming, but it just has had to be restless because it does so awfully want an abiding place and has not found it. Or if it did it was torn and harried and treated more like a wayfarer taken in for the night than the friend found at last. And until it finds such gay peace with you that I cannot imagine its going unless you expelled it. And don't think I don't realize how immensely it must satisfy you to keep itself from getting expelled. Because you should have everything the earth has to give you. I blush to think how crudely I have talked to you this summer and I hope to convince myself that I was not really myself then, when I was hard and greedy. I did really appreciate you just as much as I do now, but you seemed so distant that there was nothing for me but the desperado attitude, a kind of Captain Kidd swagger. But I seem to remember, too, long hours when I wasn't a pirate, and those console me with their delightful quality. I like the peevish and disgruntled tone least of all, and I marvel at your charity in bearing with me so long.

You must like me a great deal, and yet my sober reason still balks at imagining you could like me enough. And yet I have become so strangely unflustered about you. I am feeding on the illusion that, even if you didn't straighten out all your complications and we stayed in this wistful borderland, you wouldn't recede as long as I was fair and giving, as I should be. I have to think for myself. Well can I live on that? And it doesn't seem as if I couldn't for awhile. That is, if you aren't going to try to forget me. But you won't add to obstacles by trying yourself up in some household arrangement, will you? I wish I was with you this minute.

R

187

to Elizabeth Shepley Sergeant
(Ms Yale)

Caroline Country Club
Hartsdale, N. Y.[1]
21 Dec. 1916

It was even nicer of you to think the review was nice, for as I read it over it wasn't at all the tone I wanted.[2] I patronized a little and the "bourgeois" was certainly shockingly undiscriminating. I see now that your own preface was the best review the book could possibly have had, and I am angry that I did not say so. Still Hackett[3] liked the review and I have found him very hard to please lately. I'm sorry your cold has still pursued you. Since I left Milton I have been off to Virginia and back. Hampton is a most interesting school to look at, and a Utopia of a place to live in. My sister's husband is the liveliest kind of a modern chaplain, very modern in his theology and sociology. They have a charming new home and a marvelous baby. All sorts of grateful negro slaves, earning their way through school by labor; community heating plant; community restaurant if you want it; illimitable food raised on the model farm as part of the education purveyed; charming water front and old houses; place and the knowledge that you are in the only school I know of where practically everything is worth the doing and all the energy goes into living value. The ubiquitous Flexner has rightly discovered in it an example of his "modern school", and is about to make it his own, with a survey after he finishes Gary.[4]

I take very kindly to the black man, and took great delight in my sister's inviting the black commandant and his wife to dinner. I think the Southern white man's policy of keeping down a race whose infectious personal qualities he never was really able to resist is the least defensible thing in the world. The white race has an instinctive personal antipathy to the [?], and yet fills Southern homes with black servants, gives its children to black women to nurse, fornicates with them, and altogether admits the black race constantly to about as human and personal relationships as it is possible to conceive. Whatever the antipathy may be, it certainly is neither personal nor instinctive, and it is most irritating to try to track down what it is. It seems to be nothing more than a crude enjoyment of caste-power, and the unpleasantness of having a social group that was once your property become now potentially your equal. This is certainly the least rational of prejudices and it is intolerable that the white should be allowed to fall back for defense on "instinctive", "natural", etc. The thing is full of ghastly ironies, and I shall unburden myself of it some day.

R. S. B.

[1]Esther Cornell's family home was in Hartsdale. He was probably visiting her.

[2]"France Yesterday," *New Republic* IX (Dec 9, 1916), 156-58, was a review of *French Perspectives.*

[3]Francis Hackett was in charge of the book review section of the *New Republic.*

[4]Flexner eventually published *The Gary Schools: A General Account* (1918), which was a critical assessment of Wirt's system.

188

to Alyse Gregory
(Ms Yale)

Milwaukee
Sunday, [January 1917]

I meant to write to you days ago, but my life has been such a phantasmagoria of inefficiency that it didn't get done. This region is one of the few American scenes where I am appreciated, and I have just slid along from one hospitality to another, losing track of the days. The trouble started in Chicago, where the president of a small girls' college was in my audience. I had spoken there when I was in Milwaukee on my Gary tour two years ago. She is an impressive person, and she literally abducted me. I had a Sunday of great honor at the college, spoke in the afternoon before the girls, spent the night there, encompassed by 350 of them, and was handed on the next morning to the Unitarian minister, who is one of the most industrious propagandists of "Youth and Life." Tuesday I was lured to Madison, where I have a number of friends at the University, and spent several most delightful days of conversation and investigating. Madison is unique, a great tone to it for an American city, the provincial capital in all its brilliance, and a pretty good brilliance for this country too. You get a taste of what New York would be if the national or even the State Government were only there. My judgments are notoriously untrustworthy, but it seems to me now that my little group of friends there exceeds in charming soundness anything I even remotely apprehended at Columbia or indeed anywhere in New York. I thought so before when I was there, but I am sure of it now. I renounce Boston for Madison as my city of refuge. There was a charm in four days of stimulating and exclusively masculine society, a rather rare experience for me. I was put at the admirable University Club, and had all my obvious instincts of amour-propre continually satisfied. Max Eastman was also there at the time, making his usual innocent commotion in the university by getting the University buildings closed against him as a "propagandist".[1] This was my first chance to get acquainted with him, our Village lives never having crossed. We discovered the firm bond of a common enemy. I like him. His tempo seems even slower than mine. There was much sitting around in Horace Kallen's room with him and with admiring students of the Form and Kit Magazine circles. Then I pursued industrial education at the capitol, with the enfant terrible McCarthy blarneying me with his irresponsible brogue.[2] I don't know whether you know all these heroes or not. They bulk in my world. I had lunch with Lucille's family, most outrageously as without her knowledge and permission. I just remembered the address, and of course could not resist my curiosity. Mother, brother, & sister, both younger,—quite charmingly naive and genuine; L[ucille] appearing as a little strange and restless, outraged at their (to me) wholly harmless bourgeoisdom, not knowing at all what she wanted, lured by "exceptional" people, stung to an anxious and wholly illegitimate attempt to "improve" her family, embroiled by her delusive love of the satanic Florence, chasing will-of-the-wisps to New York when Madison offered the perfect environment for satisfying one's social rage.

I had long hours with the philosophy professor [Max Otto] whom she admired and who is half in love with her. He is a most charming soul, human, spiritual, wistful, innocent, embroiled by the material complications of life. Circumstantially he has almost everything that I have not but want to complete my life (except that we are both wifeless) and I have everything that he has not. Perhaps I was over-impressed with his charming house, full of windows that looked to the South over a wild and frozen lake, and the model and comfortable and devoted sister who kept house for him. He has just been through a crisis at the University, when the rabble of local ministers got after him for preaching atheism in his courses, and tried to have him put out. He stuck to his guns and routed them, but he thinks it killed his old German mother of whom he was very fond. He sheds an amazing influence. No sensible girl could refuse to adore him.

Milwaukee I like immensely. Social service loses its hectic, priggish note here. It's been worked into life. A hard-headed Socialist administration of practical idealists and efficient laborites gives a tone to the place. We went to see Berger, a great character, passé intellectually, but a study in political intuition. The Unitarian Minister with whom I am staying is a jolly little Nantucketer, transplanted to the Middle West. He has all the social and political ropes in his hands and has a fine time with life. It makes my flesh creep to see some of the amiable and altruistic elderly bourgeois with whom he has to associate. I could not stay with him long and live. But he is momentarily refreshing. Do you know this Mid-West innocence? It is even worse in Chicago. Wirt is a perfect type. You get it in Victor Narros' letters to the "Evening Post." It goes to my head like wine, for I can feel so relatively sophisticated and realistic. This should have been the soil in which I was raised. I shouldn't have had my confidence always damped by thickly cynical Columbia and rapid, sure New Republic. The criticisms of the NR out here are most amusing.

There is a howling blizzard outside, and I hope it will not keep me here forever. I now think of arriving home Wednesday night, omitting Washington.

R. S. B.

[1]Max Eastman was a co-founder of *The Masses* and was a Marxist. His appearance at Wisconsin created a famous incident in the history of the University, for he was denied the use of a lecture hall because of his views. The University had gotten a reputation for academic freedom, but, with the approaching war, it was becoming self-conscious of its loyal obligations.

[2]Horace Kallen and Max Otto were both members of the Philosophy Department. Kallen was an expert on William James. Otto had caused a furor because he had questioned the existence of God. Charles McCarthy was a legislative librarian and publicizer of the Wisconsin Idea. His book, *The Wisconsin Idea* (1914), was the most popular account of that system.

189

to Van Wyck Brooks
(Ms Pennsylvania)

New York
February 16, 1917

Dear Brooks,

In response to your kind note, I send you this foolish essay. Can you read it? My typewriter is broken down, or I would not send it in this form. I want to see you again. Could you not lunch with me some day, say at 47 Fifth Ave.? My phone is Chelsea 8652, if you want to call me up some morning. I have a book of yours which I should return.

Sincerely,

Randolph Bourne

190

to Theodore Dreiser
(Ms Pennsylvania)

New York
April 19, 1917

Dear Mr. Dreiser,

Why don't you get your publishers to issue a cheaper edition of "A Hoosier Holiday"[1] so that more people can get it and enjoy it. Honestly, I don't think the pictures add to its value at all; on the contrary, they lock you up in an expensive form and keep you away from an American public that needs just this sort of thing. I have been looking through it again, and am more enthusiastic than ever. It is wise and delightful, and incredibly American. That is, you have taken the small town American background and made it disgorge every drop of its juice and sweetness. The story you tell seems so typical that it is almost epic. And you do it like the artist, without the Puritan sentimentality that the poor old American small town would get lost in if it tried to tell its own story. If we could get young America to soak itself in a book like this, then I think we might really get some real fiction with some of the warmth of the soil and the beauty and sting of youth, and not the funny, motor, de-sensualized stuff that gets turned out by our young novelists. Won't you take many more motor trips through the South and West, and give us America through your temperament?

Cordially yours,

Randolph Bourne

[1]The book, an account of a motor journey from New York to Indiana with personal reminiscences, was published in 1916.

191

to Arthur Macmahon
(Ms Mrs. Arthur Macmahon)

White Plains
Wednesday [note
in another hand
"Received Washington,
D. C. 12 July 1917]

Dear Arthur,
        I was glad that you summoned the resolution to write me and let me know what you were doing. The work sounds educational and official, and you must see many intimate sides of the conduct of the war. I should like to be there to discuss it with you. Do you see Keppel and Lippmann? The N[ew] R[epublic] seems decidedly to have ceased running the war. Wilson's later utterances have knocked their strategy in the head.
        I have a good friend in Washington who would be delighted to meet you. She was part of my London sojourn. Her husband is in the Geologic Survey and very dull. She is lively, hospitable, clever. A classmate of Beard's at DePauw University! Her name is Mrs. C. E. Liebenthal [?], and she lives at 3411 Oakwood Terrace, near the end of the Mt. Pleasant Valley line. She has many young friends and will probably take you off with them on week-end tramps in the Blue Ridge. Look her up, and tell her I introduce you. I will write her about you. She is in the telephone book. She will be glad to meet you.

Then there is Joy Young, who has been in New York, working with the pacifists, and recently got arrested for picketing at the White House.[1] She is charming, with a natively terroristic mind, and looks like an angel. She could be reached at 21 Madison Place, and I know would be glad to meet you. I don't know how long she is to stay in Washington, so you had better hurry if you want to meet an unusually interesting girl.

Then there is Merz of the NR's Washington Bureau. Perhaps you know him already. He is a young man, almost too bright to live, but worth knowing. All the world must be at Washington these days. If you want entertaining society, I think you will enjoy Mrs. L. and her friends. I do hope you'll look her up.

My summer is bound to be chaotic. I planned to go to the Thayers in Dublin, but that fell through. So now I am with Agnes de Lima and her brother and Mrs. Cornell at White Plains. Esther [Cornell] is doing farmwork in Bedford. I may go away later for two weeks with Van Wyck Brooks. I can be addressed here c/o Mrs. Cornell, 24 Chase Ave., White Plains, N. Y. Which reminds me that I had dinner with our Harry [Chase] in Mt. Vernon, and saw the adorable baby Hollis.

R. S. B.

[1] The most publicized pacifist demonstration took place in early April, but there was constant agitation throughout the summer. Bourne was acquainted with Joy Young through the pacifist organizations to which he belonged.

192

to Alyse Gregory
(Ms Yale)

White Plains
Wednesday [early July 1917]

The city seems in another world, and nothing could be more serene than this rainy hill. Esther [Cornell] is working on a farm in Bedford; Agnes [de Lima] is in town; Esther's mother and I spend the day together. I sleep somewhat audaciously out on the front porch, and read and write in front of a too smokey wood fire in a fradulent fireplace. I speculate shall I go to Mrs. James, or shall I stay here? Shall I go away with Van Wyck Brooks in August? Meanwhile I can forget temporarily that I haven't stability in life. How is the cruel city treating you? Any news of Harold [Stearns]? I shall probably be in some day next week, and will try to see you.

R.

193

to Alyse Gregory
(Ms Yale)

Provincetown
27 July [1917]

I hope you have been happy and cool, though it is mere condensation to address Milligan's from Cape Cod. Brooks and I have had three delightful days in this questionably delightful place, where Greenwich Villagers are as thick as the mosquitoes. On a station-platform en route we met your friend Griffen Barry, who Brooks knew. Mary Reston Vorse is here, with an old house of her own. Susan Glaspell has another. Lucy Huffaker and Grace Potter are everywhere. Donald Tucker is writing his history of co-operative banking in a disused and diseased wharf. Stuart Morrison is coming or has been. Ida Rauh, etc.[1] What's the difference? I long for a solitary sand-dune. But we had to see Provincetown, and we are romantically settled high up over the water, "la vie litterarie" with many groans. We are both supposedly to be writing articles for the "Seven Arts," but inspiration is very feeble after so many days in the open air. I have a toothache, and life is not very interesting. We shall probably go to Boston from here. I don't know when.

R. S. B.

[1]Lucy Huffaker was a charter member of the Provincetown Players. Ida Rauh was married to Floyd Dell. She was a Marxist, a feminist, and a believer in free love. Donald Tucker's study, *The Evolution of People's Banks*, was published by Columbia University in 1922, where he earned a Ph.D. in the same year. Susan Glaspell was married to George Cram Cook, who was a co-founder of the Provincetown Players. She wrote short stories and plays. Mary Heaton Vorse was another co-founder of the Players. During this time she was writing pamphlets on the rights of small countries for the Committee on Public Information.

194

to Agnes de Lima[1]
(Ms Columbia)

August 6 [1917]

Dear Agnes,

It was very good of you to write me so promptly. You are nobler than E[sther], who hasn't sent me a line, though I sent her postals and what I thought a charming letter two weeks ago. My heart sinks and I decide that I am only a current amusement for her, out of sight out of mind. Am I not foolish to jolly myself along that there is anything deep and serious in her fondness? I must learn to be content with her wayside flowers and not expect the quiet permanent garden. Her casualness is all the stranger because she was so outraged at what she took to be casualness in me. Shall I storm in on her at Ithaca, and insist that she take me seriously? I wish I had a conviction that she had any deep and permanent feeling for me as she has for you. Meanwhile I am going to Dublin for a few days. Will I intrude on your good nature if I ask you to forward what mail there is, and also to have laundered some things I left and some things I sent back by parcel-post addressed to myself? My address will be not Dublin, but *Monadnock, N. H.* Do you mind being factotum? Brooks has gone back after a very rarified two weeks. We saw all the Players in Provincetown, but never got the charm of the place, which is frankly a hole, filled with mosquitoes and huddled shabby houses. After you have looked on one decaying wharf you are satisfied unless apparently when you are a painter or a playwright and then you cannot have enough. Being neither, we turned up our noses at the wharves and at the decaying fish in the harbor. There are, however, marvelous dunes and rich vegetation, and it was tolerably cool while you were dying by the hundreds in New York. We met a charming couple called the Ordway Teads[2] who would be perfect for a colony and are keen for it and whom I wish to get for that farm which I go right on believing Esther is going to manage. Brooks and I did a lot of enthusiastic talking about it, and it seems to be our salvation. We have a nucleus in the Brooks and Teads. We could probably rent an old house(s) with ten acres of land in Westchester. We could afford an expensive cook and perhaps a community auto. Then we would add people in the summer. There is a young vegetable expert here who is looking for a job. We could annex her if Esther doesn't like farming. The possibilities are endless. Only the servant problem remains, and the house. I should be back in White Plains looking for houses. My imagination takes wing and I already have E and am recoverd from my depression.

As ever,

Randolph

[1]De Lima, who later collected transcripts of most of Bourne's letters for Columbia University, was an educational reformer.

[2]At that time Ordway Tead was an industrial consultant. He later became an industrial management professor at Columbia. From 1938 to 1953 he was head of the New York City Board of Higher Education He was a civil libertarian.

195

to Van Wyck Brooks
(Ms Pennsylvania)

Monadnock, N. H.
August 7, 1917

Dear V. W. B.,

The woods are very refreshing after the sands and sea, and Dublin seems as charming as ever. The Thayers live in a casual way, with terrible romances with insane servants and epic conflicts with the neighbors. I shall not be able to stand or be stood very long, and then I shall return to search for our enchanted community. I hope you found the "Seven Arts" regenerated, pouring forth an inspiration that Cape Cod could not give. I sent in the article with much misgiving and hope you will not read it. Mrs. James gave me a check for a dollar, wishing the last three numbers and the next to be sent to her,—June, July, August and September. Can you get them sent?

R. B.

196

to Esther Cornell
(Ms Columbia)

Keene, N. H.
August 10, 1917

Dear Esther,

I think I will come back next Friday, and will you go to the Symphony that Sunday, the 26th? And will you invite me back to Hartsdale for the night? I have a desperate scheme to go to Virginia on the following Wednesday to visit my sister, and I should like to see you in your country setting before I go. If you are afraid to write me a letter, you can at least send me a kind of little note accepting this concert invitation, can't you? Or if you are afraid to do that, at least little Aggie would do it for you? Please ignore my heavy sarcasm, if it doesn't please you. I think of some more which I can't resist. You would love Milton, for the first thing that assails you as you step from the train is the rich and prevailing odor of hot fudge sundae. The air is filled with it, you are followed for blocks with its enthralling power. Reason, Walter Baker's chocolate factory, pouring out day and night delicious odor to the air. I go down to the village many times a day for a paper and to refresh my senses with the fudge-laden air.

I had a wild hope that you were coming to Boston. The play was actually advertised and I knew that if it came, poetic justice could not help bringing you with it, restored to Bayard and Willie, and reunited to me, everything conspiring in the most approved melodramatic climax. Imagine my dismay when I saw Arnold Daly substituted. Then I knew that you were not reconciled. Such atrocious luck means only one thing that destiny didn't want you to waste your time in that part. The thing happened so malevolently that you are obviously being reserved for something startling. It is dramatic, for destiny had to snatch you from the very jaws. Such a very close call should sober your mind. My own career is strewn with what my egotism insists on seeing as very close shaves when I almost got jobs that I was (objectively) crying my heart out for. What is your reserved fate? Perhaps the W[ashington] S[quare] P[layers] where you could immediately get a bigger reputation than a year in that old melodrama. Perhaps New Mexico. E[lizabeth] S[hepley] S[ergeant] has returned and makes Santa Fe so attractive with little hotels along the track, that I do not see what can possibly hold me when once I get out to Chicago. It would seem strange to turn my back on New York and our network of people, and definitely close a chapter in my life, but such things have to be done. I am coming to think of Greenwich Village as a poisonous place which destroys the souls even of the super-villagers like ourselves. Are you being happy?

R. S. B.

197

to Esther Cornell
(Ms Columbia)

Hampton, Virginia
Tuesday [September 1917]

This trip of mine is a disastrous mistake. I am wasting my time, my money and my good-nature. My concentrated family is unbelievably discouraging. I seem to have extracted all the meaning of the place in my first visit, and I am expecting to go to-morrow, stopping at Washington. I should have stayed entirely home and worked. If I get home in time I shall have the party. I do not see where or how I am going to live. All the talk here is most pessimistic about food and cost of living. I seem to disagree on the war with every rational and benevolent person I meet. I crave some pagan monastery some "great, good place" where I can go and stay till the war is all over. How are you? Living, I hope, and feeling.

R. S. B.

198

to Dorothy Teall
(Transcript Columbia)

New York
September 15, 1917

It is a long time since I have heard from you, and I am wondering what your career has brought you this summer. Are you going to do some more college, or are you going to plunge into writing? Won't you come and see me some day this week or next, preferably this? Tell me what time, and I will stay in for you. My telephone is Chelsea 8562.

Sincerely,

Randolph

199

to Waldo Frank
(Ms Pennsylvania)

Harrison, New York
October 2, 1917

Dear Waldo Frank,

I tried to get you on the phone yesterday morning, but there was no reply. Now I am up here until Friday. When I return, I shall certainly be glad to see you, and hear about the distressing condition of the "Seven Arts." I have heard only confused rumors of the difficulties, but hope that they are not mortal.

Please excuse pencil, but there seems to be no ink at all in the house.

Sincerely,

Randolph Bourne

200

to Everett Benjamin[1]
(Ms Columbia)

16 Charles St.
New York City
26 November 1917

Dear Everett,
         You went off to serve your country without telling me about it, but now
that two of my women-folks have heard from you it seems my duty to write you
on this your second visit to France. I should like very much to hear your graphic
account of the life "over there." If there is any humor you are undoubtedly
seeing it, although perhaps even you are not able to extract optimism out of the
situation. It was an interesting touch you gave in one of those letters about the
French market-day, and it made me envious that you were seeing the world
while I was still hibernating in New York, and living a life of selfish, if penurious,
freedom. I feel very much secluded from the world, very much out of touch
with my times, except perhaps with the Bolsheviki. The magazines I write for
die violent deaths, and all my thoughts seem unprintable.[2] If I start to write on
public matters I discover that my ideas are seditious, and if I start to write a
novel I discover that my outlook is immoral if not obscene. What then is a literary man to do if he has to make his living by his pen?
         My family having moved from Blfd I no longer visit that stimulating
town. But I cannot say I am any more enthusiastic about East Orange. If I go
there my family makes me play the piano for the edification of the co-inhab-
itants of the house, and I feel exactly like the child of ten who used to have to
show off in the parlor. Margaret is so enraged at me for my opinions [?] that she
almost put me out of the house the last time I saw her.[3] She said she would have
cheerfully used a gun on me if she had had one. You might be interested to
know that Beachie[4] has returned to her ancestral home, with husband Andrew
and child. I had not seen or heard of the T [eall] family for months when two
weeks ago Dorothy telephoned me, and told me of this important fact. She
made a date with me for tea the next day. I prepared for her coming, but with
her usual inscrutability she did not appear, nor have I heard a word from her
since. One does not explain Dorothy, one merely suffers her. I shall be interested
in seeing Beachie in her role as model wife and mother. I shall have to invite her
in to tea, hoping that she will accept with more sincerity than her eccentric
sister. I am informed that I have a new nephew, but have not had the report
confirmed from headquarters. I doubt whether the family should be increased so
rapidly on the present income, unless Lawrence is made principal of the Insti-

tute,[5] which I suggest in order to get a rise out of Ruth, who considers him unworthy of so high a position. What will you do when the war is over? I can imagine you marrying a French widow and settling down to work her vineyard or farm and to repopulate the French nation. You will certainly want something more adventurous than the Safely Insulated, etc. Are you meeting some wonderful people in your service, and greatly broadening your experience of life? From your postmark I gather that you are safe and sound, many miles from the firing-line. I went through there once on the train from Paris to Toulouse, and remember dimly the look of the station. When the war is over, wait a week or two and I will come over and take a walking trip with you. Spain is the country I want to visit now. There is a very gay Spanish company in New York now giving a play with much song and dance, called the "Land of Joy."[6] I went the other night with four friends, and in the midst of it thought of the first musical show I ever went to. It was "The Yankee Consul," and I think I must have gone with Art Lee. Anyway the point is that I had no sooner thought of him than I happened to look down the row, and there he was, sitting heavily and gloomily, four seats away. He did not see me, and I did not take the chance to resume acquaintance with my old boyhood chum. But it gave me a chance for an interesting historical survey of all that happened to me since I went to see the "Yankee Consul."

My parting advice is,—Don't buy a Blickensdorfer typewriter if you should be tempted to become literary. It is mendacious, unreliable, and delicate. It prints the wrong letters. Its only advantage is that it is light to the hand, but since nobody wants to carry it anywhere that virtue, for which I bought it, is a relatively useless one.

Do write to me, and come back when you can.

R. S. B.

[1] Benjamin was a close childhood friend.

[2] A much quoted reference to the *Seven Arts*.

[3] A cousin.

[4] Beatrice Teall, who had been living in Pittsburgh.

[5] Lawrence Fenninger, who was married to Natalie Bourne. The Institute he refers to is Hampton Institute. Fenninger later went to the Union Theological Seminary.

[6] A musical review, with American characters introducing Spanish scenes. There was a plot linking the skits together, so the performance could be considered an early form of musical comedy.

201

to Dorothy Teall
(Transcript Columbia)

New York
December 13, 1917

I don't really think you're perverse. In fact, thinking over our interesting conversation, it strikes me that you gave one of the most *reasonable* performances I've seen in many a day. I mean it, you certainly have an extremely fine working intellect, and I doubt very much your coming to grief in anything you do. Only given this very excellent machine of a mind, which is not detached, like some people's, from your personality, you are a little puzzling in finding college such a bore. Surely there must be enough intellectual nuts to crack there to get through the courses. Otherwise I should think your mind would be unemployed. I should cultivate Mrs. Putnam and her intellectual leads. You will want to understand the structure of the society you live in, and the way people behave, and the material of literatures in the past. I advise you to grind corn while you are in college, and not come out with machinery unused. And your family will forgive much if you come out with credit. And they deserve this coddling too.

Bring B[abette] D[eutsch] down some day. I must take more testimony before I judge her case. And still I don't see that it accords even with the Bloomfield Weltanschauung that Beatrice didn't even answer my invitation! This for her.

Come and see me again. You have an extremely good and affectionate friend in

Randolph Bourne

202

to Agnes de Lima
(Ms Columbia)

Boston
[Winter 1917-1918]

Dear Agnes,

I did not like it that I alarmed you and cost you a telegram, but really we must persuade her [Esther] not to go on that tour to Maine and Pittsburg and Buffalo. She has been neglecting her temperature for weeks, and her cough is very bad, *with constant raising.* She is easily tired, and there is now a dreadful man in the play who is rude to her and disturbs her. She takes her raw eggs, and says she feels fat, but I'm sure that if she continues to work she will have to go to New Mexico as soon as her tour is over, and will have to spend months regaining her health. And then we will have to be miserable without her. Why, oh why, did you let her come to Boston, after being sick in Baltimore? And why did you not see when you were here whether she was all right? You gave me such reassuring news that I was shocked to hear this cough. She cannot possibly get rid of it—no matter what it is—as long as she has to play every night on an icy stage, and she has icy drafts at every performance. Travelling in Maine in this terrible winter will be even worse for her. If she isn't already over the line, she will be then. She is stubborn, of course, and says she has spent enough money on doctors, will not be examined again, and altogether makes me very anxious. But I hope yet to persuade her to see a doctor. I am writing this in the Library. Hope you are well and happy. I have a bad cold too.

R. B.

203

to Dorothy Teall
(Transcript Columbia)

New York
January 19, 1918

I was very sorry to miss you, and sorrier to hear that there were any difficulties about the job. Oppenheim[1] said that Dr. Hinkle[2] liked you, but needed
a typist and stenog. If the job appealed to you, I should think it might pay to
learn these things this summer, as the doctor, I understand, doesn't want any
one before fall. Certainly the world seems generally to demand this ability, and
secretarial jobs aren't the worst that are offered as a beginning. If you are in
town, and will call up and leave a message, I will stay in, for I should especially
like to see you. Or I might be coming out to Jersey tomorrow, or Thursday.

Randolph

[1]James Oppenheim was a poet and the Editor of the *Seven Arts* magazine. He was a
denizen of Greenwich Village.

[2]Dr. Beatrice Hinkle was a Jungian psychologist of a good reputation. It was her
suggestion to a wealthy patient, Mrs. Rankine, which resulted in the financing of the *Seven
Arts*.

204

to Van Wyck Brooks
(Ms Pennsylvania)

[New York]
[March 1918]

Dear Van Wyck:
    I have been trying to finish up some reviews that I got belated on while I
was sick. So the letter has been delayed, although I would much rather be doing
it than the reviews, which always creak and groan until finally they stick fast.
Today is one of the sticking-days, and I am in a mood to wonder whether I shall

ever attain that divine fluency which I must have to carry out even one of the projects which we think up so regularly together. I have the same confidence in your ultimate fluency that you seem to have in mine. Mr. Sherman on Mark Twain—whom I have been reading—made me chortle with joy at the thought of how much you were going to show him when you get started. You simply have no competition. Here is a professionally critical mind, American with a painful self-consciousness, literary with a desperate purpose, and all it can find in the "democracy of Mark Twain" is the boasting, swaggering common man from the roughshod West, ignorant of everything venerated, and extremely conceited about his ignorance.[1] Mr. Sherman simply hasn't an idea in the world that Mark Twain was anything more than a hearty healthy vulgarian, expressing himself fully and with him the millions of common Americans. But you will change all that when you get started. I must begin to read him to be able to keep up with you.

When *The Mysterious Stranger* came out,[2] Mr. Sherman did have a faint pang of doubt whether his earlier criticisms had fully explained the author of the "almost entirely delightful" Huckleberry Finn. He recognizes in the Mysterious Stranger "a book steeped in irony, a dangerously atheistical book, presenting a wholly unorthodox view of the devil and a biting arraignment of the folly and brutality of mankind." Also "it lets one in to a temperament and character of more gravity, complexity and interest than the surface indicated." I think he is right. And I wonder if you aren't going to revise your judgment which you gave to W[aldo Frank] and me the other day. If there aren't parts of that book which aren't as blinding satire on the human comedy as anything Swift ever wrote, then I am a fanatical pacifist, completely obsessed by the imbecility of wars and ready to judge any book great which ridicules human conflict. I read it a year ago, but as I remember there was an uncanny intensity about the story, a sort of chivalrous exasperation at life, that made me see at once that here was that dark pessimism, the skeleton in Mark Twain's cellar, that they were just beginning to dig up. You are finding buried treasures all over the place that none of these innocent critics ever dreamed of his having. But are you going to make light of this discovery, which, because it is the most obvious and the most loudly announced, doesn't therefore have to be the least important for your purposes? I really feel a holy mission to convert you to this book. I am a little baffled by the fact that you come to it fresh from a reading of his other books and from much reflection upon him.

This is not a letter but only a note. In a few days, I hope to strike the stride that we talked about. But perhaps this will set you off.

R. B.

[1]Stuart Pratt Sherman was at that time allied with the genteel critics in their attack upon naturalism. He proved to be more flexible than Irving Babbitt or Paul Elmer More, however. Sherman had recently published an article, "The Democracy of Mark Twain," in *The Nation.*

[2]*The Mysterious Stranger* was published posthumously in 1916. It shocked many people because of its pessimism and irreverence.

205

to Van Wyck Brooks
(Ms Pennsylvania)

March 27, 1918

Dear Van Wyck:
Your fine letter made me wonder why you hadn't kept your title for this next book which is to come out of these letters. The one you are publishing now is a prelude, a clearing of the ground, for this magnificently constructive enterprise of creating a new literary leadership.[1] But the title as you keep it for the present book will give your secret away, and this is an advantage. For your readers will then know what you are going to drive at in your second and will be cordial to the answer to your questions.
Of course I feel the necessity of this leadership more than almost anything in the world. In fact, it is the only pragmatic cause to which one could give one's allegiance at the present time, with any confidence of attaining any goal or rescuing anything of value from the engulfing blackness. There is a certain superb youthful arrogance in your implication that it is we and our friends who are to be the masters. Your coming book is a pretty comprehensive demolition of the claims of any type or class of American, past or present, to hold this membership for us. You leave nobody, so that by mere process of elimination, it must be we fearless ones—and self-conscious ones—who are to hold it. Perhaps you will think that you mean that you are to be the only herald of the dawn, the John the Baptist, and would violently disavow any thought of aspiring to leadership yourself. But away with such timidities! This is not time to shy at priggishness. The New Republic's sense of leadership—the limited but influential class—is obnoxious because it comes not from youthful violence, but from a middle-aged dignity, that not only presents no clear program of values, but chooses for its first large enterprise a hateful and futile war, with a fatal backwash and backfire upon creative and democratic values at home. Our sense of

leadership would come from discontent, from the intolerable feeling that we are alien in a world that no one around is trying with intelligent fervor to set right. It would be an impressive gesture, a leap to rally disciples because neither we nor they could stand it any longer. The N[ew] R[epublic] 's priggishness showed its hoofs only after its "leadership" had succeeded. They boasted smugly about a fait accompli. Ours would be a pious hope, a youthful insolence that looked for future accomplishment. It might even be a "vital myth." Never certainly could it be weighted tangibly. Never could the influence of this peculiar kind of literary leadership be estimated. It could not point to things done. It could only be a ferment or a goad. You would not expect it to be anything else, and you would never be found pointing complacently to tangible results.

You have very cleverly designated the kinds of idealists that are with us now. The American idealist of today must be a "patriot"—comme "American jurist"—with imperialism, national "unity," strong government, lurking in the background; or "liberal," hoping decently to attain American dignity, law and order, national integration, without the poisonous elements; or join a frankly revolutionary party, doctrinaire like the Socialist, destructive, like the I. W. W. Now the difficulty with the liberal is that so far he has felt that he could ride two horses at once, he could be a patriot and still frown on greed and violence and predatory militarism; he could desire social reconstruction and yet be most reverent towards the traditional institutions. He feels that the old-fashioned individualist profiteer and old-guard politician is so terribly the enemy that we should all support liberalism in its attack. It is hypercritical to make distinctions, when this unsocialized beast is abroad in the land. It is confusion to be anxious about democracy at home while the Prussian is loose in the world. So we find only a mild reproof about our own moral backwash of war. And we find that somehow in the liberal attack upon the unsocialized beast, liberalism has accepted—in what I believe to be the vain hope of conscious guidance and control—almost every program that the bigoted unsocialized patriot has demanded. You may accept conscription from motives very different from those of the unregenerate militarist, but if the military machine is to remain in the hands of an "American jurist" ruling class; if war always fortifies military attitudes and autocratic control; if, moreover, there was almost no chance of militarism being liberalized; but if you have nevertheless thrown your moral and intellectual support to militarism—you cannot be acquitted of a share in the result. Pragmatically, the effect is no different from what it would have been if you had willed the worst.

Now it is disgust at a liberal strategy which involved at the outset a surrender of all the large positions, with a prospect of regaining them again which is becoming dimmer every day—it is this that has driven so many of the younger generation back from the liberal camp. They want an idealism which is not full of compromises, which is more concerned with American civilization than with American politics, which is more desirous for American life, liberty and the pursuit of happiness than for a model constitution and a watertight political-democratic system. These malcontents, who from education and association would be most likely to be in the liberal camp, are thrown back on themselves with a peculiarly unhappy sense of leaderlessness. The liberals are constantly disappointing them with their callousness towards the creative values which the malcontents so earnestly crave. The war has run into the sand that fine movement for progressive democracy in which so many of us found hope. It has shown up what was really nearest to the liberal heart's desire. A change in institutions not as a means to life but as something pleasing in itself! The political liberal somehow seems to assume civilization, assume national life, assume the existence of rich personal living. What his eye is fixed on is some institutional plan which in itself appears to him good. His mind moves in this upper level of schemes for social and political change or for the attainment of some social and political good like democracy. He does not ask himself whether these schemes will, conformably to our national tradition and temperament, make the individual and the group life richer. He looks only to the satisfaction of his sense of order, or his sense of organization, or of the concepts of democracy and progress which he has obtained in youth from the professor who fired his mind at college. So we find a program of social reconstruction, which some of us had believed to be motivated by a desire for regenerated American life, evaporating into a vague, misty scheme of international organization. And we find a liberal war undertaken which could not fail to do far more damage to American democracy at home than it could ever do to the enemy abroad.

Intellectualism is the "liberal" curse, the habit of moving in concepts rather than in a warm area of pragmatic life. And it is this feeling of having asked for bread and been given a stone that haunts these malcontents from the liberal camp. Do we deny that politics has no influence on the everyday personal and social life of the nation? Of course not. What we object to is the calm uncritical attitude toward this relation. Nothing arouses the curiosity of these malcontents more than this question how political systems, political changes, political manipulations, do affect that civilized life as it goes on around us. What evil and what good can we count on government doing to us and for us? The war has brought an immense and terrifying inflation to the political sphere, so that for most people non-governmentalized activity has ceased almost to have significance. But this cult of politics had been inherent in the liberal intellectual's point of view long before the war. Instead of politics taking its place in the many-sided interests of a modern mind, it had the dominant position which it occupies in the pages of the "New Republic."

This dominance may be justified, but no proof is ever brought us. The liberal intellectual examines and discusses his presuppositions as infrequently as does the chauffeur. And it is exactly during this period of war when politics fill the sky that the lid is most serenely clamped down on philosophical introspection. It is not so in England. There under a peculiarly exasperating regime of repression, speculation seems to go on with increasing boldness. In this country I can think of no intellectual effort outside of Veblen's that has not been propaganda of one sort or another. Here the repression has been exasperating enough, but it has been successful. Our free thinking is not a plant hardy enough to withstand the chilling blast of war-policy. For most discontented people the government is not obnoxious enough to make revolutionary criticism a matter of duty. In the conflict of currents they are perhaps not certain enough of their own stand to state boldly their reflections. And there is something in this hearty patriotic assistance which the middle class, in all its branches, and in every city and town, seems to be giving the government policies of thought-suppression and war-organization, that is positively intimidating. Why let your voice cry in the wilderness, when a healthy lusty and unanimous democracy not only will not hear but is almost as ready to spill your blood as it is to destroy the enemy abroad?

So that that anxious speculation which should normally follow the destruction of so many hopes, the uprooting of our convictions as to the way the world was tending, the discovery of the sinister forces still at work in what we had thought was a slowly emancipating era, has been left wholly unattended to in this country. No intellectual leader has cared to think. The defection of Dewey is typical. After years of eloquent opposition to military conscription, he accepts it without a quiver or even an explanation of the steps by which his conviction made so momentous a change. The universities made haste to blacken and drive into limbo any one who tried to exercise his mind. Labor, which has been a ferment in other countries where intellect could work to constructive purpose in formulating the aims of the masses, divided here into the sheep and the goats. The sheep sat at the right hand of the Father, while the goats were relentlessly hunted and prescribed. The socialists divided into fanatical patriots and neutral pacifists. Even the radicals who supported the international program for a democratic peace and warred against profiteering and intolerance at home were in more haste for immediate results than for the long slow campaign of thought and organization necessary to realize the ideals. Nowhere an effort to get down to a bedrock of principle, to find out very clearly what was desirable, and use the materials at our disposal to attain it! Nowhere any clear sense of whither we were drifting or how our ideas and slogans squared with the facts. On the contrary an insensate scramble for action, a positive delight in throwing off the responsibility of thought. And nowhere was this more marked than in the intellectual class.

The result is that the mind that would speculate about what is going on in American life, or what might be done with it, or what one's relation is to it, is left without any one to think its thought for it. The country must be dotted with dissatisfied people who cannot accept any of the guides offered to them. The childishness of the conventional leads is only equalled by the sterility of the intellectualist leads. It is this malcontented class that needs a new gospel. It is this class that would understand what you are driving at, and would be grateful even for a suggestion of the enterprise you suggest. I have dim notions of how that leadership could be created, but you must tell me the technique you have in mind. I imagine people must be appealed to to desire certain things mightily. Then the "leaders" will be simply those articulate souls who can express most convincingly those desired values. In any such enterprise, leadership loses all its snobbery. It becomes a true co-operation with the attentive ones in a clearing up of our spiritual mist.

R. B.

[1]*Letters and Leadership* was published in 1918.

206

to Dorothy Teall
(Transcript Columbia)

16 Charles St.
31 May 1918[1]

Dear Dorothy,

Why do you never come to see me any more? Are you looking for a job? I was asked today if I knew of a girl who would be a secretary to a doctor-lady who deals in psychiatry and psychoanalysis. She is a friend of James Oppenheim, is the translator of Jung, and rather well known in her field. She wants a very bright person, who will be interested in personal psychology. It might be rather interesting, I think. $20 - $25 was mentioned as salary, weekly I suppose. I thought of you, and if it appeals to you, will you let me know at once, so I can put you in touch with her? I don't know whether she wants to start at once, but I imagine so. My phone is Chelsea 8562. Or if you want to apply directly to Dr. Beatrice Hinkle . . . 10 Gramercy Park, or 46 W. 9th St. Mention me . . . and James Oppenheim.

I have been very angry with the world today because I am not living in the country. My friends who might go away with me are being drafted, and the others are too poor or busy. It is no fun being a free man in a slave-world.

I hope you met Ridgely Torrence. He seemed quite taken by you. I hope you were with him, as I find him very charming and amusing. I hope you will find time to look me up after college stops.

R. B.

[1]The dating of this letter is Teall's. From the context, it appears that it was written earlier than # 203.

207

to Alyse Gregory
(Ms Yale)

Sound Beach[1]
[Summer 1918]

I did really mean to see you yesterday, but I came in too late, stayed too long at the Dial, where I found Harold in revolt against Johnson, Dewey, and Marot, and of course fanned the flame.[2] Then I had to go to East Orange, and only got back in time for Paul[3] whom I had promised to have dinner with when I came down. He didn't tell me till the end of the evening that he was called to go next week, poor soul, but he seems resigned. I'm sorry to hear about the end of the G[reenwich] S[quare] P[layers] [?] but isn't this another false alarm? You won't go to Italy, will you, and leave me abandoned utterly, without Paul or anybody? V[an] W[yck], I fear, will eventually be sucked in, in some way, and there will be nobody of my old friends. I suspect that A[gnes de Lima] and E[sther Cornell] have thrown me over as a bully and a boaster, unworthy of their friendship. Will I have nothing but the Dial to fall back on, Harold or Martin? Harold seemed quite sensible and possible, yesterday, able to work with, and there is every evidence of the grandest kind of a row over the autocracy of the great moguls.

Perhaps you will up to Washington, if my unknown hostess really does go away and leave me in possession. But you won't go away or do anything without seeing me? I'm so sorry about Fr. Must he be hauled away now? Will you keep me informed about L[ucille Deming]? I do want to see her again, and see if my making her a symbol of everything lovely is fatuous or inspired.

I wish town and country could be better combined, but I see no way of combining them.

R.

<hr />

[1] According to Alyse Gregory, Bourne was staying with Brooks.

[2] Harold Stearns was then Editor of *The Dial*. Martin Johnson held the greatest financial interest. John Dewey and Helen Marot, along with Thorstein Veblen, comprised the Reconstruction Board which was supposed to set new policies for the magazine. During this summer the transition from Chicago to New York was being made. See my introduction to this chapter for more information.

[3] Paul Rosenfeld, the music critic, who had just received his draft notice. While Rosenfeld was at boot camp, Bourne stayed in his apartment.

208

to Alyse Gregory
(Ms Yale)

Sound Beach
Monday [Summer 1918]

I expected you last Sunday, and again yesterday, but you were either fainthearted or lost; so you haven't seen our log-cabin by the sea. Last Sunday I had a call from the de Wetters,[1] who had chased me all over Sound Beach, routing out the postmaster to find where I was, a terrifying thing to do to a person who is trying to escape publicity. They wanted to take me back to New Rochelle to dinner, but I pleaded the French translation, which is turning us all neurotic. I made a tacit bargain to come up and do the typewriting in exchange for my board, but 100,000 words in three weeks taxes my abilities,[2] especially when I am trying to write my autobiographical novel,[3] and satisfy Harold's demands for reviews. Am I missing much in not being around for the Dial debut? Harold as a dude must be an even more eccentric spectacle than as a Chatterton of Francis Thompson.[4] You can't blame me; there was also your hyper-susceptibility. Your salon is still the center of all intellectual life, evidently. Your weariness? So might any of the great French ladies have spoken between the acts.

I shall be turned out of this little Paradise next week, and Heaven knows where I shall go then. I will have six weeks before the gates of Martin Johnson close about my soul. A[gnes] & E[sther] have passed out of my life like rose-petals on the breeze. An era, I feel, has been closed. Nothing but work do I see ahead of me now. If I could always work under the pleasant conditions that I am working under now, I should want nothing more in my life. I wish the Thayers would invite me to Dublin, but I do not see any way to make that any more obvious than it has ever been made.

Your mysterious telegrams to Paul and me at Sound Beach will certainly get us all into trouble. The child who does the work here cannot spell. *"Perfide"* certainly looks like a code; there is nothing in English that it can mean. It is a mere miracle that Paul was not immediately interned. He has horrendous stories of Paul Strand and others.

Why don't you stop next Saturday or Sunday? Take trolley from Stamford or Sound Beach stations, and get off at Shorelands road. Walk a little distance to the stone-posts (entrance to Shorelands), and through them. We are the second house on the right, beyond the posts.

R.

[1] He could be referring to the Herman de Wetter family. The head of the household, Herman de Wetter, was of Estonian nobility. At that time he was an engineer for an American firm. Later he served on the War Trade Board. In the 1930's he founded the Photography Department at the Brooklyn Museum.

[2] He was then typing a French translation, *Jacquou, The Rebel*, which had been done by Mrs. Brooks.

[3] An autobiographical fragment was eventually published as "Autobiographical Chapter," *The Dial* LXVIII (January 1920), 1-21.

[4] This is an obscure literary anecdote. Francis Thompson, a nineteenth century British poet and essayist, had decided to kill himself with a dose of laudanum. As he was preparing to drink, he imagined that the young poet Thomas Chatterton, who had killed himself at the age of 15, was attempting to restrain him. Thompson did not go through with the suicide, and his luck soon changed. The way in which Bourne applied the analogy is unclear.

209

to Roderick Seidenberg[1]
(Ms Columbia)

Sound Beach, Ct.
12 July 1918

Dear R. S.,

When I start work in September, I shall certainly take up the subject, and imagine that your article could be incorporated in some series of general international interest. The subject is certainly the very kernal of the international situation and no League of Nations would be worth anything unless it included such a provision. If you have the articles in shorter form, you might send them in later in the summer.

I've often wondered about how you are getting along. You sound cheerful and intellectual, as usual. I hope you are keeping a journal of your experiences, for the CO's will be about the most interesting people after the war is over, and their names, I am convinced, will be remembered after most of the generals are forgotten, not to mention the petty officers. Do you get enough to read, and could I send you any books or papers you want?

Sincerely,

R. B.

[1]At that time Seidenberg was interned in a camp for Conscientious Objectors.

210

to Alyse Gregory
(Ms Yale)

Washington, Connecticut
August 2, 1918

No, everybody would be much worse off if you were not in New York. A whole little society more or less depends on you for its social focus and would be lost and disintegrated indeed without your firesides. And I should be desolate indeed. Let's hope your record is too black for the Red Cross, and too Red for any other work that will take you away from New York. Alice of course can slip with scarcely a groan into war-work, and will probably be about in khaki in a few months, like Rheta Childs Dow. Or do I misjudge her? Perhaps Nick's tutoring can support her for a while. On Handman I don't think you vouchsafed all your powers of discrimination. I first saw him at a N[ew] R[epublic] lunch, when he discoursed in a most learned and charming manner on Balkan affairs, and had Croly and the rest eating out of his hand. Then I saw him last month one evening at the Brevoort with Kallen and Goldenweiser, and I thought him even more distinguished. He is a pal of Veblen's, and the rarest of all academic types,—a human and learned young man.[1] He is simply not of the same breed as any of those as whom he is "not so bad." If you knew the various academic types as well as I do, you would see what a remarkable young man he is. Take my recommendation and don't be irritated. But a summer in New York must make any one blasé. Can't you do something more original with your salary— always a small fortune in itself, equal to my earnings for half a year—than stew in Milligan's? Get Alice to invite you to Maine, and find a place for me to stay, or something like that. Next week I am going to be left here by my hostess who returns for three weeks to her much tolerated family. The farmers are to take care of me, and Oppenheim and Dr. Hinkle are not far away. But I expect to expire of melancholy and be driven away from this lovely country, perhaps back to Sound Beach, though I should love to go to Dublin. Why don't the Thayers write me? I offered to pay board. Couldn't you get them to write us both? That would be amusing.

I have one precious month before I go to slave for Harold and Martin. Did I tell you about going in there and finding H. quite human and likable after expounding him to Van Wyck that day? I *am* your permanent appreciative friend, and my eclipses are superficial. There will be no triangle about L[ucille]. If she comes do see that she doesn't live in a hovel, and that she keeps away from F[lorence] K[ing] and the Patchins, and stays on an entirely new plane, won't you? I wonder if she will be lovely or changed after her dreamy year away from us. Has she a job in prospect, or is it just a mad descent upon New York? You are not explicit, and I know not whether you are telling me everything you know. And you never mentioned Fr. who was in such desperate straits when I last talked to you? I should really like to know what happened to him. Not a word from Paul, whom I am afraid they are ill-treating; and it depresses me to think of his suffering. Floyd[2] was a clear triumph over the powers of darkness, wasn't he? I feel in nothing but a gossipy mood tonight. The tone here has been very frivolous, somewhat to my surprise. My life is beset by women in pairs. I begin to feel a little like a parasite, enjoying the hospitality of this youthful lady I have never met before. But I take to such treatment as if I was born only to be entertained, and as if anything else were an occasion for grievance. An idle, unreal life in comparison with the worthiness of Agnes, for instance! She must be truly appalling, and only her naive admiration for the aristocracy, who, like myself, can loaf, with a seeming literary justification, saves her. She would rather do her dismal work and sentimentalize about the delights of intellectual leisure than taste them herself, with the haunting consciousness that it is as a public woman that she will most really count.

Do not think that my countenance is turned from you, or that our friendship is thin and humdrum. Perhaps in the dim past, you were somewhat merged in the unknown possibility that ever hung, despaired of yet longed for, on the horizon. When certain of the golden planets stooped to earth, I followed greedily where they led me. It was my misfortune to crave the perilous and hectic and altogether surrendering. One pays the price in violent commotions and rebounds. If you have shone steadily on in the sky, it was what you wanted to do, and it does not make you less interesting, or incapable of dealing out vast comfort. One needs the friendly light in the sky as well as the fire in which the undreading child gets burned.

Randolph

[1]Horace Kallen was still teaching philosophy at the University of Wisconsin. Alexander Goldenweiser was a lecturer in anthropology at Columbia. He had also received his graduate training there as an ethnologist. Starting in 1919 both Kallen and Goldenweiser lectured at the New School for Social Research in New York.

[2]He is probably referring to Floyd Dell, who, at that time, was Associate Editor of *The Masses*, the most popular of the truly radical papers. He also wrote plays for the Liberal Club.

211

to Van Wyck Brooks
(Ms Pennsylvania)

[Washington, Ct.]
August 5, 1918

Dear Van Wyck,

My charmers have left me to-day, and I stay alone with the farmers for as long as I can stand it. I think I shall be melancholy by next week, so I wonder if you have the place or the desire for me again. This time, of course, paying board. Paul spoke of leaving his things in his rooms and letting me use them, so I can go back there for a while, if he has really not moved, and if he is really not returning. But of course I would rather be in the country and with you. I don't know how definitely you meant your talk of my coming back, or how I may have gotten on Eleanor's nerves by being around. But if you are hospitable, it would cheer my solitude here to know I had a friendly place to come back to.

James exaggerates about my book. I have written a lot of heterogeneous stuff, some of which I may be able to keep. The novel I decided to approach differently, and begin again when this brook runs dry. The stuff I wrote is incredibly bad. If you are not launched in Mark [Twain] by the time I get back I will threaten you with collaboration.

R. B.

212

to Dorothy Teall
(Transcript Columbia)

Sound Beach, Ct.
August 30, 1918

I think I could easily and agreeably come out for some such party as you suggest. The thought of L[ucille] as a professor is stimulating. This red ink doesn't mean that I have been converted to militarism, but that it is the only writing-stuff I can find around. I never heard about the projected Amidonian visit to New York, so I suffered no grief or disappointment. I hope, however, she doesn't come without letting me know. One regresses with pleasure to moods that have pleased in the past, however sentimental the object.

I may move from Charles St. any day, so address me at the Dial, 152 W. 13th St.

R. B.

213

to Dorothy Teall
(Transcript Columbia)

77 Irving Place
Sept. 20, 1918

Dear Dorothy,

I hear you have a job, and since you have probably already seen the source of my knowledge, I can't mystify you with my clairvoyance. I met L[illian] S[oskin] in the Library the other day and her baldescent Bernie at the cafeteria on 8th St. B. smoked a big cigar and discoursed loftily of *Musical America* and President Wilson's reply to the Austrian note. I gathered that the worm will turn, that they cannot reduce a good man to mere routine on an artistic journal without righteous protest, and that the war may last a long time.

If you are in town every day, why don't you stop in and see me after hours at my new home here, my gorgeously appointed sublet home from a man of wealth and taste who has been drafted and from whose miseries I am allowed to benefit? Telephone, Stuyvesant 7497 (Paul Rosenfeld) and I will stay in for you.

Randolph

214

to Sarah Bourne
(Transcript Columbia)

New York
October 12, 1918

I have been relieved of my editorial duties on the Dial, but I am to be paid my salary just the same and continue to write. I prefer it this way as it leaves me much freer. I will send you a copy of the next number. The rich young man who put up the money to back the Dial this year [Scofield Thayer] is a very good friend of mine, and we are both in the same boat. He has strong tastes and I have strong convictions, and the man who runs the paper is very much afraid of us both, afraid we will have too much to say about the policy.

[no signature]

215

to Sarah Bourne
(Transcript Columbia)

New York
November 4, 1918

I have been classified as totally and permanently, mentally and physically unfit for military service, and when this friend returns, it will mean that practically everyone of my friends is exempted from the service in some form or other, either as criminals out on bail, or married men or psychopaths, or weaklings. Van Wyck Brooks has finally gone with his wife and two little boys to Carmel Cal. for the winter. He is the one, you know, with whom I spent part of the summer at Sound Beach. I shall miss him tremendously, because of all my men friends I like and admire him the most, I think. We used to have lunch together here in New York, or tea after his work. It is a mutual admiration. He has been tied to a desk in the Century Co., and he looks on me as one who leads the ideal, free, dignified, leisurely life of a true man of letters, making my living by my pen with no sordid job to hold down. So, when you think I ought to have a job, remember that I am admired just because I haven't one.

On the Dial there has been some fuss about my being an editor, owing to my radical views, but I am paid just the same as if I were one, and only have to write two articles a month. I seem to be in very strong with the young man who is giving most of the money to back the Dial this year. He says he gave his $25,000 on the strength of my contributions, and he was very angry at their not wanting me as a regular associate editor. So I do not need to worry apparently, as long as the money lasts.

[no signature]

216

to Van Wyck Brooks
(Ms Pennsylvania)

New York
November 12, 1918

Dear Van Wyck,

A letter coming from you to Paul announces to me your safe arrival at Carmel, but that is all. None for myself seemed to be forthcoming, so you must be waiting for me to write. But there isn't anything to tell you, except that Berger has dumped a French book on me called "Les Vagabonds de la glorie" by René Milan, being the journal of a naval officer in the Mediterranean.[1] He wants it in a month, and will pay $150, which must be ridiculously small, considering that it would cost a third of that at least to type it. Don't you think you should hold him up for higher prices? I took it, of course, subject to his approval of my first chapter. Then I found I really wasn't sure of some of the passages, so I farmed it out to an impoverished maiden lady whose version I am now awaiting. I intend to give it the literary finish, but my vocabulary is not large, and I have to do much racking of brains to get smooth equivalents. I don't think I was made for a translator, but I'm sure it is excellent practice in stretching one's own style. Do you get the papers you want, or would you like me to send you any dailies or weeklies regularly? I should be glad enough to do it.

Paul is supposed to be coming back any day now. This I get from Waldo. Then I will be homeless for fair. It must comfort him to have the draft-calls stopped, and a prospect of no more men being sent overseas. New York has had two grand orgies of peace celebration,—a premature one last Thursday and a more Saturnalian one last night. As a pacifist, I rejoice at the innocent uprising of the unconscious desire on the part of the populace for peace, and the throwing off of the repressed reluctance for the war. It was most touching, the mood in the streets. The patriots were quite disgusted. Last night was a long orgy of drunken sailors and soldiers. Everybody had a bottle of whiskey, and the lid was off. It was rather amusing.

How much blither and freer the air! Love to all.

Randolph

[1]The French novel, which was quite successful, was published in 1916. René Milan was the pseudonym Maurice Larruoy used early in his career. Bourne's translation was published as *Vagabonds of the Sea* in 1919.

217

to Sarah Bourne
(Transcript Columbia)

New York
November 21, 1918

There has been great rejoicing here over peace, in fact, two celebrations swing to a false alarm, and the second was so gay with drunken soldiers and sailors that no girl was safe on the streets in the evening.

I am quite busy with a French translation I have been given to do, and other writing of my own. Now that the war is over people can speak freely again and we can dare to think. It's like coming out of a nightmare.

[no signature]

Appendix: Two Undated Letters

218

to Karl Robinson
(Ms Columbia)

Friday Night[1]

Dear Karl,

This is not a success, but without more time I could not get it any less rocky. My attempts at journalistic style are never happy, and this sounds unusually mediocre. If you still think there might be hope with a rewriting and there is time, I should like to try again. Otherwise I will work it off on some newspaper.

As to the typewriter, I got hold of one and discovered that I could not at all handle the different keyboard. Yours being the same I thought it was useless to come in. I got hold of a stenographer lady instead and dictated to her. Thank you so much for your offer and particularly for your kindness in negotiating the affair. I only wish I was deserving better at your hands.

Faithfully yours,

Randolph Bourne

[1]A note on the bottom of this letter, written in Agnes de Lima's hand, indicates that this letter was composed after Bourne's return from Europe. Bourne mentions, letter 89, that he had sent an article to Robinson in the Spring of 1914, while he was still on the Continent, but clearly this letter was written while Bourne was in the United States. Since Bourne speaks of "coming in," perhaps this letter was written during one of the many summers in which Bourne left New York frequently to spend time in the country. A more specific date cannot be ascertained.

219

to Roderick Seidenberg
(Transcript Columbia)

16 Charles Street[1]

Dear Roderick,
    That is a most admirable letter you have in the *Post*. Those were the things that needed to be said, and you have said them with the utmost vigor and convincingness. It's the best statement yet. The American Union against Militarism ought to see it. I hope you are having reprints made. The Post ought to turn them off for you. I am proud to know you.

R. Bourne

[1]This letter was undoubtedly written while Seidenberg was interned as a conscientious objector. The letter was probably written in 1918; Bourne lived at Charles Street occasionally during the second half of the year, but, without access to the New York *Evening Post*, a more specific date cannot be assigned.

Bibliography

I

Archives consulted

Randolph Bourne Collection, John Erskine Collection, Butler Library, Columbia University.

Waldo Frank Collection, Van Wyck Brooks Collection, and Carl Zigrosser Collection, Van Pelt Library, University of Pennsylvania.

Alyse Gregory Collection, Elizabeth Shepley Sergeant Collection, Beinecke Library, Yale University.

II

Works written by Bourne, including anthologies

Brooks, Van Wyck. *The History of a Literary Radical*. New York: S. A. Russell, 1956.

Bourne, Randolph. "A Modern Mind," *The Dial* LXII (March 22, 1917), 239-40.

—. "American Use For German Ideals," *New Republic* IV (September 4, 1915), 117-19.

—. "Denatured Nietzsche," *The Dial* LXIII (December 20, 1917), 389-91.

—. *Education and Living*. New York: Century, 1917.

—. "The Excitement of Friendship," *The Atlantic* CX (December 1912), 795-800.

—. *The Gary Schools*. Boston: Houghton, Mifflin, 1916.

—. "The Handicapped," *The Atlantic* CVIII (September 1911), 320-39.

—. "Mental Unpreparedness," *New Republic* IV (September 11, 1915), 143-44.

—, ed. *Towards an Enduring Peace*. New York: American Council for International Conciliation, [1917].

—. *Untimely Papers*. New York: Huebsch, 1919.

—. *Youth and Life*. Boston: Houghton, Mifflin, 1913.

Norman, Dorothy, ed. "Some Pre-War Letters (1912-1914)," *Twice-a-Year* II (Spring-Summer 1939), 79-102.

—, ed. "Randolph Bourne: Letters (1913-1914)," *Twice-a-Year* V-VI (Fall-Winter 1940, Spring-Summer 1941), 79-88.

—, ed. "Randolph Bourne: Letters (1913-1916)," *Twice-a-Year* VII (Fall-Winter 1941), 76-90.

Rahv, Philip. *The Discovery of Europe*. Boston: Houghton, Mifflin, 1947.

Resek, Carl, ed. *War and the Intellectuals*. New York: Harper and Row, 1968.

Schlissel, Lillian, ed. *The World of Randolph Bourne*. New York: Dutton, 1965.

III

Secondary material

Anonymous. "Editorial," *Seven Arts* I (November 1916), 54-56.

Barzun, Jacques, ed. *A History of the Faculty of Philosophy*. New York: Columbia University Press, 1957.

Brooks, Van Wyck. *Fenollosa and His Circle*. New York: Dutton and Co., 1962.

Butler, Nicholas Murray. *Scholarship and Service*. New York: Charles Scribner's Sons, 1921.

Dos Passos, John. *1919*. New York: Harcourt, Brace and Co., 1932.

Forcey, Charles. *The Crossroads of Liberalism*. New York: Oxford University Press, 1955.

Frank, Waldo, *The New America*. London: J. Cape, 1922.

Gregory, Alyse. *The Day Is Gone*. New York: E. P. Dutton, 1948.

Joost, Nicholas. *Scofield Thayer and The Dial*. Carbondale, Illinois: Southern Illinois University Press, 1969.

—. *Years of Transition: The Dial 1912-1920*. Barre, Massachusetts: Barre Publishers, 1967.

Keppel, Frederick. *Columbia*. New York: Oxford University Press, 1914.

Lasch, Christopher. *The New Radicalism in America*. New York: Alfred A. Knopf, 1965.

Mott, Frank Luther. *A History of American Magazines*, II. Cambridge, Massachusetts: Harvard University Press,1938.

Mumford, Louis. "The Image of Randolph Bourne," *New Republic* LXIV (September 24, 1930), 151-52.

Noble, David. *The Paradox of Progressive Thought*. Minneapolis: University of Minnesota Press, 1958.

Pascal, Roy. *Design and Truth in Autobiography*. Cambridge, Massachusetts: Harvard University Press, 1960.

Paul, Sherman. *Randolph Bourne*. Minneapolis: University of Minnesota Press, 1966.

Rosenfeld, Paul. *Port of New York*. New York: Harcourt, Brace and Co., 1924.

Sacks, Claire. "The 'Seven Arts' Critics: A Study of Cultural Nationalism in America, 1910-1930," unpublished Ph.D. Dissertation, Madison, Wisconsin, 1955.

Sedgwick, Ellery. *The Happy Profession.* Boston: Little, Brown and Co., 1946.

Slosson, Edwin. *Great American Universities.* New York: The Macmillan Co., 1910.

Summerscales, William. *Affirmation and Dissent: Columbia's Response to the Crisis of World War I.* New York: Columbia Teachers College Press, 1970.

Veysey, Lawrence. *The Emergence of the American University.* Chicago: University of Chicago Press, 1965.

Wertheim, Frank. *The New York Little Renaissance.* New York University Press, 1976.

Zigrosser, Carl. *A World of Art and Museums.* Philadelphia: Art Alliance Press, 1975.

—. *My Own Shall Come to Me.* Private Imprint entered at Casa Laura, Switzerland. Haarlem, Netherlands: Joh. Enschede en Zonen, 1971.

Index of Letters by Recipient

Note: The letter number is followed by the date in parentheses.

Index of Names and Titles

Note: Numbers indicate letter numbers. Numbers in brackets refer to the page
number in the introductions. Starred numbers indicate that the entry is also
footnoted.

Index of Themes

Note: Numbers indicate letter numbers. Numbers in brackets refer to the page number in the introductions.

Art

    5—Bergsonian intuition and theories of; 12—"paganism" and; 48, 50—lack of good art in England; 55—more sensitivity to art in Europe; 55—taste as element of social betterment; 70—superiority of in France; 147—difference between political radicalism and artistic style.

Autobiography

    17—in essays; 115—as method of self-analysis; [2], [13] —letters and.

Childhood

    15—ambitions to play organ; 15—and religion, socialism; 16—and Bloomfield; 17—and music recitals; 18—and career as intellectual; 20—and obligation of love; 21—and high school; 77—progress from religion to radicalism in; [7-8] —summary of his childhood.

Cities

    29, 30—Paris, lack of office buildings; 32—dirtiness of Dutch towns; 33—faster pace in European cities; 65—coexistence of old buildings and new ideas in European cities; 97—poverty of American cities compared to European; 121—impatience in; 128—need to escape from.

College

    3—glad to get back to; 15—and group of youths (Academy); 15—as liberating force; 16—Winterrowd's need for broadening experience in; 17—his feeling of oppression at; 17—letters to *Spectator* re. employees; 17—assessment of courses; 17—and connection with city; 26—dissatisfaction with last year; 40—feeling of responsibility for Winterrowd's welfare in; 49—as spiritual home; 53—activism of professors in; 56—disappointment at Winterrowd's displeasure in; 59, 61, 71—letters to *Spectator* re. fraternities; 104—realization that college friends are gone; 109—excellence of college literary magazines; 126—as way of finding destiny; 188—social

France (*see also* Paris)
   59, [16] —magnificence of French civilization; 60—quality of newspapers;
   60—French universities; 65—straightforwardness of convictions in; 66—
   superiority of literature to English; 66—appreciation of Rousseau; 67—
   universities; 68, 82—personal, emotional nature of civilization; 68, 78—
   equality of women in; 70—routine while in; 71—inferiority of American
   culture to; 72—youth in; 72, 84—inferiority of Americans in; 73—inscrutability of personality in; 73—national culture in; 76—realization of
   corruption in; 76—unanimistes; 76—social literature of; 77—wealth of
   culture of; 78—elegance of language; 79—suffrage meetings in; 80—availability of national culture in; 81—quality of intellectual life in; 83—ability of self-expression in; [101-102] —experience in.

Friends (*see also* Friendship and Index of Names)
   6—Murray; 7, 57—Seidenberg; 10—Kovar; 11, 12—long talk with Seidenberg; 21—and their youth compared to him; 26—Swain; 36—split with
   Swain; 52—solicits analysis of Winterrowd; 61—encourages Barr to publish poems; 62—feeling of distance from Winterrowd; 66—as source of
   inspiration; 81—Read Lewis; 98—feeling of loneliness among; 98—Zigrosser; 103—Teall; 116—infatuation with Amidon; 120—impatience at not
   being able to see Amidon; 120—plans meeting with Amidon; 122, 123—
   mourning after Amidon's departure; 122—appreciation of Teall; 127—
   fatherly relationship to Teall; 139—feeling of estrangement from Zigrosser; 141—effort to get Sergeant to visit; 209—Gregory; [7] —importance of
   in an assessment of Bourne; [9] —as sounding board for his ideas.

Friendship (*see also* Friends and Index of Names)
   1—his concern for; 1—his confidence in his; 8—eagerness to hear of their
   exploits; 9—wants Zigrosser's companionship; 10—gratitude for visit to
   Zigrosser's; 13, 14—women and; 14—and "pre-established harmony";
   15—as educators (Academy); 16—oppression of older generation over;
   17—his assessment of their intelligence; 17—his ideal of friendship; 23—
   therapeutic nature of conversation with; 26—relies on them in state of
   depression; 52—solicits letters from; 66—desire for while in France; 104—
   search for new circle of; 107, 201—encourages Teall; 108—advises Teall;
   109—defends literary prowess of *Monthly* group; 115—admonishes Teall;
   159—intimations of split with Zigrosser; 160, 161, 162, 163—split with
   Zigrosser; 177—encourages Sergeant; 202—concern for Cornell's health;
   203, 206—tries to get Teall a job; 209—encouragement for Seidenberg;
   210—assesses friendship with Greogry; 211—cajoles Brooks; [27-28] —
   importance of.

The Letters of Randolph Bourne:
a Comprehensive Edition

Composed in IBM Electronic Selectric Composer *Journal Roman* and printed offset and sewn by Cushing-Malloy, Incorporated, Ann Arbor, Michigan. The paper on which the book is printed is The Northwest Paper Company's *Caslon.* The book was bound in Scott Graphics Company's *Scottek C Slate Burlap* by John H. Dekker & Sons, Incorporated, Grand Rapids, Michigan.

The Letters of Randolph Bourne is a Trenowyth book, the scholarly publishing division of the Whitston Publishing Company.

This edition consists in 750 casebound copies.